Power in the Global Age

Power in the Global Age

A new global political economy

ULRICH BECK

Translated by Kathleen Cross

polity

First published in German as *Macht und Gegenmacht im globalen Zeitalter: Neue weltpolitische Ökonomie* © Suhrkamp Verlag, Frankfurt am Main 2002

This translation first published in 2005 © Polity Press

The right of Ulrich Beck to be identified as Author of this Work has been asserted in accordance with the UK Copyright, Designs and Patents Act 1988.

The publication of this work was supported by a grant from the Goethe-Institut.

Polity Press
65 Bridge Street
Cambridge CB2 1UR, UK

Polity Press
350 Main Street
Malden, MA 02148, USA

ISBN: 0-7456-3230-0
ISBN: 0-7456-3231-9 (pb)

A catalogue record for this book is available from the British Library.

Typeset in 10 on 12 pt Stempel Garamond
by SNP Best-set Typesetter Ltd., Hong Kong
Printed and bound in Great Britain by TJ International Ltd, Padstow, Cornwall.

The publisher has used its best endeavours to ensure that the URLs for external websites referred to in this book are correct and active at the time of going to press. However, the publisher has no responsibility for the websites and can make no guarantee that a site will remain live or that the content is or will remain appropriate.

Every effort has been made to trace all copyright holders, but if any have been inadvertently overlooked the publisher will be pleased to include any necessary credits in any subsequent reprint or edition.

For further information on Polity, visit our website: www.polity.co.uk

Contents

Detailed Contents

List of Tables and Figures

The Hazy Power Space of Global Domestic Politics

Today, we Europeans act as if Germany, France, Italy, the Netherlands, Portugal, and so forth, still existed. Yet they have long since ceased to exist, because as soon as the euro was introduced – if not before – these isolated nation-state containers of power and the equally isolated, mutually excluding societies they represented entered the realm of the unreal. To the extent that Europe exists, there is no longer any such thing as Germany, or France, or Italy, or Britain, and so on, as these exist in people's heads and in the picture-book accounts of the historians. This is because the borders, responsibilities and exclusive experiential spaces on which this nation-state world was based no longer exist. But if all this is gone, if all we are doing is thinking, acting and researching in zombie categories, what comes along – or has come along – to take its place?

This is the question which this book raises and attempts to answer, developing a very wide-ranging and fundamental analysis of the social, economic and political transformations of the modern age. In this account the distinction that has underpinned our view of the world to date, namely that between national and international spheres, is being dissolved in what remains a somewhat hazy power space of global domestic politics. Nonetheless, it was this distinction that helped to shape the world of the first modernity, including its key concepts (and theories) of society, identity, state, sovereignty, legitimacy, violence and state authority. This book therefore asks: how might we conceptualize a world and a set of global dynamics in which the problematic consequences of radicalized modernization effectively eliminate the cornerstones and logics of action – certain historically produced fundamental distinctions and basic institutions – of its nation-state order? The answer that is developed and explicated in the following chapters goes as follows: the new global domestic politics that is already at work here and now, beyond the national–international distinction, has become a meta-power game whose outcome is completely open-ended. It is a game in which boundaries, basic rules and basic distinctions are being renegotiated – not only those between the 'national' and 'international' spheres, but also those between global business and the state, transnational civil society movements, supranational organizations and national governments and societies.

If those things that fall within the 'national' framework are no longer national and those that fall within the 'international' framework are no longer international, then the political realism of the national outlook is a false realism. Its place is taken instead – so this book contends – by a *cosmopolitan realism*, which needs to be fully explored conceptually in terms of its logics of power. Cosmopolitan realism focuses not only on the crucial role of global economic power and global business actors in relations of cooperation and competition among states, but also on the strategies of transnational civil society movements, including 'uncivil' – that is, terrorist – networks which mobilize privatized violence against states for their own political purposes.

Cosmopolitan realism, or Machiavellianism, provides an answer to two questions in particular. First, what are the strategies by which global business actors impose their own rules of action upon states? And, second, how can states for their part win back political meta-power *qua* states in relation to global business actors, in order to impose a *cosmopolitan regime* on global political capital that encompasses political freedom, global justice, a secure social order and ecological sustainability? This *New Global Political Economy* acquires its relevance and explanatory power, on the one hand, from the fact that it is expounded as a theory of power about the strategic scope for action available in a transnational economy; on the other hand, it also takes up the counter-question suggested by this, namely, how can the world of state-organized politics (with its basic concepts, its strategic sphere of power, its institutional possibilities and constraints) be opened up to the challenges not only of the global economy but also of the global problems that are a consequence of modernization?

There are a number of signs pointing to the fact that a culture of globality is advancing upon us and possibly even gaining in dominance – among other things, the fact that, in the maelstrom of globalized modernization, global problems have long since become an everyday reality. Climate change, environmental destruction, food risks, global financial risks, migration, the anticipated consequences of innovations in genetics, human genetics, nanotechnology, and so forth, all serve to call into question in a quite tangible way the very foundations of social life. The nation-state has ceased to be the source of a frame of reference that encompasses all other frames of reference and enables political answers to be found. Moreover, the terrorist attacks of 11 September 2001 teach us that power does not translate into security. In this one radically divided world, it is likely that security will only be achieved once people's willingness and ability to see the world of unrestrained modernity through the eyes of the other, through the lens of difference, have been awakened at a cultural level and have become a part of our everyday existence. The task of creating a *cosmopolitan common sense* of this sort – a spirit of recognition of the difference of others which pervades ethnic, national and religious traditions and brings them to life in the course of mutual exchange – is, after 11 September, no longer merely an idle, naïve verbal conjuring trick, but has become much more a question of survival – not least the survival of militarily superior states.

In this respect, this book can be read as an answer to the question of how the neo-nationalist turn in many parts of the world can be countered intellectually, morally and politically. Once the power sphere of global domestic politics is opened up conceptually and politically, beyond the old categories of 'national' and 'international', prospects emerge for a cosmopolitan renewal of politics and the state.

Globalization is not destiny; it can be shaped and influenced. Indeed, it has the capacity to reinvigorate what has classically been known as 'politics' and to give it new foundations. This message is the theme of a trilogy of which this book forms the first part. *Power in the Global Age* deals with the way in which the national and international forms of 'legitimate domination' (Max Weber) are being dissolved and its rules rewritten in the globalized power game of mobile capital, states and social movements. This situation requires a change of perspective from the national to the cosmopolitan vision, one whose realism and meanings – as well as its dangers – are explained and developed in *The Cosmopolitan Vision.* In the final part of the trilogy, *Cosmopolitan Europe* (co-authored with Edgar Grande), this perspective is put to the test and illustrated by means of concrete historical examples.

Ulrich Beck

Preface

The people we elected have no power.
And the people that have power weren't elected.
Demonstrator's placard

What are the foundations of legitimate domination in the global age?[1] The worrying aspect of this question lurks unarticulated in the background of every controversy of our time and provides the impetus for this book: we think we know what we are talking about when we use the words 'politics' and 'state', and yet we know full well that we *don't* know what we are talking about. Everybody knows that politics takes place in parliaments, in governments, in political parties and in election campaigns. Yet is it not these very pre-packaged answers to every inquiry about the grounds of legitimate domination that prevent us from understanding the language of the power struggles that rock the world?

We blithely carry on believing that we know to which authorities we must appeal if we want public welfare issues dealt with at long last. But then we read in the financial pages of the newspaper that capital flows are moving here and there according to the rules of a global market that eludes all nation-state controls. Our daily lives are profoundly influenced by the export of jobs, flexible production siting, information flows, global symbolic systems and supranational organizations such as the World Bank, the International Monetary Fund and the European Union. We witness the way in which 'global ecological crises' and the 'international political economy' – key problems on which experts hold differing opinions – increasingly determine the political agenda. Listening to legal experts, we are given the impression that it is no longer states alone that create and administer international law(s). Local activist groups act globally while global corporations call the shots locally, managing at the same time to avoid their legal obligation to pay commercial taxes. States threaten – and engage in – military intervention in other states based on the appeal to human rights. And, to highlight one final example, the universalization of 'the terrorist threat' leads even democratic military powers and states down the dangerous path of granting themselves a general 'licence to kill' anyone suspected of being a 'terrorist'. We can no longer rule out the possibility that we are sliding inexorably towards an age of 'perpetual peace' in which the boundaries to 'perpetual war' can no longer be drawn – that a kind of 'peace' has set in which is worse than war. But in this context of blurred and confused boundaries and distinctions, what does it mean to speak of 'legitimate domination'?

What is currently taking place – so this book argues – is a creative self-destruction of the nation-state-dominated 'legitimate' world order. This is a highly ambiguous development, but one which also contains the possibility (alongside many other possible scenarios) of a 'cosmopolitan vision', the development of politics towards what we might call a 'cosmopolitan state'. Note, the issue is not that of a clash of civilizations, but rather of the struggle for a human culture in which very different traditions are able to live alongside one another. No wall can protect the countries of the centre from the humanitarian disasters occurring in other parts of the world. The new dangers facing humanity from the modern risk society make no distinctions of race, nation or continent.

There is a new cosmopolitan realism in the air! The concept of cosmopolitanism has been a part of Western civilization's philosophical and political tradition since at least the time of Kant, but, in order to glean a realistic critique of prevailing conditions from it, some 'dusting off' is required: the term needs to be subjected to a 'redemptive critique' (Walter Benjamin). By 'cosmopolitan' I do not mean the elitist, idealistic concept that serves as an ideological spearhead for the imperial designs of transnational elites and organizations. What I am thinking of instead are the values of an acknowledged, lived diversity that pervade every social situation and historical context, a 'cosmopolitan common sense' that takes a hold of large sections of humanity and enables them to shape seemingly unstoppable developments.

At the start of the third millennium the maxim of national *realpolitik* – that national interests must be pursued by national means – needs to be replaced by the maxim of cosmopolitan *realpolitik*, namely 'the more cosmopolitan our political life, the more national and successful it will be.' Only a politics that is multilateral is capable of opening up unilateral options for action. If global problems did not exist, they would have to be invented, as they create a common transnational context. The national zero-sum game of sovereignty that exists in many people's heads is proving to be historically false: interdependence can and must be created and understood as a plus-sum game in which all the parties involved make power gains.

It is this seemingly paradoxical core proposition of the new cosmopolitan realism that this book sets out to elucidate. In an age of global crises and risks, the politics of 'golden handcuffs' – the creation of a close-knit network of transnational dependencies – leads states to regain their national independence, along with and in spite of the power gains made by a highly mobile global business constituency.

Highly contradictory cultural currents encounter one another in very limited spaces and enter into what are often highly conflict-laden associations. Bilingualism (that is, the ability to let go of one's fixation on what is familiar), lives lived out in multiple locations, constant mobility, more and more people holding dual passports, lives that straddle more than one border – all this creates a complex web of divided loyalties, without those identities experienced as original being abandoned in the process. To have both roots *and* wings – provincialism linked with the wealth of experience gained from being an active citizen of the world – could become the common denominator of a civilization made up of societies containing heterogeneous global cultures. And, as a result, it may even provide an answer to the fundamental question on everybody's lips: what kind of order does the world need?

This acknowledgement of difference – not to be confused with state-prescribed versions of happy multicultural co-existence – opens up a multi-dimensional sphere of possibilities, but is not without its own radical internal contradictions. It is not merely an issue of the growing gap between rich and poor, of global pockets of welfare and global poverty traps between North and South. Nor is it exclusively an issue of the conditions necessary for a life lived in dignity, or of the possibility and impossibility of creating a global-sized mini-welfare state, a 'globalized Keynesianism', even if the latter were geared solely towards the *minima moralia* of basic needs. It is about much more than this. Cosmopolitan vision has to do with the way in which basic nation-state institutions can be opened up in the long term, from below as well as from within, to the challenges of the global age. It has to do with the way minorities, foreigners and the socially excluded are treated. Above all, however, it has to do with the role of the state and of governments in these contexts, a role that is fundamentally changing and whose contours still need to be defined. It has to do with the problems thrown up in the process of consolidating and reconstituting democratic societies in the global age, and the role of different groups' and parties' human rights in this. It has to do with the question of what functional equivalents there might be to the state, and in particular with the question of how outbreaks of violence stemming from people's disappointments and humiliations can be countered preventively.

Cosmopolitan vision thus combines respect for the dignity of those who are culturally different with an interest in the survival of each individual. In other words, cosmopolitanism is the next big idea to follow on after the historically worn-out ideas of nationalism, communism, socialism and neo-liberalism, and this idea *might just* make the improbable possible, namely the survival of humanity beyond the twenty-first century without a lapse back into barbarism.

The coercive dynamics of the global market economy have transformed the rules of global politics. With the removal of the boundaries around economics, politics and society, a new struggle for power and counter-power has got underway. Furthermore, the rules of legitimate domination itself are being renegotiated. However, there is no cause for jubilation at the knowledge that a new, irrevocable 'cosmopolitan modernity' is emerging, since that knowledge is necessarily accompanied by a great deal of ambiguity – indeed, how could it be otherwise after the experience of unbridled totalitarian politics in what was a twentieth century marked by one catastrophe after another? There is a specific reason for describing the whole ideology of the nation-state-based economy, society and politics retrospectively as the *first modernity* and distinguishing it from what as yet remains a somewhat hazy *second modernity* (defined by global ecological and economic crises, widening transnational inequalities, individualization, precarious forms of paid work and the challenges of cultural, political and military globalization). That reason is to overcome the 'protectionist reflex' that has paralysed Europe as well as other parts of the world, both intellectually and politically, since the collapse of the bipolar world order. Accordingly, it is the *metatransformation* of the economy, politics and statehood in the global age that constitutes the focus of this book. What had seemed to be highly stable ideals and coordinates of change are themselves undergoing a transformation, as are the foundations and basic concepts of power and domination, legitimation and violence, the economy, the state and politics as well. The key question of *how* the second modernity might become a cosmopolitan modernity is directed towards the realization of an alternative order with political freedom and social and economic justice at its centre (rather than the rules of the global market). Globalization is being fashioned by the powerful against the interests of the poor. There is no advancement of cross-cultural interaction among different societies; instead, the interests of one particular society are being pursued in opposition to those of all the others. By contrast, the cosmopolitan imagination represents the universal interests of humanity itself. It is an attempt to rethink interdependency and reciprocity beyond the limits of national axioms and national arrogance, in the sense of a cosmopolitan *realism* capable of stimulating and sharpening our faculties of perception to take in the unfamiliar, 'glocally' networked societies in which we live and act.

This book owes more to conversations with friends and colleagues than any other that has emerged from my workshop. Edgar Grande, who embodies the creativity of our jointly run 'Reflexive Modernization' research centre in Munich, helped to establish its conceptual shape in a series of conversations that went on for whole days at a time. Christoph Lau, likewise a creative pillar of our research centre and co-developer of the theory of reflexive modernization on the empirical side, witnessed the frequent appearance of each new version of this text and offered his insightful comments with characteristic humour. I also owe a great deal to workshop conversations with Boris Holzer, one of the very few people who are comfortable in very different social scientific cultures. Almut Kleine endured the many hardships associated with the writing of this book, and for her forbearance I am most grateful. Armin Nassehi, Kari Palonen, Shalini Randeria, Natan Sznaider, Bob Jessop, Mats Sørensen and Peter Wehling commented very helpfully on an earlier version.

It was both a pleasure and a privilege to be able to participate in the intellectually stimulating environment at the London School of Economics and Political Science fostered by its then director, Anthony Giddens; that environment has played a crucial role in shaping the cosmopolitan imagination of this book. This particularly includes conversations shared with Mary Kaldor, David Held, Saskia Sassen, Richard Sennett, Ralf Dahrendorf, Stanley Cohen, Don Slater, Roger Silverstone and many others besides; also, in the context of Goldsmiths College, conversations with Angela McRobbie and Scott Lash. And, last but not least, Jürgen Habermas took the time to talk through an earlier version of this book with me. I owe more to my intellectual fellow traveller Johannes Willms than I can recount here. Above all, though, this book represents a part of my never-ending conversation with Elisabeth Beck-Gernsheim, for which 'gratitude' is too weak a word.

The Volkswagenwerk Foundation enabled me to work on this book by providing a generous grant – for this, too, I offer my sincere thanks.

Ulrich Beck

1

Introduction: New Critical Theory with Cosmopolitan Intent

At the beginning of the third millennium, the future of humanity suddenly appears undecided – a turn of events predicted, among others, by Friedrich Nietzsche, Karl Marx, Immanuel Kant and Max Weber.[1]

Just 150 years ago Nietzsche urged that 'Europe ought to decide . . . that the long drawn-out comedy of its petty states and the divided will of its dynasties and democracies should finally come to an end. The time for petty politics is past: the very next century will bring with it the struggle for mastery over the whole earth – the *compulsion* to grand politics.'

Before this, Immanuel Kant evoked the vision of the cosmopolitan ideal behind this grand politics as follows: 'To consider oneself, according to internal civil law, as an associate member of a cosmopolitan society is the most sublime idea a man can have of his destination. One cannot think of it without enthusiasm.'

Karl Marx predicted that it was the process of capital becoming global rather than state politics that would break through the axioms of national politics and open up the game of grand politics. 'In place of the old local and national seclusion and self-sufficiency, we have intercourse in every direction, universal interdependence of nations. As in material, so also in intellectual production. The intellectual creations . . . become common property. National one-sidedness and narrow-mindedness become more and more impossible, and from the numerous national and local literatures, there arises a world literature.' Finally, Max Weber spelt out the implications of this for the study of history. 'But at some point there is a change: the significance of positions that had previously been accepted uncritically starts to become unclear, and well-trodden paths disappear in the gloom. The light of the great cultural problems has moved on. It is then that the academics, too, prepare themselves for a change in standpoint and conceptual apparatus, in order to look down upon the flow of events from the heights of thought.'

1.1   The meta-game of world politics

These and other perspectives, paradoxes and implications of the compulsion to grand politics can be developed and elucidated using the concept of the *meta-game of world politics*.

By 'meta-game', I mean that the old world politics, which worked by *applying* the rules, and the new world politics, which works by *changing* the rules, are fully intermeshed with one another: they cannot be separated out, whether in terms of specific actors, strategies or alliances. It is becoming clear that, in the twilight zone between the passing of the national era and the emergence of the cosmopolitan era, political action is following two completely different and yet mutually interwoven scripts. In other words, there are two different acting ensembles on the world stage performing two different plays in accordance with each perspective, such that there is a highly paradoxical interweaving between the established and the alternative political drama, between that which is closing down and that which is opening up. The realization that this is so – however easy it may be to prove – makes for confusion not only in people's thinking but also in reality itself. It is precisely this actually existing confusion of categories, scripts, plays and actors – the rewriting of the theatrical works of world politics even as they are being performed – that characterizes the essence of the meta-game.[2]

The systems of rules governing world politics can be identified according to institutions and organizations. *Institutions* refer to the underlying rules for the exercise of power (*Macht*) and domination (*Herrschaft*), in other words, formal and informal codes of behaviour that serve to facilitate or to prescribe certain forms of national and international political practice. Thus, for example, the institutions of the nation-state power game in the first modernity include state control over a limited territory, international recognition and diplomacy, a monopoly on the use of violence, and legal sovereignty, as well as welfare-state safety nets, basic civil and political rights and so on. Whereas institutions establish the basic norms and forms, as it were, of political action, that is, the categorical framework of political action, *organizations* refer to particular actors that have a certain number of members, financial and spatial resources at their disposal, and a certain legal status. By way of a rough simplification, I differentiate between three organizations that are part of the meta-game: states, global business actors and actors from global civil society.

According to the prevailing theoretical controversy, the interplay of institutions and organizations can be characterized and decoded through two logics of action, which James March and Johan Olsen call the *logic of expected consequences* and the *logic of appropriateness*. According to the logic of consequences, political action follows a rational calculus of behaviour that obeys the principle of maximizing a given set of unexplained preferences.

Examples of this include classical games theory and the neo-classical economy. The logic of appropriateness, by contrast, understands political actions as a product of power, roles and identities, which stimulate appropriate behaviour in given situations (March and Olsen 1989; Krasner 1999).

The theory of the meta-game cuts across the logic of expected consequences and the logic of appropriate behaviour by following a *logic of rule change*. This means that the old nation-state international institutional order is not an ontological given but is itself what is at stake. The relationship between institutions and organizations is turned around. Institutions no longer prescribe the space and the framework within which organizations engage in political action; instead, it is organizations – such as global business actors – that are *breaking out* of the institutional box and are forcing a reconsideration of the 'national *a prioris*' of political action.[3]

Thus, to speak of a rule-changing meta-game of world politics is to invoke a second *Great Transformation* (Polanyi 1944). It is no longer states alone that constitute the arena of collective action in the sense of prescribing the space in which political action occurs and the system of rules to which it is subject – including the indispensable social institutions for making decisions and implementing them collectively. The reflexive meta-game raises, *in reality*, the question of the extent to which the very foundations of state power *themselves* become the object of global political and global economic strategies of power. Yet this means that it is globalization and not 'the state' that defines and changes the arenas of collective action. A *second-order* transformation becomes the key issue: the Great Transformation of the state-centred order *per se*! The exclusive scenario according to which nation-states and the system of international relations between states determined the space of collective political action is broken down from both the inside and the outside at the same time, and is successively replaced by a more complex, border transcending subpolitical and global political meta-power game, one that changes the rules of power, is full of paradoxes, unpredictable and open-ended.[4] Exactly what does this mean, though?

1.2   The old game can no longer be played

Globalization has two meanings. Now that a new game has begun, the rules and basic concepts of the old game – even if it continues to be played – no longer have much connection with reality. At any rate, the old game, which goes by many names, such as 'nation-state', 'national industrial society', 'national capitalism' or even 'national welfare state', can no longer be played *on its own*. This simple game was rather like a game of draughts, where each player has a homogeneous set of pieces and is allowed to make certain moves with them. Globalization, however, has introduced a new space and framework for acting: politics is no longer subject to the same boundaries as before, and it is no longer tied solely to state actors and institutions, the result being that additional players, new roles, new resources, unfamiliar rules and new contradictions and conflicts appear on the scene. In the old game, each playing piece made one move only. This is no longer true of the new, nameless game played for power and domination. The 'capital' pieces, for example, have created a new kind of mobility for themselves, similar to the knight or the rook in chess – in other words, there are striking differences and strange polyvalencies in the strategic quality of both pieces and moves. What is more, though, the old and the new actors have first to find or invent – that is, to define and construct – their own roles and resources on the global playing board. It is not only the new *moves* in the game that are unclear, so are its new *objectives*. With draughts the aim was to get rid of all the opponent's pieces. If the new game were chess, the aim would be to place the king in checkmate. But not even that much is certain; nothing has been decided or arranged.

In the old political game of 'national (welfare) state' the aim was to achieve the greatest possible security for all. Does that still hold true? The goal of politics was to bring about a 'social democratic age' (Dahrendorf 1970), to achieve the maximum amount of social equality against a background of national homogeneity. How much cultural difference, how much social inequality should or must be permitted? In the old national–international game, it was the rules of international law that prevailed, which meant that, within state boundaries, you could do what you liked with your own citizens. Do these rules still apply? Or is it rather the case that the vague rule of 'limited sovereignty' has long since come into effect? Any state involved in 'ethnic cleansing' or serious human rights violations against its own citizens can reckon with becoming the target of 'humanitarian intervention' by the international community, based on the notion of global citizens' rights and human rights. Can heads of government, ministers or ambassadors who have blatantly violated the global civil rights of their own state citizens still rely on diplomatic immunity, or must they face the prospect of being arrested and brought before a court in the country they are visiting?

In the old game there were certain rules about fairness: anyone who throws a six either has to sit out a turn, or else is allowed to make two moves in the same turn. Then there was the rule that once one player has made their move it is the other player's turn, so that play alternates. Does this still apply? Or does it apply only in specific circumstances – within certain power relations – and not for other players under different conditions? Who decides which rules apply and which do not? In the transition from one era to the next, politics is entering a peculiar twilight zone, the twilight zone of *double contingency*. Nothing remains fixed, neither the old basic institutions and systems of rules nor the specific organizational forms and roles of the actors; instead, they are disrupted, reformulated and renegotiated during the course of the game itself. Just how far this will go is also unclear, since it depends on contingent circumstances, like the goals and alternatives of politics in general.

The thing about the meta-game argument is that the players' scope for action essentially depends on their self-definition and on their redefinition of the political. They themselves are the precondition for success. New opportunities for power can *only* be generated through critique of the nation-state orthodoxy and through new categories that point the way towards a cosmopolitan outlook. Anyone caught clinging to the old draughts dogma (e.g. the fetish of 'sovereignty') will be jumped over – or steamrollered – without even being allowed to complain about it. It is the *costs* that states incur by clinging to the old rules of draughts that provide the conditions for a cosmopolitan shift in perspective. In other words, methodological nationalism – the insistence that the meta-game of global politics is and always will be a national game – turns out to be extremely costly. It distorts our view and simultaneously prevents us from recognizing new moves and new resources of power. Indeed, the possibility of transforming the win–lose or lose–lose rules of the meta-game into win–win rules, from which the state, global civil society *and* capital can all benefit in equal measure, remains untapped theoretically, empirically and politically. In effect, it is a reversal of the Marxist principle that being determines consciousness: consciousness, or awareness, of a new situation – the cosmopolitan vision – maximizes players' options in the meta-game of global politics. The best way of transforming one's own position of power (and perhaps even the world of politics) is to change one's outlook on the world – a sceptical, realistic view of the world, but equally a *cosmopolitan* one!

The neo-liberal agenda is an attempt to capture the momentary historical gains of globally and politically mobile capital and fix them institutionally. Thought through to its radical conclusion, the capital perspective posits itself as absolute and autonomous, and thus uses the strategic power and strategic options presented by classical economics as a way of developing subpolitical and global political power. According to this scheme, what is good for capital is good for all: everyone will get richer, and ultimately even the poor will benefit, or so the promise goes. The seductiveness of this neo-liberal ideology, then, lies not in giving selfishness a free rein or in maximizing competition, but in the promise of global justice. The implication is: maximizing the power of capital is *ultimately* the better way towards socialism. *That* is why the (welfare) state is superfluous.

What the neo-liberal agenda also insists upon, however, is that in the new meta-game capital gets two playing pieces and two moves. Everybody else still gets only one playing piece and one move, as they did before. The power of neo-liberalism is therefore based on a radical inequality in terms of who may break the rules and who may not. Changing the rules remains the revolutionary privilege of capital. Everybody else is condemned to conform to them. The nation-based view of politics (and the methodological nationalism of political theory) cements capital's superiority in the game and confirms the power advantage it holds by virtue of having broken away from the national game of draughts. However, the superiority of capital is essentially based on the fact that states do not follow its lead, and that politics holds itself captive within the cast-iron framework of the nation-based draughts rules. So who constitutes the counter-power, the opponent of globalized capital?

1.3   The counter-power of global civil society

As far as public awareness and a range of studies are concerned, the role of counter-power to a capital that defies the rules falls not to states but to global civil society and its plural actors. In the old game of 'capital' against 'labour', relationships between power and counter-power were conceived of in terms of the master–slave dialectic. The counter-power of the slave – the worker – lies in the fact that he can withhold his labour. The core of this counter-power is the organized strike: workers down tools and stop working. One of the limitations of this counter-power is the fact that the workers have work and therefore employment contracts – in other words, they have to be members of an organization in order to be able to go on strike. They also face the threat of being fired (locked out) in return. This is the basis of capital's counter-power. This form of master–slave dialectic continues to exist, but is undermined by capital's new 'country-hopping' mobility. Events that occurred in Germany during the summer of 2001 offer an example of how this happens.

VW, a profitable global corporation, wanted to make new employees work longer hours while paying them less – and everybody thought this was a marvellous idea! The trade unions, Germany's Social Democratic chancellor, Gerhard Schröder, and, of course, the employers, too, all praised the new model for setting a good example, not only in the automobile industry but elsewhere as well. Soon enough the employers demanded that the salary structure be 'opened up' – in a downwards direction, of course. This meant 'flexibility', which in turn meant that working conditions and wage rates became trapped in a downwards spiral under global competitive conditions. VW had threatened to build the new VW minivan in either Slovakia or India. The reason the 'labour party' and the trade unions were celebrating was because they succeeded in preventing this from happening. It also meant, however, that in future people in Germany would be expected to work more – namely at weekends as well – for much lower wages and lower social insurance contributions on the part of the employers. *This* sort of globalization makes workers in the rich welfare states particularly nervous, as they fear being dropped from a great height. The idea of engaging in international solidarity occurred to nobody – and neither, for example, did the notion that German workers were taking away jobs from Slovakian workers.

In contrast to this, the counter-power of global civil society is based on the figure of the *political consumer.* The consumer stands *beyond* the master–slave dialectic. His counter-power results from being able to refuse to make a purchase, at any time and in any place. The 'weapon of non-purchase' cannot be restricted in terms of location, time or commodity. It is dependent on certain conditions, such as a person having money in the first place or there being a surplus of products and services available for consumers to choose from. And it is these conditions – that is, the plurality of opportunities to buy and consume – which bring down the subjective costs of penalizing *this* product from *this* corporation through organized non-purchase.

What is fatal for the interests of capital is that there is no counter-strategy to confront the counter-power of consumers. Not even all-powerful global corporations can make their consumers redundant. Unlike workers, consumers are not members, nor do they wish to become such. And the blackmail threat of shifting production to other countries, where the consumers still behave themselves and accept whatever is put before them, is an utterly inadequate instrument. In the first place, the consumer is globalized and as such is highly desirable to corporations. And in the second place, it is not possible to respond to consumer protests in one country by moving to other countries without going through considerable contortions. Moreover, it is not even possible to play consumers' national solidarity off against one another. The nature of consumer protests is that they are transnational. *The consumer society is the actually existing world society*. Consumption knows no limits, in terms either of manufacture or of use. Consumers are everything that workers are not. This is what makes their counter-power such a threat to the power of capital – and so far they have hardly begun to exploit it.

While the counter-power of workers – in line with the master–slave dialectic – is tied to direct spatio-temporal interactions and contractual relations, the consumer has none of these territorial, local or contractual ties. With good networking and carefully planned mobilization, the free, unbound consumer, once organized transnationally, can be modelled into an effective weapon. Going on strike is a risky thing for an individual; not buying certain products and thereby casting a vote against the politics of corporations, on the other hand, is completely free of risk. Nonetheless, this counter-power of the political consumer has to be organized: without advocatory actors from civil society, the counter-power of consumers remains a blunt weapon. Thus the limits of consumer counter-power lie in the limits of organizational capacity. A buyers' boycott is directed at non-members; as such, it is hard to organize and requires a carefully planned dramaturgy in the public media, a staging of symbolic politics. With insufficient publicity, it will fall apart. Money is and always will be the prerequisite. No purchasing power, no consumer power. All this places immanent constraints on the counter-power of consumers.

1.4   The transformation of the state

There is no getting away from the task of redefining state politics. The advocates and actors of global civil society are no doubt indispensable in the global game between different powers and counter-powers, especially in terms of establishing global values and standards. However, the abstract notion of the state and politics undergoing fundamental change tempts us into accepting the grand illusion that, in a world no longer bound by economic and cultural constraints, a new extra-political desire for peace will prevail. The new humanism of civil society suggests the soft conclusion that the contradictions, crises and side-effects of the current Second Great Transformation might be civilized by this new symbol of hope, namely, civil society acting at a global level. However, this conceptual figure belongs among the museum pieces of the unpolitical.

Given that this is so, the key realization is that the meta-game can *only* be transformed from a lose–lose game into a win–win game through a transformation of state politics (and of political and state theory). So the key question is: how can and must the concept and organizational form of the state be opened out and refashioned to meet the challenges of economic and cultural globalization? How does the cosmopolitan self-transformation of the state become possible? Or, to put the question differently, who are the 'democratic princes', in the sense of a cosmopolitan Machiavellianism, of the second modernity?[5] The answer is: the cosmopolitan prince is a collective actor. But which one? Are the new princes the heads of corporations who will make Schumpeter's 'creative destruction' a global affair? Or will perhaps the new Davids – the actors of Greenpeace and Amnesty International – be the ones to defy the Goliaths? Or can the heroes of the demolition of the welfare state be thought of as the princes – those who call themselves 'modernizers' as they implement the neo-liberal agenda? I think not. However unpolitical the notion is that global civil society might be capable of providing a substitute for the renewal of state politics, the notion that *civil society seizes power* is equally new and untested. It is this kind of symbiosis between civil society and state that I call a '*cosmopolitan state*'. The sought-after democratic princes of the global age would thus be the cosmopolitan renewers of the state. The key question for the stabilization of global civil society, for global, mobile capital and also for the renewal of democracy – in other words, the question as to the win–win rules of global politics – is how the ideas, theories and institutions of the state might be liberated from national narrow-mindedness and opened out to the cosmopolitan era.

In order to avoid a discussion about the false alternative between a politics of state and a politics of civil society in the global age, it is necessary to distinguish clearly between *state*-centredness and *nation*-state-centredness. No matter how right it is to get rid of the nation-state fixation – the state no longer being *the* actor in the international system, but rather *one* actor *among others* – it would nonetheless be wrong to throw the baby out with the bathwater and, while aiming critique at the nation-state-fixated outlook, to lose sight of the state's potential capacity to act and to transform itself in the global age. Thus the meta-power game means that states, too, must be conceived of, made and researched as entities that are contingent and politically changeable. The question that then arises is: how does the transnationalization of states become possible?

It is by no means the case – as is usually implied – that the politics of globalization are dictated by the globalization of the economy. In its response to the challenges of globalization, politics certainly does have strategic options, which can be identified – and this is crucial – according to the extent to which they either remain *within* the framework of the old nation-based game of draughts or else *break* with it. What is at work here is the rule that governs the decline in nation-state power: *those who play only the national card in the global meta-game will lose*. What is needed is a complete change in perspective; in other words, the following principle also holds: *the counter-power of states develops as they become transnationalized and cosmopolitanized*. Only if states succeed in catching up with mobile capital and redefining and reorganizing their positions of power and game moves can the decline in state power and authority be halted internationally, indeed turned into its very opposite.

It is necessary to distinguish between two types of transnational self-transformation of states <*false* and *genuine* transnationalization strategies.> Transnationalization can be a move within the old nation-state game; if so, it remains attached to the latter and is aimed at bringing about a 'new state reason' (K.-D. Wolf 2000). Thus, for example, alliances between the World Trade Organization (WTO) and individual states may enable the latter to gain sovereignty in terms of domestic politics, in relation to the demands of civil society for greater political involvement, for example. Domestic political opposition, for example, can be trumped using Europe, NATO or the WTO, and so on. However, transnationalization can also break with nation-based premises and assumptions to represent a first step in the emergence of a cosmopolitan state or confederation of states. It is in the latter case that I speak of genuine transnationalization.

The meta-game enables everybody to play a double game with reversed roles – the buck of failure is passed to one's opponent along with the politics of bitter pills. What arises from this is a politics of the '*cunning state*'

(Randeria 2003): state politicians deny their own power in order to be better able to exercise it. In the meantime, they hand over responsibility for the consequences of their decisions – or the lack thereof – to the other side, or else offload it onto the new carte blanche for inertia, namely globalization. As versatile converts to whatever is new, heads of government can emphasize their weakness vis-à-vis the new world powers – the WTO, non-governmental organizations (NGOs), and so on – in order to justify themselves to their own electorates, while simultaneously evading responsibility for their inactivity. Meanwhile, WTO actors swear by their old role as experts, protesting scientific neutrality and thereby forcing through their worldwide foreign domestic policy against elected governments, wherever they may be. Power holders throughout the world denounce the new 'imperialism of human rights', insisting on 'cultural difference' – in other words, the right to cultural difference – but use this as a weapon in their domestic battles to eliminate political opposition and freedom of opinion. NGOs proclaim and defend (the self-legitimacy of) human rights, but this global mission is also a tool they use in competition against one another over the begging bowls of 'global problems', from which they themselves are fed.

1.5   Terrorist groups as new global actors

Having been globalized through the mass media, the horrific images broadcast from New York and Washington on 11 September 2001 enabled terrorist groups to establish themselves at a single stroke as new global actors to rival states, business and finance, and civil society. Terrorist networks can be thought of as NGOs that are committed to violence. Like the non-governmental organizations of civil society, they act in a non-territorial, decentralized way – that is, both locally *and* transnationally. While Greenpeace tackles environmental crises and Amnesty International human rights violations committed by states, terrorist NGOs have the state monopoly on violence in their sights. However, this means that, on the one hand, this kind of transnational terrorism is not necessarily always *Islamic* terrorism: it can be bound up with all manner of goals, ideologies and fundamentalisms. On the other hand, a distinction needs to be made between the terrorism of national liberation organizations, which are tied to particular territories and nations, and the new transnational terrorist networks, which act independently of territory and across national borders, and as a result severely undermine the nation-based grammar of the military and of warfare in general.

If the military gaze to date has been focused on its counterpart, that is, on other nation-state military organizations, and on deflecting their attacks, now it is transnational threats from substate perpetrators and networks that pose a challenge to the entire state edifice. We are now experiencing in the military domain what has previously happened in the domain of culture, namely the *death of distance*; it is, indeed, the end of the state's monopoly on violence in a world shaped by the risks generated through industrialized civilization, where ultimately anything can become a missile in the hands of determined fanatics. The peaceful symbols of civil society can be transformed into instruments of hell. In principle, this is nothing new, only now everybody everywhere is fully aware of it.

In the past terrorists would try to save their own life after committing a terrorist act. Terrorists on a suicide mission, on the other hand, generate an enormous destructive force when they deliberately give up their own life. The suicide attacker is the most radical counter-image to *homo economicus* that exists. He or she has no inhibitions whatsoever, either economically or morally, and in this respect is a vehicle of absolute horror. Strictly speaking, the suicide attacker and the suicide attack constitute a *single entity*. A perpetrator cannot carry out a suicide attack more than once; neither do state authorities need to convict him or her of the crime. This singularity is sealed with the simultaneity of crime, confession and self-obliteration.

This is why the 'anti-terrorism alliance' is seeking to apprehend those suspected of being 'behind the scenes', of 'pulling the strings', of being the state patrons of the terrorists. However, as soon as the perpetrators have died at their own hands, causalities evaporate and disappear. It has been said that states are indispensable for the creation of terrorist networks. But supposing it is precisely the lack of states, the non-existence of functioning state structures, that provides fertile soil for terrorist activities? The tendency to attribute these activities to states and to people behind the scenes giving orders is possibly rooted in the old military thinking, whereas we have long since reached the threshold of an *individualization of war*, which is to say that 'war' can now be waged by individuals against states and no longer solely by one state against another.

The power of terrorist campaigns grows in parallel with a whole series of circumstances: the vulnerability of our civilization, the global mass media presence of the terrorist threat; the US president's judgement that these perpetrators threaten 'civilization'; the perpetrators' willingness to obliterate themselves; and, finally, the fact that the terrorist threat is multiplied exponentially by technological progress. In developing the technologies of the future – genetic technology, nanotechnology and robotics – we are opening up 'a new Pandora's Box' (Bill Joy). Genetic modification, communications technology and artificial intelligence, now also being combined with one another, undermine the state's monopoly on the use of violence and leave the door wide open to an individualization of war – unless effective measures are taken soon at an international level to bolt it shut.

It would not take much, for example, for someone to make a genetically generated plague, designed to threaten specific populations over longer incubation periods, rather like a genetic mini-atom bomb. And this is just one example among many. The contrast between such technologies and nuclear and biological weapons is noticeable, as well. These new technologies are based on *knowledge*; they can be readily disseminated and revolutionized over and over again, so that the possibility of monopolistic state control over certain materials and resources no longer exists as it did in the case of atomic and biochemical weapons (e.g. weapons grade uranium, expensive laboratories). This empowerment of individuals in comparison with states would also open up Pandora's Box *politically*: not only are the walls that have existed so far between the military and civil society being torn down, but so too are the walls between suspects and non-suspects, those between whom the law has made a very clear distinction up until now. If there is a danger of war becoming individualized, however, citizens would have to *prove* that they do not pose a threat: under such circumstances every individual would ultimately come under suspicion of being a potential terrorist. Thus everybody would have to put up with being checked 'for security reasons', with no immediately obvious cause. Taken to its logical conclusion, the individualization of war would lead to the death of democracy, because states would have to ally themselves with states *against* citizens in order to ward off the dangers facing them from their citizens.

1.6   The political power of perceived risks from industrialized civilization

One principle that becomes apparent here is that global *perceptions of risk* throw open a space in which new transnational opportunities for power emerge. Despite this, US President Bush has passed up the opportunity to take a bold step towards a system of cosmopolitan states. Instead, using the political power generated by a perceived terrorist threat, he has begun to create *transnational surveillance states* in which security and the military play a large role while freedom and democracy count for very little. The key question is, who defines what a 'transnational terrorist' is? The USA is not only the victim of a terrorist attack, it is also the global sheriff, plaintiff, world judge, juror and court official all in one. The threat of terrorism thus fuels the *promiscuity of power*; it seems to grant even democratic military powers and states an almost unlimited licence to hunt down terrorists – or, rather, they authorize themselves to do so in repulsing this 'threat to humanity'. Working on the premise that terrorists do not act alone[6] but need the support of 'evil' states, President Bush is developing a new, military doctrine in which the option of armed intervention against states that threaten the USA is justified as a right to self-defence. Indeed, Washington has gone so far as no longer to rule out the unthinkable, a first strike using so-called mini-nuclear weapons against states suspected of supporting terrorism.

What is the aim of the 'war against terrorism'? Ill-defined aims – to root out and destroy the 'evil' of terror – have no limits, no possible end point, and therefore amount to a *general authorization*. Fundamental distinctions between war and peace, attack and defence, are rendered invalid. The ubiquitous existence of 'suspected terrorists' makes the construction of enemy images a more radical and more flexible affair. Just as corporations can produce goods anywhere, so too powerful states can now construct a variety of different enemy images. It is not the declaration of war by an enemy state but rather the unilateral judgement of the state under threat that determines who the (next) enemy is and who must reckon with military intervention. The *concept of 'enemy'* has been made more flexible through being deterritorialized and *disassociated from state actors*, allowing a state, first, to deploy weaponry wherever it sees fit, in the interests of 'internal defence' (of the USA, but also of Russia, Germany, Israel, Palestine, India, China, and so forth); second, to make an indirect declaration of war against states, without having been attacked by them; third, to normalize and institutionalize the 'state of emergency', both domestically and beyond the state's borders; and, fourth, to suspend legal frameworks, with regard not only to international relations and terrorist enemies but also to one's own constitutional state and foreign democracies.

Furthermore, constructions of the enemy that are disassociated from state actors undermine established military–political alliances (such as NATO) because these are geared towards state enemy images. What comes to take their place are anti-terrorism alliances, which can react in a flexible way to each different construction of the terrorist enemy but need to be forged anew time after time, thereby providing a spur to diplomacy and forcing states to break away from the mentality of camps and alliances.

Constructions of the terrorist enemy 'kill' the plurality of society and of expert rationalities, as well as destroying the independence of the courts and the unconditional validity of human rights. They empower states and secret services to pursue a policy of de-democratization. The power of risk perception reveals itself not least in the fact that, even *within* developed democracies, fundamental civil and political rights are suddenly (capable of) being suspended – even with the consent of the overwhelming majority of their democratically experienced populations. Faced with the alternative of security or freedom, governments, parliaments, parties and populations that otherwise compete with or obstruct one another are quick to reach the unanimous decision to dismantle fundamental freedoms. At the same time, national sovereign rights in relation to the police and the military are being sacrificed (more or less unilaterally) to the requirements of transnational cooperation in the fight against militant terrorism.

This illustrates the fact that global perceptions of global risks from industrialized civilization trigger a political reflexivity that breaks through the national orthodoxy, opens up the space for political action and facilitates a cosmopolitan shift in perspective.

This applies (as already shown) to the perceived threat of terrorism. But it is also true of globally perceived ecological and economic threats, so that one could formulate a *law of the opposing political value of global financial risks and global risks from industrialized civilization*: global economic risks *can be individualized* and therefore encourage the process of renationalization; the ecological risks of industrialized civilization, on the other hand, *can be cosmopolitanized*. 'Globality', therefore, refers to people's experience of the threats facing industrialized civilization from its own self-generated risks, along with the realization of planetary finitude; these experiences effectively eliminate the plural oppositions between peoples and states and create a closed space for action based on intersubjectively binding meanings. As the Asia crisis of 1997–8 shows, global financial risks expose entire population groups to unemployment and poverty, but are manifested initially in millions of 'individual destinies', through the destruction of property and employment opportunities. In contrast to this, the globality of risks from industrialized civilization draws attention to the mundane meaning of a cosmopolitan community of common destiny. As such, it opens up a new kind of experiential sphere, which is at once global, individual *and* local, thereby (perhaps!) creating cosmopolitan contexts of meaning and action. This cosmopolitanization of risks in industrialized civilization is a crucial starting point for the advocatory strategies pursued by movements rooted in civil society.

1.7   Who are the 'players'?

Is it not a coarse, wilful violation of the academic commitment to rigour to speak of the practical options available to 'capital', 'global civil society' and 'the state'? Surely this involves unjustifiably simplifying the internal diversity within and obvious contrasts between the groups referred to in such sweeping terms? Who, for example, is being referred to when we speak of 'the world of business'?: specific companies?, 'capital' in the singular?, one particular 'class'?, *the* 'managers'?, *the* 'shareholders'? Is reference being made to individual actors, collective actors or cooperative actors? Is it not the case that the so-called strategies of capital, the state and global civil society belong to utterly divergent sociological aggregates and aggregate circumstances? Is it possible, as Foucault claims, that 'nobody' is acting, that the place of another 'player' at the table remains *empty*?

The answer this book seeks to explore is this: *the players are not pre-given; instead, they are made into players by the meta-game*. They have to constitute and organize themselves politically *within* the game, *as part of* the game. In other words, what is at work is an interactionist logic of reciprocal social constitution *as* players and opponents. Opponents' opportunities for power, their resources and their scope for action are not only related to one another in principle; the actors themselves are only formed in the first place by the moves they make and on the basis of their own self-interpretation, articulation, mobilization and organization – they gain (or lose) their identity and power to act in the course of mutual conflict.

The logic of the meta-game generates a specific *asymmetry of power in terms of the strategic capacity* of capital, the state and global civil society respectively. An extraordinary range of prerequisites are needed to produce political counter-power. This is just as true for the globalization of civil society as it is for the transnationalization of states. As regards capital, the very opposite is true: its particular strength lies in the fact that it does *not* have to organize itself as a single capitalist entity in order to exercise its power in relation to states. 'Capital' is a collective expression for the unco-ordinated actions of individual companies, financial flows and supranational organizations (WTO, IMF, etc.) whose *outcomes* – in the sense of *politics as side-effects* – put states under pressure in a more or less unseen and unintended way, and thereby expedite the unravelling of the old game of draughts known as the 'nation-state'. It is extremely heterogeneous; its immanent players and opponents are themselves threatened or affected by 'hostile takeovers' and globalization risks. But because of the phenomenon of politics as a side-effect, they manage to outplay states nonetheless. 'Capital' in the singular, then, does not need to exist as a unified actor, it does not need to take its place at the table in order to bring its power to bear. This place at the global political meta-game table can be occupied by 'nobody'; and this is exactly what amplifies the power of global business actors.

On the other hand, states need to divest themselves of their national orthodoxy and organize themselves collectively (in the form of the European Union, for example) in order to develop their power and the roles they play in the transnational arena. The *weakness* afflicting the countervailing power exercised both by state actors and by civil society lies in the fact that it does not exist as such, and that it first has to define, orientate and organize – that is, constitute – itself politically against all manner of resistance in the global arena of action.

Campaigns such as the following are occurring more and more frequently. The NATO states agree a weapons amnesty in Macedonia in order to extinguish the flames of the ethnic civil war there. Not only does this military recycling campaign fall strangely between the stools of war and peace, between military action and social work. It also occurs 'without resistance', as it were – perfectly smoothly, with general consent. Perhaps this example can be used to make a more general point: those who take to the streets to protest *against* economic globalization are fighting *for* the globalization of human rights, environmental protection, the right of trade unions to self-determination, and so forth. What this demonstrates is a new kind of *asymmetry of dissent and consent in the national and transnational arena*: while proactive politics – greatly mourned – becomes bogged down in 'political entanglements' (Scharpf) in the national arena, states develop the capacity to act transnationally against the background of a coerced consent that tolerates objections and resistance only as a variant of consent. 'Global problems' – human rights, the prevention of catastrophic climate change, the struggle against poverty and for justice – open up new extra-democratic, extra-state sources of a legitimacy that is self-justifying. Voting is replaced by consent, or, to put it another way, the experience of globality gives rise to the strange *law of the inescapable immanence of being 'anti'*. Globalization, in other words, devours its enemies. Those who are against it are for it – for a *different kind of* globalization.

1.8   Legitimacy undergoes a paradigm change

The paramount question that arises when the meta-game is radically thought through to its conclusion – the 'crunch' question, as it were – is: who or what decides on the legitimacy of the *change* to the rules? Does the transformation of the rules happen on the same old foundations of legitimation used in the national game of draughts? Or are the national sources of legitimacy for power and domination themselves open to negotiation in the meta-game? Who is arguing for what? Who is playing the game of 'change-the-game' and with what background assumptions?

It seems reasonable to suppose that the answers to these important questions emerge from the concrete perspectives of the different players – that is, contradictorily, according to the logic of interaction. But this would mean, at the very least, that the meta-game involving global politics is played in the shadow of a *grandiose misunderstanding*. With their belief in the secularly transcendent, insuperable legitimacy of the old national–international system of rules, the adherents of the national draughts system are playing the big new meta-game on the assumption that any set of rules, even the future one, ultimately has to have the same kind of legitimacy as the national set of draughts rules. As far as the foundations of its legitimation are concerned, the global order is an *inter*national order derived from nation-state legitimacy. To use the onion metaphor, the national draughts rules regarding legitimacy are passed on to the next 'layer', namely supranational institutions. Methodological nationalism presupposes that the nation-state, as the source of legitimacy for supranational norms and organizations, is constant and absolute. The possibility that a global order might be self-legitimating – be it on the basis of pragmatism, rational philosophy or legal positivism – is ruled out from the start.

No, some opponents say, cosmopolitan politics has its own independent sources of legitimation. The new rules and sources of rules emerge, for example, out of the combination of *human rights* and *domination* which, in cases of conflict, enforce these human rights in opposition to the national (draughts) rules. This need not mean that the cosmopolitan regime establishes itself amid the same imperialistic claims as a moral, military and economic world power – such as the USA, for example. Rather, the reverse is true: once a cosmopolitan regime is established – in terms of its commitment to peace, justice and dialogue – it creates a power space that demands to be filled and given firm foundations through military means (UN missions, NATO, etc.). What lends justification to the cosmopolitan regime – such is the intention, at any rate – is the cohesive combining of *moral, economic and military self-legitimation*; it is this that, in cases of conflict, makes such a regime capable of imposing sanctions in the face of individual states' claims to a monopoly on violence.

At this point it becomes clear that distinguishing the national outlook from the cosmopolitan outlook and juxtaposing the two not only reveals new arenas for action and resources of power, but also explains what is ultimately at stake in the meta-game, namely the foundations for the legitimation of politics *per se*. It is only in the narrow perspective of methodological nationalism, where the supranational order of actors and power is seen as the *international* order of power, that the transformation of the rules of the power game has to take place in the context of the old national draughts order. In actual fact, however, the meta-game entails the possibility of a *paradigm change in legitimacy*. This is the point at which the game metaphor comes up against its limits, however, because it is the change in legitimacy that does away with a nation-state sovereignty sanctioned by international law and opens the way to legitimate intervention by a 'military humanism', as we saw in the Kosovo war in 1999.[7] The call for justice and human rights becomes a sword that is used to invade other countries. How can one be in favour of cosmopolitan legitimacy when it leads to crises and wars and thus to the bloody refutation of the idea itself? Who will rein in the side-effects of a cosmopolitan moral principle that speaks of peace while facilitating war? What does 'peace' mean when it generalizes the possibility of war?

If it was not clear before, then this is certainly the point at which it becomes possible to recognize the shadowy zone in which the meta-game takes place – and the murky shadows it itself casts. In the spirit of republican Machiavellianism, it is necessary to make a clear distinction between *genuine* and *false* cosmopolitanism. Yet such clarity is often hard to achieve – such is the nature of the beast – because it is the compelling legitimacy of cosmopolitan law that makes it so tempting to instrumentalize the latter for national-imperial purposes. Fake cosmopolitanism instrumentalizes cosmopolitan rhetoric – the rhetoric of peace, of human rights, of global justice – for national-hegemonic purposes. This is why we can and must speak of false and/or symbolic cosmopolitanism when universal law, transcendental moral claims – such as those raised by Immanuel Kant in his tract *Toward Eternal Peace* – are merged with national superpower pretensions to become the source of legitimation for a global-hegemonic rhetoric around the 'new game'. There is a whole range of historically diverse examples of this.

Fake cosmopolitanism, instrumentalized for national purposes, was Stalin's policy. He robbed the *Communist Internationale* of its autonomy and made it into an extended arm of Soviet national interests. In the domain of philosophy, Johann Gottlieb Fichte elaborated several examples of the scandal of cosmopolitan presumption in the national arena, as Peter Coulmas recounts.[8] A completely different example is the USA, which pursues the global enforcement of human rights as the national mission of a global power. And last but not least, the return of the medieval concept of a 'just war' is a further key indicator of fake cosmopolitanism.

The difficulty of distinguishing between genuine and fake cosmopolitanism arises not least on account of the fact that the implied *existence* of the cosmopolitan regime seems to be a precondition for its realization. Switching project and reality around seems to be a particularly effective strategy for making the unachievable achievable, namely to establish the unity of the many, which the cosmopolitan regime requires. Asserting that the goal has been achieved becomes a means of achieving it. Only if globality *is assumed to be real* can it be established in the face of the continued existence of conflicts and contrasts between different nations, regions, religions, camps and conditions in the world.

Are there counter-positions *within* 'cosmopolitanism' which come to the fore the more this regime becomes established? And how do these come about? No single player or opponent can ever win *on their own*; they are dependent on alliances. The goal of the strategies of capital, for example, is, in simplified terms, to merge capital with the state in order to open up new sources of legitimacy in the form of the *neo-liberal state*. Conversely, the goal of global civil society and its actors is to elaborate a connection between civil society and the state, that is, to bring about a *cosmopolitan form of statehood*. The forms of alliance entered into by the neo-liberal state and the goals of the same instrumentalize the state (and state theory) for the purpose of optimizing and legitimizing the interests of capital worldwide. Conversely, the idea of a cosmopolitan state in civil society form is aimed at imagining and realizing a robust diversity and a post-national, indeed a post-global order. The neo-liberal agenda surrounds itself with an aura of *self-regulation* and *self-legitimation*. Civil society's agenda, however, surrounds itself with the aura of a *global morality* and struggles for a new grand narrative of radical-democratic globalization. This is the way, then, in which the meta-game of global politics opens up its own *immanent* alternatives and opposition. Hegemonic and counter-hegemonic movements line up against one another when 'cosmopolitanism' comes into play.

Within the theoretical frame of reference of the meta-game, the key concept of strategy takes on a specific meaning. The logic of rule changing means that the political game about power and domination turns into a game about double contingency; the old draughts rule system (including the foundations of its legitimacy) can no longer be relied on; a new system is not yet in force. In this hybrid state between 'no longer' and 'not yet', abstract words such as (self-reproducing) 'structures' and 'systems' dissolve 'in the mouth like rotten mushrooms' (Hofmannsthal 2000). However, into the breach between 'structure' and 'anarchy' steps the notion of 'strategies'. The concept of strategy thus becomes detached from the goals and intentions of specific (collective or individual) actors. 'Strategy' comes to refer to the mutual and contradictory interactive relationship between a closed and an open global politics, along with its internal dynamic; these are embedded in the interrelated activities of capital, the state and global civil society. Strategy in this sense is a term that describes the *real space of possibility* opened up by the meta-game for groups of actors engaged in conflict-laden interaction with one another.

In this sense, the theory of the meta-game needs to be developed in terms of a specific *game logic*, that is, as a strategic constellation of interacting, more or less collective, rule-abiding and rule-changing actors, whose positions, resources and shares of power are determined and changed reciprocally. Game logic is not to be confused with the empirical course of a game, with individual moves. The idea is to accept the logic of the different actors' perspectives and their interdependence (conflicts, contradictions, paradoxes), in other words, the logic of the capital perspective, of advocatory movements rooted in civil society and of the state perspective. Logic refers to an argument based on 'as ifs': what would happen if capital were as mobile as possible? What would happen if the state got rid of the barriers of nation-based thinking and came to understand itself as a cosmopolitan state with a corresponding institutional framework? In other words, it is about challenging one's opponents, figuring out their scope for action, their power options, making them as strong as possible.

In this situation, the order of priority between reality and possibility is reversed: you have to know what moves are *possible* in order to understand the *real* moves. Max Weber, for example, frames historical and political contingency as 'objective possibility'. The historian or the social scientist always has to speculate with unrealized possibilities so that he or she can compare them with those that have been realized: 'In order to comprehend real causal relationships, we construct unreal ones' (*Kritische Studien*, quoted in Palonen 1998).

The language of games teaches us why the realm of the possible has to be explored conceptually if the realm of the real is not to be misunderstood as the only possible reality. This approach enables us to defuse the obvious objection, namely, that by addressing the question of the logic behind the different perspectives and the ways in which they are interdependent, one becomes immune to empirical developments and objections. This is why it is important not to confuse the objective possibilities of economic or political globalization with the *real* game moves, with the empirical experience of globalization. But the opposite is also true – political action based on empiricism alone fails to recognize the contingency of political action and therefore of politics *per se*.

1.9   Blind empiricism?

The discourse of globalization tempts us to take the 'theory only' route, to return metaphysics to the centre of empirical social science. But the opposite is also true – the relationship between the possibilities of globalization and empirical study of it is often distorted by *false indicators*. An article entitled 'Measuring Globalization' (*Foreign Policy*, January/February 2001, pp. 56–65) states the following: 'Everyone talks about globalization, but no one has tried to measure its extent . . . at least not until now. The . . . globalization index [outlined here] dissects the complex forces driving the integration of ideas, people and economies worldwide. Which countries have become the most global? Are they more unequal? Or more corrupt?' The authors then list their indicators: personal contacts across national borders, measured using international travel, international phone calls, cross-border remittances, and suchlike. The World Wide Web was also measured, not only by assessing the number of users but also the number of Internet hosts and secure servers. Finally, indicators were created for measuring economic integration: the movement of goods and services was investigated by examining the fluctuating share of international trade in every national economy, and so on and so forth. The results themselves are not relevant to the present discussion (for professional empirical approaches to globalization, see the classic works by Beisheim and Zürn 1999 and Held et al. 1999). What is interesting here is the striking fact that in the example above the creation of empirical indicators presupposes the 'national–international' distinction; in other words, it follows the logic of the national outlook. As a result, there is a systematic failure to recognize the specific nature of the *trans*nationalization of production, capital flows, lifestyles, and so forth. The link between the economy and the nation-state outlook is an ambiguous one: on the one hand *homo economicus* has no nation-state ties, while on the other statistical surveys are based on the concept of the nation-state – that is, at the macroeconomic level, nation-states are the relevant points of comparison and it is assumed that the nation-state is the 'natural' institutional arrangement for supplying collective goods. The indicators derived from this easily lead to misinterpretations.

To take an example by way of elucidation, international trade measures exchanges between different nations. However, this indicator is undermined by the growing importance of transnational corporations, to the extent that it eventually becomes a fiction. This happens in two ways. Firstly, that which is still measured as 'international' trade is replaced by *intra*-company trade – investments, capital flows and services which pass from one country to another within company networks do not cross any national borders. Secondly, though, it is not a matter of international 'trade' either, as goods are neither 'sold' nor 'bought' at all, but rather shifted backwards and forwards and recombined on a corporate transnational map where national locations and borders are of strategic significance. These ways of undermining national controls (be they customs controls or official statistics) constitute the whole strategic point of transnationalization from the corporate perspective, as they enable corporations to play a double game when dealing with prices and taxes; as a result, transnational corporations pay fewer and fewer taxes in their so-called home countries. Note: the national outlook blinds us to the hidden reality of transnationalization, hidden for deliberate, strategic reasons on account of the meta-game logic. Estimates are that more than a third to a half of worldwide trade is now carried out in the form of *intra*-company 'non-trade'. At the same time, it is extraordinarily difficult to capture in empirical and statistical terms this direct cross-border trade within the transnational spaces in which corporations do business and exert their dominance, as this intra-corporation non-trade eludes all external attempts to monitor and record it (Köhler 2002). In addition, the corporations themselves have a strategic interest in *not* letting anyone look at their cards, because they are engaged in 'translegal' manoeuvrings, that is, they are operating in the grey area of (il)legality. The national view of official statistics, of course, is the view of the state tax authorities. However, the question of whether ultimately it is the wrong minutiae that are being meticulously counted is one that *cannot* be settled empirically, but rather one that requires a critique of the empirical basis of the national outlook, an empirical-methodological shift in perspective, a change of paradigm from methodological nationalism to methodological cosmopolitanism.[9]

'All in all', conclude Edgar Grande and Thomas Risse,

the empirical findings available so far in relation to the globalization debate can be summarized as follows. *Firstly*, in many spheres the pressure exerted by globalization is not as great as is widely assumed. *Secondly*, globalization is not solely about the call to 'roll back the state'; instead, in many areas of international politics – such as environmental and human rights policy – transnational actors are demanding stronger state regulation and international cooperation . . . *Thirdly*, the different responses manifested by national political systems show that economic globalization does not simply sweep away historically evolved institutions. *Fourthly* and finally, the pressure exerted by globalization has very diverse effects on nation-state capacity and autonomy. Even in business and finance policy, there is still significant scope for decision-making, which nation states can use to achieve priority social objectives such as basic social welfare and full employment. (2000: 244)

But what goes for companies goes for states as well: empirical confirmation that the old politics is still at work doesn't constitute a refutation of the argument that whoever continues to play the old game will be bulldozed, or that the option of adopting a transnational and cosmopolitan approach does *not* exist for states. For theoreticians and empiricists alike, the distinction between the logic of the game and specific moves is essential. It would be wrong to draw conclusions about the course of a game from its underlying logic, and conversely, even more so, to conclude from specific moves that such a logic is non-existent. Those who cite empirical findings in order to *refute* the scope for state action opened up in the global age are in fact basing state action on an ahistorical, abstract concept of the state while simultaneously depriving the analyses of political science and political theory of a critical outlook.

1.10   New Critical Theory with cosmopolitan intent

The distinction between the national and the cosmopolitan outlook needs to be differentiated further according to whether one is talking about the *concrete perspectives of actors* – the national outlook – or about the *scientific observer perspective* – methodological nationalism.[10] Belief in the nation-state is based on the following, largely taken-for-granted premises: society is equated with nation-state society; states and their governments are considered to be the cornerstones of political science analysis. It is assumed that humanity is divided into a finite number of nations and that these are organized internally as nation-states, while being demarcated from one another externally in the system of international relations. What is more, this demarcation from the outside world, along with competition between nation-states, represents the fundamental organizing principle of politics. The rationale for belief in the nation-state is, according to thoughtful political scientists in particular, that democracy has *only* been achieved – indeed, *can* only be achieved – within the nation-state. Without the nation-state, they say, there can be no democracy, and this is why the 'post-national constellation' – in contrast to Jürgen Habermas's (2001a) arguments – poses a threat to democracy.

On no account should *methodological* nationalism be confused with *normative* nationalism. While the former is linked to the social scientific observer perspective, the latter is linked to the concrete perspective of political actors. As far as the first modernity is concerned, it is possible to establish a characteristic merging of the national outlook of political state action and the methodological nationalism of the social sciences. This amounts to what Max Weber called a 'national value relationship' (*nationale Wertbeziehung*) which applied and continues to apply to the 'field of inquiry' of social scientific research, as indeed to the latter itself.[11]

This hidden and therefore highly stable harmony between the considerations of value and background assumptions that guide social and social scientific activity clearly no longer applies to the transition from the first to the second modernity. Two constellations need to be distinguished here: isolated flights and forays into the 'cosmopolitan outlook', 'methodological cosmopolitanism' both in the field of political players (NGOs, political parties, supranational organizations, corporations) and in the sphere of the social sciences; and the majority – the mainstream – in the arenas of national politics as well as in nation-based political science, which continues to act and research steadfastly within the axiomatic framework of the national outlook.

This, then, is where dissonances erupt that cut across the distinction between the actor and observer perspective, between politics and political science. However, these dissonances can only be perceived once the national outlook has been left behind and a cosmopolitan perspective has been mastered. The zombie science of the national outlook that thinks and researches in the categories of international trade, international dialogue, national sovereignty, national communities, the 'state nation' (*Staatsvolk*), and so forth, is a 'science of the unreal' pursued by 'national sociology'. Just as nation-based economics has come to a dead end, so too has nation-based sociology. This is because there is a failure to recognize – let alone research – the extent to which existing transnational modes of living, transmigrants, global elites, supranational organizations and dynamics determine the relations within and between nation-state repositories of power.

It is no less important to distinguish between the chances of success (or failure) of methodological cosmopolitanism and the chances of success (or failure) of a cosmopolitan regime. It is conceivable, at least potentially, that the shift in perspective from methodological nationalism to methodological cosmopolitanism will become more convincing *without* anything being implied about the prospects for a cosmopolitanization of states and societies. Thus, a person who is optimistic regarding a change in perspective may well be a pessimist regarding a change in politics. It would be ridiculously naïve to think that a change in scientific paradigm might lead to states becoming more open to cosmopolitanism.

If we make a differentiation, on the one hand, between political action and political science and, on the other, between the national and the cosmopolitan outlook and methodological nationalism and methodological cosmopolitanism, what emerges is a table divided into four parts: (1) nation-state-centred society and social science; (2) zombie science of the national; (3) cosmopolitan critique of nation-state-centred society, politics, sociology and political science: New Critical Theory; and (4) 'cosmopolitan state', 'cosmopolitan regime', and so on (see table 1.1).

However, there are many different ways of assessing the likelihood of these potential trends in politics and political science. At least where close

Table 1.1 Change in perspective and paradigm from a national to a cosmopolitan modernity and social science

		Political action	
		National outlook	*Cosmopolitan outlook*
Political science	*Methodological nationalism*	Nation-state-centred understanding of society and politics in political practice and political science	Zombie science of the national: national sociology fails to see transnationalizations
	Methodological cosmopolitanism	Cosmopolitan critique of nation-state-centred society and politics, sociology and political science: New Critical Theory	The cosmopolitan society and its enemies: what do cosmopolitan state, cosmopolitan regime, transnational surveillance state mean?

historical comparisons are concerned, for example, it is possible to consider change in political perspective and change in scientific paradigm as *both* being unlikely. However, to regard both as being likely – in other words, to claim, hope for or fear a spontaneous breakthrough of a cosmopolitan state and cosmopolitan social science – is surely beyond most people's capacity for optimism. But what remains the foreseeable task for the future, even for a sceptical view of the world, is to establish acceptance for methodological cosmopolitanism *without* any concrete political signs that the era of the cosmopolitan state has begun. What it *would* mean, at least, is the birth of a *New Critical Theory with cosmopolitan intent.*

1.11   New Critical Theory of social inequalities

I would now like to turn to a specific set of themes and an area of research that is central and yet has so far received little attention from the cosmopolitan shift in perspective, namely the sociology of inequalities. This serves well as an example in order to test and illustrate the effectiveness of New Critical Theory and its empirical approach. A World Bank report from March 2002 concerning the financial situation of the developing countries reads like an indictment by the organization Terre des Hommes of the ignorance of rich countries: falling prices for raw materials on the world market, trade protectionism and the economic downturn in industrialized countries, not to speak of the decline of worldwide tourism after 11 September 2001, have all contributed to a dramatic worsening of the situation in the world's poorest regions. The world has become a dangerously unequal place – even for the rich in the major cities of the West. Debt servicing alone accounts for $200 billion a year in currency flows from the South to the North. At the same time, flows of private capital towards the South shrank in 2001 for the fifth time in succession to settle at $100 billion below 1997 levels. Global inequalities are increasing: between 1960 and the year 2000 the proportion of global income enjoyed by the richest 20 per cent of the world's population increased from 70 per cent to 90 per cent, while the proportion of the world's income owned by the poorest 20 per cent fell from 2.3 per cent to about 1 per cent. While 1.2 billion people – nearly a fifth of the world's population – have to manage on less than a dollar a day, state development aid has fallen again by 20 per cent since 1990. How can we explain this contradiction between the growing impoverishment of ever increasing sections of the population and the growing ignorance of this problem?

Many members of the Bundestag (parliament) in Germany belong to the generation that twenty to thirty years ago pledged 'international solidarity': they were active in Third World initiatives or argued as politically active Christians for the necessity of creating 'one world' in order to eradicate need. Today, this very same generation is pursuing policies that have made Germany into a country with one of the worst records in development. Can this be adequately explained by politicians' personal flaws and failings? Or is the blocking out of global inequalities a structural issue? Is there some principle that can account for the contradictory fact that, while global inequalities are growing, they are simultaneously 'legitimized' from a sociological perspective?

There are at least two possible answers to the question of what it is that legitimizes inequality: the *merit system* and the *nation-state principle*. The first answer is a familiar one and has been both elaborated and criticized; it derives from the self-understanding of the national perspective and relates to domestic inequalities within the state. The second answer emerges from the frame of reference of the cosmopolitan perspective and relates to the 'legitimation' of global inequalities. It follows from this that it is only by systematically alternating between the national and the cosmopolitan perspective that the big blind spots – and sources of error – present in the methodological nationalism of inequality research can be brought to light (see table 1.2). Only in the context of such a New Critical Theory of social inequalities can the *fundamental asymmetry of perceptions of inequality that are bound up with the national outlook be revealed from both a social and a social scientific perspective*. This illuminates the fact that the 'legitimatory achievement' of the nation-state lies in turning people's attention exclusively towards domestic issues, thereby banishing global inequalities from the field of vision of the (relatively) privileged.[12]

It makes sense in purely spatial terms to differentiate between *large* inequalities (which in turn can be divided into transnational, supranational, international and global inequalities) and *small* inequalities. 'Small'

Table 1.2 Sociology of social inequalities viewed through the contrast between national and cosmopolitan perspectives

		Social situations	
Legitimation		Large (global) inequalities	Small (nation-state) inequalities
	National outlook	Irrelevant, non-existent	Merit system
	Cosmopolitan outlook	Nation-state principle: exclusion of the excluded	Nation-state principles governing the construction of global inequalities as irrelevant

inequalities are located within the nation-state and, for perfectly good reasons, appear to the individuals and groups affected by them to be large ones; however, from a cosmopolitan perspective they are small because they coincide with nation-state frameworks of self-description, self-ascription and self-monitoring. The merit system allocates inequalities within the state, while at the same time legitimizing them. An appropriate paradigm for describing this situation is the written examination: everybody goes in on an equal footing but comes out again on an unequal footing (with different positions in the marking hierarchy). With the merit system, for example, income distribution can be both unequal *and* legitimate. In contrast, to speak of the nation-state principle as a 'legitimation' of social inequalities means that the nation-state focus on national inequalities makes global inequalities *disappear* – legitimation through erasure. Large inequalities are banished beyond the bounds of the national perspective. What follows from this is that they can both grow into and be 'legitimized' as institutionalized irrelevance and unreality. Thus, large inequalities are 'legitimized' not so much through a lack of concern and debate about global inequalities, but rather through concern and debate about 'small' national inequalities.

The distinction between 'large' and 'small' thus relates to spaces of perception and population figures. Of course, this law of the nation-state exclusion of global inequalities is an overstatement of the issue – the national particularity of a state does not generally rule out the possibility of universal principles and perceptions. Nonetheless, it is true to say that the nation-state outlook 'frees' people from having to look at the misery in the world. It works on the basis of a *double exclusion*: it excludes the excluded. The stability with which the large inequalities suffered by humanity are 'legitimized' in silent complicity between state authority and state-fixated social science, through organized non-perception, is astonishing.

Whereas the merit system facilitates *positive* legitimation of 'small' inequalities, the nation-state principle effects a *negative* 'legitimation' of large inequalities. 'Positive' legitimation means that the merit system brings a *reflexive* and *reciprocal* form of legitimation to bear; in other words, social inequalities may, in principle, win the consent of the underprivileged. The legitimation brought about by the nation-state principle is 'negative' by contrast, because it is *non*-reflexive and *non*-reciprocal and therefore cannot win the consent of the underprivileged and excluded. The nation-state is a principle that seeks justification for global inequalities in the dark. The nation-state principle is based on a lack of reflection, not, as with the merit system, on reflection. Negative legitimation that is achieved through institutionalized silence and by looking the other way ultimately lacks legitimation, therefore, because it excludes the consent of those whose consent is needed the most: the poor, the degraded, the excluded. The nation-state does *not* legitimize global inequalities. Rather, *non*-legitimized global inequalities are banished from the field of vision and are *thereby* stabilized. Historically, this means that the European nation-state represents the institutionalized forgetting of colonialism and imperialism, to which it owes its ascent. But what lends stability to this negative 'legitimation' through silence in the face of the growing permeability of borders? What destabilizes it? Four principles of the nation-state construction of irrelevance and unreality can be identified additionally here.

The first of these is the *principle of nation-state fragmentation and attributability of global inequalities*. As long as there is no global authority responsible for monitoring global inequalities, they disintegrate into a patchwork of nation-state inequalities. For every one of the roughly 200 states that exist, there are roughly 200 frameworks for observing and assessing the relevance of small social inequalities. However, the sum of these domestic inequalities recorded by each individual nation-state by no means equals the total of large, global inequalities because the logic of the national outlook is not the same as the logic of the cosmopolitan outlook. In particular, nation-state self-ascription and the associated assumption of endogenous causality contradicts the cosmopolitan point of view, which also draws on transnational interdependencies, power relations, decision-making bodies and causalities to explain nation-state domestic inequalities.

The South Commission report (1990, quoted in Falk 1995: 50), argues as follows: 'Were all humanity a single nation-state, the present North/South divide would make it an unviable, semi-feudal entity, split by internal conflicts.' This is both right and wrong at the same time, as it fails to recognize that the nation-state world order structurally ignores and thereby 'legitimizes' global inequalities.

The nation-state principle is the analytical key to understanding why the connection between globalization and poverty has been so little researched within nation-based sociology. As long as the national outlook holds sway in the sphere of political action as well as in social scientific analysis, poverty and wealth will be localized in the national context as a matter of course. The very possibility that the negative consequences of globalization might make themselves felt in different historical contexts – in the form of growing inequalities, erosion of incomes, exploitation of natural resources and the undermining of democracy – is ruled out *analytically*. As far as social scientific research on inequality is concerned, then, the principle of nation-state fragmentation is linked to a large source of error: the danger of *reaching false conclusions from nation-state premises*.

The second principle is as follows: the *perception of social inequalities presupposes norms of equality*. In the nation-state perspective, the stability with which large inequalities are excluded is based on the validity of national norms of equality, be they defined in terms of culture, ethnicity, law or politics. The objectivity of global social inequalities is not called into doubt politically as long as they stand in the shadow of institutionalized norms of equality (Stichweh 2000). It follows from this that, as national norms of equality are replaced by cosmopolitan ones, so the necessity and urgency of giving state legitimation to existing large inequalities grows. On what is this equality within Western welfare states based in the national paradigm? On the formal equality implied by the status of being a citizen: differences in income between men and women, or differences in where people live, and so forth, should not provide grounds for grading citizens in terms of their status. All the members of a nation have the same rights and responsibilities. This legally sanctioned equality among state citizens is backed up by the nation-state model of cultural homogeneity (same language, history, cultural traditions). These national principles of inclusion and exclusion serve both to determine and to stabilize the limits to people's perception of social inequalities.

This leads to a third principle, that of the *non-comparability of social inequalities between nation-states*. The national perspective and the 'functional capacity' of the nation-state to legitimize global inequalities rest not least on the fact that politicizing comparisons can be brought to bear only *intra*nationally and never *inter*nationally. Delegitimizing comparisons, on the other hand, presuppose national norms of equality. In this sense, for example, differences in income between Nigerians and Germans, South Americans and Finns, Russians and Chinese, Turks and Koreans, can be as large as they like, even given the same qualifications and job descriptions, but the delegitimizing potential of these comparisons is only felt if they occur within a common framework of perceptions of institutionalized equality. This might be the case, for example, with membership of a nation or of a global corporation.

The interesting issue that emerges from all this is the extent to which international differences in income within the European Union can continue to be legitimized in future by the principle of non-comparability; or the extent to which, with increasing European self-awareness (and the institutionalization of European self-observation), the inequalities that have thus far been blocked out internationally will now be perceived as *intra*national inequalities and therefore have to be legitimized. As the barriers to comparing inequalities between nation-states come down (for whatever reasons), the European Union may be expected to enter a phase of acute turmoil, even if conditions of inequality remain constant.

However, the role of the nation-state in the system of global inequalities is by no means exhausted in its so-called legitimizing function. The fourth principle is: *erasure legitimizes inaction*; or, rather, it legitimizes *action* that makes large inequalities worse because, for the national outlook, these 'external' effects find expression in a predetermined unreality, that is, electoral irrelevance. By talking about social inequalities exclusively as 'home grown' inequalities, it becomes possible to pursue a global politics of redistribution in which the risks are externalized and passed on to weaker Third World countries, while any benefits are maximized within the national context.

While Western statesmen were enthusing about the fact that we had enjoyed a *decade of unexpected peace and prosperity*, a growing number of countries were sinking further into debt and unemployment and were witnessing the decline of their health and social services as well as urgently needed infrastructures. What may well be helpful to Western corporations, such as a rigorous enforcement of deregulation, privatization and greater flexibility in developing countries, is often disastrous for the latter themselves. To pick out just one example: the World Bank, the extended arm of the G-7 states, promoted contracts with private energy suppliers in Indonesia and other countries. 'These contracts entailed provisions where the government was committed to purchasing large quantities of electricity at very high prices.' International corporations pocketed the profits while the risks were loaded on to states that were poor to begin with. Both the US Treasury Department and the World Bank strongly promoted this type of private commercial activity. 'That was bad enough. But when the corrupt governments were overthrown (Mohammed Suharto in Indonesia in 1998 . . .) the U.S. government put pressure on the [new] government[s] to fulfil the contract, rather than default or at least renegotiate the terms of the contract. There is, in fact, a long list of "unfair" contracts, which Western governments have used their muscle to enforce' (Stiglitz 2002: 71).

To sum up these principles: the nation-state world order fragments global inequalities; national norms of equality exclude global inequalities; the intra-national comparability of inequalities guarantees international incomparability; and the irrelevance of large-scale inequalities is predetermined. All these principles make it possible for powerful and rich nation-states to pass on the risks entailed by their decisions to poor states, a practice stabilized not least by the fact that the methodological nationalism of the social sciences confirms and supports actions based on the national perspective. Inequality research based on this approach compounds national myopia and turns itself and the object of its research into nation-state 'native science'. Something that is considered elsewhere to be problematic from a scientific point of view – self-oriented research – is raised here to a methodological principle. At best, this national autism is extended into a comparative autism along the lines of international comparative studies. But even this comparative methodological nationalism remains wedded to the big mistakes of methodological nationalism itself. However, this social and social scientific fabrication of the unreality of growing global inequalities in national sociologies is becoming increasingly problematic.

- The errors of the national outlook are starting to become apparent to the extent that borders are becoming permeable and interdependencies across all manner of boundaries are growing exponentially. This can be illustrated by looking at the obvious contradictions in which restrictive migration policies become entangled. On the one hand, the rich countries of the North are plagued by a spectacular decline in population, with the familiar consequences of an ageing population, pension and health systems under threat, and political conservatism. On the other hand, these very same countries are busy turning themselves into fortresses so that they can fend off the real and imagined migration flows from the poor South. At the same time, military, economic and political interdependencies are growing worldwide, triggering new flows of migrants and refugees. So any measure that is taken is doomed and brings with it predictable 'side-effects' that can easily run completely counter to the original aim. In the aftermath of the terrorist attacks of 11 September 2001, for example, the political will to control migration flows to the USA in particular, but also to many European countries, has become stronger and more focused. However, this curtailment of civil liberties merely serves to undermine politicians' willingness to authorize more immigration in order to solve the problems caused by a falling birth rate and an ageing population.
- The national outlook is also called into question by processes involving the internal globalization of nation-state experiential spaces. The following developments play a part in this: human rights are no longer associated predominantly with citizenship status; and inequalities in life opportunities are not experienced solely within national contexts. People with an international education are an example of this, as are the growing numbers of bi-national marriages, children and parenting arrangements, as well as the increase in transnational working and living situations (Beck-Gernsheim 2000). Ultimately, the national outlook also fragments

with the increased mobility of communication, information, money flows, risks, products and services, and as even the remaining group of immobile locals see their personal domains of experience transnationalized through mass communication, advertising, and so forth (for empirical data on this, see Beisheim et al. 1999; Held et al. 1999). Furthermore, supranational institutions such as the World Bank, UNESCO, and various NGOs systematically generate data that bring the large inequalities into full global public view, thereby calling into question the mechanisms of national unreality-making.[13]

- The errors of the national outlook become clear as new patterns of inclusion and exclusion become more important, along with new ways of distinguishing between them. More and more mechanisms of inclusion and exclusion no longer match the classification of inequalities based on classes and population groups whose boundaries coincide with those of state borders. Important new patterns of inclusion and exclusion are emerging in relation to, for example, (a) supranational trading blocks (European Union, NAFTA, etc.), (b) diasporic cultures based on particular ascriptions (e.g. 'Black Atlantic' (Paul Gilroy)) and (c) living conditions in global cities (on this point, see the analyses of Sassen, Castells, Albrow, Eade, Dürrschmidt). These are all cases in which the arguments used to defend the national outlook also break down.

  In his essay 'Living on a Lifeboat' (1974), Garrett Hardin provided an early and famous defence of the national outlook and a critique of the cosmopolitan outlook. He compared nation-states to differently equipped lifeboats in which the survivors of a shipwreck are seeking refuge. Hardin argues that it is left to each person in the lifeboat to decide whether they will offer a seat to the host of people struggling for survival in the raging sea. But no obligation is implied, not least because, if those shipwrecked were taken on board, it would contravene the safety rules of the lifeboats themselves, thereby putting everybody at risk. While still proving to be very effective even today, this 'the-boat-is-full' argument is wrong for the simple reason that there are fewer and fewer nation-state lifeboats of the sort implied by the national outlook. There is a failure to recognize the actually existing situations, modes and causal mechanisms of post- and transnational inequality. What makes the cosmopolitan perspective distinctive and demonstrates its superiority is not so much its moral critique as its ability to expose the misdiagnoses of the national outlook.

- The errors of methodological nationalism also become discernible to the extent that the distinction between 'large' and 'small' inequalities – or, to put it differently, between the cosmopolitan and national perspective – itself becomes dubious. What we are increasingly dealing with is the *internationalization of national models of class*. As the permeability of national borders increases, so too does competition within and between different national domains. Correspondingly, the winners and losers of globalization are distributed according to whether they are located in production sectors that are protected from or exposed to the market. The opaque term 'globalization' is often used in the *struggle of national elites against transnational elites* as they vie with one another over positions and resources within national arenas of power.

- The walls are crumbling in international terms too: if it was hard to exclude the excluded before the terrorist attacks, it has now become much harder, as global poverty increasingly comes to be perceived as an *internal* national problem affecting the rich countries of the West as well – although with what practical consequences remains to be seen. The terrorist threat that defies national borders also removes the blinkers limiting the nation-state's field of vision, revealing the ominous growth of global inequalities.

There is no doubt that these developments are too much for individual states to deal with on their own. Not only do they not have appropriate ways of intervening; they do not even have appropriate means of observation, let alone ways of exerting any kind of causal control (Stichweh 2000). The central paradox of a cosmopolitan reorientation can thus be explained – by way of self-critique – as follows: as the boundaries between 'large' and 'small' inequalities become more permeable and no longer coincide with national borders, so the mental block – the institutionalized non-perception of large inequalities – acquires greater significance. Why? Because this is the only way of bridging the growing asymmetry between expectations of state intervention and states' capacity to fulfil them. In an age of widening global inequalities and growing global public awareness of them, renationalization is the rich states' 'functional' response.

Conversely, we can deduce that if the nation-state 'legitimizes' global inequalities according to the Brechtian principle 'for we do not see those who dwell in the dark', then this legitimation collapses when the state becomes cosmopolitanized. The cosmopolitan state, which – however selectively – integrates those who are culturally different, thereby unleashes as a 'side-effect' an avalanche of legitimation problems, even in the most favourable case of constant inequalities. Why? For the simple reason that it is loosening or removing the barriers to non-comparability of social inequalities. However, this means that, with cosmopolitanization, there is a greater temptation, and greater opportunity, to 're-ethnicize' and renationalize both society and politics. It is precisely *because* barriers and boundaries begin to come unstuck that the perceptual block in people's minds becomes firmly re-established.

So can we mark down the nation-state principle as an achievement or is it just the opposite, a trap? Whichever way the answer turns out, it is clear that, when the state and social science unite unreflexively in making global inequalities invisible, it affects political and scientific actors in very different ways. Whether or not the national outlook is attributed to the nation-state as an aspect of its functional capacity, it certainly perverts the social sciences. They come to be identified as national sociology or national political science, and as such lay themselves open to critique; moreover, they become entangled in an ever more obvious contradiction in relation to their goal and ethos, namely to investigate reality. What they are doing is committing themselves (often unseen and unwittingly) to making reality unreal. The silence of social scientific analysis on global inequalities is nothing short of a scandal.

In this global era, the New Critical Theory with cosmopolitan intent is faced with a key task: it must reveal and dismantle the wall of methodological nationalism built into the category systems and research routines of the social sciences so that, for example, it can bring into view the legitimatory role of the nation-state within the system of large inequalities. The established domestic maps of national social inequalities are elegant and highly detailed and may generally be adequate for managing the resultant potential for unrest among the relatively privileged part of the world's population at state level. But the demons that inhabit the large, unfamiliar, utterly under-researched worlds of inequality are no longer mere decorative motifs that serve to embellish the margins. Belief in the nation-state, along with the national narratives that dominate public commentary and academic research, certainly cannot be overlooked or ignored. But since the terrorist attacks of 11 September, if not before, many people have come to realize that chipping away at the perceptual block that stands between the 'small' and the 'large' inequalities is not much different from looking down the muzzle of a gun.[14]

Ultimately, New Critical Theory is also a self-critical theory. The idea is that only the cosmopolitan outlook, with its commitment to reality, can reveal the *disasters* that threaten us at the start of the twenty-first century. Critical Theory inquires into the *contradictions, dilemmas and unseen, unintentional side-effects* of a modernity that is becoming more cosmopolitan; it draws its critical definitional power from the tension between political self-description and social scientific observation of the same. The theory goes as follows: *the cosmopolitan outlook opens up spaces and strategies for action that the national outlook closes off.* This interpretation gains greater plausibility through the fact that the space for action opened up by the cosmopolitan outlook stands in contradiction to the lack of alternatives diagnosed by politicians and social scientists alike in the national perspective.

In this respect, we can identify four major errors to be demonstrated and tackled by the New Critical Theory. Its task is, first, to name and expose the *forms and strategies by which cosmopolitan realities are rendered invisible; to criticize national circularity,* that is, to expose the fact that the nationalization or 'ethnicization' of political options can never justify the methodological nationalism of the social sciences; to overcome the *ahistorical self-perpetuation of social scientific sets of concepts and research routines* by creating alternative concepts and research strategies; and, finally, to make a contribution towards *reimagining the political* and to encourage others to do so – in other words, to establish and bring to bear the difference between the national outlook of political actors and the cosmopolitan outlook of the political and social sciences.[15]

The main issue in the debate about globalization is *not* the significance of the nation-state and its sovereignty (as is widely implied, among others, by Scharpf and Offe); rather, it is about gaining a new cosmopolitan perspective on the entire field of power and thereby highlighting the new actors and networks of actors, power opportunities, strategies and organizational forms of an unbounded politics. The cosmopolitan critique of nation-state-centred and -cemented politics and political science, undertaken from the point of view of New Critical Theory and empiricism, is both empirically and politically central. There are two fascinating aspects to the argument: the global political power game is an open-ended one, and it requires a cosmopolitan shift in orientation in social scientific theory and empirical practice to demonstrate the ambiguity surrounding this open-endedness of the foundations, goals and alternatives of global politics and to give it political expression. This book therefore raises the question: how can power and domination, politics and the state be redefined for the twenty-first century? Who or what are the new democratic princes, the Machiavellian innovators of the cosmopolitan age?

2

Critique of the National Outlook

Tell me what you dissociate yourself from and I'll tell you what you stand for.[1] The opponents of globalization may not be any more far-sighted than its proponents, but they have set about constructing and combating an image of globality – of global or cosmopolitan or world culture – that has its roots in their negative imagination and about which one thing can be said for sure: as a horror image of the 'global dream', it has been elaborated, especially by its opponents, specifically for the purpose of being rejected in simplified terms. According to this image, the signs of the new era can be read as symptoms of a globalizing culture (I globalize, you globalize, he globalizes), one that has lost its heritage, its home, its memory. Paradoxically, this (nightmarish) dream of global culture leads towards something that modern literature, in its drive towards universalization, has also produced, namely, a 'place' of its own that is both a generalized 'somewhere' and a generalized 'nowhere'. This synthetic world culture has become arbitrary and is desperately searching for new patterns of identification, but all it is left with – so it is said – are the surrogates of a global homogeneity.

Many advocates of a future cosmopolitan regime hope that, as frameworks of experience and social circles are opened out transnationally, and the nation and the state are decoupled, the nation will become a purely cultural or 'folkloric phenomenon', divested of all political significance.[2]

2.1 The 'cosmopolitan' is at once a citizen of the 'cosmos' and a citizen of the 'polis'

The concept and history of nationalism are rooted in the *most recent* history of modernity, developing their myth-creating potency in eighteenth- and nineteenth-century Europe. The concept and history of cosmopolitanism, by contrast, is as old as political thought itself. The terms 'cosmopolitan' and 'cosmopolitanism' are inventions of Greek antiquity. They go back to Diogenes, who – in a highly modern way – argued polemically against the distinction between Hellenes and barbarians in the sense of 'our people' and 'strangers'. Not only does he criticize this 'us' and 'them' opposition, he also answers the question as to what takes its place. He derives 'cosmopolitanism' from a mobility that both transcends and blurs boundaries. Rather like today, then, it was the mobility of the Hellenes that placed a question mark against the common antithesis of 'us' and 'them': the Hellenes and the 'barbarians' began to mix.

Viewed in retrospect, the conceptual construction of the 'cosmopolitan' person revolutionizes the commonplace logic of distinctions. The distinction between 'us' and 'them' is no longer an ontological one and in this respect neither prescribes nor establishes any absolute exclusion. This notional figure of an *exclusive* distinction – the 'either/or' principle – comes to be replaced by the notional figure of an *inclusive* distinction – the 'both/and' principle. In other words, the other, the stranger, both loses *and* gains their difference beneath a horizon of equality. Thus 'cosmopolitanism' means that the 'us and them' distinction is at once nullified and renewed by the construction of a *dual locatedness for all*.

In terms of both social and philosophical ideals, the cosmopolitan lives in a dual homeland and possesses dual loyalties: he is *both* a citizen of the *cosmos* – a world citizen – *and* a citizen of the *polis* – a citizen of city and state. For the Stoics, the cosmos was infused with the power of the 'logos' and was their homeland; everyone had a share in it, whether they were freemen or slaves, Hellenes or Orientals. Each person is both a citizen of the world *and* a citizen of the city; each has both roots *and* wings, is both equal *and* different, at home in a particular place and at home in the cosmos; in other words, everybody lives in the 'cosmopolis'. This is essentially conceptualized as a political unit that crosses all boundaries of ethnic belonging, culture, religion and class in a kind of 'as-if equality' – in the sense, in fact, of a '*rooted* cosmopolitanism' (Cohen 1997; Beck 2002a), that is, a locally rooted and proactive cosmopolitanism. Those who have experienced more and who are more far-sighted are more likely to recall the specificities of their existence and to rely on them. Exposure to the global scene creates an awareness of familiar horizons. The cosmopolitan identity does not betray national or local identity (as the national outlook pretends and accuses it of doing); on the contrary, it *makes them possible*. By *cosmopolitan common sense* I mean the taken-for-granted way (though it is anything but taken for granted) in which, both culturally and politically, people experience and live out apparently contradictory identities and loyalties, *without* this being experienced as contradictory either in a person's own mind or in others' expectations. This is why, for example, one speaks of the USA as a 'nation of many nations' or a 'nation of many peoples' in which (at least according to the prevailing model) it is natural to be both American and African, American and Irish, Spanish, German, Japanese, and so on.[3]

It is of no little importance to separate off this kind of inclusive distinction from what at first sight appears to be a similar notional figure, namely the *dualism between Christians and heathens*. The Christian view of the human being also does away with ontological difference; Christianity relativizes and negates myths of origin. In the Christian faith, distinctions of race, ethnic belonging, class, sex and age lose their validity in the image of the Christian community – although, unlike cosmopolitanism, it presupposes each person's *professed commitment* to the Christian faith. Ontological opposition is replaced by an opposition, based on decision and faith, between Christians and *heathens*, one which *renews* the distinction between 'us' and the barbarians in the context of baptism, repentance and excommunication.

In contrast to this, the inclusive both/and distinction between 'us' and 'them' achieves two things in the context of cosmopolitanism. First, the idea of a dual homeland holds for *everyone*, regardless of decisions and distinctions. In this respect it anticipates the idea of general human rights. Second, the otherness of others [*die Andersheit der Anderen*] is not universalized into non-existence, as with (Christian) universalism, but is instead acknowledged in the context of a perceived equality. What lies at the core of cosmopolitan value-consciousness and self-awareness, as well as of cosmopolitan realism in relation to specific (life) histories, is an acknowledgement of the otherness of others; this includes both a measure of realism regarding the dilemmas and the potential for violence unleashed by such an acknowledgement, as well as the *dialogic imagination* that goes with it.

The concept of the 'world citizen' became the buzzword of eighteenth- and nineteenth-century Europe. People argued over the extent to which the linking and merging of cosmopolitanism and nation, universalism and particularism, was significant, necessary or useful. Nearly all the great European thinkers – poets, philosophers, social and economic theorists – participated in this debate, albeit *before* nationalism had conquered people's hearts and minds. Thus, the foundations and intellectual traditions of a *post*-national, *cosmopolitan Europe* were created during a pre-national era and rooted in a pre-national controversy. Today, in the context of the global age, the challenge is to rediscover these foundations and traditions and to revive them in the face of the ultimately short-lived dream of the everlasting nation.[4]

2.2   The public world is everything that is perceived as an irritating consequence of modern risk society's decisions

As early as 1927, John Dewey continued this tradition by embarking on a 'search for conditions under which the Great Society may become the Great Community.'[5] In other words, he poses the question: what exactly is 'political' or 'public' about the actions of those individuals – and this is where his framework is highly relevant to the cosmopolitan constellation – who do not belong to any community, in terms of natural rights or ethnicity or nation? In his search for a public space that is at once transnational *and* anchored in the actions of individuals, he proposes a dual approach: first of all, he distinguishes (in the terminology of political theory) between collectively binding *decisions* on the one hand and their *consequences* on the other. He links this with the theory that a public sphere only ever emerges at the focal point of public communication, *not* out of any general interest in collectively binding decisions – but, rather, triggered as a result of their *consequences*. People remain indifferent to decisions as such. It is not until individuals perceive and start to communicate with one another about the problematic consequences of decisions that they become worked up and anxious; communication shakes them out of their complacency and makes them worry, it pulls them out of their indifference and their egotistical existence, creating a public sphere of action based on commonality and community. The extent to which this is maintained depends on the extent (for whatever reasons) of concern and communication about these consequences. This is a variation on the sceptical insight formulated by Epictetus: it is not deeds themselves that distress human beings, but the public words spoken about these deeds.

People, Dewey argues, get together for all manner of reasons. But no single element and no sum of their social actions in and of itself can generate reflexivity about the public nature of their actions. This arises 'only when the *consequences* of combined action are *perceived* and become an object of desire and effort, just as "I" and "mine" appear on the scene only when a distinctive share in mutual action is consciously asserted or claimed. Human associations may be ever so organic in origin and firm in operation', but they develop a reflexive, 'public' quality only when their consequences, to the extent these are known about, become the subject of appreciation or striving, 'or of fear and rejection' (1954: 151–2; see also Krüger 1996).

In response to the question of how political action is possible in multi-ethnic, transnational, cosmopolitan contexts, Dewey says the following: the binding power, the sensory system and the nervous system of politics, which generates and binds together people's attentiveness, morality and willingness to act, emerges *only* in the course of public reflection about consequences. Its scope of influence does *not* coincide with national borders; instead, *the public world is everything that is perceived as an irritating consequence of modern risk society's decisions*. In a word, it is risk – or, to be more precise, the perception of risk – that creates a public sphere across all boundaries. The greater the mass-media-projected omnipresence of the threat, the greater the boundary-breaching political force of risk perception. Thought through to its conclusion, this means that the everyday experiential space known as 'humanity' does not come about in the form of everybody loving everybody else. It emerges instead in the perceived problem of the global consequences of actions within the risk society. In other words, it is the *reflexivity of the world risk society* that creates the reciprocal relationship between the public sphere and globality. Regardless of all the borders and rifts that separate nations, the constructed and accepted definition of planetary threat and its global mass-media-projected omnipresence create a common arena of values, responsibility and action which, analogously to the national arena, *can* (though need not necessarily) give rise to political action among strangers. This is the case when the accepted definition of threat leads to global norms, agreements and common action.

Having said this, the reverse is also important: risk definitions are always controversial. If they do create commonality, this presupposes the presence of a shared set of values. Thus, culturally shared (socially constructed) risk definitions also produce at *trans*national level a proximity and normativity that imply social obligation. This is because reflexivity about risk opens up the issue of reciprocal obligations in a transnational way: from whom can I expect to receive help if the worst comes to the worst? To whose aid am I expected to jump if they are in danger or distress? How can norms of transnational justice on the one hand and preventive precaution on the other be institutionalized? Thus, the public sphere, in the sense of a reflexivity restricted to *dialogue*, becomes *political* only when it creates and organizes practical action in order to make some sort of impact.

The public sphere generated by the consequences of the risk society also comes into being because all that is annoying, irritating and threatening is given voice by it (this, too, is part of the concept of risk). What has been shown to be true for modern nation-states – that they can be kept in shape only through constant communication about the threats they face – seems to hold true for the as yet informal fashioning of planetary norms as well. *The awareness of global norms that gives rise to political action emerges as a by-product, so to speak, of their own violation.*

The Holocaust in particular has opened our eyes to the depths of barbarism possible in a technologized civilization and has impressed on us the need for cosmopolitan standards, which have since become the global moral horizon of 'reparations' (Sznaider 2000; Levy and Sznaider 2001).

Paradoxically it is precisely the unimaginable nature of the Holocaust that contributes to its decontextualization, such that it is able to become a model for 'good and evil', for 'guilt and innocence'. The Holocaust thus forms a global point of reference for remembrance. This reflexive form of remembrance is a necessary precondition for the transition from a nation-state memory to a cosmopolitan one. The Americanization of the Holocaust plays a central role in two respects here. On the one hand, the American media landscape transforms the Holocaust into a consumable product; and on the other it transforms the Holocaust into a universal precept that makes general human rights a politically relevant concept in the consciousness of those participating in this new form of remembrance. This is not to say, of course, that we adhere to the naïve belief that the politics of the USA is guided by the imperatives of human rights. But neither do we want to fall prey to the thoroughly instrumentalized belief that political interests and the world of emotions (as in the case of human rights) are mutually exclusive. Instead, we are concerned to demonstrate how the Americanization of the Holocaust has contributed towards making the memories of this event into a globally valid value. Applying the historically specific Holocaust to a future-oriented globalized politics with the capacity to provide a basis for enforcing human rights in general (which in turn serves to prevent a new Holocaust from occurring) also entails the dislocation of political sovereignty. This means that the 'Americanization of the Holocaust' is simultaneously its cosmopolitanization. The way a state treats its citizens has now become an issue of general human interest, and the conflict between international law, which guarantees state sovereignty, and human rights, which limit this sovereignty, marks the latest developments in this. (Levy and Sznaider 2001: 150f.)

The atom bomb disasters of Hiroshima and Nagasaki and, in a different way, the Chernobyl nuclear reactor disaster have similarly forced states to come together out of necessity to address their consequences and have led, at least in the case of nuclear weapons, to non-proliferation treaties (albeit inadequate ones). NATO's intervention in Serbia, as the world's policeman, to prevent genocide being committed against the Kosovo Albanians created and sharpened a general awareness of the fact that only a set of laws grounded in the figure of the world citizen is capable of ensuring that action taken on behalf of persecuted people and population groups does not remain merely a matter of morality.[6]

All these cases illustrate that a globality of experiential spaces arises, first, out of a breaching of the norms that safeguard everyone's moral survival and, second, from the perceived consequences for everybody, that is, for each individual. A cosmopolitan sensibility or morality does not automatically set in when the world becomes interconnected; rather, it comes about through the concrete realization that one's own survival and that of others can no longer be separated. Public outrage over the global consequences of public decisions and a resultant acute awareness of norms creates – possibly! – 'the public-political element of action' *after the fact*, that is, retrospectively.[7] At least three phenomena now exist which suggest that the globality of an awareness of consequences actually does lead to political action among strangers from different nations. These are: the institutionalization of a global morality of the Holocaust, supranational governmental organizations and courts of law, and international non-governmental organizations.[8]

2.3 The communitarian myth

The realization that there is such a thing as a global public reflexivity about perceived threats to humanity dispels what one might call the *communitarian myth*, namely that community ties – both prescribed and assigned – must exist *first* in order *subsequently* for political action to be possible in these –

that is, national and ethnic, territorially *limited* – frameworks and spaces. This temporal and logical priority of a prescribed collectivity, which is sup- posedly the only form in which first communal action and then, through this, political action become possible, confuses the non-binding power of decisions and collective action as such with the politicizing effect produced by the perceived risks of consequences.

Methodological nationalism is based not only on a fixation on the state, but also on a *fixation on ethnicity*. By focusing on the alleged givenness and priority of 'community', which then creates the political identity needed for individuals to engage in political action, the social science of the national falls prey to a misapprehension; it refuses to face the Dewey question: how does a public sphere and, with it, political action become possible, *independently* of prior essentialist decisions? The communitarian myth thus establishes an intellectual paralysis that prevents the crucial issue from even coming into view, namely how a space is created that is characterized by a transnational public sphere, a politics involving individuals in actively caring for and having obligations towards one another. Political action does not break down if collectivity can no longer be assumed. What *emerges* (possibly) is a new form of both individualized and globalized public awareness of risk which comes about (perhaps worldwide) through the confrontation between modernity and its self-generated consequences and threats.

One key objection to the affirmative theory of the national and of the nation-state reveals the *monologic-national self-misunderstanding* of this view: the history of violence, the myths and the imaginary of the national came into being *across* borders, *in violation of* borders, that is, they can only ever be reconstructed and decoded *trans*nationally and, ultimately, within a cosmopolitan frame of reference. National history, when it is not doubling the frame of reference of the national, is *trans*national history; it is the bloody history of imperialism, of colonialism, of subjugations, wars, attacks and defences, the history of perpetrator societies which see themselves as per- petual victims. In short, *only* those who leave behind the nation-state para- digm can recognize the hidden transnationality of national myths. The task of decoding nationalism and its idea of the state can only be achieved as a cosmopolitan enlightenment project. Nationalism can only be adequately de- and reconstructed as a global principle of order of the nineteenth and twen- tieth century in a post-national context and through a transnational change in perspective.

Anthony Smith (1995) paints a picture of an 'autistic', introverted nationalism, because he analyses nationalism on its own territory; however, this is a one-sided non-concept of the national, as it fails to recognize its integral imperial aspect. Nation-state modernity is an expansionist project whose emotional and therefore political strength comes from the fact that boundaries – those of the nation, of the market, of knowledge and of technology – are continually being jumped over. What Anthony Smith completely overlooks is that the bloody history of national communities and their political capacity for mobilization can only be decoded from the standpoint of a post-national age and its historical and social science, and that this enlightenment concerning nationalism is a *central methodological project of the cosmopolitan enlightenment*. If they exist at all, there are as yet merely the beginnings of German–Jewish, German–French, French–Algerian, British–Indian, Irish–British, North American–South American, Polish–Russian, Japanese–Chinese, etc., projects of communication, institutionalized and dialogic forums for remembering, in which the traumas and myths of the national epoch *might* be exposed, unravelled and perhaps even overcome.

What is needed in order for this to happen is the methodology of the *meta-standpoint*, in which the different national standpoints are compared and contrasted with one another in such a way that each national standpoint is placed in its own context and there is a systematic (ex-)change of perspectives. Not until this happens can the mutually isolated monologues of national public spaces, where stereotypes of self and other become fixed through a process of perpetual circularity, be opened up to one another so that one's own standpoint can be appreciated as being specific.

Once liberated from its national container, 'history' can no longer be a history of glorious deeds. Suddenly, a sceptical historical narrative stresses the past wrongdoing of one's own nation: guilt is established. Cosmopolitan remembering means acknowledging the history (and the memories) of the 'other' and integrating them into one's own history. This perspective pushes the narrative of the self-righteous nation into the background. The heroic narrative of the first modernity is the narrative of the 'active perpetrator'. By contrast, the narrative of the second modernity will become the narrative of the 'non-active' victims. Something is or was done to them, and this constitutes their moral superiority. In the first modernity, the distinction between the remembering of the perpetrators and the remembering of the victims was an important aspect of a mutual lack of understanding and served to fence people off from one another. In the second modernity, a compromise comes about which is underpinned by mutual acknowledgement of the history of the other. It is this act of reconciliation that becomes the central experience of remembering. Thus, in many ways it is no longer solely an issue of the actual states that have committed crimes (especially as those affected have often already fallen victim to biological time), but of how their descendants deal with these histories and memories. In other words, by including the other, we defuse the distinction between the memories of the perpetrators and those of the victims. What remains is the memory of a common history. A cosmopolitan memory of the past is constituted not in a common community of destiny driven by some mythic desire or other and existing for purposes of continuity, but by the act of deliberately and willingly incorporating the suffering of the other. Thus new moral-political responsibilities emerge out of communication and interdependence. And that is not all: new cosmopolitan attitudes also emerge in the second modernity. Using cosmopolitan memories as an epistemological starting point also calls so-called 'methodological nationalism' into question. (Levy and Sznaider 2001: 236f.)

In this context, the cosmopolitan regime means that the national monologues of victimization that are celebrated as national memory are systematically replaced by transnational forms and forums of memory and dialogue, which also enable the innermost aspects of the national realm – the founding of myths – to be opened up to and for one another. National modernity, with its fixation on homogeneity, minimizes the identity-forming power of international, inter-ethnic, inter-religious debate – the (often painful and paradoxical) dialogic imagination. This is precisely what the cosmopolitan outlook explores and institutionalizes. In other words: national locations are transformed by stealth into (compulsory) world locations in which the conditions for encounter have to be created and established for this public sphere. Transnational organizations based on common interests and global political parties active both nationally and internationally need to be founded, or else existing parties reoriented and reorganized in such a way that they reflect and reinforce transnational domains of experience and sets of values. The immediate proximity of unfamiliar certainties is an inexhaustible source of creativity and conflict. Without placing experiments in transnational conflict regulation *at the centre* of nation-state, political and corporate organizations, the danger is that the phase that lies before us will either trigger renationalizing reflexes or lead to a post-political era of high technocracy.

2.4   Methodological nationalism as a source of error

Methodological nationalism entails five systematic errors in particular, which a New Critical Theory is capable of revealing and correcting, and in relation to which it can assert its own theoretical profile and prove its empirical fruitfulness.

First, the boundaries, categories, notions of order and variables of the national outlook are unquestioningly accepted into the social scientific perspective of observation and analysis. To take just one example, if the boundaries of politics and society are breached and if they are detached from the *a prioris* of the state, the result is that what is considered 'national' and 'international' can no longer be separated out, and apparent sameness – the sacred inner space of nation-state power – becomes the immediate field of intervention for international, supranational and transnational actors and organizations and for 'crises'. It can no longer be suggested, for example, that national inequalities and conflicts can be adequately analysed nationally, and neither can it be assumed that the actors, issues, bureaucracies and authorities of 'domestic politics' coincide with the actors, issues, bureaucracies and means of influence silently implied by the national outlook and methodological nationalism alike. In contrast to this, the concepts employed in New

Critical Theory reveal that the classic boundaries between domestic and foreign politics blend and blur, that political science sub-disciplines such as international politics and national governmental studies need to be liberated from the dogma of the national outlook and connected with one another, and that government studies need to be reformulated from a cosmopolitan point of view. What have classically been seen as 'external factors', such as global risks, global norms, supranational actors, the situation of people living in Africa and the Arab peninsula and the human rights violations there, turn into 'internal variables' and need to be systematically related to the way they are reflected in the national public sphere, the politics of national and international lobbies and NGOs, etc., 'while at the same time the state-centredness of previous international relations research needs to be overcome'. In view of the fact

that governing increasingly takes place in 'unbounded spaces', the division of 'domestic politics' from 'foreign politics' and 'Governmental Studies' from 'International Relations', which is repeatedly questioned but still characterizes the discipline, becomes obsolete once and for all. It is not only a matter of integrating national explanatory factors into analysis of international political processes, or of reassessing the significance of the international determinants behind national political processes, as this has been done in numerous approaches over the past few years; instead, it is a matter of problematizing the 'domestic'/'foreign' division itself.

What is needed, then, is a realization that 'traditional concepts such as "domestic policy" and "foreign policy", or "society" and "the state", are less and less suited to getting an analytic grasp on the challenges associated with globalization and "unbounded governance"' (Grande and Risse 2000: 251f.).

Second, the mistakes, errors and distortions of national-centredness and nation-state-centredness. The important point here is to imagine the apparently impossible possibility that what appears as 'decline' and 'downfall' in the national perspective can be seen and analysed in the cosmopolitan perspective in terms of a contribution to a new order. The denationalization of economic activity may undermine the nation-state's capacity to influence the economy, but it may be an important step towards the transnationalization of the nation-state. The denationalization of the state facilitates the national pluralization of society and – possibly – by the same token, the cosmopolitanization of the state. Similarly, the denationalization of the legal system may initiate a variety of forms of the transnationalization and cosmopolitanization of the legal system and the state.

This is not to claim, of course, that these developments will occur, still less that the collapse of the nation-state order *causally* generates a cosmopolitan order. What is crucial, however, is that perspectives are broadened and that there should be a process of alternation between the national and cosmopolitan perspectives. In an unbroken methodological nationalism, phenomena and processes that break with these frameworks of order *have to be* either ignored or identified as decline – whereas in the cosmopolitan perspective, the question as to how far the supposed collapse is an essential element of transformation, that is, of the emergence of a new order, can and must at least be posed and examined. It is also possible that apparently cast-iron research results gained in the experiential space of the nation-state cannot be transferred to the transnational experiential space. Thus, political interconnections in the national and transnational domain of power may display *opposing* qualities and functions, such that it becomes harder to act at national level and easier to act at transnational level (on this, see pp. 252–7).

Third, the ahistoricity and abstractness of the state and the concept of the state. The new thing that the cosmopolitan outlook reveals, and for which it is necessary to open up the theory of political action, is the globalization of contingency (Palonen 1998), or, to be more precise: *the 'becoming contingent' of state politics* – indeed of the *concept* of the state and of politics – through economic, cultural and political globalization. The so-called side-effects of globalization are achieving something worldwide from outside the national context that revolutionary movements domestically have been unable to do, and something that to Max Weber was unthinkable, namely to break open the cast-iron shell of dependence on the nation-state and to make it a political issue.

This reinvention of politics does not have to remain limited to the national level and to the sphere of welfare-state politics. Examples of globalization *and* politicization can also be found in human rights and environmental politics. In both spheres, the globalization of social movements based in civil society and that of non-state actors (INGOs) creates the preconditions for domestic political enforcement of international norms[9] . . . It is thoroughly conceivable that the days of the hierarchically structured nation state are numbered, whereas the organization of political domination in network-shaped contexts, where nation states are 'suspended', opens up new practical options in a globalized economy and culture. (Grande and Risse 2000: 241, 245)

This does not mean that the 'state' no longer plays any role at all, but that the role the state plays and what the word 'state' stands for becomes blurred and open-ended: a competition state, a neo-liberal state, a business state, a neo-national state, a simulation state, a glocal state, a cosmopolitan state, and so on.

Fourth, a clear distinction needs to be made between nation-state-centredness and state-centredness. New Critical Theory opposes the detaching of political thought from the state and inquires after the preconditions and opportunities for a *cosmopolitan self-transformation of the state*. This issue gets distorted in many different ways:

- by the *neo-liberal agenda*, according to which the state has not died but, on the contrary, has the power to transform itself, although it uses this power one-sidedly, to bring itself into conformity with the world market. This it does, for example, through privatization (the transfer of ownership and control of public services, such as health, transport and telecommunications, into private hands) and deregulation (the breaching of national boundaries and protected spaces that comes with the movement of capital and with financial exchanges). This position is surprisingly similar to the one held by its most fierce critics, namely

- the position of those who support the *international political economy*. Here, too, it is the overriding imperative to economize that is the dominant factor: the nation-state, if it wants to survive in the world market economy, has to transform itself into a 'business state', 'a competition state' or a 'neo-liberal state'. The more closely a national economy is integrated into global markets, the greater are the costs for an economic policy aimed not at liberalization and deregulation, but rather at an expansionist financial and fiscal policy, in order to achieve full employment;[10]

- and also, finally, by the emphasis on *governance* in contrast to *government*, as well as a reliance on global civil society to democratize supranational power and domination and, qua *deus ex machina*, to solve global problems.

Fifth, the national way of looking produces a distorted view of the key question: what are the legitimatory foundations that underpin the transformation of rules between the national and the cosmopolitan epoch of modernity? To put the question differently: how are supranational power and domination justified?[11] Methodological nationalism projects its understanding of legitimacy onto the new, transnational level of the formation of power and counter-power. According to this, the legitimacy of supranational power is power *derived* from the nation-state order. Supranational domination is conceptualized and legitimized as nation-state domination *writ large*. Contract theory provides the model for this: the legitimacy of supranational power concentration arises out of contracts agreed between assumed nation-state subjects. However, methodological nationalism closes itself off in this way from the key question of the extent to which a *change in the legitimatory foundations of political action* takes place in the transition from the national to the cosmopolitan epoch. A world citizens' regime is *not* a magnified nation-state regime, at least not necessarily and probably not even empirically. This being the case, however, a number of tricky problems arise. To what kind of legitimacy can a regime lay claim which, on the one hand, undermines nation-state-legitimated domination and transforms its very foundations while, on the other, holding sway not only in relation to a particular territory (as with the national form of domination) but universally, i.e. globally? Can the transnational law on which the cosmopolitan regime is based be reconciled with the idea of democratic governance? Or does it elude the idea of democracy and put other modes of legitimation – such as that of self-justification – in its place?[12]

This is why a change of paradigm characterized by the two opposing concepts *international* and *cosmopolitan* is needed. The world acquires a new shape as a consequence of this distinction. The national cosmos was divided into a clearly definable 'inside' and 'outside', at the centre of which the nation-state governs and creates order. In the internal experiential space, the issues of work, politics and cultural identity and the conflicts arising from them were perceived and worked through in the context of the nation as a forum for collective action. This was matched internationally, in the external experiential space, by the image of 'multiculturalism', in which the national self-image is reflected and reinforced by marginalizing and excluding strangers. Consequently, the national/international distinction was always more than a distinction; it functioned more as a permanently self-confirming prophecy.

The antithesis posed by cosmopolitanism breaks open this framework of meaning from the inside out. In the perspective of methodological cosmopolitanism, it suddenly becomes clear that the national cannot be clearly distinguished from the international and that, consequently, homogeneous units cannot be demarcated from one another either. This is how the nation-state repositories of power are broken open from inside and out, how a new point of view emerges, a new perspective on space and time, new coordinates of the social and the political, a new shape of the world that justifies a new concept for a new era, namely that of the second modernity.

What distinguishes the second modernity from postmodernity? The authors of postmodernity emphasize the *removal* of boundaries – through '*networks*' (Castells), '*flows*' (Bauman) and '*scapes*' (Appadurai) – whereas the theory of the second modernity focuses on the question of the ways in which other kinds of context-specific (variable, plural) boundary constructions emerge, given the fact that state sovereignty is becoming less clearly defined. Thus the cosmopolitan perspective *contradicts* the postmodern dissolution of boundaries. It is precisely at those points where the world becomes 'bound(ary)less', where the distinction between national and international becomes blurred, that decisions *have to* be made – not least, who is to decide how responsibility is to be attributed (Beck et al. 2001). This demarcation of boundaries between the national and transnational attributing of decision-making and responsibility becomes unclear, leading to ad hoc attribution, random attribution, plural responsibilities, along with political instrumentalization of the same. The crucial point is that this *transnational meta-power politics of plural boundary demarcations*, this dialectic of

Table 2.1 Paradigm change in the social sciences from the first modernity to the second modernity

	First modernity: *methodological nationalism*	Second modernity: *methodological cosmopolitanism*	Postmodernity: *methodological pluralism*
Boundary	Congruence of boundaries: the national distinction between inside and outside dominates across all issues; political membership is prescribed and exclusive.	Politics of boundaries: inside and outside become mixed in relation to specific issues; boundaries need to be redrawn and justified; plural political memberships which to some extent can be chosen.	Dissolution of boundaries: 'networks', 'flows', 'scapes'
Class/social inequality	State-centred national sociology: social inequalities are addressed *only* and *exclusively* within the nation-state context – 'consonant hierarchy'; ethnic–national distinction between mobility and migration.	Transnational sociology detached from the state: social inequalities are addressed at the level of world society and in their many dimensions: (a) globally, (b) transnationally, (c) intranationally; 'discrepant/dissonant hierarchies'; 'migration' = global social (upwards) mobility.	Cultural theory of the global; global culture industry, local exclusion ('useless poor')
Ethnicity/culture	Hegemonic either/or culture: majority-dominated premises of homogeneity; 'problems with minorities'; hidden essentialism; universalism 'blind to difference'; race and space form a potentially deadly discourse; aim of politics: assimilation and integration	Limited both/and culture; typology of transnational life forms; dilemmas and contradictions of cosmopolitan culture; quantitative and qualitative transformation of majorities into minorities and vice versa; recognition of ethnic difference; de-essentialized	Unbounded both/and culture; non-hierarchical plurality ('hybrids'); universal co-existence of cultural differences, de-essentialized, identities open to change

Ethics	Ethic of exclusion: the absent Other; dominance of the particular as opposed to the universal	Ethic of inclusive exclusion: the present Other; dominance of the universal as opposed to the particular ('cosmopolitan nation')	Ethic of universal relativism; incommensurability of context-specific ethnic standpoints
Economy	Distinction between home-based economy and industry (family and market) *within* the nation-state framework; transition from agrarian societies with local markets, in which production techniques remained unchanged over centuries and social cohesion was grounded in a common faith and religious rituals, to a national modernity, in which market economy, democracy and national culture mutually impact on and dominate one another.	Distinction between nation-state and global economy: de- or ex-territorialized reorganization of the economy *without* a global state framework; emergence of a world, market and 'me' society, in which capital but not labour is endlessly mobile, populations for the most part urbanized, religions and ethnicities pluralized and social inequalities radicalized.	Cultural crises and contradictions of global – postmodern – capitalism
State/politics	Apparently necessary merging of space with politics: state = territorial state = nation-state; equation of sovereignty with autonomy: state independence, national self-determination and dealing with important national issues (welfare, law, security) coincide.	Decoupling of space and politics: despatialization of state and society – 'cosmopolitan state'; distinction between sovereignty and autonomy: national issues have to be dealt with transnationally; loss of autonomy may lead to a gain in sovereignty.	Post-political global view

strategies for cosmopolitanization and renationalization, can be brought into view as such, deciphered and systematically examined neither in the national nor in a postmodern perspective, but rather in a cosmopolitan perspective.

It is not the case, however, that the paradigmatic opposition of (inter)-nationality and cosmopolitanism provides a rationale for any logical or temporal exclusiveness; rather, it suggests a conflictual co-existence of transition, a new form of simultaneity of the non-simultaneous. This should not be thought of as a negative-sum game, as a situation in which what is forfeited in national terms is won back in cosmopolitan terms, and vice versa.

The same is true for conflicts around sex, class, ethnicity and homosexuality which, while they may have emerged from the national context, are no longer really at home within it but instead overlap and interconnect transnationally. The cosmopolitanization of social movements is evident as well – as is the fact that they have become the vehicles for global insights, values, conflicts, demands, rights and obligations.

The argument so far can be summarized as follows: 'globalization', when taken to its logical conclusion, means that the social sciences must be grounded anew as a *reality-based science of the transnational* – conceptually, theoretically, methodologically and, incidentally, organizationally as well. This includes the fact that there is a need for the basic concepts of 'modern society' – *household, family, class, democracy, domination, state, economy, the public sphere, politics,* and so on – to be released from the fixations of methodological nationalism and redefined and reconceptualized in the context of methodological cosmopolitanism. Table 2.1 offers just a brief overview of this, using a few key terms (and indicating where the difference to postmodernism lies). These issues will be developed in the following chapters, using the key concept of *'power'*, that is, by exploring the relationship between the nation-state and global business.

3

Global Domestic Politics Changes the Rules: On the Breaching of Boundaries in Economics, Politics and Society

How can or must the key concepts of 'power', 'domination' and 'violence' be reinterpreted and reconstructed in a cosmopolitan perspective?[1]

3.1 The meta-power of global business

What is the meaning of cosmopolitanism in this context? For one thing, it is a perspective that opposes the abstract, historically deep-frozen concept of the state and politics embedded in assumptions about the meanings and impacts of political and economic boundaries; for another, it opposes the abstract notion of global capital as something that irrevocably colonizes state-organized politics. If these concepts are taken as a basis for analysis, a picture emerges in which politics and economics are placed in a static, deterministic relationship to one another. However, this blocks out the very factor that the cosmopolitan perspective makes central, namely the politics of plural boundaries and the openness of the context in which global business actors and state actors alike pursue their goals. In the cosmopolitan view, this game about changes in the positions and bases of power in the global arena needs to be conceptualized by making the reciprocal relationships between political and economic arenas the focus of attention. This means it is necessary to examine how the political dimension of global capitalism and the economic dimension of global politics may be decoded and placed in relationship to one another. Accordingly, the state can no longer be seen as a pre-given political unit; instead, we need to analyse how – in what sense – states (and the concept of the state) are being hollowed out and how their (its) meanings and functions are being redefined and transformed. Disciplinary boundaries and theoretical positions separate the state from the economy in order to ask how they are related to one another, thereby generating an apolitical, abstract analytical framework. What gets distorted in the process are the strategic interactions through which politics is transformed, as well as the consequences entailed by such transformations for shaping and reshaping the social meanings of boundaries; this includes the question as to which new opportunities are thereby opened up for state capacity in the global age.

We are witnessing one of the most important changes there has been in the history of power. Globalization needs to be decoded as a creeping, post-revolutionary, epochal transformation of the national and international state-dominated system governing the balance of power and the rules of power. [A *meta-power game* is in progress in the relationship between global business and the state, a power struggle in which the balance of power and the rules of power governing the national and international system of states are being radically changed and rewritten.] It is the world of business in particular that has developed such meta-power by breaking out of the cage of the territorial nation-state-organized power game and mastering new strategies of power in the digital domain in contrast to territorially rooted states. 'Meta-power game' refers to the fact that the nation-state rules of global politics are being radically altered in the course of disputes and struggles over power.

Anyone pursuing the question of where the strategies of capital acquire their meta-power encounters a curious situation. The basic idea was expressed in the headline of an Eastern European newspaper on the occasion of a visit by the German chancellor in 1999: 'We forgive the crusaders and await the investors.' It is this exact reversal of the calculation on which classical theories of power and domination are based that enables transnational companies to maximize their power. It is not the threat of *invasion* but rather the threat of *non-invasion* of investors, or the threat of their withdrawal, that constitutes the means of coercion. There is only one thing worse than being overrun by multinationals, and that is *not* being overrun by multinationals.

This form of domination is tied no longer to carrying out commands, but rather to the possibility of investing more cheaply elsewhere – in other countries – and thereby evoking the threat of *not* doing something, namely of *not* investing in *this* country. In this sense, the corporations' new-found power is *not* grounded in violence as the *ultima ratio* for imposing one's will upon others and is therefore much more mobile, being independent of any specific location; this in turn means that it can be deployed anywhere in the world. The potential for blackmail entailed by this kind of domination perfects the logic of economic action and economic power: always and everywhere *not* to do anything, not to invest, without being subject to any public obligation to offer justification – *this* is the crucial lever of power that global business actors hold in their hands.

It is not imperialism but rather non-imperialism that constitutes the essence of global business power. Thus, the deterritorialized maximization of business power needs to be neither won nor legitimated politically. It occurs independently of the monitoring bodies of developed democracies, such as parliaments, courts and governments. It has no need of military mobilization. The power of global business interests is based, therefore, on exactly the opposite of the sources of nation-state power: democratic elections, public legitimation, a monopoly on the use of violence. The power formula of transnational business interests is, by contrast, *deliberate, targeted non-conquest*. This violence-free, invisible, fully intentional and ubiquitous 'not' of withdrawal is neither subject to consent, nor is it capable of winning consent.

To put it differently again: the non-political *per se*, namely *not* doing something, changes the nation-state rules of power, the power architecture between states and business – it maximizes *and* covers up the expansion of global political power on the part of global business actors. Withholding investments, along with targeted inaction, forcibly brings about conformity to the global business agenda everywhere, regardless of borders; and it fosters a variety of 'pre-emptive' neo-liberalism – among states, political parties, churches, trade unions, employees, and so on. At the same time, hardly any obstacles lie in the path of investment decisions, as they realize their collective binding power in the most effective way conceivable, namely through a policy of *faits accomplis*.[2]

To put it briefly: the meta-power that global business interests have in relation to nation states is based on the *exit option* (Hirschman) that capital has appropriated for itself in the digital domain. It is the experience – one understood by everybody throughout the world – of actual or threatened *exclusion of states* from the world market that demonstrates and maximizes the power of global business in contrast to isolated individual states; large areas of Africa are all too familiar with this experience, and it is also still being practised towards certain successor states of the former Soviet Union. This meta-power falls in between the categories of legal and illegal: it is neither illegal nor legitimized, but is rather 'translegal'; it possesses the power to rewrite the state-dominated rules of legitimate domination in the national and international arena.

How is this possible? What is it that triggers this situation? The exit option that decides the weal and woe of states comes about through the competition between states for global investors and capital flows. As a result, first modernity nation-states which were primarily military rivals turn into second modernity competition states that are primarily global economic rivals. The key to power is no longer military might but a state's position in the global market. This means that state domination *as such*, both with regard to its internal and external stability, and indirectly with regard to its legitimacy, is mediated by the global market.

The analogy that exists between the military logic of state power and the economic logic of state power is quite striking. The volume of investment capital is the equivalent of firepower and weaponry, albeit with the crucial distinction that the threat *not* to shoot increases power. Product development is the equivalent of developing new weapons systems. Instead of military bases and the diplomatic service, large companies establish branch offices in many different countries. The old military rule that attack is the best means of defence is recast to mean that states must invest in research and development in order to make the most of the offensive force of capital. As research and education budgets grow, so too – it is hoped – does the clout wielded by the state in the global arenas and organizations of global politics. Above all, however, old-fashioned ideological warfare has been supplanted by the discourse of globalization. The key to winning over minds is to anchor the maxims of neo-liberal globalization in people's identity and in their image of themselves as their 'own boss'.

This theorem of meta-power can be developed, in one way, as a *mirror image* of the classical theories of power and domination for which Max Weber laid the groundwork. Thus, global business meta-power is exercised in relation to states, that is, the sovereign, self-justifying vehicles of legitimate violence. However, this meta-power eludes the definitional criteria of state domination because it is based

- not on force
- not on military strength or intervention
- not on democratic consensus

and because it instrumentalizes nation-state law.

All these seemingly 'essential definitions' of state domination tacitly presuppose the *territorial principle*: they map out and formulate the territorial understanding of society and domination within the frame of reference of methodological nationalism. This tacitly implied political significance of space is the only way of comprehending the opinion apparently held unanimously, regardless of theoretical differences, that ultimately domination is always and necessarily based on access to the means of violence. 'All politics is a struggle for power; the ultimate kind of power is violence', writes one of the most critical thinkers in sociology, C. Wright Mills, thereby simply following Max Weber's famous definition of the state as 'a relation of men dominating men, a relation supported by means of legitimate (i.e. considered to be legitimate) violence'. In this context, Max Weber explicitly quotes Trotsky, who said: 'Every state is founded on force', and Max Weber adds: 'That is indeed right' (Weber 1946).

But in fact that is *wrong*, specifically with respect to the *de*territorial meta-power of global business actors. And that is exactly what makes it so difficult for an outlook wedded to methodological nationalism to recognize and analyse these actors as a 'quasi-state', an 'ersatz state'.

The principles of territoriality and violence set clear limits to state power. The weakness of violence lies in its *inflexibility*. In contrast, wealth is *highly flexible* as a means of power available to global business actors. Unlike violence, which can only be practised *negatively* in the sense of actual or potential punishment (killing), wealth can dispense rewards and punishments alike, it has the potential for both positive and negative applications and dosages. In addition, wealth elicits consent via self-interest, it goads people into eager obedience based on self-interest. If wealth becomes linked with two other instruments of power, *efficiency* and *knowledge*, the result is the ultra-flexibility of economic meta-power. Knowledge can be used to change the political agenda, stimulate new needs, create markets, redefine goals, convince, persuade, indeed, even transform enemies into allies. 'Knowledge is power' (Francis Bacon) – to the extent that time is money, this principle not only acquires greater acceleration and becomes a maxim of capitalism, it also acquires greater significance, because knowledge, in the form of investment in research and technology, both undermines *and* accelerates knowledge production.

The other aspect of this theory of meta-power is that the globalization of globalization discourse is probably globalization's principal achievement. This *discursive* power of capital – the global power of targeted non-conquest – can be very much better understood, however, in terms of Foucault's theory of power. This differs fundamentally from the classical definitions of power, which make the latter the central point of reference and presuppose the presence of clearly distinguishable actors. 'Power' in the Foucauldian understanding, however, is not something someone can either have or not have; it is not a possession but is, instead, present everywhere in social interactions. Power is exercised by the rulers as much as by the ruled, through everyday discursive practices. It becomes invisible and taken for granted to the extent that it is integrated into people's identity.

The power of threatened non-investment is indeed present everywhere nowadays. Accordingly, globalization is not an option. Globalization means domination by nobody. Nobody started it, nobody can stop it, and nobody is responsible. The word 'globalization' stands for organized irresponsibil-ᐸ ity. Keeping a lookout for someone you can contact, someone to whom you can make a complaint, someone you can demonstrate against is a lost cause: there is no institution, no telephone number, no e-mail address. Everybody either is or sees themselves as a victim – nobody is the perpetrator. Even the corporation bosses, the 'modern princes' who want to be wooed, see it as part of their allotted role to sacrifice their thinking and acting at the altar of shareholder value if they themselves do not want to be fired. The more the discourse of globalization flows into every capillary of social life, the more powerful global business actors and strategies become.

One significant way in which this discursive meta-power of globalization acquires concrete form is in the TINA principle: There Is No Alternative. TINA There is plenty of talk nowadays of 'multiple modernities' – the Eurocentric Western monism of modernity has been broken, not least by postcolonialism, but also by an awareness of transnational ways of living, networks and identities, as cultural theory and research have revealed. But this multiplicity of culturally divergent 'DIY modernities' and modernity mosaics is at best manifested in visions of alternative capitalisms rather than in alternatives *to* capitalism. The hegemony of globalization discourse reveals itself paradoxically in precisely that which seems to contradict it, namely in the international debate about the new diversity of modernity options. This covers up and remains silent about what is excluded here by virtue of being taken for granted: neo-liberal monism, the sole, inevitable orthodoxy of the global market.

Conflicts over modernity are as old as modernity itself. After the collapse of the socialist alternative to modernity, however, current controversies over the substance, aims and institutions of a future modernity are not only postmodern or postcolonial, they are above all *post-revolutionary*. The image of the 'world market society' that globalization discourse conveys and naturalizes does not have – as the national, democratically constituted society does – (at least) one two-party system, a dialectic of government and opposition and a two-way dialogue, all struggling for the future of humanity. Instead of debates over alternative futures, it is the TINA discourse of globalization that predominates, and with it the moralistic black-and-white opposition between the *world's good guys* – the 'modernizers' – and the *world's bad guys* – the anti-modernists. The latter entrench themselves in the no-go zones of the major cities and global society, where – as in all good haunted castles – the ghosts of the daily evening news, share prices, the international drugs trade, terrorist intrigues and life-threatening killer viruses go about their dastardly, humanity-threatening deeds.

Drawing on Michael Mann's theory and history of power (1986, 1993) we might put it more precisely as follows: the meta-power of global business actors is *extensive* and *diffuse* rather than *intensive* or *authorized*. It is *extensive* in the sense of the discursive hegemony of neo-liberal globalization. The latter establishes, beyond all boundaries of nation, ethnicity, religion, sex, caste, class, space and time, a context of generalized power relations, a minimum of worldwide relations of competition, dependency and cooperation. This context of power is *not intensive*, because it does not prescribe or set down any hierarchical coercion in terms of, say, obedience to commands. At the same time, it is not an authorized power but rather a diffuse power, *diffuse* because it is anonymous and lacks a centre, attributability and clear structures of responsibility.

Finally, meta-power is not '*authorized*' (in Mann's sense, but also in the sense of Max Weber's 'legitimacy' of domination) because it has no legitimacy (of its own), the consequence of this being that belief in the legitimacy of global business meta-power always remains in doubt on the part of the 'ruled' themselves – states, countries, cultures, societies. Indeed, it is even the case that the bigger, more extensive and more diffuse the power of global business actors is or seems to be, the more clearly their need for legitimation and lack of legitimation comes to the fore.

This is how new kinds of economically defined meta-power formations emerge in the global arena – highly fragile, highly flexible and legitimated neither democratically nor by the state; they are *no longer* solely business actors, but they are *not yet* states: they are '*quasi-states*', highly prone to worldwide movements of resistance and anti-globalization coalitions of the most heterogeneous kind on the one hand, and to market collapses resulting from these on the other. It is this issue of legitimacy, this legitimatory crisis of global business meta-power, which grows along with global business itself and bursts to the fore with a multitude of political consequences. One such consequence is that meta-power makes global business much more prone to violence and therefore much more dependent on state violence.

Global business meta-power brings about a vulnerability to and dependence on violence

Hannah Arendt referred to the opposition between power and violence that becomes more radical as modernity unfolds. 'Politically speaking, it is insufficient to say that power and violence are not the same. Power and violence are opposites: where one rules absolutely, the other is absent. . . . [T]o speak of non-violent power is actually redundant. Violence can destroy power; it is utterly incapable of creating it' (1970: 56). 'Violence can always destroy power; out of the barrel of a gun grows the most effective command, resulting in the most instant and perfect obedience. What can never grow out of it is power' (ibid.: 53).[3]

Thus, *violence* consists of the means and procedures of physical coercion, whose ultimate consequence is aimed at life itself. When organized militarily, it constitutes the worst case scenario on which Carl Schmitt bases his concept of the political. *Power*, however, emerges from the sum of the *consent* accorded to actions and decisions. The stability of power is based not least on the unquestionable nature of consent. Power that comes from unquestionability disappears from the horizon of consciousness. To be more precise: *there is a positive correlation between the taken-for-grantedness of power, the forgetting of power, and the dimensions of power*. One could almost say that, wherever nobody is talking about power, that is where it unquestionably exists, at once secure and great in its unquestionability. Wherever power is the subject of discussion, that is the start of its decline. Wherever consent is withdrawn in relation to power, the control of violence is eroded – either the privatization of violence sets in, or else the use of the police and the military to tame outbursts of violence can no longer count on the requisite approval. The point at which meta-power conflicts escalate into outbreaks of violence and anarchy is when the legitimatory crisis undermines the state's monopoly on violence. This is why (the unquestionability of) power disintegrates in the meta-power game and there is an increased danger of violence erupting and escalating.

It is surely no coincidence that around the same time as Hannah Arendt was writing in the 1960s, two other theorists of modern society, namely Talcott Parsons and Ralf Dahrendorf, were arguing analogously that power is dependent on consensus; in so doing, they even systematically predicted the collapse of the Soviet empire: 'But power', writes Parsons,

in the strict sense of a general social medium, essentially contains an element of consensus. This is because power is based on the existence and use of institutionalized opportunities to exert influence; through opportunities to exert influence and through the exertion of influence, the system of power is furnished with consensus in the context of social values. It is *not* the general *legitimizing* of power and domination that is the special achievement of democratic institutions, but rather the mediation of *consensus about the exercise* of power and domination by specific persons and groups and through quite specific binding decisions; no institution that is fundamentally different from democratic institutions is capable of this achievement. A form of legitimation that is merely general is not sufficient, especially in highly differentiated societies and systems of government. In this respect the decisive function of the system of democratic association is to organize the participation of members in the choice of leaders and to arrange the formulation of political principles; to make sure there is an opportunity to be heard, to exert influence and to have a genuine choice between alternatives.

It is clear to me what follows from this view, namely, that the totalitarian communist organization probably cannot fully match 'democracy' with its political and integrative capacities in the long term. Indeed, I venture to *predict that the communist organization of society will prove to be unstable* and either will make adjustments that tend towards electoral democracy and a pluralist party system or will 'regress' to less developed and politically less effective forms of organization; in the second of these instances the communist countries would develop much more slowly than in the first instance. This prediction is based not least on the fact that the Communist Party everywhere has emphasized the task of educating the people for a new society. In the long term, its legitimacy will surely be undermined if the party leadership is not willing to *trust* the people that it has educated. In our context, however, trusting the people means entrusting them with a share of political responsibility. This can only mean that the monolithic unitary party will have to give up its monopoly of political responsibility in the end. (Parsons 1970: 70f.)

Even Ralf Dahrendorf – *the* Parsons critic of the 1960s – ultimately puts forward an analogous argument:

In a certain way, it follows from the 'definition' of the totalitarian state that conditions for the organization of oppositional interest groups are not given within it. To be more precise: although the social and the technical conditions exist, the political conditions are lacking and there is no freedom to form coalitions. At this point, the significance of the resistance put up by the government of East Germany to free elections becomes just as clear as the situation in which totalitarian states in general are threatened with the danger of violent, probably revolutionary political conflicts. If latent conflict groups are given the opportunity to organize – whether explicitly, as in Hungary, or merely in actual fact, as on 17 June 1953 in Berlin – the whole edifice of totalitarian states will collapse. Moreover it seems highly likely that this possibility can acquire concrete form at any moment in any totalitarian state; in modern totalitarian societies founded upon ideological state parties, there is a constant danger, especially from the point of view of the ruling elites, that the one permitted organization, the state party, will itself become the source of oppositional movements and revolutionary conflicts. (Dahrendorf 1970: 120)

This is exactly what came to pass, personified in the figure of Gorbachev.

If the dependence of power upon consent can be proven historically in such an impressive manner in relation to the full military arsenal of the state, then it does not take much courage to predict that the triumph of the meta-power of global business, as fragile and dependent on consent as it is, makes the latter susceptible to violent attack. The growing opposition between power and non-state, privatized violence in the second modernity can also be demonstrated by showing that even 'consensus-proof' power can be provoked to the extreme by small groups of utterly fearless violent criminals (suicide terrorists). Global cultural conflicts provide a host of reasons for fundamentalists and terrorists to engage in their extremist responses, which confront the entire technologically sophisticated world with its inevitable vulnerabilities. Even extensive electronic controls repeatedly show up new gaps and opportunities for attack. Considering the general vulnerability to which global economic production is subject, one has to wonder why this powerlessness in meta-power and the opportunities for violence which it offers to small extremist groups have not yet been exploited with very much more horrendous consequences. In the world that is fast approaching – a united and yet divided world with many obvious contradictions – this susceptibility to and dependence on violence on the part of highly organized economic superpowers could indeed contain a new dimension of conflict, which could have an impact on the whole picture and change its entire complexion. As the response to the terrorist attacks on New York and Washington indicates, the <u>perceived</u> threat of terrorism brings with it an opportunity to reverse neo-liberal power relations – to deprive global business actors of their power and to empower states.

A pacifist and a cosmopolitan capitalism?

Two further consequences of these processes of meta-power formation are worth noting. In the risk society's laboratory – the global economy – both a *pacifist* and a *cosmopolitan* capitalism (among other things) are being experimented with. Whether or not these will become established in the face of the harsh, militant reality of worldwide economic and political upheavals and expressions of anti-globalization is questionable, however.

World history is a history of madmen either potentially or actually jumping at each other's throats with the intention of preventing madmen from achieving domination. World politics is the politics of violence. This principle – that the anarchy of power holders and states is a bloody and imperialistic one – has held true throughout the ages. By contrast, the new meta-power of global business is, in and of itself, *essentially pacifist*, although possibly not in terms of its consequences.

As we have explained above, the power of global capitalism comes not from invasion but from the exit option. However, this ex-territoriality of capital investment is only half the story: if you take your money out *here*, you have to invest it *there*. In other words, capital always has to put down roots somewhere, it has to become 'localized', and in this respect it always acts 'imperialistically'. Yet this is no military imperialism, it is an imperialism based on the 'spirit of trade', one that those being overrun desperately need, even if they rebel against it. It is the *masochism of economic self-interest* running amok amid the delights of the consumer society – even as it denounces and demonizes the same – that the power of the global market provokes and instrumentalizes, and to which it owes the fragile consent it enjoys. Immanuel Kant wrote about this theme more than two hundred years ago:

The spirit of trade cannot co-exist with war and will sooner or later seize hold of every nation. The reason is this: of all the powers that are subordinate to the power of the state, the power of money can be said to be the most reliable. Hence, states see themselves compelled (admittedly not by the motivating force of morality) to promote the nobility of peace and, wherever in the world there is a threat of the outbreak of war, to prevent it through mediation . . . In this way, nature itself guarantees the Eternal Peace through the mechanisms present in human inclinations; albeit with a certainty that is insufficient to foretell the future of the same. (Kant 1964: 227)

Kant derives from this the 'obligation' to act *as if* this were possible.

In similar fashion, Auguste Comte and Herbert Spencer also theoretically conjured the 'essentially unwarlike' character (Schumpeter) of capitalism – too soon, as it turned out, for *soon afterwards* the long, bloody eras of imperialism, colonialism and world wars began, and counter-theories of *military* capitalism were able to point to the co-existence of war and global trade between nations, even up to the present day.

But is this also true of the transnational economy of the second modernity? In times gone by, warlike peoples would conquer trading peoples; nowadays, it is the other way around. The way the GDR joined West Germany can also be seen in these terms. It is the separation, or opposition, between the state and global business and their new rivalry over power that *possibly* makes the unwarlike meta-power attached to the withdrawal of investment a new force to be reckoned with. At any rate, amid what are often heated public debates over the new role of global corporations, we ought to take note of the fact that these are the forms of conquest of a pacifist capitalism, which acquires its superior power in relation to localized, territorially organized states *from this very pacifism*. While we can also speak of the 'structural violence of non-investment and non-intervention', it would be pointless to do so because that would be to obscure the specificity of this form of domination – a highly flexible, deterritorial, non-military form of coercion *not* based on obedience to commands.

Additionally, global capitalism is *polyethnic* at heart and in this respect it calls into question the national ontology of society and culture. Thus, what is in the process of emerging, against the grain of dominant critiques of capitalism, is not only a pacifist but a *cosmopolitan* form of capitalism. National societies trumpet their belief in cultural homogeneity, in the necessity of bounded, guarded territories, friend-and-foe relations, myths of origin and a collective public memory oriented towards them. Only in this way, so it is said, is society, or 'integration', possible, and with it politics, democracy, a public sphere, social justice, history, and so on. According to this view, global companies are ultimately doing the devil's work because they demystify these myths using the persuasive power of a global business rationality that creates *faits accomplis*.

The logic of exclusion characteristic of nation-state politics comes into conflict with the logic of inclusion entailed by global business rationality. Rather than separation, it is the mixing of races, ethnic groups and nationalities that becomes the source of creativity and profit maximization and therefore the dominant labour market policy pursued by transnational companies. The antidote to stagnation is hybridization. The melange approach is trumps and becomes the norm – at least within transnational organizations' sphere of power. Mobility within a company means mobility across borders and boundaries. Anyone who wants to make their career in a 'German' global corporation not only has to speak English in Erlangen but also has to 'kill distances' every day and be prepared to move to different continents. Global corporations acquire their capital and recruit their management elites from many different nations, create jobs in (nearly) every part of the world and distribute their profits to shareholders in very different countries. Thus, the belief in a national socio-ontology of society is *empirically disproven* by real-life experiments – not with the morality of multiculturalism, but with the money argument. It is *global business* cosmopolitan realism which, using the language of profit maximization, facilitates the breakthrough of the following maxim: cosmopolitan societies are simply more creative, more productive and, in this respect, superior to national societies in global market competition. Note, however, that it is the meta-power of capital that puts companies in a position to turn their transnational organizations into real-life experiments with polyethnic co-existence and cooperation – often *in opposition to* the resistance of nation-states, national laws and national authorities. To put the point somewhat provocatively, unbounded capitalism is both a source of chronic tax evasion *and* a school for cosmopolitanism.

To speak of the emergence of a pacifist and cosmopolitan capitalism will seem to many to be more than a little illusory, not least because (or when) it involves remaining silent about its flip sides. Thus, for example, the fact that the global market requires cosmopolitan flexibility and sensitivity also works as a mechanism of exclusion. Generally speaking, those who are already mobile in the first place always end up getting more and more in a 'winner takes all' scenario. All those others who are unable to compete are faced with the threat of 'drift' (Richard Sennett): aimlessly roaming from place to place, person to person, job to job. This generates narcissism and puts family relationships, love relationships, friendships, people's ties to particular places and their social capital at risk. More freedom makes for more homelessness, more mobility makes for less loyalty and more transnationality makes for less democracy. In other words, the collapse of the national socio-ontology by no means automatically signals the advent of a cosmopolitan age; it does not mean that curiosity about and respect for difference will increase. Such a collapse can also lead to atomization and hatred of foreigners. Both diametrically opposed scenarios, that of *atomization* and of *renationalization*, as well as that of *cosmopolitanization*, have to be kept in the field of view. There are worlds between them, potential global crises and catastrophes.

All power generates counter-power. The emergence of cosmopolitan societies and that of their enemies are two aspects of the same movement. The 'translegality' of global business meta-power lends legitimacy to global anti-globalization and anti-modernization movements – after all, they are the ones defending national institutions of legitimate domination (the state and democracy) against the subversions of global capital. Modernizations and their associated ruptures and eruptions have always evoked nostalgia for lost certainties, the defenders of traditional values and virtues. In nineteenth- and twentieth-century Europe this 'dialectic of modernization' frequently led to xenophobic rejection of cosmopolitan internationalism and its liberal values; this was linked to the fear of moral decadence that was supposedly inherent in urban global society. This dialectic of modernization is emerging today with fresh intensity, not only within the USA and Europe, but on a global scale as well.

In many non-European cultures globalization is equated with *US Americanization*, which is seen as the driving force behind all the evils that infect their societies. The relentless upheavals caused by global economic and social transformation have already led in many parts of the world to a degree of squalor and destruction that eclipses even nineteenth-century Europe's 'proletarianization' (Karl Marx) – and will do so even more in the future.

For those who believe in the national socio-ontology and who want to preserve their culture from internal decline, globalization is the 'Great Satan'. The more pride a nation has in conjuring up the myths of its cultural heritage and insisting on its independence, the greater is its resentment of 'American globalization' and 'global Americanism', which, as far as those with a nostalgia for the nation are concerned, constitute a permanent violation of national dignity. Global counter-movements against modernization thus extend from the diplomatically sophisticated animosity of the French, through a range of paradoxical coalitions of opposites, as between environmental and xenophobic movements, for example, to the new internationale of ethnic and religious fundamentalisms. What is more, their influence grows in tandem with the expansion of meta-power and with the social and political upheavals the latter causes around the world. It does not bear thinking about what would happen if the sparks of a new global economic crisis were to be dropped into this powder keg!

With the war in the Middle East, conflicts in Afghanistan and countless regional hotspots in Africa and South America, the world in the early years of the twenty-first century is draped in a net of tensions and dangers that could escalate out of control at any moment. Even nuclear scenarios have assumed a degree of probability that was not even conceivable towards the end of the Cold War. The Kashmir conflict between nuclear newcomers India and Pakistan, an Israel threatened by weapons of mass destruction, a suicide attack by a fanatic with a so-called dirty nuclear bomb in the middle of New York – since 11 September 2001 nothing is inconceivable any more. So surely one must be blind to speak of an 'exit capitalism' no longer based on military conquest? On the contrary, one must be blind *not* to speak of it. It is necessary to keep *both* in mind at the same time, especially since war really has become almost unthinkable in the central arenas of economic globalization where transnational corporations and states compete and cooperate. Military might really has become less important here. At the same time, it is true that, because of the growing power of globalization, states are still based on an imaginary 'we' that excludes 'the others'. In the blind spots of global politics, where old territorial conflicts continue as virulently as ever, war and the threat of war serves to inflame hatred and enmity.

By contrast, the theory of meta-power asserts that the categories of state-centred power, domination and politics, taken as given in the neo-realism of the social sciences, are *zombie categories*. They are not capable of grasping the new situation – the new actors and strategies, the new quality of power struggles and their associated social and political upheavals, paradoxes and ambiguous prospects (within as well as between nations). After the nightmare of the twentieth century we have to expect the worst. But we also need to open our eyes and sharpen our conceptual tools to appreciate the ways in which the historical preconditions of nation-state domination are being eroded in a world infused with global business meta-power and values, and how the rules of global politics are being rewritten in conflict-laden interactions between states, global business interests and civil society movements; and that this is happening without democratic legitimation, by 'translegal' means and (something that is unprecedented and unthinkable within neoliberalism) in an unwarlike, 'pacifist' manner. Because of this, the category and theory of the state in the second modernity need to be reconceptualized accordingly.

3.2   The meta-power of global civil society

The autonomy of the nation-state is called into question not only by the meta-power of global business actors but also by the meta-power of global civil society. Its meta-power is based on establishing the validity of human rights in opposition to the nation-state-based apparent taken for grantedness according to which states can do whatever they please within their own sphere of domination. The politics of human rights also opens up an arsenal of strategies for silently revolutionizing the international system. Whereas in the global business frame of reference the foundations of state sovereignty (meaning states recognized by international law) are relativized and undermined by the power of mobile capital to say 'no' to investment, in this instance the normative, legal and political anticipation of a 'cosmopolitan' ('weltbürgerlich') condition calls into question the independence of the nation-state. By demanding observance of human rights, not only NGOs but also any group of states committed to cosmopolitan values are able to exert influence beyond their own borders on issues of authority and legitimation inside other states. In other words, there is a dramatic expansion in the sphere of influence available to cooperative cosmopolitan states. This comes about because the human rights regime transforms the arena of power of 'global domestic politics' (Weizsäcker) from one fragmented into nation-states into a boundless space in which 'foreign' states as well as NGOs can interfere in the 'domestic politics' of other countries and completely alter their institutional power structures. This strategy is particularly successful when domestic resistance groups oriented towards cosmopolitan ideals are encouraged and empowered through the human rights regime and corresponding regional conventions, or when human rights policies are linked to economic or military sanctions.

In this sense the language of human rights opens up a highly legitimate, authoritative discourse of power which, on the one hand, allows oppressed and endangered groups to legitimize their rights and, with the help of external, global public support, (possibly) to get them enforced in domestic struggles. On the other hand, it also gives governments and non-governmental organizations a permanent and fundamental right to intervene in both word and deed anywhere in the world.

The distinction between genuine and fake cosmopolitanism is crucial in this context as well. The possibility of fake cosmopolitanization – that is, for instrumentalizing the global enforcement of human rights in the interests of a national mission – clearly exists for the one remaining world power, namely the USA. Most governments in the European Union, on the other hand, operate a policy of human rights more with the aim of creating a generally binding legal framework for international relations that successively changes the parameters of national power politics towards a cosmopolitan regime grounded in 'global domestic politics and citizenship' (cf. Beck 2004: ch. 1).

Today, Western states with a cosmopolitan orientation hold all the trumps and have more than ample opportunity to make the most of the new resource of power contained in human rights. The issues of concern to global civil society provide Western states active on the global stage with the requisite ideological tools for launching global economic and military crusades. This new combination of humanitarian selflessness and imperial power logic is manifested particularly in the 'humanitarian interventions' that have enabled a highly ambiguous 'military humanism' to become established (along with the corresponding arming and reorienting of the national and transnational military forces entrusted with and equipped for this task).

The founding of the UN and the declaration of human rights, along with the threat of punishment for wars of aggression and crimes against humanity, emerged from the sense of shock elicited by the Nazi concentration camps and summed up in the historic cry 'Never again!'. What also emerged from this, in retrospect, was a normative global consciousness concerning the inviolability of the rights of each individual, as a response to the experience of the inconceivable brutality with which they had been violated. Thus, human rights politics, which began after the Second World War and deliberately made the rights of individuals (rather than just the protection of minorities) central, is a response to the out-and-out failure of nation-state-oriented international law in the catastrophic history of the twentieth century, when it shed its innocence and forfeited its legitimation. In the catastrophic aftermath of this failure there arose something that Hannah Arendt called the 'new thing', the 'being able to begin' of the political. 'If the meaning and purpose of politics is freedom, then this means that we do indeed have the right, in this space and in no other, to expect miracles. Not because we believe in miracles, but because people are capable, as long as they are able to act, of achieving all manner of improbable and unpredictable things, and constantly do so, whether they know it or not' (Arendt 1993: 35).

The new thing that comes into existence as a result can be characterized with good reason as a creeping revolution, because ultimately this is about a human rights regime gaining priority over the right of nations (*Völker*) to self-determination and thereby overthrowing the political world order. The so-called domestic affairs of a state are now everybody's affair. Not even the leader of the Soviet Union and the Warsaw Pact, Leonid Brezhnev, was able to 'restrict' the sovereignty of the communist bloc states and thereby open them up in principle to Soviet intervention, and yet this is precisely what is happening now on a global scale, with the anticipation of a human rights regime applicable to all the world's citizens. In cases when a state engages in state terrorism against its own citizens, such a regime inevitably triggers intervention and therefore, ultimately, preventive action in the case of potentially flagrant violations of world citizenship rights (*Weltbürgerrechte*). Governments can thus forfeit recognition of their sovereignty under international law in the context of cosmopolitan human rights. Given that a guilty conscience on human rights is often the flip side of a nation's self-confidence, states are aware that this situation is potentially always given, with respect both to themselves and to other states. But this ultimately means that everybody can – indeed must – always interfere in every situation. And yet *everybody cannot* interfere everywhere, only those with the requisite economic and military means to do so. As a result, the global power to define what constitutes and does not constitute a violation of human rights is essentially dependent on the economic and military strength of states.

The universality of individual human rights not only does away with the borders between states but also enables them to be joined together and combined as the strategies of power demand. As a result, the global politics of human rights sets up a permanent battlefield of political power between or within states, in which the rich 'good guys' interfere in the affairs of the poor 'bad guys'. In this way, the rules of domestic and foreign policy are suspended in the power sphere of human rights, and new 'both/and' rules – about foreign policy from within and of domestic policy from outside state borders – introduced instead. This can be observed today in the unresolved conflicts between East and West and between North and South, and in the constant wrangling over the status and definition of human rights in Asian and Islamic cultures. It is manifested not least in the different domestic political arenas – in Europe, for example, but also in the USA – where the fusion of human rights issues with global economic issues has become a permanent source of conflict. In particular, the human rights regime lends oppressed groups, classes, ethnic communities, minorities, and so on, all around the world a global public voice, supported by non-governmental organizations both within and outside the countries concerned.

The transition from a nation-state to a cosmopolitan world order is achieved not least through a change in priorities between international law and human rights, a change prompted by the need to prevent terrorist abuse of nation-state power. The principle that applied in the nation-state first modernity, *international law overrides human rights*, is replaced by the cosmopolitan principle of the second modernity – the consequences of which have not yet been thought through – *human rights override international law*. This means that, in cases of conflict, a person's world citizenship rights are upheld in opposition to nation-state sovereignty anchored in international law.

The revolutionary consequences of this move are now starting to become apparent. The distinctions that sustain the international order as we know it – between domestic and foreign policy, between war and peace – are collapsing as the human rights regime turns against international law, directing itself not towards peoples and states but towards individuals, and postulating a *legally binding world citizen society of individuals*. This, however, stands in competition and conflict (if not always or in every situation) to all the state citizen societies of sovereign nations. The long-term impacts of this are speeded up

- in situations where human rights in the national and international arena are enforced and upheld through appropriate instruments of observation and control (for example, by independent experts or non-governmental organizations) and where this process is guaranteed – if necessary against the opposition of individual states;
- in those instances in which human rights activists within and beyond a single state's borders become organized in international networks; domestic institutional power structures can be circumvented and transformed in this way, by networks of actors spun between local and foreign groups being mobilized and expanding their power base through their interconnectedness with media audiences inside and outside the country, with state institutions and with global business actors.

This is also achieved to the extent that the relevant power holders and publics have committed themselves, at least verbally, to 'modernity and democracy', and where a linkage is established between the enforcement of human rights and economic sanctions. The big success story that serves as an example of this is South Africa, where collective economic sanctions were imposed with the goal of ending apartheid. The United Nations took the initiative with this form of sanctions in 1962 and were joined between 1970 and 1990 by more than a dozen countries under the leadership of the USA. The important thing, however, was that nobody in the world defended apartheid and that resistance was practised in a large alliance consisting of states, non-governmental organizations and corporations.

Above all, however, it is the actual or threatened linkage of global human rights policy with military intervention – as occurred spectacularly in the 1999 Kosovo war under the military leadership of NATO – that has opened a new chapter in power politics, namely that of an interventionist human rights policy that will ultimately help the contradictions of 'military humanism' – contradictions that up to now have remained latent – to emerge.

The defence of human rights on foreign territory using exclusively civilian or, in borderline cases, military means currently occurs against the background of the 'under-institutionalization of cosmopolitan law' (Habermas 1998). NGOs in particular (in cooperation with open-minded states) have a crucial role to play in systematically observing and recording human rights violations within individual states, for purposes of imposing sanctions if needed. Amnesty International, for example, has not only systematized and improved the effectiveness of networks of observation focused on human rights violations throughout the world, including the Western states; it has simultaneously developed considerable skill in revealing domestic state terrorism, using the vivid testimony of individual biographies, and retrospectively highlighting the scandal of human rights violations using global media publicity. In this way it has created a global awareness of human rights and sharpened the global conscience. This cannot, however, disguise the fact that Amnesty International is also among those that constantly engage in humanitarian intervention in foreign states using non-military means.

There is a whole string of parallels that can be drawn between the human rights regime and the neo-liberal regime. Both work according to the model of the self-fulfilling prophesy, inasmuch as both are the midwives of a new order of power and legitimacy. Both attempt to make nation-states and national societies permeable – both to capital flows and cycles of production and consumption on the one hand, and for the enforcement of human rights on the other.

Clearly both regimes can be connected to one another, whether from the one side or the other. Thus, the proposal has already been put forward to make states' human rights violations a criterion for investment decisions, so that the human rights regime can be enforced using the global economy as a whip.

With the advent of the new Western power politics of ethical and economic globalization, sovereign rights in the nation-state modernity are undermined and are subordinated to 'global responsibility'. It is precisely *because* world-wide demands for the upholding of human rights are considered highly legitimate, and consequent interventions such as that in Kosovo seen as selfless, that the astonishing extent of overlap with the old-fashioned goals of imperialist global policy often goes unrecognized. What this means, however, is that human rights leave the door wide open to *fake* cosmopolitanism, to a hegemonic instrumentalization of human rights.

The path towards this new hybrid form consisting of humanitarian selflessness and the logic of imperial power is laid by developments that can be characterized as a 'circle of globalization' – economic, cultural and moral globalization working together to reinforce the decline of nation-state institutions, which for their part can lead to devastating human tragedies and wars, as was the case in the 1990s in Somalia, West Africa, Yugoslavia, Albania and parts of the former Soviet Union. Even if the weakening of the West's centralized power cannot be regarded as an outcome of the human rights regime, nonetheless it is becoming apparent that a hidden vacuum of state power and legitimation is being intensified in this way and may break out into the open. This includes the possibility that nation-state compromises between ethnic groups may lose their binding power and that conflicts which had been kept latent may eventually erupt into civil war. However, since all this takes place 'before the eyes of the world', that is, in the global context of perceptions of 'global responsibility', the looming potential for violence and chaos is accompanied by the growing possibility of 'humanitarian intervention'.

In the circle of globalization, then, the 'necessities' of the world market and the 'good intentions' of global civil society become linked to a chain of 'unwanted side-effects' and turn into a global civilian-military-humanitarian threat, along with all the dilemmas this raises on every front. The more successful the actions of the prophets of the global free market and the Davids of human rights (which includes the erosion of national and territorial state structures), the greater the threat (now motivated by cosmopolitanism) to ever larger sections of the world population from the West's 'humanitarian interventions'. The contradictions of this 'military humanism' also come openly to the fore, making the Kantian rationale of a *'peaceful*, even if not friendly, thoroughgoing community of all nations on the earth that can come into relations affecting each other' (Kant 1996: 121) lose credibility on account of a renaissance of the medieval doctrine of the 'just war'. In the global system of weak states, as propagated and created in the course of neo-liberal global policies, nothing more stands in the way of imperial misuse of the cosmopolitan mission.

This is taking place in a context of radical historical non-simultaneity, so that the linking of global ethics, economic strength and military might creates a sharp cultural dividing line that runs between the champions of the new cosmopolitan world order – that is, the states of the 'original' West – and the 'global others' who are unable to meet these standards. Those countries excluded from the cosmopolitan order, those of the so-called Second, Third and Fourth World, have inherited the political legacy of European nationalism; and many states are compensating for their unstable domestic situation by exercising authoritarian domination and a policy of ethnic exclusion. They are predestined to take the role of 'global underdogs' in the cosmopolitan age, measured and excluded by the standards of both the neoliberal regime and the human rights regime.

The contradictions of this interventionist politics of human rights are obvious: for one thing, in a world in which human rights are constantly and flagrantly being violated, intervention can only ever occur *selectively*. In view of the erosion of state authority, civil wars in which the rights of people are treated with contempt (to put it mildly) are an increasingly likely occurrence; at the same time, intervention becomes increasingly unlikely, while the selectiveness with which interventions are undertaken is bound to foster suspicions of instrumentalization for purposes of power consolidation, which abound in any case. On the other hand, the states with a 'clear human rights conscience' become tangled up in the contradictions experienced by those who sit in glass houses and throw stones. In looking out for others' human rights violations they overlook their own human rights violations. Disputes over the substantial definition of human rights are therefore an expression of anticipated disputes over the West's double standards regarding human rights.[4]

At the same time there is the beginning of a process – again involving a deep-rooted asymmetry between different parts of the world – that appears utterly unreal, paradoxical and indeed perverse to a consciousness fixated on the nation-state: *the reform of military affairs along the lines of civil society.* The tasks of the military are being completely reprogrammed and now essentially consist in the continuation of global civil society by military means (cf., for example, Bredow 2001). In order to confront the challenges of radical non-simultaneity, 'the armed forces of Western countries need to be fundamentally transformed. This transformation is so far-reaching and profound that what we are dealing with, in effect, is a completely new and slowly evolving category, the *New Armed Forces*' (ibid.).

These are effectively armed forces committed to *de*-escalation whose task is neither to defend their own country against foreign attack nor to conquer foreign states, but rather to re-establish and secure the democratic order of civil society on foreign territory. These 'civilian armed forces' are there to defend the free, democratic, cosmopolitan basic order on the territory of *other* states against conflicting parties, *both* of which are usually engaged in targeted and unscrupulous violation of human rights. Max Weber would characterize this in terms of 'ethically minded armies' that have to be equipped and trained to establish respect for human rights, much like a military referee, under conditions imposed by foreign cultures, states and legal systems.

These armed forces are no longer sworn to any national loyalty, but form multinational military units – in terms of both their organization and field of operations – that are committed to the code of human rights. As a consequence, the key military concept of 'victory' (or of 'defeat') loses its romantic, myth-creating aura. The aim is not to conquer and subdue foreign countries and states, but to put out the flames of ethnic civil wars. It is this military firefighter function that takes the place of the archaic logic of conquest.

This historically unprecedented transnational merging of civil society and the military finds expression in a number of vivid Orwellian forms of speech, in which the language of war speaks with the tongue of the angel of peace: 'peace mission', 'humanitarian intervention', 'peace support operations' and 'military operations other than war'.

Armed forces committed to de-escalation do not fight for victory against an enemy; instead, their role in the theatre of war is directed at containing the violence between warring parties. The main reason for their combat deployment is not to threaten their own country but to threaten the civilian population in another country and to threaten world peace. The primary objectives of deployment are to protect the population, monitor aid measures and begin to rebuild structures of order compatible with human dignity. (Bredow 2001)

This goal cannot be achieved by acting in isolation, only through military–civilian networks and collaborative efforts. It is not only the armed forces of other countries that are involved in this but also – and this, too, is a crucial feature of cross-border transnationality – humanitarian and other non-governmental organizations, representatives of the conflicting parties, and reporters from the national and international media. Accordingly, in terms of their composition, objectives and organizational structure, the armed forces effectively turn into miniature cosmopolitan social experiments.

This means, however, that the entire moral and political cosmos of the military becomes obsolete at a stroke. If the opposition between enemy and friend seemed as indispensable to national mythology as the cultural homogeneity of the soldiers, then 'military civilian workers' stand for just the opposite: for a transnational solidarity of human rights, for multinationality and targeted cooperation with non-governmental organizations and official bodies from civil society, with the purpose of fulfilling 'peace missions'.

In this sense the New Armed Forces, on account of their objectives and the manner of their deployment, become the forerunners of cosmopolitan armed forces, new hybrid entities of 'military humanism'; they become, so to speak, truly secularized 'salvation armies'.

3.3 Translegal domination

Global business actors act 'translegally', in other words, their actions are neither illegal nor illegitimate. Their power is maximized in the form of a 'revolutionary usurpation' (in Max Weber's terms) in the digital arena. Translegal domination denotes constantly having a more or less institutionalized opportunity – regardless of national boundaries between systems and functions – to influence the outcome of state decisions and reforms so that the priorities expressed in them are consonant with those required for exercising power in the global market. To adapt Max Weber's definition of domination, it is an opportunity to work towards the self-transformation of a community of states that has (in extreme and successful cases) internalized the neo-liberal world market regime as an internal compass for state politics; it is a transformation wrought not with the tools of command and obedience but, among other things, with a selective policy of refusal – of non-investment and non-intervention. This point is reached whenever politicians and states adapt their policies to conform to the world market and claim this constitutes a political obligation vis-à-vis public welfare.

The historian and philosopher David Hume lent early expression to his amazement at the ease with which the few succeed in imposing their will on the many in a lasting way – *even with their consent*. Max Weber accordingly based his theory of domination on the question of what kind of 'belief in legitimacy' leads those ruled to recognize the domination of the rulers on a permanent basis. Due to his specific interest in the forms of stable domination, he paid little attention to the in-between, hybrid forms of unstable domination.[5] 'Translegal domination' is exactly this type of unstable hybrid of domination, corresponding to a specific 'neither/nor' scenario: 'translegal' is neither illegal nor illegitimate; at the same time, though, 'translegal' is neither legal nor legitimate. However, this double negation does not add up to a positive definition because the 'authority of global business' has *no* global belief in legitimacy at its disposal to which it can appeal.

In this sense one could speak of 'translegal' domination as 'alegal' or 'alegitimate' domination, if what is meant by that is this in-between status – neither illegal nor legal, neither illegitimate nor legitimate. The meta-power of capital owes its existence to and is expanding by means of the new opportunities offered by information technology for shortening time horizons and abolishing distances – *without* formally contravening any laws and *without* the consent of parliaments and governments. It stems from what David Harvey (1989) calls the 'annihilation of space by time'. To put it in figurative terms: *states have roots while investors have wings*. It is this new asymmetry between rooted and winged forms of power that facilitates the unwarlike conquests of global business.

Thus, translegal domination does not mean a kind of domination that stands *above* the law, as was the case with kings and queens who ruled by the grace of God. What we have here instead is a particular combination of features:

1 Translegal means *transnational* meta-power, inasmuch as the latter reflects and systematically exploits the cooperative advantages and hidden niches of different national legal systems for purposes of expanding global business power.
2 Translegal means *law-making* meta-power. Corporations do not want the law of the jungle to apply, but international rules either are too weak or are non-existent, while national rules contradict one another. So corporations make their 'own law' – this applies as much to technical standards as it does to labour standards, contract law, international arbitration procedures, and so forth. It may still be correct (as laid down by German Basic Law) that 'All state authority rests with the people' (Article 20,

paragraph 2, section 1), but what is no longer correct is that all author-ity rests with the state. In particular, the power to make laws, the author-ity over authority – in other words, the right to decide who may decide about what in a binding way – no longer lies with the 'sole legitimate' power of the state. Instead, forms of *divided sovereignty* come into being, divided between states and global business actors (organizations). This means that, in the context of the private global economy, new organiza-tional forms of non-public power are being created, a power that stands above sovereign states without itself making any claims to state sover-eignty, yet still having a partial degree of law-making power.

3 Translegal power also means *quasi-state* authority over authority – with one crucial consequence: transnational companies, as 'quasi-states', have to make *quasi-political* decisions. Such authority is clearly revealed, for example, in genetic technology. The issue of whether and under what conditions experiments may be conducted using the genomes of animals or even of human beings is one of fundamental importance to humanity and is at times the subject of heated debate in the various national arenas. In actual fact, however, national governments and publics are more like observers when it comes to making these decisions. Corporate managers ultimately make their decisions and execute them immediately *without* the consent of governments or publics. If a nation-state institution attempts to restrict a corporation's options, the latter simply seeks to relocate its operations. Taken to its logical conclusion, then, the question is no longer whether something is allowed to happen, but rather merely *where* it will happen. In extreme cases, then, global business actors make genuinely political decisions without any democratic legitimation.

4 'Translegal' is the meta-power of *innovation*, that is, having systematic access to the institutional and cognitive conditions and opportunities for *producing new things*. This means, first of all, acquiring and maintaining power over the productive and innovative force of science. To the extent that global business corporations and organizations succeed in making use of this monopolistic social resource for creating technological inno-vations and 'truth', they do indeed hold quite a few trump cards in the poker game for global social power. They can create and destroy jobs, create new products and markets, circumvent or evade state regulations and controls, eliminate competitors, and much more besides.

5 The *limits* to translegal power arise from the fact that translegal domina-tion is *translegitimate* domination, since, *without* a framework of global state order and *without* sources of democratic legitimation, it *lacks* a global belief in legitimacy of its own. From where do global business actors draw legitimation for their decisions? What is the nature of their mandate? Essentially, global business actors take their justification from the criteria of economic rationality associated with *market success*. The 'mandate' of global business is based on the economic vote of the

shareholders, manifested in profits and losses made on the world's financial markets; and it is based, *mutatis mutandis*, on the encouragement and support of consumers who, through the act of buying, are always able to make use of their right to vote, to give vent to their loss of trust (in politics) in most effective fashion by changing over to the competition. Nonetheless, this *economic* legitimation presupposes the legitimate laws and legitimate authority of the nation-state and does not authorize global business meta-power *in opposition to* states. In particular, the meta-power game acquires its themes, its dynamic of conflict, its lines of development and its unforeseeable consequences from the fact that the boundary between the state and business – the authority and the right to decide who may make binding decisions about what – gets broken down, strategically negotiated, shifted and fixed anew. If we agree with Jean Bodin that 'sovereignty' is to be understood as having the authorization – self-justifying and non-derivative – to make collectively binding decisions and, in particular, to make laws, then global business actors and organizations practise a form of *non*-state, *supra*-state, economically determined *'quasi-sovereignty'* within the transnational, global arena of economic activity. This has to do with the legal vacuum of global action, a vacuum that arises, on the one hand, from the non-existence of a world state and, on the other, from the fact that state sovereignty over law-making is limited *nationally*.

This means that legislative authority is at once *privatized* and *transnationalized* in the de facto sovereignty of global business organizations. However, the transnational 'authority over authority' of global business is simultaneously always a national one.

Legal changes are the order of the day in advanced capitalist societies as much as in former socialist ones and in the countries of Africa, Asia and Latin America, which are reshaping their legal norms and institutions under the tutelage of the IMF and the World Bank. But the state no longer enjoys a monopoly over the production of law. A range of new actors (corporate law firms, arbitration bodies, international institutions, donor agencies and NGOs) are contributing to the diversity of forms of regulation, to the variety of settings of rule creation and to the proliferation of methods of interpretation and application of norms and standards. Non-state quasi-legislators are both the product as well as the engine behind the transnationalization of domination. While national legal fields are being increasingly transnationalized, transnational legal regimes are penetrating into national arenas. (Randeria 2001: 25)

Human rights, property rights, patent rights and environmental rights are the key issues in relation to which the boundaries between national and transnational contexts become blurred and disappear, to be redrawn in such a way that in both the national and transnational arenas negotiation occurs over transnational and national zones of influence, areas of responsibility and commitments (Goldstein et al. 2000; Zürn and Wolf 2000).

As a consequence of this, the organization of political domination, which in the first modernity was determined exclusively by the rules, principles and procedures of the nation-state, is transformed and pluralized in the second modernity from the inside. 'Governing', in the sense of actually solving problems, increasingly takes place via the private sector as well (Cutler et al. 1999; Grande 2000; Schlichte and Wilke 2000).

Consequently, transnational companies become private sector *quasi-states*, which on the one hand make collectively binding decisions, and on the other mutate into fictitious decision-makers and virtual organizations. The old companies used to be regulated via markets and hierarchies, their power and their decisions defined in economic terms and limited accordingly, making them exempt from legitimation. As quasi-states, however, companies also have to make political decisions, while at the same time relying to a large extent on negotiation and trust, which is why they are thoroughly dependent on legitimation.

Although not democratically organized or legitimated, anti-globalization initiatives seem to many people to be a kind of Robin Hood movement. When young people are asked, for example, which political actors they admire, movements such as Greenpeace and Amnesty International appear at the top of their list. This means that there is a *paradox between power and legitimacy*. Transnational corporations and business organizations have a great deal of power but little legitimacy. Social movements, on the other hand, have only little power but a high level of legitimacy. The increasing pace of global economic integration is accelerating the decline in legitimation affecting global business meta-power. This *'legitimation trap'* in which global business power is caught provides considerable potential for politicization. Chronic problems of legitimation make world markets *highly unstable*, since corporations themselves exist within relations of dependency. The more they 'emancipate' themselves from voters and state institutions, the more dependent they become upon consumers and their trust, on markets and competitors. Credibility thus becomes a crucial form of capital, as world markets presuppose the existence of trust – on the part of both the public and consumers. Once their trust has been frittered away, the whole thing can pose a threat to markets, to corporations, even to the US economy and therefore to the global economy as a whole. This is currently the situation facing large corporations that fiddle their balance sheets, the genetically modified food industry, mass meat production and large-scale agriculture (with their attendant food scares), nuclear energy, and so forth. The fragility of shareholder and consumer trust points to the fragility of global corporations' legitimacy. This is their Achilles heel, and this is what social movements have in their sights when they embark on their spectacular campaigns. Even the neo-liberal US government sees itself forced to counter this dramatic loss of trust in the business world with an anti-neo-liberal politics of conversion to (at least symbolic) regulations and controls.

From what source do advocatory movements such as Greenpeace draw their mandate for action? They, too, lend themselves authorization and lay claim to some degree of 'non-state sovereignty' by demanding that responsibility for the environment be assumed at a global level, particularly in the face of nation-state and global business egotism. But they have no electoral mandate to do so and violate within their own organization the very rules of democracy for which they are fighting worldwide. They draw their legitimacy from the celebratory mass media representations of their efforts to avert the self-generated threats emanating from technologized civilization (see this volume p. 253). They receive their mandate from their commitment to the key issues facing humanity: environmental destruction, global financial risks, human rights violations, civil rights, the struggle against increasing global poverty and flagrant violations of the unwritten rules of a 'global justice'. These 'global problems' do not constitute the 'domestic affairs' of nation-states or international corporations. This is why it is legitimate for these movements to become involved – even to the extent of deliberately contravening nation-state laws – and, with the aid of the mass media, to alert the global public around the world to the issues at hand and spur it into action.

The global public may have few ways of exercising influence in relation to states, but where corporate power is concerned it potentially has a great deal of influence, inasmuch as 'global public', in economic terms, equates with the political consumer becoming aware of his or her power. The sleeping giant, the consumer, awakes and transforms the act of purchasing a product into a vote on the global political role of corporations, thereby striking the latter with its own weapons – money and non-purchase.

Consequently, the mandate of social movements is always a *post hoc* mandate. Social movements act in anticipation of the defence of global values and responsibilities, an anticipatory move that may be confirmed in retrospect – for example, in an international consumer boycott – or else it may not. Their mandate is therefore that of a self-confirming or self-refuting prophesy. Here, too, the same rule applies: nothing is so successful as success, and nothing does as much to destroy credibility as failure.

However determinedly individual groups – particularly in the anti-globalization movement – may argue in favour of protectionism and against worldwide economic integration, their own activities do not stop at country borders either. The struggle against globalization has long since become a globalized struggle. It was only when they began to make use of global networking and global information technologies and mass media that social movements became a political opposition to be reckoned with in the dominion of global business. Corporations against movements – these are the two large blocs that face one another on the international stage of the new political world.

Among the instruments of power available to networks in this – in addition to demands for global responsibility – is the *truthfulness of information*. In a world in which lies are told as a matter of course, and with predictable regularity at that, anyone who dares to call a spade a spade poses a danger. States and corporations deal with the truth in a strategic way, meaning that they hush up those facts that are harmful to them and propagate those from which they hope to gain an advantage. They maintain a huge and expensive apparatus for this task. In contrast to this, the 'legitimatory power' of social movements is based on their constant credibility as 'witnesses at the scene', who help to bring the 'perpetrators' to justice using their reliable information. If all goes well, then global social movements are acting in experimental anticipation of a cosmopolitan morality and cosmopolitan reforms that will put ideas generally considered to be 'unrealistic' on to the global political agenda and test their relevance to reality, while also lending a voice to ordinary people and their civil rights.

3.4 The neo-liberal regime

During the era since the Cold War, neo-liberal globalization has become not only an influential force in world politics but also a crucial one in normative and political terms. The promise that all who obey the commands of the world market will be blessed with earthly riches is renewed time and time again at the altar of the all-powerful god of the market. In what is ultimately a revolutionary vision, the political and normative claims of neo-liberalism contain the promise of creating an opportunity for eliminating the global hierarchy of power and the division of labour, in the form of corporate realpolitik. The 'neo-liberal regime' not only encompasses political principles that optimize economic egotism, but is also based on the aim of implementing a new, worldwide politics of distributive justice. Thus, neo-liberalism has established itself as a quasi-global party that makes its presence felt within very different national parties and political arenas, while claiming to represent and defend global values rather than the interests of business. The real-life utopia it implies is one in which the domination of the neo-liberal regime makes it possible to release millions of people worldwide from the chains of poverty, by generating win–win situations rather than a winner-takes-all dynamic. But the persuasive power of the neo-liberal regime is tied to its success and dwindles away whenever failure threatens. With the emergence, or rather the perception, of worldwide crises and risks that lead to global conflict and upheaval, the opportunities for power available to cosmopolitan counter-movements grow.

How does the triumphal march of neo-liberalism relate to the national and cosmopolitan outlook? The neo-liberal steamroller generates national resistance and contradictions but it also – potentially – opens up the space for a cosmopolitan age, by means of a global policy of boundary removal. The legacy of neo-liberal contradictions does not have to be the renationalization of the world; it could also be a self-critical cosmopolitanism. How can we gauge the extent of the power of the neo-liberal regime, how can we tell where it ends and how it is called into question? What indicators point to the rise and which to the fall of neo-liberalism in world politics? The neo-liberal regime rules out options and modes of behaviour that *do not favour*, but rather impair and prevent, links to global structures (and markets, institutions). This is the reason why strategies of economic nationalism – the nationalization of key industries, legal measures that favour home-grown business, laws concerning 'permitted' levels of foreign capital shares, etc. – have actually become discredited. Even in those places where they are still practised, they have now become subject to justification. One might say that, whereas the national once had a taken-for-granted exclusiveness about it, this has been replaced by the dualism of protectionism and cosmopolitanism (*Weltoffenheit*). All attempts at minimizing or completely severing links to the global order (even on the part of such populous states as the Soviet Union and China) have swung in the opposite direction. The Chinese vision of a 'socialist market economy' was aimed above all at opening up China to global interconnections and institutions so that it could have a share in them. Not exclusion but inclusion in global flows (of capital, information and communication, knowledge, technology, tourism, but also of migration and criminality and so forth) has become the dominant policy worldwide. The model of the autarchic state is passé.

The neo-liberal regime decides on inclusion and exclusion in the global economy. Its power is based on the potential economic and moral exclusion of entire states and of their populations. And it is not only states that exclude other states. In the context of a neo-liberal regime, non-states exclude states and their populations simply by not doing something, namely, investing there.

The actual or threatened exclusion of states and national societies is related to a variety of things: success or failure on the world market, for example, or being praised or punished in front of the global public. In the first instance they are excluded from the circle of 'investment-friendly' countries, which robs them of their material basis for survival, and in the second from the group of recognized countries, which robs them of their dignity. The non-state power of global business actors does not have to be deliberate; it is not exercised – to put it in legal terms – with intent.

The scope and binding power of the neo-liberal regime can also be gauged by the fact that its norms are conceived as *global* norms and thus include nation-states as 'local executive bodies'. The IMF has created a system of surveillance in which the norms of 'good' budgeting are applied at national and local government levels. The neo-liberal regime provides for globally binding decisions against individual states' resistance, and a universally valid and applicable 'policy mix' is propagated accordingly. This means that political reforms should be oriented towards economic objectives – low inflation, a balanced budget, the removal of trade barriers and foreign currency controls, maximum mobility for capital, minimal regulation of the labour market and a lean, adaptable welfare state that urges its citizens to work. These are *the* reform objectives of the neo-liberal regime. Meanwhile, economic domination can remain 'unpolitical' because the task of conforming to the international economy – to the global financial markets in particular – has become the internal compass that guides the 'governing' politics of nations.

One litmus test for assessing the growing domination of neo-liberalism, then, consists in the extent to which the 'decision-making signals' sent out by global markets have become the standard of 'rationality' for political decisions and reforms. To the extent that this happens, the neo-liberal regime can be said to have merged with the common good.

Political science makes a distinction between *party* and *ideology*. Parties, as organizational units that shape informed political opinion, can face one another in opposing camps – as government and opposition, for example – whereas ideology (political aims and objectives) is currently becoming *increasingly* standardized across all party and national boundaries, as is maintained, for example, by the theory of the 'social democratic age' (Dahrendorf). The neo-liberal regime achieves its objectives as a global standard ideology in a similar way, transcending the boundaries of every party and every nation. Neo-liberalism rules not only in the boardrooms of global corporations and in global financial organizations such as the International Monetary Fund and the World Bank; it is also active and plays a dominant role *within* national parties, parliaments and governments. This is manifested not least in the fact that the contrasts between political parties worldwide on key issues of economic policy, the labour market, education and social welfare policy have all but melted away. In this sense, parties with extremely different agendas have been divested of their principles and objectives and, behind the façades that carry the same old names, have been more or less transformed into branch offices of a *single* political ideology, that of neo-liberalism. This happens in the following ways.

Firstly, the global economic aims and principles of neo-liberalism break through national specificities and borders from the inside and accelerate processes of reform aimed at opening up the nation to global interdependencies.

Secondly, the programme of economic globality is put into practice in national political arenas in opposition to national political priorities through inter-party competition.

And finally, neo-liberalism is a transnational ideology in the sense that the global concerns of the market are implemented in the interaction between national parties at both intranational and transnational levels. Thus, in countries such as Britain, the USA, Germany, France, Japan, South Korea, Argentina, Brazil, and so on, we see the phenomenon of estranged twins at work, represented by the ruling neo-liberal 'social democrats' on the one hand and the opposition neo-liberal 'conservatives' on the other. All of them are struggling together, in the various niches of global society, to establish the neo-liberal regime in the national and transnational arena.

The seductive power of neo-liberalism thus lies in a twofold impulse. On the one hand it rewards the promise of cosmopolitanism (*Weltoffenheit*) with wealth, or else it strengthens transnational institutions, actors and organizations by way of counteracting national self-interest, that is, it *establishes a transnational principle of order for the global age*. At the same time, politics is entering a negative phase: it is ultimately engaged in making itself redundant, in line with the motto 'global market modernization or bust'. This is why it is appropriate to speak of the *trap of the neo-liberal understanding of politics*.

What we are experiencing, then, is by no means the 'end of politics', but rather the beginning of global politics based on economics: the neo-liberal regime is being realized in the form of a global politics of reform (Sklair 2000). It is fighting for a vision of a world without frontiers – albeit not for labour, but for capital. These neo-liberal futures have been strongly criticized. One argument goes: there are good reasons for doubting that the neo-liberal regime is in a position to reproduce itself at all. The following are the principal factors that constitute the driving force behind this instability (Pieterse 2000).

- Financial instabilities that are provoked by the *economic* world risk society: this is evidenced by the run of financial crises in those regions that have opened themselves up to the global market.
- Unemployment, precarious forms of employment, automation and the new manifestations of 'unemployment growth': associated with this is the well-founded impression that states have been left with a much narrower range of options, reduced to the dilemma of either paying for increased poverty with higher unemployment (as in most European countries) or else accepting spectacular levels of poverty for somewhat less unemployment (as in the USA).
- Accordingly, inequality and poverty are growing within and between societies, leading in turn to a range of different social and political conflicts, upheavals and risks.
- The list of environmental disasters and technological risks threatening the world is growing ever longer: climate change is happening more quickly

and with greater severity than expected (as reported by the UN's working group on climate change). Floods and droughts threaten, along with wars and increasingly scarce water resources, etc.

- As corporations become more mobile, so corporate taxation declines; by the same token, territorially limited governments are having increasing difficulty in bringing their tax laws to bear in relation to transnational business actors.
- Consequently, the difficulties of financing public welfare, both nationally and globally, are also on the increase.
- Contradictions are emerging everywhere between freedom and capitalism, and democracy and the market (Beck and Willms 2003).

The trinity of deregulation, liberalization and privatization has no solutions to offer in the face of these self-refuting prophecies of a rosy neo-liberal future. This is the point at which a central contradiction rears its head: it is in the interests both of global business and of states and their political parties to have a minimum amount of standardization and regulation in the global political context. Without taxation there can be no infrastructure; without taxation there can be no decent further educational institutions or affordable health care. No taxation – no functioning public sphere. No public sphere – no legitimacy. No legitimacy – no security. And to close the circle: without forums and forms for dealing, both nationally and globally, with conflicts in a regulated way – that is, in a way that enjoys widespread recognition and is not based on violence – there will eventually be no global economy at all, in whatever form.

What a *cosmopolitan* regime can learn from the neo-liberal regime is that, in order to be successful, regulations need to be globally binding – nothing else is good enough. However, to be powerful enough to be accepted and implemented globally, rules have to be acceptable – on both sides of the North–South dividing line. Such a regime would have to contain an agenda for a global development perspective and in this way address the interests and specific situations of small and weak states on the periphery of the global economy.

3.5   The dialectic of global and local issues, or the crisis of legitimation in nation-state politics

There is a new dialectic of global and local issues that do not fit into the scheme of national politics. As these kinds of global problems increasingly impact on people's everyday lives and yet are dealt with either inadequately or not at all at the national level, the crisis of legitimation in nation-state politics deepens.

'Global transformations' (Held et al. 1999) in this area need to be understood in terms of revolutionary change, in the dual sense of a paradigm change in both science *and* politics – by which is implied that precisely this diagnosis is a highly controversial one. Moreover, globalization is often understood as global networking, that is, as a process that ultimately entails nothing other than establishing and multiplying the technological prerequisites for globality. Arguing against this approach, Martin Shaw suggests that the mechanisms of worldwide networking are by no means as new as some 'globalizers' think, and that, while they constitute the necessary conditions for global transformations, they are by no means sufficient on their own. Globality, Shaw asserts, is a conscious process, the key to which is the worldwide development of a common human awareness of the global, not in the sense of an abstract, moral or intellectual affair, but deeply rooted in social struggles and linked with social processes such as democratic change that are normally viewed in isolation. In this sense, he says, we can actually observe a diffuse, non-simultaneous and incomplete global revolution occurring, as well as several manifestations of an anti-globalist counter-revolution (Shaw 2000: 230).

The theory of meta-power can be rendered more precisely in this context. It does *not* assume that globality in itself creates the commonality of a global consciousness of globality. Instead, globality must be decoded as a meta-power conflict over the *definition* of globality. The strategies of capital, of the state and of advocatory movements not only open up a field of conflict in which the boundary constructions of nation-state politics become a project of negotiation; they also establish globality, by way of a self-fulfilling prophecy, as a frame of reference in the process.

Three consequences are associated with this. Firstly, globality *cannot be presumed* to be a global 'community of destiny'. Rather, secondly, globality (in line with the meta-power theory) needs to be decoded as a manufacturer of global conflicts and thus *as a factory of global reflexivity*. This means, thirdly, that the meta-power theory claims to determine neither the direction nor even the outcome of global change; still less does it imply the existence of a global historical subject of cosmopolitanization. Instead, it opens a window on many different, contradictory responses to global problems, both theoretically and empirically, and shifts them to centre stage. At the same time, however, the meta-power theory points to the auto-dynamic of global processes of negotiation that generate the minutiae of a politically effective, *normative context of expectation* regarding transnational governance. The main problems that concern people are *global* problems, not only in the sense that they have outgrown the national scheme of the political in terms of their origin and consequences, but also in the sense that they throw up *mundane* issues here and now, in this place, in this town – for example, issues around nutrition, construction or investment; and this new transnationality of issues that are both mundane and political grows in step with the triumphal march of neo-liberal politics. Over the past few years, industries that are subject to large amounts of regulation have been liberalized – telecommunications is a prime example of this; other examples are energy, food and finance. The worldwide competition unleashed by this trend has brought national standards authorities into conflict with one another. The free-flowing traffic of goods has made the problem into a global one. And this is only the beginning. Other sources of conflict are already starting to become apparent – global environmental, financial and labour market standards and so on – in other words, agreements need to be sought in areas of activity where regulation is even more important and more difficult on account of being highly sensitive politically.

This is where the flip side of neo-liberal politics reveals itself: the first wave of national deregulation forces a second wave of transnational re-regulation. Thus, those things that were devalued in the 1980s have now been accorded new value: the state and politics. What is needed is the exact opposite of neo-liberal deconstruction, namely, *strong* states, so that transnational market regulations can be pushed through both within and outside country borders. The differences within the North, as between the USA and the European Union, for example, concerning the wholesomeness and safety of food, already appear incapable of being bridged. But these sorts of difficulties become that much greater the wider the differences are between cultural backgrounds, levels of income and political systems in the countries involved. At the same time, since such agreements have to be negotiated, found or invented, globality becomes normative dynamite for conflict, not only in politics and business but also in people's everyday experience. This increases the impact of the mechanism named above: while global problems strike like lightning in people's experiential spaces and turn their priorities upside-down, they can only be dealt with inadequately or not at all at the national level.

The following questions therefore arise. Who is actually authorized and entitled to take decisions and to create institutions that are capable of managing international financial flows? What kind of consensus is necessary and who has to be involved in order appropriately to address global climate change? Can the struggle against AIDS (or the lack of one), where millions of lives are at stake, be decided in the private sphere through an institutionalized lack of accountability? What kind of political actor or political institution should ideally be put forward for such tasks, at what level and with what kind of mandate? How are the different authorizations to make decisions at global, transnational, national and local levels related to and yet separated from one other? Who, in other words, actually establishes norms and regulations and what these should look like? Who is legitimated to do so, over the heads of nation-states and in a way that is binding for the latter?

There is a growing realization that new, global institutions are required to tackle global environmental destruction, arms control, the financial order, migration flows, poverty and injustice, and the upholding of human rights. What needs to be taken into account with regard to each measure or each institution, however, is that these global problems also have a regional aspect to them, meaning a national and a local aspect. Who ought to monitor these actors? To whom are they responsible? To nation-states alone? To which parliaments? Which public? The United Nations? NGOs?

Let us take one example: the statement from the United Nations that climate change is occurring more quickly and with greater severity than had thus far been assumed. One initial reaction to this might be to reject this prognosis – after all, perhaps the Cassandra-like voice of the UN becomes louder the more public pressure is applied by its critics. Wasn't there a greenhouse effect back in the Middle Ages? But this escape route is cut off. 'What is stated in the UN report is unequivocal and was approved by more than one hundred states', says the president of the UN group for climate protection, Robert Watson. Floods and droughts (to mention only two consequences) pose an increasing risk and in turn trigger unexpected and unpredictable synergistic effects.

The scientifically grounded assertion that humanity's future is under threat is directed not only towards every government and every manager in the relevant industrial companies, but towards all the people around the world. *Everyone* is called to change their behaviour immediately and drastically. Global problems are *moral maxims with cosmopolitan intent* in scientific disguise. The language used to argue and debate the hole in the ozone layer, climate change, BSE and so forth may be a scientific one, but the message is clear: *we* have to act!

The devil, though, is in the 'we': who are 'we'? States? International organizations? Europe, the USA, the Third World? The automobile industry? Scientists? Consumers? The mass media? Is it all about legal issues? Transport issues? About expanding the motorway network? About the competitive strategies used by manufacturers of catalytic converters in the European markets? About issues in Asian agriculture? About potential wars? About the scarcity of drinking water in parts of Africa and Latin America? Are the Netherlands and Bangladesh going to be swallowed up by the sea? Or is it about the number of beds available in the Bavarian tourism sector? The problem with this problem is that it is a little bit about *all* of these things at the same time, which is why no one can say for sure what it really is. At least, not without provoking determined objections from neighbouring industries, neighbouring states, neighbouring disciplines or from the Third World.

A 'we' that is this open-ended is not only incapable of acting, it doesn't even exist. Global problems such as impending climate change raise this very dilemma. *Neither a global consensus nor appropriate global institutions exist.* This is what gives rise to a growing awareness of the urgent need to act – with *no way* of doing so.

In Europe alone, any form of politics that really seeks to get serious about transnational problems such as climate change, alternatives to nuclear energy and legal regulations for human genetics, as well as immigration and human rights and so forth, is faced with a range of complicated issues. All these issues are both domestically highly sensitive *and* domestically insoluble. They force politicians to take a quantum leap, namely to relinquish national autonomy in order to create cosmopolitan sovereignty for solving national problems. Resistance can be mobilized successfully against this at the national level; however, if this transnational opening out of national politics does not occur, people's trust in nation-state political capacity will be permanently undermined.

3.6 The nationality trap

In the global age, states fall into a 'nationality trap': if they cling to the postulate of nation-state sovereignty, then competition among states for investment increases and the state's ties to the nation become a bind when it comes to inventing and developing a transnational politics.

In summarizing the argument thus far, we find that there is a central paradox in the neo-liberal understanding of politics and the neo-liberal model of the state. On the one hand, the latter is oriented towards an ideal image of the *minimalist* state whose functions and autonomy are supposed to be tailored towards enforcing global business norms. A state that accepts and conforms to the rules of the world market needs to be readily replaceable and completely interchangeable; it must exist in a relation of competition with as many states of the same ilk as possible and it must have internalized the neo-liberal world market regime institutionally, as it were. On the other hand, though, market deregulation and the privatization of public services *cannot* be achieved by a weak state. What is called for, instead, is a *strong* state, as the legal systems that conform to the needs of global business have themselves to be sanctioned by states and established *in opposition to* resistance within society. A further task consists in modernizing the institutions of surveillance and suppression – reinforcing border controls, for example, and being prepared for terrorism, the weapon of the weak. Above all, the state must be able to make it absolutely clear that the mobility of capital in no way entails a comparable mobility for labour.

Thus, a further paradox is this: *globalization goes hand in hand with an emphasis on and reinforcement of borders* and an intensification of border controls. However, these new borders do not work like the old ones used to: they are more like Swiss cheese, with holes and uncertainties systematically built into them on account of the need to guarantee the flow of information, capital and people (tourists) all at the same time (see this volume p. 8). So the political power and autonomy of governments must on no account be curtailed. Instead, states must be placed in a position to bring their societies to a point where they accept the rules of transnational power. Indeed, states must even provide *post hoc* legitimation for decisions that have often come about in totally undemocratic ways and the outcomes of which take power away from national politics and give global business carte blanche. Thus, in order to achieve the goal of restructuring the world along neo-liberal lines, one would have simultaneously to minimize *and* maximize the power of states.

In win–win situations, where *both* parties – states and global business actors – *benefit* from the redistribution of power, this paradox is likely to remain hidden. In times of crisis, on the other hand, it is likely to become a source of conflict. Serious protectionist reactions – as a response to post-national terrorist threats or impending global economic recession – could not only radically destabilize relations between states and global financial organizations but may also endanger cooperation between the leading states in the global economy. And what happens if militant movements exploit anti-globalization sentiment and threaten the workers and facilities of particular global corporations caught in the crossfire with acts of violence? To whom would management then turn to plead for protection? Would they create their own armed 'corporate police force'? Or would they simply leave their investments in the lurch?

Why do states find it so hard to exploit these contradictions of neo-liberal politics for the purpose of revitalizing democratic politics? Business corporations that are mobile and operate in global networks are in a position to play off individual states against one another and thus to weaken them. It is that much easier for them to consolidate their 'translegal domination' the more the national point of view predominates in the thoughts and actions of people and governments. Thus, the existence of (methodological) national-ism in daily life, politics and academia reinforces and strengthens the transnational power of corporations. When national rivalry, egotism and competition are stirred up, the community of states becomes divided and is prevented from finding and consolidating the tremendous power of state cooperation and giving it institutional shape. This in turn enables global business actors to play isolated nation-states off against one another, according to the principle of 'divide and rule'. In this respect, *politicians' fixation on the national arena constitutes a critical aspect of self-obstruction.*

This cat-and-mouse game between global business and the nation-state can really only be resisted if states follow the lead of 'delocalized' compa-nies and extend their state activities beyond existing national borders. This can happen either in line with the old imperialist-military logic or in the form of inter-state cooperation (federation). These kinds of collaboration between states are based on the reciprocal insight that binding international treaties and regimes help prevent a situation in which states seek to outdo and/or undermine one another, which is damaging to all involved. Transnational strategies of cooperation therefore serve two goals at once: to increase competition between global business actors and to reduce competition between individual states.

To investigate the extent to which the strategies of states are capable of countering the power of capital's strategies, it is helpful to introduce a distinction between *potential* power and *actual* power. The actual power of states is paralysed by self-obstruction – that is, by neo-liberalism and nationalism. *Potential* state power, by contrast, arises from the sum of all the strategies available to states and governments when they break through this dual self-obstruction and thereby open up new transnational possibilities of power and control for themselves. As they succeed in developing ideas and embarking on paths towards the *despatialization* of the state and politics, so they are able to find political responses to the new global economic geography.

But what does the 'despatialization' of the state mean? When governments negotiate agreements that are binding under international law or when they come together – as in the European Union – to form new, cooperative transnational executive bodies, each government can be said to be acting in transnational space because the commitments entered into are binding for all those involved. What emerges from this process are transnational formations of states cooperating with one another, that is, spaces of 'cooperative sovereignty', which are capable of dealing with both global problems and global corporations by creating new sets of coordinates for action (Zürn et al. 2000). However, this strategy comes at a price.

If states want to appropriate new policy and sovereignty options for the purpose of governing, that is, if they want to extend the scope of their political sovereignty and control, then the price they have to pay is active 'self-denationalization', a reduction in national autonomy. Thus, under the conditions of economic globalization, states fall into a *nationality trap*: if they cling to the potential for sovereignty offered by nation-state politics, then competition for investment among states increases *along with* the danger of the global market being dominated by monopolies, which in turn disempowers state actors. If, on the other hand, they are able to reduce competition among themselves by forming political alliances based on mutual commitment, in order to strengthen their position in relation to global business, they need to relativize their national autonomy. The state's nation-based conditioning and parochialism become an *obstacle* to inventing and developing forms of politics and statehood at the transnational level in the age of economic globalization.

This paradox expresses a key experience of the cosmopolitan constellation: those elements that were joined together in the national paradigm – the independence of the state, national self-determination, and the execution of key tasks by the political establishment (welfare, law, security) – become independent of one another and yet at the same time linked in a new way.

Governments have to relinquish national independence and enter into cooperative agreements that entail tying one another's hands in order for key national tasks to be dealt with more efficiently and in order to discover new avenues for action, not only internationally, but also in relation to the opposition and the public *within* the national arena.

3.7   The transnational surveillance and citadel state

The terrorist attacks of 11 September 2001 on the World Trade Center in Manhattan and the Pentagon in Washington, along with the reactions to these attacks, provide an instructive example of the form that resistance to the transnationalization of key national institutions may take. However, they point not to a cosmopolitan opening but rather to the transnational construction and consolidation of citadel states. The crucial point to realize is this: the discovery that state power can be increased through transnational cooperation is a politically ambiguous one. It can be used either to construct transnational surveillance and fortress states or to build cosmopolitan states. In both cases, however, a dismantling of national autonomy and an increase in national sovereignty are by no means mutually exclusive – they may even reinforce one other and speed up the process. The logic of the zero-sum game, which applies equally to empires, superpowers, colonialism, economic and cultural imperialism, independent nation-states and military blocs, has lost its explanatory power. In the cosmopolitan perspective, the creation of political sovereignty for dealing with transnational problems needs to be conceived of and organized as a cooperative extension of national policy options by means of the plus-sum game of post-national 'European' sovereignty, for example.

September 11th symbolizes an unimaginable event, unimaginable even long after it happened because, once again, words fail us. What was it? A 'crime'? The outbreak of a 'war'? A 'battle'? It was, at any rate, the most dangerous attack on the United States in its entire history. Out of the blue. Without any declaration of war. Not the hostile act of another state. No missile defence system could have prevented this attack. Even the term 'terrorism' is, strictly speaking, wrong – after all, the objective was not national independence for some group or other. The perpetrators were not fighting for a better, more just world. They simply wanted to wipe the symbols of Western power off the map. It is equally wrong to conjure up an image of the terrorists as murderous madmen, because people who, armed with pocket knives, turn four passenger airplanes into suicide missiles in such a carefully planned way are not mad. Neither are they 'cowardly murderers', as US President Bush says – they are just the opposite. They have the barbaric courage of men who turn themselves, their own lives, into a highly accurate weapon of mass destruction. All this is neither war nor peace, neither crime nor terror, neither murder nor revolution. It is a transnational network of what might be called 'violence NGOs'. These organize and carry out non-state (private) military acts of opposition against the superpower USA. Their biggest weapon is that they act uninhibited by any moral qualms. Neither their own lives nor the lives of others count. In this sense, what we are dealing with is absolute nihilism (measured by Western values); or, to be more precise, a combination of nihilism and religious fanaticism that eludes Western understandings. What the Western observer is utterly incapable of comprehending is the way in which fanatic anti-modernism and anti-globalism are directly merged here with modern global thinking and acting.

Up until now, the military gaze has been directed at its own kind, that is, at other nation-state military organizations, and has focused on repulsing them; now, states everywhere are faced with the challenge of a transnational threat from substate perpetrators and networks. We have already seen the *death of distance* in the cultural sphere – now we are experiencing it in the military sphere; indeed, we are witnessing the end of the state's monopoly on violence in a highly technologized world where anything can ultimately become a missile in the hands of determined fanatics. Terrorists have perfected the art of instrumentalizing the vulnerability of the Western risk society.

The concept of luck has lost its innocence in the process: we have all become unwilling participants in an ever-present lottery of (bad) luck, in which 'being lucky' means having escaped this time around. Anyone can be just as much a neighbour as a murderer. There is no definitive sign (a uniform, a passport, education, language, religion) that distinguishes the one from the other.

The experiential world of modernity is full of all kinds of global threats, and in this respect it is used to them to a certain extent. The way in which threats are presented to us in the world risk society compels us to become indifferent and immune towards them. Thus, we learn to live with the eco-logical dangers that humanity brings upon itself just as we do with global, economic threats – as long, that is, as they have no tangible impact on us. However, these dimensions of the world risk society – ecological and eco-nomic risks – need to be clearly distinguished from the new, perceived threats of terrorism. Whereas the former ills can be seen as unintended side-effects of intentional action, the new terrorist activities represent a *deliberate* insti-gation of catastrophe. The perpetrators who transform civilian objects into weapons of mass destruction wear no uniforms and are invisible. The days when airplanes served merely to ferry passengers to their destinations are gone once and for all. The image of the twin towers of Manhattan bursting into a fireball created by civilian airliners has led the fatal ambiguity of every object to enter the collective consciousness. The horror of these images is expressed in the absolute defencelessness with which an invincible nuclear power, the USA, was laid low in cold blood. The lesson sent out to rebel-lious youth on the streets of Islamic countries is this: a small group with simple means, determined to go to any lengths, has demonstrated the profound vulnerability of the great, invulnerable, all-powerful, satanic USA. Thus, the principle of accident and coincidence, which up until now has shaped our understanding of risk, has been replaced by the principle of violent intentions.

At the same time, the perception of a global terrorist threat has meant that the principle of active trust has been replaced by that of active mistrust, although the rule that applies here is that perceptions of risk pave the way for new opportunities for power. Despite this, President Bush has declined to use this historic *moment of truth* to take a bold step towards a system of cosmopolitan states. Instead, using the political power inherent in the perceived terrorist threat, he has begun to build transnational surveillance states in which security and the military play a large role while freedom and democracy count for very little. A prime example of this is the way US bureaucracy deals with terrorists, as reported by Rajiv Chandrasekaran in the *International Herald Tribune* of 11 March 2002: persons suspected of transnational terrorism and who have been identified and arrested in a foreign country by US secret services and military personnel are transported, under US control, to third countries where they can be subjected to certain interrogation practices – including torture and threats to their families – without any of the democratic controls that apply in the USA. 'Since September 11th these sorts of movements have been used on a permanent basis', says one US diplomat. 'It allows us to get information from terrorists in a way we can't do on US soil.' As this admittedly extreme example shows, states can use transnational cooperation to employ certain practices against suspected terrorists which, in the context of democratic states, are considered illegal and are accordingly subject to criminal investigation.

Even if local secret service agents have been at work, diplomats say, it is better to deal with the suspects in secret because this avoids long drawn-out judicial conflicts and minimizes publicity that might forewarn other suspects. Interrogating or passing sentence on people suspected of terrorism in a third country, particularly in Muslim nations such as Egypt or Jordan, also makes it easier to circumvent political controls and concerns in the home country, diplomats say. If a suspect were to be taken to the United States, there would be bound to be objections from government departments, afraid of giving any publicity to such an act because it may trigger certain counter-responses by fundamentalist Islamic groups.

As this example makes clear, it is thoroughly misleading to assume that state sovereignty and globalization are necessarily irreconcilable with one another. What is certainly true, however, is that states that want to open up and appropriate new options for acting in the global arena are dependent on cooperation with other states. A loss of national autonomy can *increase* state capacity and influence. It is only in the national outlook that economic, ecological and military globalization coincide with political paralysis. In the interchange between national and cosmopolitan perspective, systems of negotiation certainly can, in the context of global norms and global consensus, contribute to state capacity (at national level) (Mlinar 1997).

In order for thought and action to break free from the nationality trap, it is necessary to introduce an essential distinction between *sovereignty* and *autonomy*. (Methodological) nationalism is based on the equation of sovereignty with autonomy. In this view, economic dependency, cultural diversification, and military, legal and technological cooperation between states automatically lead to a loss of autonomy and therefore to a loss of sovereignty. However, if sovereignty is measured in terms of the political power to shape events, if the main criterion is the extent to which a state is successful in increasing the prosperity of its population and making headway with pressing problems such as unemployment, the fight against crime, environmental protection and social and military security, then greater integration and cooperation – that is, loss of autonomy – will result in a *gain* in sovereignty in practical terms. Governments' capacity to influence events will increase as prosperity increases and as they acquire greater technological and global economic power, all of which is facilitated by inter-state agreements. In other words, sovereignty that is shared and combined does not spell reduced sovereignty – on the contrary, it increases individual states' sovereignty.

Pooling sovereignty pays off in many different ways, including an increase in security and stability, a reduction in fear and conflict, lower military costs and greater economic and technical cooperation. It is therefore in the 'national interest' to denationalize and to pool sovereignty for the purpose of solving national problems.

The crucial insight as far as the cosmopolitan regime is concerned is this: *a formal loss of autonomy and a gain in practical forms of sovereignty can mutually reinforce one another*. Globalization implies two things: an increase in actors' sovereignty when, for example, they acquire the capacity to act over greater distances and thereby gain access to new options, and, the flip side of this development, the loss of autonomy of entire countries. The practical sovereignty of (collective and individual) actors expands as their autonomy, in formal terms, declines. In other words, during the course of political globalization, a transformation takes place from autonomy based on national exclusion to sovereignty based on transnational inclusion. What is crucial in this is not the fact *that* a network of inter-state relations is created and woven ever more densely, but rather *how* this is seen, judged and organized. In the national outlook, cooperation between states and state networks figure as a burdensome evil, a zero-sum game between the national and international level. Questions such as the following abound: how far are we relinquishing competencies? What are they allowed to do? What are we allowed to do? The more they do, the less we can do. In the cosmopolitan perspective, by contrast, interconnections figure as a plus-sum game: the more they can do, the more we can do.

The new politics starts by breaking through the 'national sound barrier'. Indeed, in view of the stark, day-to-day relevance of global problems, politics in the national space can *only* be reinvigorated by shedding national parochialisms. Transnational states are *better* nation-states. This is because they gain access to the plus-sum game played in transnational spaces and contexts, the better to solve both national and transnational problems. This does not necessarily have to lead to an expansion of Orwellian citadel states; it can also entail working with a 'cosmopolitan nationality and statehood' in which national traditions are at once broken open, protected and extended by cosmopolitan means.

3.8   The cosmopolitan state

One political response to globalization is the 'cosmopolitan state'. This is grounded in the principle of the state's neutrality towards nationality and allows national identities to exist side by side through the principle of constitutional tolerance.

The argument thus far has led us to the following question: how can the concept of the state and state theory itself be broadened to deal with the internal, cosmopolitan globalization of national frameworks of action and the challenges posed by the transnationalization of life, work and politics? We can pose the same question in a different way: who will prevent the next holocaust from occurring? My experimental answer is this: possibly the *cosmopolitan state*, one based on the principle of *the state's neutrality towards nationality*. Just as the Westphalian Peace put an end to the German religion-based civil wars of the sixteenth century by separating religion and the state, a response to the nation-based world (civil) wars of the twentieth century – so the theory goes – could be to separate the state from the nation. Just as the areligious state enables different religions to be practised at all, so the cosmopolitan state ought to guarantee the co-existence of national identities via the *principle of constitutional tolerance*. Just as the scope and context for political action were redefined at the beginning of the modern era by forcing Christian theology into a secondary role, so today national theologies and teleologies need to be tamed to the same end. And just as this was utterly out of the question for the theological outlook in the middle of the sixteenth century – indeed, it effectively spelt the end of the world – so today such a thing is just as unthinkable for the 'theologians of the national', signalling as it does a break with the basic premise of politics, namely the friend-or-foe system. And yet if we take our cue from the ideas bequeathed to us by Jean Bodin and Johann Althusius, who demarcated state sovereignty from the encroachments of religion and opened it up to history and politics, it becomes possible to reground this *cosmopolitan sovereignty* theoretically and develop it politically, in opposition to the historically discredited premise of national homogeneity, so that it enables real diversity to flourish.[6]

But what does the ancient and suddenly revitalized adjective '*cosmopolitan*' mean when placed in relation to the weighty noun '*state*' to make the 'cosmopolitan state'? For one thing, it marks itself off from *constitutionalism* and establishes the fact that a purely constitutional transnational order, that is, one based on general or constitutional law, will remain internally unstable as long as it is not supported by a corresponding consciousness in the population, by a *transnational identity, culture and statehood*. What is cosmopolitan about the cosmopolitan state, then, is that the creation of a transnational order depends on a genuinely cosmopolitan community whose influence profoundly shapes the politics of its member states. For this to occur, though, it is necessary to overcome the notion of a *single*, homogeneous, territorially bounded home nation fenced off from those who are culturally different, and to replace it with the notion of a *dual homeland*. Both elements are possible and necessary: cosmopolitan state entities are reliant on nationally rooted cosmopolitanisms.

The adjective *national* insists on self-determination. The cosmopolitan question in response, however, is: self-determination – *against whom*? How are the victims of (national) self-determination integrated into the same? In what terms are the impacts of self-determination on those who are culturally different spoken about within a 'national' community? How can the 'barbaric freedom' of sovereign communities (Kant) be transformed into a cosmopolitan freedom in which the voice of the other is present in the experiential and cultural spaces of the national self?

In an era of cultural globalization and ethnic-national plurality, this can only become possible through a post-national, plural-national state that is neutral towards and tolerant of nationality, one that acquires its legitimacy from the traditions of nationalities that have been opened up and reformed in line with cosmopolitan values. It can only be achieved by a cosmopolitan sovereignty which

- takes account of rapidly accelerating global interdependency;
- explores and develops the cooperative sovereignty of states for purposes of solving global-national problems; and
- establishes peace amid the diversity and rivalry between ethnic groups and nations while also protecting this diversity.

Cosmopolitan, then, means acknowledging both equality and difference at the same time and feeling committed to the planet as a whole. The global problems faced by those who are culturally different must be present, they must be heard, they must have a voice – culturally as well as politically – in the political community.

To nationally trained ears, this sounds like a completely unrealistic utopia, and yet in many of its basic elements it is already a reality. The path towards a cosmopolitan state is followed every time a country puts democracy and human rights above autocracy and nationalism; where efforts are made to incorporate firmly within the decision-making process itself the impacts of decisions on those who are culturally different; where attempts are made to harmonize and make a new connection between the rights of minorities and majorities, between universalistic and particularistic rights. The process by which international law has been relativized in relation to the new prominence of human rights (with all the maddening developments and confusions this entails) also points in this direction.

In this context Europe can really only be thought of – albeit counterfactually! – as a new variety of transnational, cosmopolitan state entity that draws its political strength from the act of affirming and taming European national diversity, with all its endearing parochialisms. The 'Brussels Convention' must dare to draft a cosmopolitan constitution so that – as Benjamin Franklin recommended back in 1787 – American success can be repeated in completely different historical circumstances. 'I have participated for four months in the convention that has worked out the constitution. If it is successful, I wouldn't know why you in Europe shouldn't put into practice the plan of good (French) King Henry IV by also forming a Federal Union and a great republic of all your different states and kingdoms, and this by means of a similar convention; for we too have had to reconcile many interests.' In March 2002 – 215 years later – a European convention in Brussels set to work. As different as the situation of the European Union of the current time is compared with that of the United States in 1787, the fundamental issue, then as now, is how to organize a polity that is made up of several states and combines domestic and foreign political capacity with the greatest possible degree of subsidiarity. Having said this, Europe today can and must go a crucial step further. It needs to redefine and redraw the boundary between particularism and universalism, between the nation and cosmopolitanism, other than the way this was done in the nation-state model of the first modernity. The notion that a particularistic state can simply be treated as a universal one, as a natural foundation on which all the contradictions of human existence can in principle be resolved, has been refuted historically. Neither is the optimistic notion that human beings eventually become humane – or even world citizens – as they become members of particular nation-states any longer tenable. It was Immanuel Kant who gave expression to the hope that, even though we remain tied to particularisms, we might become capable of acquiring and safeguarding universalism in particularism, that is, of acting on the basis of universal laws. However, this is the hope that needs to be rethought, after the violence and barbarity of the twentieth century, and corrected in such a way that priority is given to an identity-creating, cosmopolitan world citizenship over against national particularism.

The objections to such a cosmopolitan draft constitution for Europe that are raised today are quite similar to those with which the American convention had to struggle in Philadelphia in the year 1778. At that time, the issue that was the subject of heated debate up until the very last was whether the loose union of thirteen American states needed a powerful central legislature, executive and judiciary. Even the subsequent ratification of the draft constitution was achieved only by a narrow margin. Those who wanted more centralized authority were accused of being 'oblivious to the wishes of the people'. The South distrusted the North, the small states distrusted the big ones. Everyone was busy defending their own sovereignty. But ultimately all the parties were winners by dint of realizing that federalism brought about an *increase* in sovereignty, an insight that may – or perhaps even will – eventually put a cosmopolitan Europe on the road to success. It is the increase in practical sovereignty and in political capacity in the global age that more than makes up for the loss of formal autonomy.

Imagine Europe as a cosmopolitan confederation of states which work together to curb the excesses of economic globalization and which demonstrate respect for difference – especially the difference of their fellow European nations – rather than denying it or bureaucratically negating it: this could be, or become, a thoroughly realistic utopia.

The theory and concept of the cosmopolitan state are distinct from three positions: the dangerous illusion of a nation-state that fends for itself, the neo-liberal idea of a minimal, deregulated business-led state, and the unreal temptations of a unified world state.

The concept of the cosmopolitan state represents an appropriate response to the twentieth-century history of right-wing and left-wing regimes of terror, as well as to the endless history of colonial and imperial violence. Bodin conceived of state sovereignty as an authority that creates order amid the tumult of a post-religious world. He could not know what we know today, namely that the antidote to the anarchy he so feared – state sovereignty – has infinitely increased and perfected the potential for horror, hatred and anti-human violence.[7]

One concrete example of the concept of the cosmopolitan state in action is the *struggle for a political Europe*, one that is more than just a conglomeration of nation-states that jump at each other's throats at regular intervals. It is a matter of overcoming ethnic nationalism and the nation-state, not by condemning them, but rather by protecting them within a constitutional scheme that affirms different cultures and facilitates peaceful co-existence.

In order to achieve this, the European continental ethos of democracy, the rule of law and political freedom needs to be renewed and cultivated for the transnational era (Held et al.). Metaphorically speaking, Europe must absorb the 'American dream' that says: you can be whoever you want to be. You are not determined by your origin, class, skin colour, nation, religion or gender!

A cosmopolitan Europe of national differences – what does that mean, say, in relation to Britain? In my view, the islanders' Euro-scepticism does not warrant critique on account of their desire to hold fast to their own national civilization, but rather because of their inability to understand that a cosmopolitan Europe, far from dismantling it, actually safeguards it. A Europe without the British version of civilization would not be Europe. The most important historical event of the twentieth century, the overthrow of the National Socialist regime of horror, would have been unthinkable without British determination to defend European values in Europe against a German people incited by fascist forces. This was a product of British history, an example of *British cosmopolitanism*, which needs to be preserved as the founding act of a new Europe rather than overcome. In similar fashion, now is the time to discover a cosmopolitan France, a cosmopolitan Germany, a cosmopolitan Italy, Poland, Spain, Greece, and so on, and to encourage them to be partners in a cosmopolitan Europe.

3.9   The regionalization of cosmopolitan states

The architecture of a cosmopolitan union of states might also point the way out of a politics of false alternatives in other regions of the world, especially in regions where chronic ethnic-national conflicts rage.

The key historical example of state cosmopolitanization is the European Union's struggle for a political structure capable of overcoming the same old alternative posed by the national outlook – federalists versus intergovernmentalists. But is the idea of the cosmopolitan state not applicable to other regions of the world as well? This possibility becomes clear when we compare the political architecture of the transnational cooperation state with that of national federalism. Both demand a highly differentiated yet balanced power structure in which *functional spheres of sovereignty*, such as law and order and education, as well as cultural autonomy and local government authority, are organized in a decentralized way – within nation-states in the case of federalism, and between different states or quasi-state organizations in the case of transnationality. Likewise, it is also possible to conceive of in-between, hybrid forms of a transnational or cosmopolitan architecture of state confederation, which, in both small and large steps, would successively do away with the apparently solid unity of nation and state by means of the plus-sum game of transnationalization, without generating a power vacuum in the process.

In many contexts, there have been only two alternatives until now: *either* national – and therefore state – self-determination *or* subordination to national – and therefore majority-dominated – apparatuses of state institutional power. In these instances, a new option has now emerged, that of *cosmopolitan state federalism*. In zones and regions of the world, for example, where there is chronic ethnic-national conflict – such as the endlessly complicated and intractable dispute between the Israelis and the Palestinians – or again, in the face of impending annexation – as in the case of Hong Kong or Taiwan by China – such an option makes it possible to pursue a 'third way' that is neither exclusive nation statehood nor annexation.

Initially, of course, this is *a purely intellectual possibility* and one that seems utterly unrealistic given the very real conditions of violence, expulsion, terrorism, war, hatred and exclusive territorial claims that exist. Nonetheless, the idea of cosmopolitan co-existence between states in the global age alone may be capable of unblocking people's minds and opening up new paths for action and negotiation.

Perhaps the idea of the cosmopolitanization of nation-states can generate a new strategy for finding peaceful solutions to chronic conflicts over nationality and imperial dependencies, since two things can be achieved by it at the same time. Firstly, the loss of nation-state autonomy can be compensated by extending the pooled sovereignty of participating governments and countries; this in turn makes it possible, secondly, to create bridges of prosperity and legal frameworks that foster the co-existence of mutually exclusive cultural claims, certainties and traditions. This new cosmopolitan extension of state authority, conceived as a response to globalization, creates and reinforces economic and legal interdependencies and to this extent is able to operate as a strategy of prevention. Cosmopolitanization is an antidote to fundamentalism (whether it be ethnic, religious or nationalistic), which, as is well known, flourishes in conditions of poverty and underdevelopment and territorial exclusivity. What is more, inter-state cooperation makes it possible to clamp down on local political elites' attempts and temptations to instrumentalize these conflicts for the purpose of accumulating power.

3.10 The asymmetry of power between financial risks and risks associated with technologized civilization

Is the idea of a cosmopolitan state purely a thought experiment or does it actually have real historical significance? If it is not merely a voluntaristic postulate, which political forces and movements are working towards such a state and which against it? This question can be answered using the theorem of the asymmetry of world political power *between global financial risks and risks associated with technologized civilization. Financial risks cause individual property and individual property rights to be devalued and in this respect they can be individualized and nationalized; they provide opportunities for movements aimed at re-ethnicization and renationalization to acquire power and therefore represent a boost to the opponents of cosmopolitanization. By contrast, risks associated with technologized civilization violate and thereby intensify a global consciousness of norms, create a public sphere and in this respect render irrelevant the national set of premises governing thought and action, offering cosmopolitan alliances – between non-governmental organizations, states and corporations – new practical options and new opportunities to acquire power.*

As long as financial risks do not exceed a certain, indeterminate point at which they become politically explosive, rather like a 'global economic Chernobyl', it is clear that they foster renationalization movements – this can be seen not least in the fact that nation-states disaggregate global social inequalities in such a way that they appear not as global but as national phenomena.

The opposite applies to global risks associated with technologized civilization: the world risk society is a latent revolutionary society in which the limitations of the national outlook are dissolved in actual or potential catastrophes.

A paradoxical connection exists between globalization and the individualization of social inequalities: as a result of financial crises in the global economy and their social and political after-effects, both the exclusion of individuals and the individualization of exclusion become intensified. To the extent that the boundaries to national societies and inequalities are falling away, methodological nationalism paints a *false image of reality*: the origins of global financial crises remain beyond the horizon, while there is a doubling of the nation-state individualization of global inequalities. What then occurs is a paradoxical series of self-concealing errors: domestic inequalities which, as Saskia Sassen shows, undermine the boundaries between centre and periphery, between North and South, and which lead to the 'Brazilianization' of the USA and Europe (to take one example), are attributed to the nation-state context, whereas external inequalities that actually or potentially undermine nation-state boundaries do not even enter the spotlight of methodological nationalism.

The critical question, without a doubt, is who are economic globalization's particularized *losers* at national level – the answer to this will enable us to assess the actual power relations within and between states with regard to the implementation of a cosmopolitan regime. Two initial hypotheses suggested by the theoretical framework described here may help to answer this question.[8]

Firstly, the situation in which globalization's national losers find themselves can be linked – in direct contrast to *mobile* capital, which appropriates transnational space – to the *immobility* of capital and labour, as well as to (political) activities, ways of life and life worlds in general; in other words, it is linked to territorial ties (however these may be grounded).

Secondly, this constellation of territorial immobility in certain professions and production sectors (as well as that of forms of political domination and ways of life) intersects with the increasing degree to which the *boundaries* of capital, labour, politics and culture *fall away*. It is in this crossover zone between immobility and the shedding of boundaries that the reservoir of globalization's losers comes into being, one that offers political movements and parties committed to ethnic-national isolation the opportunity to garner votes and power.

National boundaries *provide protection* against competition. The removal of boundaries (as in the liberalization of markets, and so forth) *intensifies* competition, albeit a particular kind of competition, namely that between people who are equals in terms of their profession and yet strangers in terms of national belonging. Nation-state boundaries are of crucial importance to individual members of a profession (or office-holders): they reduce and channel competition *within* the system of professional qualification. Metalworkers are not in competition with financial advisers but with all other metalworkers – and much more so with the latter because they are in a narrow field of competition. The way professions are constructed and 'tailored', then, defines spheres where competition exists and spheres where no competition exists. In this sense, national borders are similar to professional boundaries. German metalworkers are not in competition with Turkish, French, Polish or Russian metalworkers, they are in competition only with all the other German metalworkers. However, once boundaries are removed, competitive pressure is generated *within* specific labour markets in relation to people from other nations. The patterns of inequality that arise from this display – hypothetically – the following characteristics:

- They are defined by sector, meaning that they affect certain production and service sectors more than others.
- This pattern of distribution by sector means that in the 'losing sectors' labour and capital are affected in equal measure: the situations in which globalization's losers find themselves *cut across* the old oppositions between labour and capital, splitting existing social structures down the middle along the fault lines of territorial immobility and global competitive pressure.
- Also included among globalization's losers are those sections of the *political and bureaucratic elite*, the source of whose livelihood – national bureaucracies, organizations and professional positions – is placed on a precarious footing by supranational organizations (Europe, WTO, IMF, UN, etc.) and by the threatened withdrawal of corporations and departments.

Sectoral mobility or immobility, then, does not coincide with class mobility. National economies contain sectors both relatively open to the market and relatively protected from the market, in which income and social position depend crucially on the maintenance of nation-state boundaries and protected spaces. The argument outlined here affects rich welfare states in particular, because the removal of boundaries, along with global competitive pressure, brings the prospect of a considerable drop in living standards as well as lowered expectations; poor states, on the other hand, have no need to fear this competition, although this means they are excluded from the global market as a result. It is not hard to name those who oppose cosmopolitanization, and at first sight they appear extremely powerful. But who might be considered a supporter and sympathizer of such a cosmopolitan transformation?

Several questions can be derived from the foregoing diagnosis. Could modern cosmopolitanism turn into a creature of global capitalism? Or is the opposite the case, namely, that radicalized global capitalism *destroys* the prerequisites for cultural diversity and sources of political freedom? Is it even conceivable that self-globalizing capital might bring itself to become an actor in the cosmopolitan renewal of democracy? Would it be possible for the sub-politics of investment decisions to be formed into an instrument of power with the aim, on the one hand, of enforcing global rules on unfettered capitalism and, on the other, of encouraging nation-states to open themselves to cosmopolitan values and practices? Is it at all conceivable that the right to strike might shift from the workers' movement to a company managers' movement and become transformed into a cosmopolitan investment policy that not only serves the purposes of positive advertising but also spells out anew basic rights, democracy and justice in a joint pact with regulatory cooperation states? Or is this merely to conjure up false hopes and a false consciousness once again?

It is a well-known fact, particularly in the social sciences, that there is nothing more risky than making a prognosis. However, if we shift the growth in global corporate power and, with it, the issue of the legitimation – the legitimatory decline of global companies and global financial organizations – to centre stage, we can experimentally derive a short-term and a long-term prediction from this diagnosis.

In the short term, the protectionist forces may triumph – that heterogeneous collection of nationalists, anti-capitalists, environmental activists, defenders of nation-based democracy and of state authority, as well as the xenophobes and religious fundamentalists. In the long term, however, a paradoxical coalition consisting of the supposed 'losers' of global economic liberalization (trade unions, environmental activists, democrats) and its winners (corporations, financial markets, the World Trade Organization, the World Bank, and so on) could indeed bring about a cosmopolitan renewal of democracy, if both sides recognized that their respective interests are best served by a *cosmopolitan regime*. If this were to happen, labour representatives, environmental activists and defenders of democracy would actively support the establishment of cosmopolitan legal systems and institutions. The same goes for global companies, too. Ultimately, they can only operate successfully in business terms in a context that guarantees them and others economic, legal, political and social stability and security. *Only* a cosmopolitan expansion of the state, politics and democracy – in whichever institutional form or global division of labour – is capable of safeguarding companies' profit interests in the long term. This is admittedly a development that will be characterized by setbacks and breakdowns. But the only way of making it possible is, as Immanuel Kant taught, to act *as if* it were possible.

The all-important question in this is not *whether* a cosmopolitan regime can be established, but rather *how* it will be established, and above all how it will gain democratic legitimacy, that is, the consent of the people. To what extent and in what way will a consciousness – a will, a community – emerge that supports the creation of a cosmopolitan regime? Peace in the twenty-first century depends on the emergence of such a cosmopolitan common sense among people, and not on the economy, states or supra-state political organizations.

3.11 Seeing issues of risk as issues of power

As already mentioned, the world risk society is a latent quasi-revolutionary society. A shift in focus is crucial in order to develop this perspective: the source of politics lies not in decisions about technology itself but rather in its unforeseeable consequences. In a risk-sensitive global public sphere, the issue of power is ignited especially by the knowledge that consequences cannot be predicted in advance. The foundations on which decisions are made in the current technological revolutions are being delegitimized in highly effective media representations of risk crises, protest movements and consumer boycotts, which plunge the world economy into a crisis of confidence.

As global risks increase, so too does the global fragility of markets. The more fragile and unpredictable world markets become, the greater the threat to investment capital, the more frequently shareholders jump ship, and the more urgent the issue of power – that is, the question of 'relations of definition' – becomes for all those involved. In a context of global uncertainty concerning the consequences of new technologies, who gets to decide, and on the basis of which legally defined norms of liability and proof, what counts as a 'risk', who counts as the 'responsible party' and who, therefore, is to pay if the worst comes to the worst? How can the system of *organized irresponsibility* be disrupted and the burden of proof redistributed in such a way that corporations have to be made responsible and liable for the global uncertainty that they have so far passed on to consumers and the environment? It is not experts' opinions about technical safety or benefits, nor ethics that is the crucial issue with regard to so-called problems of acceptance in relation, say, to genetically modified foods; it is power and legitimacy in the global age.

The ever-present assumption contained in claims of control on the part of state bureaucracies and legal systems within technologized civilization is that technical control of the consequences and dangers presented by new technologies is a part of that control.[9] If research into artificial intelligence is combined with nanotechnology, for example, what emerges is a world of miniature machines that build other machines and thereby construct other forms of life. Eventually, a world of computer-generated artificial life systems comes into existence (Clark 1996). In this way, the vision of a 100 per cent efficient, economically streamlined form of industrial production acquires a force capable of shaping reality. Its special feature lies in helping to control the diseases, viruses and other dangers associated with technologized civilization.

However, this vision of completely self-monitoring, open-ended technological systems capable of existing independently of human intervention ultimately only reinforces the ambiguities of technologized civilization. On the one hand, such systems perfect the promise of security; on the other, though, they open up previously inconceivable dimensions of risk – particularly regarding the new quality of complexity and contingency which they provoke, as they bring about the transition from closed systems to open, self-constructing systems. The latter have the capacity to adapt to conditions which are undergoing complex, turbulent and multidimensional change at such a speed that human intervention is out of the question.

The definition of the world risk society is therefore as follows. The very power and characteristics that are supposed to create a new quality of security and certainty simultaneously determine the extent of *absolute uncontrollability* that exists. The more efficiently and comprehensively the anticipation of consequences is integrated into technical systems, the more evidently and conclusively we lose control. All attempts at minimizing or eliminating risk technologically simply multiply the uncertainty into which we are plunging the world.

The first modernity was based on a simplification: technical objects and worlds could be constructed *without* unexpected consequences, and these objects were capable of replacing the old, bad ones. The more science and the more technology were brought into use, the fewer disputes there were because the 'one best solution', optimum economic benefit, was an achievable goal on the horizon.

In the second modernity, we find ourselves in a completely different playing field, inasmuch as, whatever we do, we *expect unexpected consequences*. Expectation of the unexpected, however, changes the quality of technical objects. Changes that are seemingly simple and minimal – those any newspaper reader finds confirmed every day when science and technology add their own uncertainties to the uncertainties that exist in general, instead of minimizing them – bring about a situation that is hard for many to comprehend: science and technology do not simplify the debates about new technological worlds. Far from putting out political fires, they actually add fuel to the flames by pouring on the oil of ethical, ecological and political controversy.

We can see how this is the case if we take the example of the BSE crisis, which incidentally provides a model for 'risks' associated with food in general. Despite considerable effort on the part of researchers, all we know is that we *don't* know how the sequence of contagion works, what incubation periods can be expected, and whether there will ultimately be 500 or 5,000 deaths in Europe alone. One aspect of the alarm generated by BSE in Europe lies in the experience that the promises of safety issued by science, politics and industry are built upon the shifting sands of a *known lack of knowledge*. Thus, the world risk society is an era of civilization in which decisions that affect the lives not only of the current generation but also of future generations are made on the basis of a known lack of knowledge.

When it comes to determining what should be regarded as a 'risk' and what should not – and who should be made liable for it – cultural values and stereotypes play a much more decisive role in relation to non-quantifiable uncertainties than to predictable risks. For example, many people regard the AIDS risk in Africa as an insidious variant of Western imperialism, if indeed it is not denied outright (with the disastrous consequence of its spreading further unchecked). If, by contrast, we shift the focus to an expectation of the unexpected, we discover that the category of risk stands for the *public sphere principle*. Thus, as early as the start of the twentieth century, the pragmatic philosopher John Dewey swept away the fear that technologists and technologized civilization had of risk and discovered in risk itself the *principle of hope*.[10]

The theory of economic interpretation as it is commonly presented fails to take into consideration the transformation that can be effected by meanings; it overlooks the new medium that places communication between industry and its eventual consequences. It is obsessed with the illusion that has long since overthrown the 'natural economy': an illusion based on non-consideration of the difference made to action by the perception and publicizing of *consequences*, both real and potential. It thinks in terms of what has occurred, not what might occur; it thinks in origins and not in outcomes. (Dewey 1996: 134ff.)

It is dissent over the unforeseeable consequences of decisions – not consensus about them – that gives rise to a global public discourse, a global context of values and norms and a desire for coordinated action, all of which extend beyond every nation's borders. According to Dewey, then, worldwide controversies over technological consequences and global conflicts over risk have an *educational function*. Large-scale industry *externalizes* global consequences. Amid the turmoil of worldwide modernization, isolated local communities are bulldozed, broken apart and renetworked through the perceived globality of risk. Transnational communities of risk and risk publics spring up and become established in relation to long-term technological consequences and expectations of the unexpected, which are felt well beyond national borders, and they may lead towards a political process of experimentation with new solutions and cosmopolitan norms.

From the perspective of industry and of nation-states, it seems like the end of the world whenever social movements disregard national laws in order to draw attention to long-term impacts and to demand publicly that corporations take their social responsibilities seriously as a result; however, if we apply Dewey's view to the present, such situations become *civilization's laboratory for institutions of the future and institutions with a future*. Thus, global risks can turn into global sets of values, networks and movements which, rooted in regional and local cultures and conflicts, are capable of articulating and implementing visions of how to live (and survive) and visions of democratic self-government.

In this sense, risks can be understood as *negative* communications media – in contrast to the positive communications media of money, truth and power. Whereas the latter create intentional contexts of action across all system boundaries, the negative communications medium of risk forces communication to take place between those who do not want to communicate with one another. It allocates commitments and costs to those who refuse to accept them (and who often have the law on their side when doing so). In other words: risks break through the 'self-referentiality' of partial systems (Niklas Luhmann) – of the economy, science, politics and everyday life; they overturn the priorities attached to their respective agendas and orders of business and create contexts of action between camps that are mutually ignorant or mutually hostile.

The curious counter-power of risk made public – its capacity to tear down the façades of organized irresponsibility in the full flashbulb glare of the public media at least for a second (long enough to shock the world), and to force the ignoramuses together – points to the existence of *political reflexivity about risk*. Risk publics thus generate a *quasi-revolutionary situation*, an inverted mirror image of social order as reality.

In searching for a metaphor for this political reflexivity, the image of supping from the honey pot suggests itself. Everybody dips into the honey pot containing promises of a technological paradise in order to pinch a bit for themselves; then, in order to get rid of the residual honey – residual risk – they wipe their hands on their clothing and on all kinds of objects and people, so that they entangle themselves and others in an increasingly tight net of sticky risks. It is this (measured against existing norms) 'perverse' sweet-as-honey logic of hope associated with risk communication that constitutes its politically explosive dynamic. The only thing that technical experts in industry and politics can do in the face of it is make the sign of the cross and call in the exorcists.

The world has not necessarily become a more dangerous place. It is systematic *loss of trust* that makes consumers see 'risks' everywhere. The less trust there is, the more risks appear. The greater the awareness of risk, the more unstable global markets become. The more unstable global markets become, the greater the boomerang risks are for everyone – including corporations and governments.

Unpredictable technological risks, then, are like a contagious disease, a 'social virus'; they become transformed into economic and political risks that tyrannize the innermost areas of social life by way of revenge for denial of the consequences of social decisions. Corporations that pass on the unpredictability of consequences to others get caught up in the vicious circle of unpredictable world markets and overnight devaluation of billions' worth of investments. The blanket loss of trust faced by corporations and governments in relation to their handling of the risks they produce and then pass on as 'residual risks' can hardly be made good by the solitary actions of individual corporations. Ultimately, even powerful corporations have their backs to the wall when fighting against activist networks. In order to realize just how difficult it is, even for powerful corporations, to triumph over these oppositional movements, one has only to remember how loss of trust can be instrumentalized politically time and time again. For example, in a contract negotiated and signed by the secretary-general of the United Nations and a group of major corporations in the year 2000, the latter committed themselves to upholding environmental standards in return for being allowed to use the blue UN logo. This contract was immediately criticized by social movements for being inappropriate because it failed to include any effective means of self-monitoring. Activists rejected it as an attempt by corporations to 'bluewash' themselves. This neologism is a variation on 'greenwashing' as well as a reference to the UN flag, and was used in order to highlight corporations' wrongdoing in comparison with their 'green' advertising.

Incidentally, the lesson of the Brent Spar affair – the so-called Shell shock – is that, once a corporation has stood accused in public and has lost its legitimacy, not even government support, including legal and police powers, can help it any more. Shell had the British government, including its police force, on its side but had to back down when a transnational consumer boycott of Shell fuel stations escalated.

One of the great misunderstandings on the part of companies, as well as politicians and scientists, is that conflicts over risk are 'single-issue' affairs – protests against an oil drilling platform, genetically modified foods, child labour, against the flagrant violation of workers' rights and environmental norms, to name but a few examples. What lies behind these accusations of 'single-issue' protest is the view that protest movements are self-absorbed, monomaniacal and politically naïve, whereas the directors of multinational corporations and central governments see the 'big picture' and, in weighing environmental costs against the benefits of economic growth, new jobs and international competitiveness, are able to reach a 'rational' view.

The aims of protest and protesters alike are portrayed as unrealistic, utopian, economically fanciful and bearing no relation to the demands of modern governance. The opposition movements that spring up, for example, whenever new patents are granted in genetic technology or when genetically modified crops are planted are suspected of being 'NIMBYists' ('not in my backyard') – such people are happy to enjoy the comforts of modern life and economic growth but are not prepared to accept the risks that inevitably go with them.

In contrast to this view, protest groups attach symbolic significance to the 'single issues' they are concentrating on, particularly in relation to account-ability for consequences and the *global responsibility* that arises out of this. As the public controversies over Brent Spar and over 'Frankenstein food' in Britain teach us, it seems that indisputable scientific knowledge plays a far less significant role in public perception than does the plea for global responsibility.

Risks are not things. They are social constructions in which expert knowl-edge as well as cultural values and symbols play a key role. In order to unravel the power conflicts that lie behind conflicts over risk, it is necessary to raise the issue of 'relations of definition'. I use the term 'relations of def-inition' in parallel to the term 'relations of production' used by Karl Marx. What is meant by it are the kinds of resources – and the access to them – needed for defining (away) risks in a socially binding way.

A whole series of questions points to this substructure of risk-defining power: who has what to prove? In other words, who bears the burden of proof in any given situation? What qualifies as causal evidence and as 'proof' under conditions of cognitive uncertainty? Which norms of accountability apply? Who is responsible? Who must carry the costs? As we begin to examine these cognitive power bases of the relations of definition, we gain a deeper insight into the connection between risk and power; we also get some indication of how changes in the power relations of definition – such as a redistribution of the burden of proof, or product liability regulations – can influence the political dynamic of risk conflicts. Transformation of the power relations of definition may not only improve the chances of opposition movements but may also make global companies take social responsibility for the unknown consequences they trigger.

3.12   European and non-European constellations

The notion of a second modernity raises a genuine misunderstanding. For one thing, it appears to introduce a new problematic evolutionary periodization, whereby one era comes abruptly to an end and a new era begins. This new era would supposedly be one in which all the old relationships disappear forever at a certain point in time and completely new ones come into being at the same moment to replace them.

In addition, this evolutionary misunderstanding is directly linked to a second one which implicitly draws the conclusion that the constellation of a second modernity applies equally to all continents, regions and cultures with their diverse histories.

Naturally, neither of these notions is intended. If the distinction has any meaning at all, then it is purely as a heuristic tool for raising the issue for the social sciences of new categories and theoretical frames of reference for change, while at the same time enabling the social sciences to distinguish systematically between different, contrasting constellations of the second modernity that are nonetheless tangled up with one another in contradictory ways.

The old concepts of the First, Second and Third World are also turning into zombie categories. This means, first of all, that the context of globality is now everybody's starting point. Globality refers to the experience of threat emanating from the self-generated risks of technologized civilization and to the realization that the earth is finite; this eliminates the plural oppositions between peoples and states and creates a closed space of intersubjectively binding meanings. However, within this context of globality, extremely different locations have emerged for historically contingent reasons, which, due to the challenges of globality, are drifting ever farther apart from one another. It may be, for example, that a sub-Saharan African living in the new cosmopolitan constellation not only faces an even more dramatic threat to his or her already modest livelihood (perhaps even on account of this new constellation), but that he or she also gains a few new minor opportunities as well; nonetheless, the improbability of that individual seeing out his or her days in the Ritz Hotel has increased to an unimaginable extent.

The *African situation* – according to the cosmopolitan perspective – is neither modernity's 'before' nor its 'outside', but is rather intertwined with the European, Asian, and South and North American conflicts of modernity: it is a matter of *entangled modernities* (Randeria). If we want to talk about the European constellation of the second modernity, we have to begin with Africa. This is because the historical fate of Africa – the destruction wrought by colonialism and imperialism – is the suppressed dark side of European nation-state history in the first modernity. The fate of Africa, then, is an inseparable part of the emergence of the first European modernity (even if this is denied in the self-image of European autarchy through an act of historical forgetting); by the same token, however, the cosmopolitan constellation of the second modernity acquires a totally different meaning for Africa, namely that of a second *without* a first modernity, because it is here that the key European institutions of the nation-state constellation – states, law, science, democracy, the welfare state with full employment, national unity – are only ever present in the form of a self-refuting *dream* of an African modernity *without* European imperialism. But there can be no doubt whatsoever that, in the meta-power situation of global business dominance, Africa too must reclaim its voice.

Although colonial domination disrupted the process of state building in Africa, African societies remain plurinational by nature. The pre-colonial nations – that marked out the identities of these multinational states – survived; even though they were parcelled out and often dispersed among several states, it was not impossible to reforge a societal link. On the contrary: the crisis of the Western nation-state creates an opportunity that may be decisive for the African situation, namely, to separate the state (still a 'gift' imposed by the colonial powers) from a territorially fragmented African national diversity that still exists in the historical memory of its people. Reinstating these 'nations' will make it possible to bring to an end the crisis of national consciousness and identity that is ravaging Africa, and will in future prevent political manipulation of disputes over nationality. (Tshiyembe 2000: 14)

Between the beginning of the twentieth and twenty-first centuries, the *European constellation* underwent dramatic change. At the turn of the twentieth century the world was dominated by the nations of Europe, and they were geared up for war. Nowadays, however, Europe is no longer the centre of the world, and a war between the major member states of the European Union, while not completely impossible, has become highly improbable at the very least. Europeans are a peaceable and prosperous set of people and tend to get upset about the poisons in their food. The nationalistic culture of war has been 'corroded', as Carl Schmitt would cuttingly remark, by the spirit of trade; indeed, this has even reached the point where the philosopher's dream of 'eternal peace' – already dreamt long ago by Immanuel Kant – has at last come within reach, at least for Europe.

Perhaps it is more accurate to say that the unimaginable horrors unleashed on the European continent by the Second World War, and in particular the horror of the Holocaust, have not only broken the inner pride of European nationalism but have also opened Europe up both to a cosmopolitan renewal and to a renewal of cosmopolitanism – unlike, for example, the religiously and territorially loaded complexities of the dispute between Israelis and Palestinians, which are mired in origin and end-time scenarios. Thus, the European constellation is ultimately about the historical experiment of a 'transnational state', a 'cosmopolitan state', as a response to globalization.

This needs to be clearly distinguished from the *Asian constellation*. It would be a complete misunderstanding of the latter were we to assume that economic and political openness to the free play of global capital and neoliberalism are characteristic of it. It is precisely the huge economic success of the 'tiger states' that in many different ways has reinvigorated cultural heritages and traditions and made them fashionable – contrary to simplistic models of modernization; it has by no means led to the creation of a cultural space for Western-oriented democratic movements. The historical changes taking place in this region need to be understood in direct relation to their own history, as a rejection of the postcolonial state and an embracing of a new kind of synthesis of Asian modernity, linking transnational familial ethical identities and institutions with the challenges of global capitalism (Ong 1999).

Regional inequalities with regard to the *way people are affected* by the problems arising from modernization have to be seen in their tension-filled relationship to the fact that these problems are *common to all*. While the collapse of global financial markets or changes in climatic zones have a very different impact in different regions, this does nothing to alter the fact that in principle *everyone* can be affected – and that the task of overcoming these problems demands *a global effort*. This can be interpreted as the principle of 'globality' (Albrow 1996) – in the sense of a growing consciousness of global interconnections – becoming increasingly plausible and valid. Thus, for example, global environmental problems may encourage the earth's population (both in the present and in future generations) to perceive itself as a 'community of fate'. The latter is by no means free of conflict when, for example, the question arises as to how far the industrialized countries are justified in demanding that developing countries protect important global resources such as rainforests, while they themselves simultaneously use up the lion's share of energy resources for themselves. But these very conflicts *themselves* have an interactive function, in that they emphasize the fact that global solutions need to be found and that these need to be brought about not by war but by negotiation. Without new global institutions and regulatory mechanisms – and thus a certain degree of convergence – it is barely conceivable that solutions can be found. Transnational publics that are aware of the consequences of technological risks are sparked into existence as a result of boundary-transcending long-term consequences and expectations of the unexpected, leading in turn to an involuntary politicization of the world risk society.

Yet this is only one possible consequence of globalized dangers. It is possible to come up with other positions that draw exactly the opposite conclusion from the dilemmas posed by global threats, namely that what we need to pursue is not an adequate global modernity but rather improved, 'other' modernities. Politicians such as Malaysia's Mahathir or Singapore's Lee Kuan Yew do not simply put the case for rejecting modernity – they certainly do want to promote modern production methods, mass media and science. But they are also toying with the idea of dipping only selectively into the 'package' of Western modernity. What distinguishes these alternative modernities from the Western version is, interestingly enough, their attitude towards the *problematic outcomes* of Western modernity, so that Western modernization, along with all its 'flaws', becomes an indispensable foil and category of reference for these countries' own visions of development (Holzer 1999: ch. 4).

The role played by the problematic consequences of Western modernity is therefore a thoroughly ambiguous one. On the one hand, they are the essential transmission belt for globality, while on the other they provide a cause and a rationale for demarcating other modernities from Western modernity. This is the necessary outcome of a historical situation in which the uncertainties of a cosmopolitan second modernity are interpenetrated by and intertwined with the different regional starting points of a partially developed, partially still sought-after and partially already relinquished first modernity. It is precisely out of this dissent over the unforeseeable consequences of modernity that a global public discourse arises in the new 'overlapping communities of fate' (Held 2000: 400), one that extends across all national borders and brings with it an expectation of coordinated action.

3.13   Cosmopolitan realism

The argument at the heart of this book is not directed towards a cosmopolitan idealism or even towards romanticism; rather, it is an attempt to substantiate a cosmopolitan realism *which adheres to the principle that political action and political science make us blind without cosmopolitan concepts and ways of seeing the world.*

True, the shimmer of a normative-political theory of self-critical cosmopolitanism comes through here as well – a *cosmopolitan imagination* – but the central concern of the book is an empirical and analytical one, namely to show, first, that the national outlook is *wrong* and, second, that only the cosmopolitan outlook *adequately fits with reality* and provides an *adequate basis for action*. This applies both to the sphere of political action and to that of political science (see table 3.1). Those who remain caught up within the national outlook will find they have lost out.

If the national outlook *does* become caught up in a *cultural pessimistic cycle of self-confirmation*, then national axioms will generate global problems that cannot be dealt with using the conventional nation-based tools, indeed they cannot even be perceived as such. The cosmopolitan outlook, though, is neither optimistic nor pessimistic but sceptical and self-critical. The world that appears within its field of vision is neither darkened by cultural pessimism nor illuminated by a belief in progress. There is no attempt here to persuade us that we are on our way towards a world of general human benevolence. Indeed, just the opposite is the case: disasters lurk at every turn, and yet there is also an enticing glimmer of new beginnings – usually it is impossible to tell whether or not the future holds both at once. The main feature of the cosmopolitan outlook is simply that it is *different*. So what characterizes the *structure* of the cosmopolitan outlook? What are its conceptual forms and ways of looking at the world, what are its coordinates, its boundary constructions, its horizons of expectation, its values, at what

Table 3.1 On the distinction between the dimension of reality and the dimension of values

	National outlook	*Cosmopolitan outlook*
Dimension of reality: empirical-analytical theory and research	Nation-state frame of reference; endogenous causality; national situations and problems; is empirically wrong; zombie science of the national; cultural pessimistic self-confirming circle	Transnational frame of reference; global interdependencies and causalities; interaction between national and global crises and inequalities; is empirically correct; *cosmopolitan realism;*[11] critique of the national outlook; cosmopolitan theory of meta-power
Dimension of values: *Normative and political theory and utopia*	*Normative nationalism:* Theory of the nation-state and of nation-state democracy; political realism in relation to power	*Self-critical cosmopolitanism:* Principles, opportunities, dangers and legitimatory problems of the cosmopolitan regime[12]

points has the loss of boundaries led to negative outcomes, what are its built-in dilemmas and contradictions?

To exaggerate the point somewhat, even an ethnic nationalist fighting against both cosmopolitan cultural and financial elites and the civil rights-based nation-state would have to take the cosmopolitan outlook on board if they wanted to make their mark in an unfettered world; this would mean locating and making use of their opportunities to act within a transnational framework and a transnational arena. This is because they are, in effect, 'sandwiched': the politics of ethnic exclusion and isolation stands in contradiction to global economic dependencies, transnational flows of information and culture, global risks and crises, as well as global political actors' opportunities for intervention. In other words: even someone clinging to the (nightmarish) dream of ethnic absolutism would have to be a cosmopolitan realist.

This cosmopolitan realism can be understood through the following dimensions, or issues (see table 3.2).

(1) At what level do I form, or select, concepts? Not at the national/international level but at the transnational level, which focuses on the interaction between global business actors, civil society, supranational organizations

Table 3.2 An unfettered world in transition: transformation of political conceptual forms and ways of looking at the world

	National outlook	Cosmopolitan outlook
Level of concept formation (coordinates/ frame of reference)	Politics within borders: the political system in the nation-state frame of reference; state-centred outlook; national/ international	Politics of boundaries: boundary-transcending interaction between side-effects; transnational point of view, political level and political arenas; not state-centred; not system-centred
Norms and rule systems	Nation-state regime; system and ideal of the Westphalian Peace; the organization of humanity into sovereign, territorially exclusive nation-states; political realism regarding power	Cosmopolitan regime: historically open meta-game of global domestic politics; internationalization of nation-states; conflicts over the regulation of the global economy and over the enforcement of human rights and the transnational renewal of democracy
Actors and strategies	Nation-state, government, parties, international organizations; international diplomacy; formal positions in the political system	Mobilization and organization of common interests across borders; increase in new power centres above, below and parallel to nation-states; institutionalization of extended networks of inter-state politics, including global business actors and strategies and civil society actors and strategies
Legitimation	Forms of legal domination; democratically legitimated national politics; anarchy of nation-states	Forms of translegal domination; not (directly) democratically legitimated; fragmented system of power and counter-power
Culture	Ideal of national homogeneity; positive integration	Cultural diversity; the extent to which apparently distant cultures and societies overlap with one another, live alongside one another and conflict with one another at local level; 'critical integration' of very varied traditions
Military	State-centred enemy images; either war or peace	Enemy images no longer tied to state entities: transnational terrorism; humanitarian intervention; both war and peace; political realism as cosmopolitan realism

and, of course, nation-states. The boundary constructions that are also necessary in the transnational sphere (e.g. those of 'domestic foreign policy' and 'foreign domestic policy') do not follow the nation-state script but have, for their part, to be repeatedly renegotiated and legitimated politically and strategically under changing circumstances and in relation to specific themes, likewise in transnational interactions.

(2)   What does 'politics' mean in the transnational context? The *politics of plural boundaries* – in the context of fluid, equivocal boundary demarcations. The necessity of constructing transnational boundaries raises new problems around decision-making (conflicts between boundaries and responsibilities), and both emerges from and consists of a double interaction. On the one hand, the rules of the old national game overlap with the new (still diffuse) rules of the cosmopolitan regime; on the other, transnational boundary politics results from the *interaction between the side-effects* of capital flows, cultural flows, migratory movements, risks, terrorist acts, religious fundamentalisms, anti-globalization movements and ecological and economic crises. Thus, transnational politics refers to a level of organized, more or less informal domestic, foreign, inter-state and substate politics that mirrors all other phenomena – global economic power relations, crises and strategies, nation-state situations and the reactions of individual countries and country groups, interventions on the part of the global public, civil society and the military, environmental threats, and so on. Transnational politics cuts across national politics. It *contains* nation-state politics, just as the reverse is true: nation-state politics becomes the site where transnational politics is worked out. As far as the relationship between them is concerned, the following principle applies: *nation-state politics without cosmopolitan vision is blind, while cosmopolitan vision without nation-state politics is empty.*

Cosmopolitan realism can and must, then, be specified in detail in relation to different global domestic political ('glocal') levels and to different historical and geopolitical constellations (figure 3.1): globally, nationally and locally, but also in relation to different regions of the world (Asia, Europe, Africa, North America). In general, it can be said that transnational politics is institutionally and infrastructurally *under*developed politics; in other words, it is characterized by *un*satisfactory legal structures and infrastructures, forms of democracy and legitimation, as well as unsatisfactory intermediary institutions of global domestic politics (e.g. those of jurisdiction, of parliamentary and party political representation, and of the balance between global regional power blocs). A further characteristic feature is the diversity and inequality of the actors; for example, not all members of transnational civil society are civil or even representative. Furthermore, the actors differ radically in terms of resources, power, and access to information and centres of decision-making. Thus, transnational politics is *polycratic* politics, in other

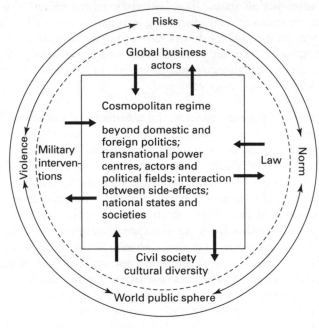

Transnational political arena

Figure 3.1 Cosmopolitan realism: the structure of the cosmopolitan outlook, or politics in the world society

words it is pluralistic, familiar with contradictions, informal and subpolitical rather than formal, integrated into multiple interdependencies, and yet effective, because it governs different national contexts.

(3)   What does 'interaction between side-effects' mean? The notion of the 'meta-power' of economic actors is ambiguous. It can mean: (a) business turns into politics, economic activity is transformed into political activity. This is not what is meant here. What *is* meant is this: (b) in terms of its self-definition, global business activity remains economic, that is, *un*political activity. This, however, generates interactional phenomena between side-effects, which in turn do away with the boundaries, basic distinctions and institutions of the first modernity and are negotiated transnationally in the context of *politics* as rule-changing meta-politics.[13] Let us take the example of the court of arbitration at the World Trade Organization. In what capacity do the judges encounter one another? They represent quite different legal systems and legal traditions. As different as these are, the judges dispense justice in the context and on the basis of transnational politics.

I am *not* talking about global business as politics, but about a transnational politics that arises from interactional phenomena between side-effects. This is what fuels the mobilization and organization of common interests across boundaries as well as the integration of new power centres above and beneath the level of nation-states and parallel to them.

(4) What becomes of nation-states? Far from being dismantled, they are instead reinterpreted, losing their old significance and acquiring a different, new significance in the transnational arena of power. The interactional 'system' of transnational politics obeys neither the rules of classic international law nor those of the cosmopolitan world society, neither territorial state boundaries nor the maxims of national sovereignty. Accordingly, the forms, formulae and forums of a transnational security policy and architecture based on limited state autonomy have not yet been developed. Enemy images no longer linked to state entities open up national arenas, on the one hand, to the possibility of new, flexible forms of alliance ('anti-terror alliances', which undermine 'inflexible' forms of alliance such as NATO), and, on the other, to the possibility of permanent military intervention, that is, for 'new wars' (Kaldor 1999) that entail no declaration of war and no possibility of ending such intervention through peace negotiations or peace treaties.

The term 'cosmopolitan realism' has three meanings, then. First, it means realism *based on the science of reality (wirklichkeitswissenschaftlich)*; second, realism *based on power politics*, by which I mean, third, realism *based on boundary politics* – in other words, not the dismantling but rather the *pluralizing of boundaries* as meta-power politics. The points at which domestic state power struggles, inter-state power struggles and non-state power struggles dovetail with one another can no longer be located within the frame of reference of either 'national' or 'international' arenas. The political theory of national political realism is empirically wrong. What takes its place, though, is not cosmopolitan idealism, but rather *cosmopolitan realism*, meaning that this meta-power politics – a politics that cuts through and blurs boundaries, as well as setting new, fragile boundaries – needs to be conceptualized and analysed as a New Global Political Economy. This is the subject of the following chapters.

4

Power and Counter-Power in the Global Age: The Strategies of Capital

The message is this: the game is an open-ended one in the radical sense that neither can the old game continue to be played, nor have the new rules of the game been negotiated. Indeed, it is not even clear whether the framework of the old order can be replaced with a new one, or to what extent the contingency of politics should or can be approved, legitimized and placed on a permanent footing by a global cosmopolitan legal order.[1]

The strategic space to be elaborated by category in this and the following chapters relates to the *strategic game logic* that exists in the dynamic interdependency between the three actor perspectives of global business, states and global civil society. The actor status of each of these is constituted (or not) through the mutual rivalry involved in the rule-changing meta-power game. Note, we are *not* talking about empirical game scenarios.

In this context, the space, or concept, of strategy refers to a 'neither/nor': neither structure nor chaos, but rather the reciprocal and contradictory relationship between meta-power strategies involving a non-ontological concept of power. 'Neither/nor' also means that strategies are to be understood as *quasi-institutions* – neither the old nation-state order nor a new global state order or world citizens' order holds sway. In other words, 'strategies' exist only as forms of action based on the contingency of politics, and these are differentiated according to different groups of actors – capital, global civil society, states.[2] Strategy is another word for the lack of a world state, combined with a cosmopolitan founding era: the struggle for a global system of rules. To put it in terms of a typology of theory, then, what is presented here is a theory of action with global political power intent, an initial contribution to a cosmopolitan realism and Machiavellianism rooted in theories of power.[3]

4.1 The global politics of global business

The opportunities for different groups of actors to be constituted as political actors in the meta-power game are unevenly distributed. This asymmetry of strategic capacity, which favours capital especially, lies in the logic of its position of power and exercise of power, and allows us at the same time to answer in a highly differentiated way the question of which individual or collective actors are hidden behind the broad-brush term 'capital'. In order to exercise power as players of the game, global civil society actors and states have first to be constituted politically through a public political process in the global arena, as active subjects with specific political objectives; this is not true for capital. For example, it does not have to form political parties or go through the process of democratic elections in order to exercise economic meta-power in relation to states. The power of refusal neither presupposes a political objective nor requires political justification. It works according to actors' self-perceptions based on the criteria of economic action. However, this in no way lessens the political meta-power of global business actors – on the contrary, it increases it. What sense are we to make of this?

Economic power becomes transformed into political meta-power by way of a side-effect: global business actors set about toppling the world order by following a model of *politics as side-effect* (Holzer and Sørensen 2001: 16). This political game with the side-effects of global business activity maximizes the meta-power of capital for at least three reasons.

First, the politics of side-effects spares those who benefit from it the trouble of having to organize and legitimize themselves as political actors, without necessarily forfeiting any political power in the process. It is possible to act (politically) as a (political) non-actor, indeed highly effectively, with the power that creates *faits accomplis* (or threatens to do so). The politics of side-effects, then, is a form of '*domination by nobody*'. 'Nobody' is doing politics here, and they are doing so in a very effective and often deliberate way.

Second, global politics as a side-effect of economic decision-making allows for a considerable heterogeneity of actors. It is not necessary to assume that transnational corporations, or banks, or medium-sized businesses, or – to put it even more absurdly – global financial markets and capital flows are pursuing a particular 'strategy' or 'policy'. Rather, the political meta-power 'of capital' results from the collective impact of very heterogeneous actors, markets, capital flows, supranational organizations and so forth, each of which understands itself to be making decisions in its own interest on the basis of economic considerations.

Third, the strategies of capital as a side-effect at global political level by no means rule out – indeed they rule in – the possibility that they themselves may fall foul of 'hostile takeovers', incalculable global financial risks, the contradictory demands of shareholders, and perhaps in future the organized power of consumers as well. So even the so-called actors of economic globalization may see themselves as 'victims', and may be uprooted and frightened by the force of change. Nor is the *internal* meta-power game of global business a game of victors, either, but rather a game played between actual and potential losers. Those who emerge as victors from the worldwide takeover battles of today might end up being 'swallowed up' the day after tomorrow. And even the new head offices of victorious business empires have to deal continually with bad news – the sense of crisis is never far away. After all, there is always some fire that needs putting out somewhere in the world. The grand objective pursued by heads of corporations – a global presence in every market – is bought at the price of permanent turmoil in an economy characterized by uncertainty. Nonetheless, it remains true that this maximizes rather than reduces the power of global business actors generated via side-effects.

In addition to overcoming political boundaries, side-effects can also generate 'overflow' (Michel Callon) with regard to institutional boundaries. This is the case when property serves not only as an indicator of the availability of capital but also as an indicator of *political* power. We are less interested in the most obvious form in which this can occur, that is, when property is used deliberately for political purposes. This is dealt with both in everyday speech and juridically in a certain word – corruption – albeit care is taken that this boundary transgression remains the exception. . . . What is much more interesting, on the other hand, is the case in which the use of property is expressed in politics *as a side-effect*, since in this case precautionary measures against corruption have no impact. While corruption still works with the instrument of positive sanctions (someone is paid for doing something specific), the mobilization of economic resources to influence a political community occurs, for example, through the threat of withdrawing industrial production, in other words, through negative sanctions. When that is the case, we are faced with *subpolitics*. This very use of the latter function of property, however, seems to be acquiring ever greater significance. (Holzer and Sørensen 2001: 16f.)

Is capital self-legitimating?

Economic globalization not only creates economic facts by means of global political, world-changing side-effects; it also opens up new sources of legitimation for economic action. The 'strategies of capital' can maximize their global political power whenever they succeed in establishing a connection between capital and the law, or capital and the state. In the 'logic' of the capital perspective, then, the idea is not only to put states under pressure by instigating competition between potential production locations, or to tame competition on the global market by forming cooperative networks; it is essentially a matter of gaining access to new sources of legitimacy. This can be achieved via two basic strategies that contradict one another in certain respects:

- on the one hand, through the *neo-liberalization of the state*, in other words, the economic self-transformation of politics in the sense of self-colonization;

- on the other, by *decoupling law(-making) from the state* and thereby *decoupling authority from the state*, thus enabling new rules and sources for rules to be generated, along with legal instruments for guaranteeing contracts and regulating conflict.

This is fundamentally a dual strategy. Empowerment and disempowerment become mutually intermeshed: capital is empowered while states are disempowered, and states are delegitimated while capital becomes self-legitimated.

An outstanding example of the way the power of capital legitimizes itself by means of the law is the international system of arbitration.

Courts of arbitration are private courts established by contract; they come into play when there is a breach of contract between companies or between companies and states. The composition of the court also follows an agreed procedure . . . Arbitration proceedings may be regulated by law, as in Germany (§§ 1025ff. Code of Civil Procedure), but this form of regulation specifically does *not* refer to the set of laws to be applied. One of the benefits of choosing this kind of procedure, especially when the disputing parties are from different states and legal orders, is that they are free to agree which set of laws applies. A further advantage is the fact that disputes are settled more quickly than they would be before a state court, and that the judges are better informed about the issues. In view of the rapidly increasing importance of international arbitration proceedings, one strongly suspects that what is emerging here from below, as it were, and by means of legal casuistry, is a form of transnational law, independent of nation-state or supranational legislation. This transnational law of trade (*lex mercatoria*) therefore enjoys the status of a paradigm for the transnationalization of law beyond the nation state. (Günther and Randeria 2002: 38)

Gunther Teubner (1997) speaks in this context of 'global law without a state': 'Multinational companies enter into contracts with one another which they no longer make subject to any national jurisdiction or any national material set of laws. They agree to make their contracts subject to a court of arbitration that is independent of national laws, which in turn is supposed to apply the norms of a set of transnational trading laws' (Teubner 1997). In Teubner's view, this is not a nation-state legitimated source of law but rather an *autonomous* source of law that lies beyond the purview of political legislation.

Thus, capital acquires a form of *legal sovereignty*, through which it makes itself independent from all external, state-based legitimatory grounds and sources. This 'self-justification' of contracts in arbitrational practice thus implies a paradox.

The transnationalization of law becomes a deconstruction of 'law' in its nation-state sense. And it is exactly that which, within the nation-state outlook, turns the world upside down: anything that should not exist does not exist. However, this view fails to recognize what is ultimately at stake in the meta-power game: the decoupling of legitimacy from the state and the creation of an autonomous, transnational set of laws for the self-legitimization of capital.

The question is: to what extent are UN organizations, including the large transnational financial and trade organizations (IMF, World Bank, WTO, and so on), acting as midwives to a new order of legitimacy and power? That is, how successful is the attempt to make nation-states and national societies into mere instruments of capital flows and production–consumption cycles? The growing prominence of supranational legal orders and regimes, international organizations for conflict regulation, law-making firms and, not least, direct intervention on the part of the World Trade Organization and other supranational financial organizations have created a complex, ambiguous and polyvalent structure of legal spaces and of authorities that make and administer the law, in which jurisdictions and boundaries frequently overlap within and between national territories: this is, in effect, the legal version of the politics of boundary pluralization.

The fact that the actors, spheres of influence and claims to validity associated with this new plural-sovereign form of legislation are becoming transnationalized and multiplied does indeed have consequences for our understanding of *law as such*, as they raise the *question of legitimacy*: from where do 'legal systems' and 'laws' draw their binding, legitimizing power if they are no longer conceptualized within the terms of nation-state sovereignty? What is it, in fact, that legitimizes 'law' *in the absence of* state democratic authority? What 'means of coercion' can a non-state system of law for global business 'self-legitimation' fall back on? To what extent can these global business 'laws of convention' (bilateral, multilateral agreements or protocols that are supposed to have or to develop quasi-legal binding power) still be understood as 'law' at all in the sense in which this term has been coined and institutionalized within methodological nationalism?

Are we to view this pluralization of legitimatory sources of law as a regression, measured against the standards of democratically constituted states based on the rule of law? Or is it just the opposite, an embryonic form of capitalist quasi-statehood in a transnational arena without any state sovereignty?

Since 'private business authority' has no access (so far, at least) to state means of violence or coercion, the question then becomes, what gives rise to its *obligatory momentum* and in what does this consist? A whole range of partial answers can be found here along the spectrum from *persuasion* to *coercion*, more or less coupled with *consensus*. However, quasi-statehood (which also, of course, points to the lack of transnational statehood) means that laws and norms have to possess and develop a kind of 'self-coercion', some capacity to convince and to gain acceptance for themselves. Ultimately, however, that will be possible only if the self-confirming prophecy of their own legitimacy is based on a claim to validity that goes beyond economic egotism, beyond the self-interest of global business actors. In other words, since the binding power of the legal self-legitimation of global business activities is not based on state means of coercion, this must be compensated for by the power of persuasion. To exaggerate the point somewhat: the main component of successful economic activity consists in the de-economization and self-politicization of the business world, and in the acceptance of responsibility beneath the global public gaze of consumers. This is why, in summary, I assume that the neo-liberal regime is characterized by the following key features.

- Capital acquires access to the sources and norms of legal self-legitimation, allowing it to create legitimate systems autonomously and to institutionalize corresponding ways of regulating conflict; capital and the state thus merge into the 'capital-state', in which states, as 'autonomous units', make themselves the objects and subjects of a world order geared towards optimizing the interests of capital.
- The attempt is made to establish a transnational, institutionalized authority above the level of the state, whose purpose is to advance the neo-liberal self-transformation of states in order to make global capital accumulation easier to achieve; to stage a game of politics as side-effect, both discursively and in reality, in order to keep divergent and resistant social forces in check and to establish the discursive hegemony of the neo-liberal regime.
- The mode of self-legitimation is thus based on the moment of a *universal inclusivity* that combines self-legitimization with a universal set of laws, an indifference towards cultural differences and an economic-pacifist concept of invasion. Self-legitimating capital is 'a machine for universal integration, an open mouth with infinite appetite, inviting all to come peacefully within its domain. (Give me your poor, your hungry, your downtrodden masses . . .)' (Hardt and Negri 2000: 198).
- A global society based on merit comes into existence, in which global inequalities between countries, states and regions are allocated according to economically measurable 'principles of merit', in line with the maxim that every country is the architect of its own destiny. In this way, both poor states – and regions – as well as rich ones are allocated their place in the hierarchy of global society via images of the self and the other. Upwardly mobile regions such as Asia and, perhaps in the future, China provide the 'proof': those excluded from global society are – ultimately – to blame for their own exclusion.

Strategies of capital – an overview

Viewed from the perspective of global business, then, the 'ideal' state policy would possess the following features.

1   The state must be easily replaceable and be fully interchangeable: autarchic strategies;
2   it must be in competition with the greatest number of comparable states as possible: substitution strategies;
3   it must have internalized the neo-liberal world market regime: strategies that establish a monopoly on economic rationality for global business, that is, monopolization strategies;
4   it must not engage in military conquests but use its legitimatory resources for politically (democratically) sanctioning and legitimizing the decision-making autonomy and binding power of global business actors: strategies of preventive dominance.

This 'ideal image' of a state that conforms to the demands of the global market has its counterpart in the fact that state actors (as well as NGOs, and so on) are *excluded* from certain options, while other alternative decisions are *dictated* to them. In other words, meta-power limits the range of options in terms of what political alternatives remain available at all.

Thus, the meta-power of global business *excludes strategies of economic nationalism and isolationism*; these would at any rate amount to committing nation-state hara-kiri. This means, conversely, that, if nationalism and re-

Table 4.1 Global economic strategies of capital

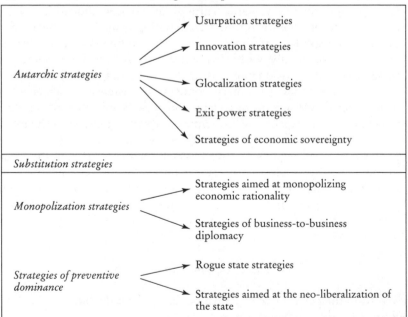

ethnicization are capable of maintaining their presence within global market competition at all, then it is only in a form in which political nationalism becomes contradictorily linked with the neo-liberal regime of cosmopolitan (*weltoffener*) markets, something with which Haider is experimenting in Austria and Berlusconi in Italy. The collapse of the Eastern bloc and East Germany, but also the opening up of North Korea, an autarchic communist state, thus symbolizes the beginning of a newly established world market regime.[4]

On the other hand, this *global economic power of exclusion* can be read off from the kind of options to which the sphere of political action is reduced, or between which it is forced to choose: *either 'proactive globalization'*, based on the formula: if you can't beat globalization, 'join' it – put it into practice – in order to share in the opportunities it offers – *or resistance* to globalization. Thus, a few countries of the South have openly attempted to circumvent the policies of international institutions, refusing in particular to bend to the demand that they actively subject themselves to a neo-liberal catalogue of norms. The World Bank and the Western funding bodies, however, are capable of countering this kind of resistance by appropriate means, and those who have spoken out in favour of this 'state resistance' against the global neo-liberal regime have, one by one, buckled and stepped back in line, without having a single solitary cent of their burden of debt to the 'international community' waived.

One can try to escape this choice between conformity and resistance by accepting and perhaps even glorifying the sole remaining option of *mass marginalization*. However, this glorification of the exclusion and marginality of entire regions of the world clearly bears the stamp of global economic meta-power. Fanto Chero, for example, argues that African marginality need not necessarily be seen as something negative. 'It could instead provide a compelling occasion to redefine African priorities away from global integration and toward self-reliance and new regionalism, to recognize informal economies, and to encourage informal politics, particularly civil society at a regional level' (Chero 2000: 123). And he cites Claude Ake: 'Perhaps marginalization, so often decried, is what Africa needs right now. For one thing, it will help the evolution of an endogenous development agenda, an agenda that expresses the aspirations of the people and can therefore elicit their support. Because of exogeneity, and its contradictions, Africa does not even at this late stage have a development agenda' (Ake 1996).

However, this exaggerated elevation of exclusion by the restrained pathos of the development of a 'decolonized imagination' bears the unmistakable stamp of global business power. Taking this train of thought as far as it will go, the obvious conclusion is that the scope for action available to states becomes squeezed between two types of conformity, eagerly proactive and reluctantly ponderous. And yet this fails to take into account the fact that the world of business and the state are in a position of mutual dependence, just as it does the fact that states for their part have ways of winning back a kind of meta-power in relation to global business.

In fact, state politics and the world of business have always been mutually intertwined. For example, globalization not only presupposes a certain political course set by states, such as the liberalization of markets. Politics itself also acquires an enhanced image and significance as a response to the expansion of market power, not only by virtue of being the only legitimate form of dealing with social conflict but also through being capable of *influencing and shaping* globalization.

The options available to states in terms of responding to global economic challenges are often blocked off theoretically. For example, in the term 'competition state', 'competition' usually refers to relations of competition between states themselves with regard to the performance bonuses offered by the global market; rarely does it refer to states' competition *with* and *against* global business actors for practical alternatives at global political level. If it is correct that individual states, in their fixation on the nation, are indeed tied into a certain field of options that has shrunk to the (phantom) alternative between conformity and resistance, then it is just as correct and important to see that a confederation of states that rediscovers and develops the cooperative power to shape political events is also capable of appropriating new ordering functions and modes of influence in relation to global business.

Thus, the notion of a 'competition state' is directed at global business's ideal image of the *neo-liberal* state. Ultimately, it is the eager, anticipatory 'market state' that is the extended arm of the global market, the continuation of world market policies by state means.

An essential distinction is lost in this, however: the need of states to prepare themselves for direct competition in the world market is falsely equated with a lack of alternatives. The possibility of a 'transnationalization' or 'globalization' of state policy is ruled out *analytically*. In those theoretical approaches bound up with the national outlook, the meta-power game is explored in a *one-sided* way, namely from the perspective of what may turn out to be the temporary historical dominance of global business actors. In contrast to this, the necessity of redefining 'the state' and 'politics' for the age of globalization remains unexplored.

For some decades now the debate about politics has been conducted on the assumption of the unchanging nature of society. At the close of the first modernity, politics seems to be defined in curiously *negative* terms: it is dominated by '*imperatives of avoidance*' (Offe), meaning that the only task remaining is that of eliminating dysfunctionality and avoiding 'system-endangering crises and risks'. According to a widespread lament, politics does not sit happily with reform and is geared not towards expanding its practical options or realizing practical goals, but solely towards solving technical issues. It is stuck in an 'administrative rut'.

Yet this picture proves to be a deceptive one if the perspective elaborated below is correct. Even neo-liberal politics is the opposite of a politics of the status quo. Neo-liberal politics pursues systemic transformation within the terms of *self-detachment from the state*, and 'grand politics' must be prepared to redistribute and defend power within society, as between the global, national and local level, for example – and find ways of doing so.

But the opponents of neo-liberalism are also feeding off a *Hercules-like concept* of politics: after all, they say, it is only a matter of such 'trivialities' as the transnational opening out and reshaping of nation-state democracy, the creation of cooperative alliances between states in order to place preventive legal constraints on global environmental and technological risks on the one hand, and on turbulent financial markets on the other. Anyone following public political debate nowadays is constantly struck by this schizophrenia: while constant laments are to be heard about the end of politics, this occurs in the guise of the very opposite, namely in the context of a grand politics which, because it is ultimately conceived as global politics, breaks apart not only the institutional framework but also the categorical framework of political thought and action.

4.2   Strategies of capital between autarchy and preventive dominance

Autarchic strategies

If we inquire after the rule-changing logic according to which global business actors act, rather than focusing on isolated moves in the game, it becomes apparent that the strategies of capital are aimed at minimizing capital's dependency on individual states and indeed on the international community of states as a whole, and that they are aimed either at persuading states to undergo their own neo-liberal transformation and/or at developing capital's own legitimatory sources of norms and conflict regulation. These kinds of *autarchic strategies* effectively terminate the alliance that had been forged in the first modernity between the market, the nation-state and democracy, the message being: if we need politics at all, then it is the neo-liberal variety. We don't need a state – we've got the market. But we'll organize the culture of freedom in a variable way. We'll pay little attention to political freedoms and give pride of place to consumer freedoms, so that the difference gets submerged amid the spectacle of being able to choose between ten or fifteen different kinds of butter or pizza.

'Autarchy' does not mean autonomy, but *radicalized* autonomy, a kind which denies or seeks to minimize the indispensability and irreplaceability of the state and of politics and is aimed at making the rationality and domination of the market self-legitimating.

Autarchic strategies thus imply the desirable possibility of the self-legitimation of global business domination. This goal would be reached if three things could be achieved:

- the merging of capital with *law*;
- the merging of capital with the *state*;
- the merging of economic *rationality* with personal *identity*.

In this sense, autarchic strategies amount to a rule-changing global experiment involving the neo-liberalization of law, the state and society in line with the maxims of classical economics. With the emotional appeal to 'economic emancipation', they are directed towards liberating business actors and enterprises from national, state and social constraints. To put it another way, the strategies of capital transform the very *concept* of capitalism and the *concept* of the state.

As is so often the case, this is an ambiguous development, for what comes to light here is a historic source of legitimation for the strategies of capital which has so far been somewhat neglected, both in the national perspective of politics, the public sphere and political science, and in the economistic self-perception of capital itself. Any answers proffered in response to the throwaway question of who is in a position to bring a civilizing and humanizing influence to the bloody madness of the national era must surely rule out one actor in particular: the nation-state itself. In fact, if neither global civil society actors, nor intellectuals, nor the public, nor migrants, nor those deprived of their rights and stripped of all human dignity, nor those excluded from society can be expected to fulfil this Herculean task, then there really is no actor in sight who might be entrusted with our historic liberation from the immaturity of national politics, for which it is itself to blame. If we conduct a thought experiment and ask how it might nonetheless be possible to make the transition towards a situation in which the egotistical violence of the nation-state is tamed by cosmopolitanism, all that remains is the figure of global politics as a side-effect. The attacks by global business and finance on the community of states – shall we call it a hostile takeover? – could, in a politics of unintended side-effects, signal the *dawning of a cosmopolitan regime*. Humanity ought more or less to stumble into this highly conflict-laden yet happy condition. An 'enlightened' global capitalism (brought about as a side-effect) would condition societies, states and political parties, in the face of the global power of refusal (non-investment), to give up the parochial attitudes of the national outlook step by tiny step. This should make it possible to 'invade' the national spheres of sovereignty, something the latter (in spite of resistance) *have to* long for, so that the *de*nationalization of thought and action can occur by way of *self*-denationalization, that is, in eager, anticipatory obedience to business interests. The way to catch mice, as we all know, is to use a little cheese – perhaps opportunities for global market success may be the way, in the long term, to 'catch' nationalistically oriented cultures, countries and states. Objectively speaking, at any rate, the strategies of capital have an inherently non-interventionist, coercive character which *might* be capable of awakening the mercantile spirit even in belligerent states, and tempting them onto the rugged path of political self-transformation into transnational cooperation states. The economic authority of anti-militaristic global market power could – when it is not aimed at abolishing politics, the state and democracy – provide the conditions for their cosmopolitan renewal.

The current era has already glimpsed, as a side-effect of its successes, at least a few gruesome fragments of its own destruction and can therefore guess the extent of its full-blown brutality. Because of this, the most it can hope for, even with the power of its trusted helper, the side-effect, is to advance towards a cosmopolitan modernity not with bold strides but more with an awkward stumble. This *possibility* that the global business strategies of capital may have an emancipatory side-effect comes about *because* the power relation between states and global market actors is an asymmetric one; that is, it comes about only as long as the influence of economic power on the nation-based thinking and acting of states is stronger than the other way around.

However, the exit option not only establishes competition between states, it also gives global business the *power of exclusion*: those who fail to fulfil the catalogue of norms required by neo-liberal reform policies, or who do so only inadequately, are threatened with being cut adrift from the lifelines of global investments and capital flows.

Conversely, however, global business usurpation strategies (of technological revolutions, state research funding, legal competencies, and so forth) – to the extent that they are successful – lead to the *self-politicization* of global business; the latter thus takes on quasi-state tasks and functions at the transnational level and, consequently, within the national arena and framework as well, using the economic pretext of 'capitalist rationality' – without being legitimized to do so. Accordingly, autarchic strategies bring about *state privatizations*. The 'autarchy' at issue here is not an economic one, but rather a *global* and, at the same time, a *sub*political one. Whereas the economic autarchy of global business is directed inwards, as it were, and is aimed at the economic rationalization of *every* sphere possible, political autarchy pursues the goal of establishing the preconditions for a global economy without states – or, to be more precise, a global economy in which the controls exercised by and between individual states are minimized, while maximum support is given to the development of global business power. The strategic objective of establishing such an economically constituted global domestic politics is served by the following autarchic strategies.

First, appropriation of the transnational arena: *usurpation strategies*.

Second, control over science and technology as the 'power of innovation' – the 'source of options'; that is, control over 'technological advantage': *innovation strategies*.

Third, independence from state controls is maximized when specialization and globalization are combined in such a way that transnational companies concentrate on a few tasks (core competencies) but fulfil them on a big scale throughout the world: *strategies of denationalization and glocalization*.

Fourth, while the power of states grows as they conquer foreign territories, the power of global business actors increases in exactly the opposite way, namely by the latter putting themselves in a position to leave a given national territory: *exit power strategies*.

Fifth, since state politics is still organized nationally, or, at best, regionally (as in the European Union), global business actors are discovering and experimenting with the right to legislate, and are themselves organizing collectively binding decisions in the transnational arena (from cartel decisions through financial controls to protection of the atmosphere): *strategies of economic sovereignty*.

Usurpation strategies

Strategic competition between private companies and expanding markets, on the one side, and the state, on the other, is not a new phenomenon. It goes back to the Middle Ages when European royalty chartered private (ad)venture capitalists, so to speak, to open up foreign countries and exploit their resources. Thus, conflict-laden cooperation between the state and business, aimed at reciprocally maximizing benefits and profits, is an early social innovation that can be traced back through the centuries and has merely found its most recent form of expression in present-day corporatist globalization.

The 'global business versus the state' relation is comparable to that of 'market versus *oikos*' (Weber 1978: 1214), that is, the liberation of market towns in thirteenth-century Europe. In both cases – the breakaway of the town market from the dominating grip of the principalities and of the global market from that of the nation-state – *homo economicus* is, as we have said, more or less forced into becoming *homo politicus*. Neither the 'market versus *oikos*' opposition nor the 'nation-state versus global business' opposition should be thought of as an economic 'struggle' between the respective political authorities and market actors. In the case of the medieval towns, Max Weber emphasizes the ambiguous and overlapping nature of interests, something which, applied here, is also true of the 'release' of global business from the location-based paradigm of the nation-state. A prime example of the way in which power has migrated away from state governments and towards corporate management (occurring as a largely non-controversial, unspectacular process) is that of the telecommunications industry being released from nation-state controls and subsequently embarking on a triumphal march through the global market (a move that is now encountering a degree of mistrust on the part of shareholders).

At the height of society's 'colonization by the state', states assumed the right to control information – sometimes openly, in the form of censorship, and sometimes through a monopoly on information media (post office, telephone, travel). This censorship on the part of states concerning what goes on in the minds of their citizens – frequently trivialized in terms of 'state sovereignty over information' – has become prone to a radical process of decline over the past two decades. The reason for this (from the state perspective) is the 'subversive' convergence of changes in information technology, market demand and government deregulation policies, which began first in the USA but soon spread to more and more states and countries. This *informational disempowerment* of states was instigated and advanced by the latter themselves, with the USA leading the way, and it was carried out under the flag of economic liberalization, with the promotion of private sector business. However, this triggered an avalanche which buried the options left open to national governments, while the range of options available to the global producers and operators of telecommunications technologies expanded in leaps and bounds.

If these companies are successful in building up monopolies or quasi-monopolies, they are, firstly, in a position to dictate to states the conditions under which the latter may access the global network – something as crucial to them as the air we breathe. Secondly, they also exercise considerable influence over the *content* of information, so that – in the long term – private sector brainwashing, in the form of advertising and shallow entertainment, comes to take the place of state censorship.

The 'autarchic strategies' employed by market towns in the Middle Ages to escape the control of the princes were at first a clever mixture of widely dispersed settlement and economic attractiveness – the carrot-and-stick method, so to speak: the masters of the town and the economy evaded the prince's stick while giving him the carrot, in other words, allowing him a share in the economic fruits of their new-found independence. Later they made their own laws (as global business is doing today) and set up their self-monitoring organizations (the police and the military), something that has no equivalent as yet in the 'emancipatory movement' in which global business is engaged in relation to states. Global business power does not have to separate itself off in territorial terms. Although it has to rely on the forces of the state to protect its property and its workers against attack if need be, it can quite happily set up its company headquarters and develop its operations at the centre of national power, in direct proximity to governments, police and the military, without thereby endangering its independence or the possibility of disengaging from the national milieu: its 'autarchy' is grounded *deterritorially* and in this respect is utterly immune to the fact its immediate neighbours are the 'masters of the nation'.

On the contrary, nurturing a neighbourly relationship with the elected 'princes of the nation' gives corporations a better opportunity to play on the devotion to business displayed by nationally oriented publics and governments, and to get them singing from the hymn sheet of economic and scientific nationalism – with such lines as 'Germany's biotechnology sector is gearing up to compete with the Americans'. All they then have to do is pocket the freely flowing billions of national funding and use them to consolidate their deterritorial inaccessibility. What politics and public alike are incapable of grasping, trapped as they are in their national parochialism, is the fact that every dollar, every yen and every euro that goes towards funding, say, the biotechnology revolution, contributes towards the *denationalization* of the economies concerned, so that taxpayers are actually financing their own disempowerment.

It is the same everywhere in the world, the same contradiction catches one's eye every time: globalization implies that nationality (particularly that of corporations) is no longer important, and that mobile corporations are owned by anonymous shareholders throughout the world. But those politicians and heads of corporations who preach and practise the maxims of globalization also appeal to the national interest whenever it comes to seeking funding for corporations that have already long been operating in the transnational arena.

There is indeed a double contradiction at work here: state funding for corporate giants not only stands in glaring contradiction to the neo-liberal understanding that globalization-friendly governments and managers have of themselves. More than this, the national reflex is even used in instances where funding for national companies and industrial sectors has long since become a fiction. National industrial policies that make use of a range of instruments (research funding, the issuing of long-term loans, tax concessions, targeted government contracts, and so on) are rather like 'phantom policies': the long since detached arm of 'national economic interests' still reaches into the tax pot to fund and feed the expansion of global business markets, that is, the autarchy of global business actors.

Siemens is a perfect example of the way the huge sums of taxpayers' money that are spent in the name of state industrial policy support a process in which companies eventually break away from the national business community by entire sectors. Siemens's company strategy, like that of any other corporation, has to be geared towards progressively loosening its connections and reducing its obligations to the country it started out in, withdrawing from national demands and expectations. The countless billions that Siemens has received from the German state over the course of the last fifty years, especially for developing nuclear technology, have hastened the company's emancipation from Germany. . . . This is happening today in every European state, so that year on year they are becoming less and less like industrial nations. England, the land that gave birth to the first Industrial Revolution, has been leading the way in this for the last twenty years. Foreign capital and foreign management are required to build the few cars and ships the country still produces. This one-time industrial nation earns its money above all in the international finance industry, with global hotel chains and real estate, and with North Sea oil. And when the French cockerel crows on its perch above the country's profitable industrial sector, it does so in spite of the fact that large parts of the latter are owned by foreign capital. We saw what this means . . . when the takeover battles between the large French banks took place – and likewise in Germany, where Mannesmann lost its independence and its control over the company's destiny because foreign owners had other ideas. And when governments in either country cautiously get involved, it is to no avail and merely serves to demonstrate that they have become too weak to implement any kind of industrial policy. (Koch 2000)

Yet it is not only national industrial policy that becomes phantom-like. Something similar also occurs with such emotive and conflict-laden terms as 'economic nationalism', 'neo-colonialism' and 'imperialism'. In many countries on the periphery, globalization continues to be equated with a new kind of Western or American imperialism. But who or what is 'imperialistic', if the 'mega-profits' from a corporation with operations in Venezuela subsequently go to 'investors' based in Japan, South Africa, Brazil or even, possibly in the not too distant future, China?

Another (hypothetical) case: a transnational corporation is nominally 'localized' in Liechtenstein or in Malaysia, and its shares are constantly changing hands between a hundred thousand different shareholders from a dozen countries, traded on the share markets in Bombay and Sydney, Paris and Hong Kong – who is the 'neo-imperialist' in this case? What if institutionalized investors are themselves transnational, if managers from every region and culture in the world are working right alongside one another? Which country, which nation is then the 'capitalist aggressor'?

In other words, in the deterritorialized, denationalized economy, nation-based friend-or-foe models are no longer relevant, although it certainly doesn't stop these stereotypes from being used.

The gradual detachment of global business market expansion from the national stereotypes of the logic of conquest is a lengthy process; moreover, it is one which, in the non-simultaneity of the simultaneous, that is, in the competition between national and transnational business, encounters a great deal of resistance. Nonetheless, it involves the intersection of two developments. First, national accountability becomes less important as national economies and corporations become globalized. And second, corporations are less reliant on the basic elements of territorial exploitation – raw materials and natural resources – because they are offering highly technologized industrial products and services and selling them throughout the world.

Incidentally, the image of transnational companies has also changed in the magnetic field created by the growth of global business power. While they are still considered to be the 'cause' of national impoverishment in many countries, opinions are becoming increasingly divided, so that what some condemn, others long for. This change in role from imperialist bogeyman to bringer of fortune comes most clearly to the fore where competition for scarce capital investment is intense and the extent to which individual countries depend on it is growing at the same time. What is striking about this is that territorial (and therefore military) size is not especially relevant in the competitive struggle for scarce capital investment. Even small territories such as Hong Kong, Malaysia and South Korea have transformed themselves from economic dwarfs into economic giants on the basis of their internalized capitalist dynamic. The key factor in this seems to be how effectively countries can *attract* foreign capital and hold on to it in the long term.

A fascinating issue arises in view of the parallels and differences between the town economy of the Middle Ages and the global economy at the start of the twenty-first century. In endeavouring to achieve political autonomy, the towns aroused the suspicion of the princes and kings, which eventually led to the decline of the towns. Perhaps one day people will speak in retrospect of the 'brief interlude of global business' at the start of the twenty-first century, when the business world's struggle for political autonomy provided grounds for making the leap from nation-states to cosmopolitan states, which in turn made global business subject to new restrictions.

Innovation strategies

However, the power of global business is not only a deterritorial power that thereby eludes the controls of territorially bound state power; it is also able to acquire 'wings' by having *systematic access to the institutional and cognitive conditions and possibilities for producing new things*, and that means, above all, *access to the productive and innovatory power of science*.

So far, we have managed to assemble quite a few answers to the question of what constitutes the key characteristic of global business actors' meta-power, and, of these, the following one is essential: it is the combination of self-globalizing capital coupled with self-globalizing science and technology that gives global business a head start against states in the race for practical options.

Technological innovation has always been a crucial strategy deployed by capital in relation to markets and power. The reasons for its current significance lie, on the one hand, in the historically new quality of technological options (e.g. in genetics, human genetics and nanotechnology, and so forth) and, on the other, in the way science and technology, given the availability of the exit option, can be put to use translegally and transnationally, while the problematic consequences and legitimatory difficulties associated with them can be unloaded onto the countries in question.

There is no longer any doubt about the fact that the range of practical options developed by the sciences since the second half of the twentieth century has acquired a new, 'anthropological quality'. This is especially true, for example, with regard to nuclear fission and the nuclear weapons to which it gives rise, to the peaceful use of nuclear energy, as well as in relation to debates over the ethical and 'post-human' consequences of genetic technology. In the debate about technology at the start of the twenty-first century, there is a considerable degree of consensus among the experts and publics involved that modernity is already a *technologically constituted* world, and one that will become even more so in the future.

In other words, the triumph of modernity is linked to a double movement. As traditional securities and frameworks for everyday life start to unravel, this is accompanied by increasingly dense technological and global integration, and by new ways of organizing the conditions in which people live. Even if we don't know much else about the potential 'cosmopolitan regime' of the future, these two characteristics are apparent even today: it will be *oriented towards the global market* and it will be constituted *technologically*. *Both* aspects lie outside the scope of state control and are located within the power sphere of global business and scientific actors.

The construction of technological worlds also opens up the prospect of a 'post-human world', in which human values have been relativized and replaced by more powerful, artificial 'cyborgs' that not only carry out certain tasks and interact independently of humans, but also drive forward developments towards a post-human civilization.

These developments are in every respect ambiguous. They may not only further disempower states, they may empower them in new ways, as in when they set up electronic systems of control and surveillance in every last corner of technologically constituted worlds (of which the 'electronic eyes' currently being tested at trouble hotspots in large cities are but a feeble omen). It is also conceivable that these technologically constituted worlds may give rise to a completely new concept of democracy that is at once global and direct, presenting counter-power movements and civil society with new opportunities for expanding their role. What is emerging, then, is a technologically defined space of possibilities that is ambiguous in itself, but whose diversity is dramatically restricted by virtue of being occupied by global business. Realistically, then, we can expect neither that global business profit interests will coincide with an extension of 'cultural citizenship rights' (Featherstone 2000), nor that the flip side of technological innovation – its unforeseeable dangers – will be taken seriously or be seen as an occasion for global regulations, perhaps even a modernization of taboos. Conversely, it seems reasonable to suspect that our inability even to imagine the consequences of a 'post-human' civilization is being used as an excuse, indeed a justification, for doing nothing. The chaos of technological development ultimately stands and falls with the new neo-liberal rhetoric of deregulation: leave it to free market forces, they'll sort it all out!

Bill Joy, a leading computer scientist *and* someone who warns of the dangers of computer science, was asked: do you think that in our fragmented, greedy world it would still be possible to generate a collective will to act and, with it, a historically aware scientific sphere that sets limits on its own activities? His response was: 'If we don't come to a collective understanding, then clearly we face the threat of being wiped out.' It is no longer the individual or the politician or the government or some other person who has too much power.

The science of technology gives power to the imagination and therefore to each individual person. That is why the balance between the individual and the collective must be brought back to a collective mechanism. This is the only way of banishing danger for the individual. The fact is, we live in a civilized society, which means that we will go without something in order to get something else that promises us security and certain benefits. But society can't protect us from other people because the new technology has acquired a superior degree of power, and the fundamental compromise from the eighteenth century has lost its validity. I realize that is a bold statement. But science now has to create the basis for a new social contract.

Some areas, including certain aspects of nanotechnology, are so dangerous that we would be better off leaving them well alone. The question is, how do we best set about doing that . . . I don't see any realistic possibility of putting a stop to all economic activity in these critical areas. But we have to limit the free availability of the knowledge gained from them. The best compromise would be secure laboratories under international control. (Joy 2000: 53)

As Mike Featherstone stresses, it is certainly important not to allow the future of technologically constituted civilization to end up being an either/or vision between nightmare and salvation. Also, we must get rid of the notion that society and technology, or society and nature, exist in opposition to one another and that the one 'colonizes' the other. A whole range of social scientific studies have clearly demonstrated that technologies as such contain cultural codes and behave as 'actants' (Latour 2001), that is, as quasi-subjects. In this respect, technologies incorporate cultural norms and power relations. This can be seen not least in the fact that the Internet is an *American* invention and that American cultural values – such as equal access for all – have been realized in the technological aspects of its social architecture. In contrast to this, a French version of the Internet that did not come into circulation provided for an internal hierarchy and many different ways of separating domains off from one another.

Typically, however, what does and does not turn into a political issue is historically variable in itself. This requires a little closer elucidation. The sixty-four thousand dollar question is this: who legitimizes *decisions* about technological development, and who legitimizes the *consequences*? In other words, it is important to distinguish between the 'legitimation of decisions' and '(non-)legitimation of consequences'. It is at the join between the two that the contradictions and limits of the power strategies associated with global business and global science become apparent.

Let us look first at the legitimation of decisions. According to the fairy-tale version of democracy, this takes place in the arenas of the public sphere and of politics, specifically in parliament and government. However, the exit option open to global business plays a crucial role here: the public spheres and national parliaments of different states can be played off against one another and in this way ultimately be forced into anticipatory assent.

If, on the other hand, we distinguish between 'state' and 'non-state' legitimation of technological developments, then it becomes clear that individual states are continuously losing legitimatory power in the face of the exit option held by global business actors. Corporations are usually able to circumvent nation-state norms and regulations (for example, the German Embryo Protection Act) by going to states where there are fewer or no restrictions regarding the application of a technology. It thus becomes possible to stage the spectacle not only of economic competition but also of ethical competition between states, the upshot of which is the emergence of 'low ethics countries' (in a kind of 'moral dumping'). The mere threat of this, along with the anticipation of this threat within society, undermines the public spheres of individual states.

Thus, ethical debates in national public spheres – to the extent that they are conducted at all – take place in a peculiar atmosphere of unreality, since it is not clear whether or to what extent the possibilities for decision-making being publicly argued over still exist within the national arena at all, or whether they have long since migrated elsewhere. Using the power of the 'exit option', however, the 'ideal nation-state' – that is, the sum of individual states' consent – can only ever be obtained by devious means or by coercion as a *post hoc* legitimation. The collective binding power of transnational decisions is based not least – this much becomes clear once again – on the *'translegitimacy'* of global business innovation.

As a result of this, the practical options left open to individual states are ultimately reduced to two ways of legitimating what is happening in any case: they can either appeal to and renew people's faith in progress, or else they can put forward the argument based on *pre-emptive globalization*, which sweeps aside all concerns by saying, in effect: since globalization rules out the possibility of nations going it alone, we (unfortunately) have to insist on an accelerated timescale for implementation of problematic technologies, as it is in our own economic interests to do so.

State politics is thus brought into play as a resource for legitimizing globally binding decisions over which it has little to no influence in the high-speed system of global market-oriented modernization. Instead of trying to put the brakes on the dangerous pace of development of new risk technologies, instead of sharpening people's awareness of the dangers and problematic consequences they entail, and instead of massively supporting the search for alternative technologies and giving society a larger role in political decision-making about technology, the political approach to the dangers and risks of new technologies falls victim to international competitiveness and the hope that new jobs may be in prospect. In this respect, state politics – by conforming to neo-liberal global market priorities – is stepping on the accelerator rather than on the brake with respect to the implementation of high-risk technologies. This eventually rebounds on politicians at the point where predictably unpredictable consequences and dangers become the focus of public concern and thereby the source of economic and political turmoil.

Glocalization strategies

As the economy becomes global, something paradoxical and ironic occurs, namely, the planned economy returns to the new global corporate decision-making centres of power. It is only a slight exaggeration to say that, while the planned economy has died out in the communist East, it has been resurrected in the midst of the global market economy – in the form of centrally planned, global corporations that set up a worldwide network consisting of a centre, strategic bases and subsidiaries, and holdings and partnerships. This is organized more or less hierarchically, with the power concentrated at the centre, its integrating influence spread to the farthest flung outposts of local production using sophisticated information technology and command structures. The largest among them – the Daimler-Chryslers, Wal-Marts and Sonys – produce and move goods at a value of 50, 100, 150 billion US dollars every year, more than the gross domestic product of a medium-sized nation-state such as Denmark.

The current wave of mergers has already led to a situation in which the elite among these global corporations have put a considerable distance between themselves and the rest of the field: only a handful of corporations now dominate the global markets for oil, minerals and agricultural products, and about 100 companies the industrial and service sectors. These few companies make all the decisions about the norms that are to apply in the global economic society, they decide what is good and evil, right and wrong, who are the 'overdogs' and who the 'underdogs' in the new 'community of states' – they constitute the *'global capitalist planned economy'*.

A particular pattern emerges here in terms of how companies are structured, namely the *'glocalization'* of company policy. The idea is not so much to merge as many different business sectors as possible – whether nationally or internationally – into a single company, as in tying together the automobile industry with the insurance sector and high-tech companies. Instead, the aim – according to current management theory – is to make a few key areas of expertise the core element of a particular specialization at global level, and possibly to form a monopoly out of them – in other words, to set up these areas of expertise (product manufacture, services) on a large scale and offer them for sale throughout the world. This compromise, or hybrid, between globalization and production specialization is intended as a way of increasing corporations' independence from the incentives provided by nation-states, while simultaneously preventing them from turning into lumbering giants.

Moreover, this organizational strategy of glocalization enables corporations to maximize profit margins by minimizing the prices for individual products or services. Glocalization possesses a strategically significant polyvalency, making several things possible at the same time: corporations can play the game everywhere in the world and thereby consolidate their power in relation to nation-states; at the same time, they are able to make the process of production cheaper and raise global profit margins by exploiting transnational opportunities for rationalization. In this process, however, global company strategy soon comes up against internal limitations and contradictions, as it seeks to keep a globally spun network on the go in commando style: this hierarchical strategy of globalization is not only too expensive, it also disregards the significance of the new cultural and political autonomy of location. Accordingly, the current fashion among corporate strategists is something that has come to be packaged in such strange terms as 'multi-local multi-national', 'global local' or 'glocalization'. Regional managers are required to deal with as many tasks as possible in their own location and to familiarize themselves with the local market and competition, while nonetheless drawing on the resources of the corporation with its worldwide network. This might mean, for example, manufacturing particular products in large quantities at lower prices at one single location in the world only. But what these glocalization strategies provide companies with, above all, is a *cosmopolitan experiential context*: they can now learn globally from local experience. For example, if something proves a success on the Indian market, the aim is to replicate that success in Brazil or New York. In addition, the top corporations also gather all the latest knowledge about rationalization that they can in order to benefit their own business specialization; this involves spying on universities, institutes and competitors in order to obtain the optimum knowledge and to put every new development into practice almost before it has even seen the light of day.

The new information technology facilitates these glocalized corporate strategies as well. Not only is it possible to keep in close contact with colleagues (via video conferencing, e-mail and so on); whenever necessary, head office can also assess which product in which supermarket in which town in the world is selling best and which internal and external circumstances are the reason for it. This can also be done by examining chains of production through to suppliers – who in formal terms are independent – for any additional opportunities for rationalization. This in turn makes it possible to resolve one contradiction, or at least to incorporate it productively: namely, to produce goods, coordinate operations and monitor processes in a decentralized way, that is, both locally and centrally – in other words, globally.

Exit power strategies

The power of the market town was very limited. The existence of the market was generally based on a concession on the part of the landlord or prince and on his willingness to provide protection.

On the one hand these political masters are interested in a regular supply of foreign articles and craft products on the long-distance market, and in the tolls, the escort moneys and the other protection fees, the market taxes and the fees from law suits which the fairs give rise to. On the other hand, they might also hope to profit from the local settlement of taxable tradesmen and merchants and, once a settlement rises around the market, from the ground rents which this produces. (Weber 1978: 1214)

In this respect the ruling interests of the prince and the interests of the town regarding economic autonomy did indeed coincide. Economic development served the purposes of both, making the town economy autonomous and increasing the power of the prince. However, this clearly had its limits, since 'more decisive was the inability of the city to bring military-political means of power into the service of its interests, such as the patrimonial-bureaucratic prince could apply' (ibid.: 1330). The situation is a very different one when it comes to the competitive struggle for domination between the nation-state and global business. Here, the domination of global business is, by its very nature, completely and utterly *a*military by nature. So what is it that constitutes the much trumpeted domination of global business actors? How do they manage to outdo the nation-state? How does the state become privatized? What kind of 'power' and 'domination' is emerging here? In order to answer these questions, it is necessary to clarify the distinction between state power and transnational economic power in relation to the distinction between territorial and deterritorialized domination. State power acquires its dominant position and keeps it stable by controlling a territory along with its population and resources. Global business, on the other hand, does just the opposite: it acquires its power by becoming *independent of place*, thereby maximizing ex-territorial domination and bringing it to bear against territorialized state power.

As a result of the revolution in telecommunications technology, transport routes are becoming detached from territory. It is not (necessarily) that nation-state boundaries have become more permeable, but rather that the *concept of space is being revolutionized*. From this point on, it is not domination over a given territory that is important, but rather access to the network. Trading via the electronic network is certainly not a power-forming process in itself, but it certainly is when it becomes a counterweight to the territorialized power of state and labour, and when it is combined with capital's power resources. Trading on the net kills distances and facilitates a new kind of routeless, feather-light mobility, an ability to be in two places at one time.

The traditional (nation-state) concept of domination is essentially a territorially based one. As in the case of social relations in general, so too the concept of domination (as famously formulated by Max Weber, for example) presupposes spatial-physical proximity. As Timothy Luke puts it, organic metaphors are often used in order to illustrate traditional ways of viewing certain actions: conflicts are dealt with 'eye-ball to eye-ball'; disputes are verbal 'fisticuffs'; justice is done on the principle of 'an eye for an eye, a tooth for a tooth'. We show solidarity with someone by standing 'shoulder to shoulder' with them; community is based on 'face to face' encounters; friendships are conducted 'arm in arm'; change takes place 'step by step'. In the end, domination is also based on the use of physical violence, is organized through a 'ruling class', presupposes 'membership', ruling 'desires', 'means of coercion', 'obedience', and so on – that is, a territorial understanding of the social which is rendered irrelevant in digital space. The concept of space that emerges here is one in which the fixity of place is no longer given or allocated, not in the sense that production and communication can now take place in a completely delocalized way, but that social relations can be built up multilocally and can thus transcend borders and boundaries. While such direct mobility is despatialized and makes distance irrelevant, it does presuppose communication in zero time; in other words, contacts between different locations in the world are established in the immediate present. As a result, a social space is formed in the digital 'now' in which contacts and ways of influencing events become possible and real and whose success is no longer tied to the natural obstacles of geographical distance. The distinction between here and there loses its constitutive meaning in the construction of social relationships. This is also true of relations of domination, in particular those that emerge in the relationship between the nation-state and global business.

The power of business is grounded above all in being able either to set up or to cut off the lifelines of national politics and society – jobs and taxes – by means of its investments (protected by the institutionalized freedom these enjoy). The weakness of state power is grounded in something that constitutes the state's strength, namely being tied to a specific territory. As long as they act nationally, that is, as isolated, sovereign territorial states, nation-states can do little to counter the process of being played off against one another in the basic survival issues of taxes and jobs.

The crucial point is this, however: whereas the power of states grows when foreign territory is conquered (in accordance with the national calculation), the power of global business actors, by contrast, increases when they make themselves capable of *leaving* their 'own' national territory. This in turn can be achieved only to the extent that transnational companies become *exterritorial* entities. State power, then, is not undermined, overwhelmed or broken by state power – in the form of military threats or conquest – but rather deterritorially, exterritorially, by the feather-lightness of transnational trade and activities in digital space. This delocalized concept of domination turns the logic of the traditional understanding of power, violence and domination on its head.

The deterritorialized power of business has no legitimatory sources *of its own*. It therefore remains reliant, at the very point where global business actors intervene in national contexts, on *hidden* second-hand legitimation, namely on the silent *post hoc* legitimation of decisions made by political-democratic authorities.

Deliberate non-conquest, deliberate non-investment – in this formula lies the answer to the question of where deterritorialized business acquires the power to enforce its own will, while democratic reform policies – by way of a comparison – so easily and visibly fail along their veto-strewn obstacle course. The negative character of non-intervention makes several things possible at the same time, including the politics of non-politics: this is where something is not done – indeed, nothing is being done – that requires or is even capable of winning political legitimation. At the same time, the important boundaries between the *real exercise of power* and the *potential* threat of power are levelled out, as both threat and execution coincide in the act of doing nothing. Threatening to do something, but doing nothing oneself, forces others to take action. At the same time, there are no obstacles hindering the implementation of exterritorialized investment decisions, since they acquire the collective binding power of their decisions in what is the most effective way conceivable: through a *politics of faits accomplis*.

As a consequence of this, states are increasingly subject to external control by exterritorialized financial elites whose location in the world of electronic networks can no longer be determined at all. Their interest in a country that is no longer bound by its national origins can blossom just as quickly as it can fade.

This is where a crucial paradigm change becomes manifest, from the national to the transnational – or internally globalized – mode of production. The 'global market' is not something that is 'out there'; rather, it migrates, so to speak, into the centres of production and labour organization. A change takes place from production geared essentially towards a local or national market to production geared towards a global market (or at least several national markets). The crucial point is not that individual companies turn into transnational corporations, but that markets and modes of production become transnationalized. The *internal* globalization of production and the way it is geared towards the larger global markets has transformed countless national and local companies into 'transnational corporations'. In this situation there is little left of the territorial basis, and therefore the national basis, of the authority of business.

This new form of internal globalization of production (within and between nation-states) can be depicted using the example of teleworking in shifts. This form of work involves a division of labour that takes place between company branches in different time zones and is mediated via computer networks. For example, whatever outcomes have emerged at the end of the working day in a European workplace will be taken over by the US organization and, once they have finished work, passed on to a division in Asia. When workers in Europe begin their new day, 'their' project has progressed by way of two transnationally organized normal working days – without any shift work having to be introduced at all. This kind of company-wise transcontinental division of labour may not be suitable for every product and may raise a host of coordination problems, but it is nonetheless clear nowadays that those companies that 'never sleep' are better placed in terms of rationalization compared with fixed location forms of production, work and cooperation common in industrial society in the first modernity.

Assuming the existence of free trade and fair competition, less developed countries have the opportunity of choosing a short-cut along the path of catch-up development. This has been demonstrated not only by the 'little tigers' of South-East Asia, which have long been seen as an example of such development. Other regions, too, in Latin America and China especially, are now registering an increase in the average annual rate of growth of their gross domestic product: from 4.5 per cent over the period 1977 to 1986 to 5.5 per cent from 1987 to 1996 for all developing countries as a whole, and from 6.7 per cent to 7.7 per cent for Asia.

The fact that these figures in particular reflect the rise of those countries that have opened themselves up to world trade, capital imports and integration into the 'global factory' (Gereffi 1989) proves that low or 'falling standards of living are not the consequence of increasing global economic integration, but are indeed a sign of insufficient world market integration' (Pries 1997: 7). The disastrous economic situation in some African countries as well as the financial crisis in South East Asia point to the importance of being adequately equipped in institutional terms for sound future development. (Wiesenthal 1999: 512)

What needs to be borne in mind, however, is that the transnationalization of production does not occur on the basis of a freely made political decision on the part of corporations, but is based on the need to prove their competitive credentials on the world market. Corporations can only increase their turnover if they expand their share of the world market. This in turn presupposes the liberalization not only of commodity exchange but also of the circulation of capital, in other words, the opportunity to invest, produce and lend money wherever the most favourable conditions exist. In the competition between corporations, those with an advantage are the ones that face the fewest controls and constraints on their mobility by nation-state interference. Thus, the disempowerment of states is not a direct objective; rather, it is the *competitive imperative of the global market* that accelerates economic liberalization and thereby intensifies the contradiction between the interests of capital and the interests of nation-states.

The political arena (meaning that of nation-states) and the economic arena (that of global business actors) no longer coincide. And, when global business is set free from 'economic nationalism' (Reich), this leads inexorably to both the disempowerment of nation-states and the self-empowerment of global business actors.

Strategies of economic sovereignty

In accordance with the axioms of political science, a clear division of responsibilities exists between the state and private business. *Only* the state has military-political means of violence and a monopoly on enforcing law and order, *only* the government operates foreign policy, domestic policy, education policy, and so forth. Autarchic strategies are directed at untying this bundle of state responsibilities and privatizing the functions of state in line with global business priorities. Such *strategies of state privatization*, the transfer of state functions to (the control of) global business – that is, questions regarding global economic 'foreign policy', 'domestic policy', 'technology policy', 'legal policy', 'democracy policy', and so on – constitute a violation of the political science credo.

This privatization of state functions can be illustrated by the following comparison. The communists had assumed that the state is all-conquering and that in it a 'dictatorship of the proletariat' must prevail. Strategies of state privatization are aimed in the opposite direction: global business 'usurps' state functions, not only making itself dependent on the state in the process, but quietly transforming itself – to overstate the issue somewhat – into a kind of '*global private state dictatorship*'.

Fundamentally, it is not at all a matter of conquering states but rather of conquering the *transnational arena*. It is not the relativization of state power but rather its *absence* altogether that gives global business actors the right to be the first to legislate. The other aspect of the power of capital consists in *global statelessness*, which includes the lack of any centralized monopoly on the means of violence as well as the absence of any centralized monopoly on the rule of law. The democratic, constitutional nation-state achieved the civilizational feat of taming political violence and economic power by legal means, a feat that is historically open to reappraisal now that business has started on its way into the transnational arena. Whereas the national arena, with its emphasis on specific locations, bears the imprint of the state throughout, the transnational arena, with its emphasis on flows, is not only stateless but is almost inaccessible to individual territorial states. Thus, global business has broken out of the two-dimensional arena of state control and has begun to enter a three-dimensional arena of anarchy.

Global business actors justify their actions on the basis of the right to be first to legislate in the legally sparse, indeed empty, arena of the transnational. However, since this right to legislate is a *state* privilege and right, global business actors are in fact combining elements from the opposing spheres of the public and of private action; the form this action takes brings together those things that have until now been mutually exclusive: business and the state, economics and politics. These turn into private, transnational *'quasi-states'* *without* democratic or political legitimation (examples in Günther and Randeria 2002). One might describe the mode of legitimation being made use of here as the *authoritarianism of efficiency*. This is a sub-form of self-legitimation – based not on an acceptance of the self-evidence of reason (as used in the justification of human rights), but on expert rationality and the self-determination of the 'rich guilds' of global business. This authoritarianism based on efficiency is dangerously related to the efficiency of authoritarian regimes (such as in China), which draw their legitimation from economic growth while simultaneously suppressing basic democratic rights.

Thus, *efficiency and power* overlap with one another in the emerging architecture of norms and institutions of transnational capitalism, in order to force through the norm-creating and norm-setting violence of the private transnational state, which becomes the ordering force of anarchic global politics.

Efficiency-type explanations suggest that private authority may be effective at reducing transaction costs relative to atomistic arm's-length markets where no such authority exists, and relative to public authority based in states and interstate institutions. For instance, in atomistic markets the emergence of private authority can allow firms to better cope with strategic interdependence by enhancing commitments to joint activities or by providing sanctioned behavioral prescriptions around which coordination can occur. Private authority can mobilize firms to jointly press for public policy changes that would be unobtainable for firms acting individually. Private authority can establish, monitor, and even enforce performance standards that may enhance the confidence of an industry's customers. These efficiency advantages of private authority can bring its production about either by firms recognizing these advantages and acting to construct or comply with authority, or by a competitive process whereby interactions subject to authority displace those that are not. (Cutler et al. 1999: 352)

These declarations of efficiency by no means exclude a declaration of power, however. Firms and global economic actors can merge to become transnational government cooperatives – *guilds of the global age*, as it were – precisely in order to secure market power for the future that was an outcome from the past, and thereby establishing and reproducing their power in the transnational arena as well. However, this accumulation of power does have a *dark side* to it: private authority relativizes, or replaces, publicly legitimized authority, not only because the former is more effective than the latter, but also because this is the way powerful business actors find the means to legitimize their particularistic interests *without* facing any demands for accountability, *without* having to assume responsibility towards the public and *without* obtaining democratic consent – that is, *without* the legitimatory obstacle course characteristic of authority derived from the constitutional state.

These are early forms of an '*economic sovereignty*' that needs to be understood as a mirror image of state sovereignty, by all means in the sense of a new, *non*-public organizational form of private, law-making violence that stands above sovereign states without itself possessing state sovereignty. This *supranational governance of business* constitutes a special kind of political connection and exists, initially, on the basis of the 'legitimatory flow' that it draws from the sources of its private authority. To speak of 'economic sovereignty' is justified inasmuch as the transnational, quasi-state foundations of global politics are being shaped by the sovereignty of private business, according to the principles of economic rationality.

At the same time, these institutions of non-state law also operate within and between nation-state regulations and courts of law, and in this respect make decisions within the *national context* that are binding for the same. These regulating authorities have emerged out of lawyers' organizations, which have developed a new category of 'private courts' – transnational arbitration organizations dealing with global business conflicts – through a specific set of 'private laws', the so-called *lex mercatoria*.

It is crucial to understand that meta-power not only decouples the arena of territorial power from the arena of power of transnational mobility, it also *connects* these two arenas of power in a specific way. The transnational arena of power is best understood as a virtual space that opens up strategic options and opportunities particularly within the *national* arena. In this respect the distinction introduced above between *internationality* and *transnationality* is essential, as it emphasizes the fact that, in the international state system, the borders between states are constitutive, while in the transnational space of options nation-state borders are eliminated, undermined, redrawn and mixed up. Transnationality focuses on the processes by which borders, the pluralization of borders and allocations of responsibility are juggled politically in an unbounded space. Whereas in the international state system the spheres of national and international power conflicts are clearly demarcated from one another, in the meta-power conflict national and transnational theatres and practical options become intertwined. Although this collision and intertwining of spaces and strategies of power cannot be unravelled or deciphered in a few words, nonetheless it is remarkable that the transnational power sphere intervenes in *many* – one is tempted to say in *all* –

nation-state territorial arenas of power. This is, after all, what makes it possible in the first place to establish a neo-liberal regime with claims to global
validity.[5]

In the face of this potential trend, an old enemy image has cropped up
once again: the new 'traitors of the fatherland' are the multinational companies. They spread their tentacles right across the world, so it is said, like a
giant octopus. A broad political coalition of anti-globalization activists,
ranging from the extreme right wing to the extreme left wing and encompassing such heterogeneous groups and initiatives as the globalized women's
and environmental movement, left-wing and right-wing protectionism, globalization's losers, the governments of the periphery, neo-nationalist groupings, and so forth, has come together, united in their common concerns about
globalization. The pages of the daily newspapers are regularly filled with
questions such as: don't large corporations that grow larger by the day decide
long in advance which goods will be produced in the world and who can
afford to buy them? Don't they decide which technologies will become a
reality and which will be rejected, which poisons will be universalized by
entering the food chain and the environment, who owns the rights to human
genetic material, what is taught at schools and universities, which aspects of
science are to be promoted and which neglected, and which forms of development are to be pursued in the so-called Third World? In other words,
hasn't the question of how we want to live long since migrated away from
the arena of politics and the public sphere? Aren't all the decisions taken in
a space that is devoid of politics and closed off to the public, one that has
become global business actors' 'natural' arena for action?

While this question is certainly justified, it fails to recognize one crucial
point: it is precisely *because* – and only as long as – the nation-state remains
tied to a specific territory that *global business quasi-states* come into being
which, on a private sector basis, take on and organize certain necessary
regulatory functions at both transnational and national level in the global
business arena. What I mean by these *state privatization* strategies is not only
a politics that dismantles trade barriers and obstacles to investment in the
national context, but also the opportunity – available historically for the first
time and likewise exploited by the corporations and their federations for the
first time – to create legal, regulatory structures that bring order to large,
regional markets and can potentially be implemented on the global market
as well.

In the classic sense of autarchy, then, the issue is one of economic management and of the prerequisites for and problematic outcomes of globalized economic management decisions. These are forms of a specifically
'self-reflexive' economics, one which is in the process of reorganizing its
state political foundations, institutional environment and problematic consequences in private business sovereignty, in accordance with the principles
of economic rationality.[6]

There is a general tendency that comes to light in this: self-globalizing private enterprise necessitates the creation of regulatory institutions and generates problematic outcomes, both of which need to be regulated in a binding way at global level – from decisions made by cartels, through controls placed on financial markets, to protecting human working environments and the atmosphere. These preconditions for and outcomes of global business activity and decision-making can only be brought under control by globally valid regulations. Yet it is precisely on this point that the territorially limited organizational and legitimatory forms of nation-state politics that have existed to date are failing. The resultant vacuum is filled by a variety of non-state actors who bring their peculiar brand of (non-)politics to bear, a politics that establishes certain foundations. These include non-governmental organizations on the one hand and, especially, global business actors and their lobby on the other. In the grey area between politics and business, political Potemkin villages are being built under the catchword of 'self-regulation': to the outside world, governments often retain responsibility while in fact it is a corporative technocracy which – simply by virtue of being ahead of the game in terms of expertise and information – prepares the ground for and dictates decisions, thereby advancing the politics of state privatization by hidden means. Corporations and their experts are just as much involved in organizing the international financial market as they are in setting voluntary standards for environmental protection. They send their representatives to sit on national and international committees of experts whenever treaties regarding the protection of the ozone layer are to be signed, or whenever investment agreements or the rules of the World Trade Organization are being discussed. Global business actors and their federations put their long years of experience and powerful resources to work in this power game – putting them way ahead of the Greenpeacers and trade unionists of this world, who struggle bitterly to exert an influence. At the same time, they are aided in this by something one might call politicians' (and politics') *loyalty to business*. Aware of the existing neo-liberal hegemony, the majority of politicians in different countries are already predisposed to follow the lead of the transnationals, working on an antiquated assumption that the global economy has lately rendered invalid: anything that is good for business is also good for jobs and therefore good for the country.

This embryonic, supranational private state is spreading further and further into the newly emerging transnational *and* national arenas through the self-organizing efforts of global business actors and following the model of government politicians' sanctioned commitment to neo-liberal ideology. This represents the first ever manifestation of a (quasi-)*state without territory*, whose power impacts upon existing territorial states from the outside, but which also creates a new political space beyond their borders. This is an utterly *un*political state, a state *without* a public sphere, indeed a quasi-state without a society, located in a 'non-place', pursuing 'non-policies' which it uses to restrict the power of national societies and to break them up from the inside.

There are limits, of course, to these state privatization strategies, as there are to all the other strategies. For example, transnational corporations have no means to exercise – and still less a monopoly on – a legitimate use of violence. This remains the prerogative of the state. Neither are they in a position democratically to legitimate the decisions they make that impact upon the centre of nation-state politics. Consequently, the lack of legitimation of global business actors' autarchic strategies is highly susceptible to setbacks and to the collapse of market power, in contrast to state policies. Global business actors are highly effective, by comparison with nation-states, at making collective decisions and establishing them as binding, both within and outside national contexts, but this effectiveness is bought with the absence of public involvement or debate. This means that the flip side to the power of *faits accomplis* available to global business is an inability to justify themselves to a vigilant consumer public. This results in a *chronic crisis of legitimation* that may be activated by two opportunities, or counter-strategies. First, the legitimatory vacuum in which global business actors operate may be revealed by perceptions of risk represented via the mass media (terrorism, technology, climate change), different kinds of consumer boycotts or worldwide consumer movements, and may lead to the highly painful collapse of the respective companies' global markets. In very general terms, this is a starting point for social movements for whom the question 'how do we want to live?' is at the heart of politics and yet is sidelined or not addressed at all by the state and by global business. This field of ethics and values has been vacated by state politics and global business alike, and is being appropriated instead by the new 'moral entrepreneurs' of social movements who claim that they have an answer to human beings' profound need to anchor their lives in specific, meaningful communities.

Second, the upturn in the global economy is linked with one significant consequence: the national context is disintegrating *without* any global context or cohesive system being within reach to provide a guide to action. As economic globalization advances, the incidence of social and political *conflicts* and *crises* increases. This development may be driven forwards to a point where *social* upheavals are imminent or actually occur in various parts of the world – as was the case in the South-East Asia crisis of 1998–9, as is in danger of occurring in Russia and Latin America, and as has long since become everyday reality in sub-Saharan Africa. It is when this boiling point has been reached that the quietly dominant economistic hubris of 'managing' economic globalization by economic means *alone* is exposed.

This means, conversely and paradoxically, that state power *can be revitalized* by the experience of *political crisis*. At the point of political crisis, if not before, something becomes clear that has actually been clear all along to those with the ability to see it: global business, just like the market in general, presupposes the existence of politics and the state for the purpose of creating a regulatory framework that also applies, among others, to business and the economy; in addition, though, as an endemic source of conflict itself, global business requires the legitimatory force of a democratically organized transnational renewal of politics, so that the disparities and anomic circumstances to which it gives rise can be regulated in legitimate fashion.

Global business actors' efforts to achieve autarchy in relation to the state and politics are fundamentally limited for at least two reasons. First, global business actors have no resources that would enable them to legitimize their own actions politically and democratically. Neither is it foreseeable how any conceivable course of events might ever make this kind of autarchy achievable. On the contrary, as global business internalizes state functions, it is simultaneously burdened with the political task of dealing with and shaping global business in a deterritorialized way *without* being in any way legitimated to do so, or even being capable of such legitimation. And yet this means that the arena of translegal domination, while devoid of legitimation, is filled with highly fragile social structures and quasi-political institutions which could quite easily collapse like a house of cards in the tiny breeze generated by public curiosity.

Second, autarchic strategies are limited for a reason to do with economics itself: they only make sense for global business actors so long as the temporal, institutional and material expense demanded by 'self-regulation' does not exceed the costs that would be incurred by global business if the state failed to intervene in crisis situations. To a neo-liberal utopianism that assumes economic self-regulation to be the answer to the problematic consequences of global business expansion in the long run (or, to quote Keynes: when everybody is dead), these 'costs' may appear calculable and capable of being kept to a minimum for a private, supranational capitalist quasi-state. Still, such dangerous optimism will be the first thing that comes to mind when it comes to 'compensating', not just economically, but also socially and politically, for the collapse of entire regions of the world. This is where it becomes apparent that the one thing global business has never reckoned with is crisis; its calculations have always been based on the *externalization* of costs that get chalked up as state expenditure for 'public welfare' and which include, in particular, belated compensation for the social and ecological consequences of global business investment decisions.

Substitution strategies

Even though they can ultimately be used only to a limited extent, autarchic strategies test out the parameters of the minimal state, which by the same token would be the maximum parameters for global business. Why, such strategies ask, shouldn't there be 'simulation states' and 'simulation democracies' that essentially concentrate on 'politically legitimating' global business priorities and decisions *post hoc* (or in eager anticipation of them)? In doing so, they could deploy all the resources of parliamentary democracy, the police, mass media Caesarism, and so forth at their disposal, and put buffers in place to ensure that these priorities and decisions are indeed implemented, in spite of any social resistance in the national context. However, such attempts must *ultimately* always fail on account of the fundamental dependency that exists between global business on the one hand and the state and politics on the other. Just as states are dependent on global business actors, so too are the latter fundamentally dependent on the dictates, restrictions, interventions, standardizations and relevant provisions made by the state, a dependency which remains a thorn in their side as far as the 'emancipation of the state' in the interests of global business is concerned, and one that can never be eliminated. Global business actors will thus seek to extend these limits to their power and control by means of other strategies, in order to ensure that global business is independent of state dictates.

Globalizers in the world of business need to endeavour to bring about a situation in which states and state provisions are *all the same*, or interchangeable. This would bring a twofold benefit: competition between states for foreign investment would increase, while investors would be able to optimize their own choices from among similar state packages on offer.

To put it another way, the structural power of global business can be increased and safeguarded as long as the international community of states develops according to a *unitary norm*. If it were possible to establish the *same* transport systems, legal systems, education systems, belief systems and political systems everywhere in the world, competition between states would increase along with the range of options available to global business investors from which to choose. In the opposite case, where only a few states come into consideration as lucrative investment locations and these provide global business investors with very variable sets of conditions, the situation for corporations in terms of markets and power gets worse, as does the competitive situation between them.

In this sense, *substitution strategies* are aimed at subjecting states – like eggs (and screws, and consumption, and the law) – to a global common standard, in order to make them streamlined and 'flexible' for investment purposes. This is why the idea is to avoid, if at all possible, the existence of 'elite' state packages – whether they consist in indispensable varieties of expertise (e.g. specialists in high-tech symbolic analysis) or in portfolio strategies. However, these are conditions that are by no means easy to establish, given the very different historical situations and development paths taken by states in different regions of the world. The foremost concern with regard to the substitutability of states and the decision-making priorities for worldwide investment is to ensure the removal of any obstacles that might hinder the 'free flow' of capital investments and financial transfers – in other words, a conclusive end to all protectionist policies. What is remarkable is that, in the strategic scenario projected as an ideal by global business actors, this maximization of nation-state container societies' permeability to global business interpretations applies *universally* and therefore *reciprocally* to *every state alike*. This stands in outright contradiction to the inequality and hierarchy inherent in global protectionism, which works according to the motto: just because the master is allowed to do something, it doesn't mean the slave is allowed to follow suit. While weak states are expected to dismantle barriers to global business, economically powerful states insist on erecting and maintaining protectionist barriers in order to repel the 'foreign incursions' of weak states. One example of this is the USA, which steadfastly refuses to recognize the universalism of transnational market agreements and to implement them. Yet the main goal of substitution strategies is to create basic conditions that are the same everywhere. For example, if the fundamental principles of parliamentary democracy were to be implemented worldwide, this would generate a kind of political calculability entirely conducive to the aim of organizing the world's states in line with investors' priorities. The call for human rights and democracy is therefore entirely congruent with a politics that makes states into investment paradises and is, in a material, profane sense, 'credible in economic terms'.

On the other hand, substitutability certainly doesn't have to mean sameness *in every respect*, not least because the element of difference can be put to use to maximize profits and therefore offers some key opportunities. For example, the notion that all states should train and supply high-tech specialists *exclusively* could conceivably turn into a hellish situation for investors, as it would eliminate any possibility of using differences in qualifications, ethnicity or gender to save costs. In contrast (and for these reasons), it is certainly conducive to the functioning of the market for state substitutability to be limited by a worldwide division of labour on the global market that includes hierarchies – a 'global class system', so to speak.

If we see this first in relation to the hierarchy between capital and labour, then it becomes clear that spectacular inequalities continue to exist. Whereas the globalization of capital has been elevated to the status of a general norm and any violation of this norm faces the threat of punishment via worldwide sanctions, labour markets are anything but global. If the thoroughly mobile worker wants to cross over any borders, he turns into an 'immigrant', an 'asylum seeker' or an 'economic migrant', for whom 'detention camps' and a highly armed border police unit lie in wait. Resistance to such measures, by contrast, is anything but vigorous.

Nonetheless, it is apparent that, in the area of labour mobility, nation-state protectionism does indeed meet with resistance – conceived in rigorous, directly economic terms – from global business actors. Any calls for *equality of mobility* between capital and labour and any policy based on the same will inevitably meet with bitter resistance from national actors, such as the trade unions, but can definitely count on the support of powerful global business actors – that is, as long as they follow their own rational economic self-interest.

On the other hand, a global division of labour such as the one that is emerging in the information economy – in the form of a strategy of *limited substitutability* – offers global business actors considerable benefits. If we base our reasoning on a model of the global division of labour developed by Manuel Castells in relation to the information economy, investors can exploit the following different labour market segments: 'The producers of high value, based on informational labour; the producers of high volume, based on low cost labour; the producers of raw materials, based on natural endowments; and the redundant producers reduced to devalued labour' (Castells 1997: 268).

What is striking here is that this global division of labour does *not* spring from any internal logic to do with the development of information technology, but rather presupposes global inequality and the historical-cultural backgrounds and paths of regional (groups of) states – *and reproduces them*. But quite independently of the way social science may explain this division of labour, it nonetheless offers global business investors optimum benefits as a scheme based on limited substitutability: it enables them, on the one hand, to play different states off against one another and, on the other, to translate the exploitation of global-sized inequalities and non-simultaneities into profit-maximizing cost savings. To put it differently again, it is not equality, but rather inequality among states, particularly with regard to taxes, legal supervision, standards of dignified work, technical safety and environmental protection, that optimizes global business substitution strategies.

If, for example, the same norms regarding health and safety at work and environmental protection apply in all countries, this would eliminate the strategic options available to global business for playing states off against one another and initiating competition to lower standards. *Only* as long as this sameness is *not* given and states are *not* substitutable in terms of their labour and environmental standards can they be played off against and 'substituted' for one another. This is why the continued existence of radical social inequalities between regions and cultures, as well as *within* nation-state societies, is an essential prerequisite for global business substitution strategies. In accordance with the logic of these strategies, the governments of various countries are pursuing a *political strategy of downwards mobility* in order to attract foreign capital and hold on to it in the longer term. In other words, they are systematically pursuing a politics of deregulation, tax cuts, reductions in safety regulations, and reductions in contractual and trade union-approved standardizations and forms of organizing human labour, in order to reduce competition from developed, expensive welfare states and to create a kind of 'monopoly' for themselves on cheap – and thus wretched – working conditions.

On the other side of the global hierarchy, but in keeping with a similar projected scenario, rich niche states safeguard their position in the world by pursuing a *tax haven strategy*. This parasitic strategy is aimed at attracting and holding on to global capital flows by establishing 'bank confidentiality', by minimizing taxes and by providing favourable – and therefore often quite dubious – loans. Apart from the immediate advantage of lower taxes, this also gives global business actors an indispensable strategic advantage: it allows them to exploit non-substitutability – that is, the difference between 'tax oases' and 'tax deserts' (high-tax states) – in such a way that the former can be 'substituted for', that is, 'played off against', the latter. Were states to pursue policies aimed at dismantling these kinds of differences and creating sameness, they would have to reckon with bitter resistance on the part of global business actors. In other words, there is a hidden, indeed almost *perverse, coalition* between – classically speaking – 'the exploiters' and 'the exploited', between the low-wage countries and their capitalist beneficiaries, one that is likely to put up extremely tough resistance to any cosmopolitan politics intent on establishing dignified standards of living for everybody.

Both strategies, it must be said – that of downward mobility as well as the parasitic strategy of the state tax haven – are laden with considerable risk. The problem for states that devalue themselves in order to survive in the global market is that this strategy is only successful as long as the number of such states remains very limited. As the number of such states increases, the danger is that selective and therefore limited downward mobility tips over into a policy of 'free fall'. As the number of low-wage countries that find they are forced to sell out their humanitarian ideals in order to survive in the global market increases, so downward competition also increases and the state's efforts to exploit its relative advantage over other states suddenly become entirely counter-productive. Conversely, a policy that facilitates capital flight and provides cover for it – particularly when the boundaries between legality and criminality become blurred or are deliberately removed – can easily be denounced in the global media as parasitic. However, it is hard to see how these tax havens, which even pose a threat to rich states themselves, can be closed by an international financial coordinating body introducing comprehensive regulatory standards for, say, taxation as well as for health and safety and environmental protection. Any serious attempt at international coordination and cooperation would in any case have to face the likelihood that those who refuse cooperation gain a twofold advantage:

First of all, they can save themselves the time and effort of participating in difficult negotiations, and secondly, they can make their mark by jumping on the bandwagon and exempting their economy from any regulations that are agreed. It is impossible to imagine a situation analogous to the development of national social policy that could signal the birth of a global welfare state as long as those who break the rules escape effective sanctions. (Wiesenthal 1999: 521)

Thus, the strategy of substitution, viewed from the perspective of the expanding global economy, assumes some thoroughly contradictory forms. This can be seen especially in *the way differences are dealt with*. Again, this contradictoriness can be demonstrated by reference to the fear that, if cultural development follows the lead of global business priorities, we might all end up being *McDonaldized*. On the one hand, it appears as though the global market is forcing specific locations to construct themselves as *different* in order to stand firm amid the competition between different 'place packages' – towns, regions and nations – on offer. It is easy to imagine this scenario. The key thing here would be to cultivate and highlight the particular history of a place, to give it an incomparable flair, to foster and celebrate the diversity of (world) cultures, and to design a programme of theatre, entertainment, dance and erotica in an imaginative and colourful way, one that is *not* geared towards uniform global norms. Being different would be the trademark that makes a place more attractive to mobile capital. However, as competition between different locations for nomadic capital becomes dominant, there is also a greater compulsion to level off that difference and replace it with a kind of recursive and routinized 'same place-ness', leading to a situation in which every location begins to approximate to the negative ideal of 'non-places' – like airports and intercontinental hotels, motorways and shopping malls – which enable a globalized globalizer to find his or her way about and settle down anywhere according to the same logic each time and without any special local knowledge. The major shopping streets and outlets look the same everywhere in the world. If we want, we can buy the same global brands, from Coca-Cola to Benetton, in any major city in the world, always promoted by the same advertising slogans, whether for the benefit of Eskimos, Africans, or even Bavarians.

The strategy of substitution thus leads to a paradox: the more the significance of spatial boundaries fades, the more sensitive global business actors become towards the particularity of different locations, the greater the imagination locations and states need to demonstrate in order to cultivate their cultural specificity – and yet the harder it becomes for local politics and politicians to predict who or what might make a location attractive to capital flows. This often leads to a fragmented policy, which in turn reinforces the fragmentation of a location and cements its inequalities and non-simultaneities.

Projected onto a large scale, this means on the one hand that the processes by which education, law, standards of democratic politics, and the upholding of human rights and environmental protection are standardized and formalized worldwide are thoroughly congruent with a global political strategy of substitution pursued by global capital. On the other hand, the demystification of tax havens and the implementation of minimum wage regimes stand in stark contradiction to these very strategies of substitution, because it is only this non-interchangeability of states that enables global business actors to play the latter off against one another.

Monopolization strategies

While global business actors find competition among states useful, they do need to be careful to avoid competition with other global business actors. This means that the power of individual corporations grows in line with their ability to monopolize a certain share – and specific aspects – of global power. *The maximizing of competition between states is complemented by a minimizing of competition between one business and another.*

It should be self-evident that the possibility of direct monopolization is open only to those global business actors that have reached a certain size – in terms of both their capital assets and their market presence. Global market monopolies mean that all the other global business actors *and* all the states that depend on the particular services, technologies or know-how in question are at the mercy of decisions made by the corporation concerned – certainly if serious consequences are associated with going without the relevant product. Corporations can attain this dominant position of power on the global market either by monitoring or by eliminating other suppliers (indicating how important the conflict of interests between global business actors themselves is), or else by agreeing a modus operandi with them. This necessitates the development of a kind of 'global political business diplomacy' among global corporations. There are at least five areas in which global monopolies are most likely to be established:

- monopolies on technology; these demand enormous amounts of capital, which only the giants of the global market have at their disposal – and, even then, they often need to rely on being fed huge sums of money from rich states;
- financial controls over *worldwide financial markets*;
- monopolistic access to *natural resources*;
- *media and communications* monopolies; and
- monopolies on *weapons of mass destruction* (although these global monopolies lie not only in the hands of private global business actors but in the hands of states as well).

It is worth remarking that there are always those states that share in or profit from these kinds of global monopolies, from which it follows that such monopolies produce and reinforce hierarchies of inequality and life chances around the world. They force countries which already find themselves allocated a slot at the lower end of the global hierarchy to subjugate themselves even further. This brings about 'supplier relations' and 'forms of subcontracted work' on a global scale. Monopolies reinforce and thereby manifest worldwide polarizations between the haves and the have-nots.

According to the latest estimates from UNCTAD, about 60,000 international corporations exist throughout the world with 500,000 subsidiaries. They are responsible for the largest proportion of business transactions worldwide. They make the most investments abroad and are responsible for the lion's share of technology transfer. At least one transnational corporation is involved in two-thirds of all international trade, while one-third of all trade takes place within the same company, despite traversing nation-state and continental borders.

The large number of multinationals is, of course, misleading. An elite of very large corporations has long since set itself apart from the mainstream. According to UNCTAD's latest figures, the largest one hundred global corporations alone (excluding finance companies) have sold goods valued at $2.1 billion throughout the world and have employed 6 million people abroad – and these are just the figures outside their home countries. Ninety per cent of these big players come from Western industrialized countries, although companies from Venezuela and Korea have also now made the leap into the top one hundred.

Global market monopolies alter the shape of global political power structures: states become less significant overall, so that the relationship between the state and the world of business comes to be replaced by the business-to-business relationship. And states themselves become less dependent on one another than on global economic authorities when it comes to fulfilling their national tasks. Thus, transnational firms provide many states with the ticket they need into the world market. As long as a company has (a) control over technologies, (b) access to global capital resources, and (c) access to the large markets of the USA, Europe and Japan, states (on the periphery in particular) are reliant on them in their capacity as mediators. If states (and corporations alike) can only attain wealth by appropriating a share of the world market – and they have to do so, because national markets are too small to make the necessary profits to survive – then *diplomacy between states and companies*, 'foreign business diplomacy', becomes a central precondition for success in domestic policy and government success at election time.

To turn the issue the other way around, monopolization strategies are also strategies for reducing competition. Reduction of competition is aimed at two possible addressees. On the one hand, it is aimed at the state–business relationship, where the elimination of competition signals demonstrative evidence that *business, and business alone – not* the state – is capable of producing according to the dictates of 'economic rationality', that it is efficient, cost-conscious, quality-based, customer-oriented, and so forth. The aim here is to eliminate the state as a competitor in the organization of utilities and services, something that global business strategies aimed at the monopolization of *economic rationality* are geared towards. On the other hand, monopolization strategies can, as already mentioned, be identified in the context of business-to-business relations. These *strategies of business-to-business diplomacy* typically turn into forms of what is known, tellingly, as 'hostile takeover', or else entail cooperative arrangements.

Strategies aimed at monopolizing economic rationality

In the bipolar world of the East–West conflict, competition also existed between two different forms of economic rationality, namely, the private enterprise capitalist form in the West and the state economic and state socialist form in the East. It was not until the collapse of the Eastern bloc that private enterprise actors were able to establish a *global monopoly on economic rationality*. This had – and continues to have – consequences, not only for the countries of the former Soviet Union; it also means that within the centres of Western capitalism, and spreading out from here to the entire world, aspects of the state economy are coming under pressure. The *strategy of privatizing* state-owned companies – from the industrial corporations of Central and Eastern Europe, through railways, telecommunications and the postal system in the USA and Western Europe, and much more besides – provides the proof of this success story of the systematic monopolization of economic rationality by business actors and global business actors. As global business eliminates the state as a rational economic competitor, so it becomes possible to split off more and more state-organized services from the state and to place them under the direct control of private enterprise. Governments may even 'sell off the family silver', including famous places and national cultural treasures, in order to plug holes in the state budget. The 'privatization' label also includes efforts to establish favourable conditions for *new business monopolies*.

To put it another way, comprehensive critique of the state economy and discourse that is critical of the state in general support the global business monopoly on economic rationality and make it possible – paradoxically – to establish new monopolies. These bring with them new bottlenecks in provision and threats to health and safety, such as those that have almost come to be taken for granted nowadays in the utterly chaotic privatized railway system in Britain, with its incessant repairs, constant delays, inadequate provision and multiple collisions. To put the issue somewhat provocatively, the state's monopoly on under-provision has been replaced by a private enterprise monopoly on mismanagement. If this kind of situation begins to take hold in sensitive areas such as high-risk technologies (nuclear power plants), the situation could easily turn into a political disaster.

Strategies of business-to-business diplomacy

As states begin to lose power to global business actors in any case, so negotiations between firms take on an ever greater significance, so that intercorporate diplomacy eventually becomes more important than state–corporation diplomacy (Strange 2000: 64ff.). This diplomacy that goes on within the world of global business may take place within the same sector (such as aircraft construction) or between different sectors (such as between the computer industry and satellite construction). The goals of this global business diplomacy are clear and can be read off not least from the merger fever that has gripped the big players. Their goal is to build secure global monopolies by means of agreements, cooperative ventures or even new symbioses, so that they can consolidate their structural position of power in terms of their relations both with other businesses and with states, and protect it from competition. '*Swallow or be swallowed*' – this motto seems to encourage a 'big is beautiful' approach on the global market, although the opposite might also be valid: *swallow and be swallowed* – as when the largest fish in the global market power poker game are swallowed up by even bigger 'mega-fish'. In this sense, the 'theory of international relations' ought really to be reformulated and redeveloped as the 'theory of transnational business relations'. This would enable us to shed some light on the 'Vienna Congress' of global business and to ask: which conflicts and contradictions predominate here, and what opportunities exist to either prevent or prepare the ground for 'economic wars'?

Strategies of preventive dominance

All the global business strategies outlined so far are always also doomed to *failure*, no matter how convincingly they reveal and expand the potential power of global business actors. No matter how hard global business tries to break, minimize or replace the power of states, it will always come up against one immovable barrier: *without* the state and *without* politics, there can be no global business activity. One could even say that it is in the very best interests of capital itself that the strategies of capital should fail. It is global business itself that needs a strong, (trans-)state, global political guiding hand capable of setting a regulatory framework for it, since public acceptance and, with it, the power of transnational actors will otherwise fade away.

Let us put this in terms of a thought experiment. Assuming that all the endeavours manifested in the power strategies of capital already mentioned are successful, this moment of complete success on the part of global business would simultaneously be the point of its collapse. The world of business is not elected by any population. On the contrary, it ultimately practises and perfects its translegal domination – following this thought experiment – *without* (democratic) legitimation. Once business has made the state into a zombie and has abolished democratically organized state politics, it effectively pulls the rug from under its own feet and sets in train a number of incalculable political reactions. What happens, for example, when globalization's losers rise up in revolt all over the world, when global economic crises erupt, or when the principles of global business become subject to justification and consensus, just like religious creeds – how will global business actors respond then?

In other words, it is precisely the success achieved by global business strategies of domination that drives us towards the realization that politics and the state are *indispensable* and *irreplaceable* and are in the economic self-interest of global business. They are indispensable because, in pursuing its profit interests and throwing every social and political structure and every self-evident proposition into disarray along its revolutionary path, global business becomes absolutely dependent on legitimation, and therefore threatened by a lack of it. And they are irreplaceable because all the autarchic strategies and monopolization strategies of global business ultimately fail in the face of the fact that *only* state-constituted, democratically organized politics is capable of making collectively binding *and*, at the same time, legitimate decisions about the structure and future of societies.

If it is correct, then, that the worlds of difference between the state and the market and between politics and business cannot be eliminated or erased, the key question that arises in the course of global business pursuing and achieving its objectives is this: how can the state and politics be recognized as autonomous and indispensable on the one hand, while being integrated at the same time into the process of establishing the objectives of global business on the other – how can they be mobilized and encouraged to serve this purpose? How can the feat of organizing state politics so that it both operates in line with global business priorities *and* remains autonomous be achieved? How is it possible to persuade politics and the state to continue the expansion of global business power by autonomous means? The answer lies in strategies of *preventive dominance*. These transfer the problem of domination between capital and labour onto the relationship between capital and the state, which adds a truly explosive element into the mix, because now it is the lion who is trying to crack the whip over its tamer.

Two strategies of preventive dominance can be identified in particular. First, there are *rogue state strategies*, or what one might also call the '*Springfield strategy*'. In this case, an inter-state system of prestige is established within the global economic 'world merit-based society', in accordance with a hierarchy of ranking based on the norms of neo-liberalism. Taking the small-town milieu of the US Midwest as a model, it divides states into freedom-loving 'good countries' and world peace-endangering 'rogue countries'. The second type of strategy is the *neo-liberalization of the state*. In this case, autonomous state politics is organized in the image of anticipatory, neo-liberal obedience.

Rogue state strategies

One might well ask how any inter-systemic coordination between global business and the state can be successful when each follows a different 'logic', neither of which is reducible to the other. The first answer to this is one that has been worked out in the national context but can now be projected onto the global social context. There is an elementary sociological insight which says that norms – that is, values that have real currency – are based not simply on a subjectively internalized acceptance and understanding of the moral quality of these values but rather on prior domination, because, if norms are to be enforced, there need to be appropriate sanctions available, both positive and negative. There are doubtless many different reasons why people make certain values and norms their inner guide to action. The point of the theory, though, is this: no matter what reasons we put forward, there can be no explanation for an existing system of norms, and prestige can be found without also referring back to pre-existing structures of domination. The reference to domination does two things: it explains the existence of choice between two different value systems, and it answers the question of who has what means at their disposal for 'rehearsing' these values – that is, for ensuring that they are internalized under the influence of both positive and negative sanctions.

Strategies of preventive dominance on the part of global business make use of precisely this idea. According to this approach, what is commonly referred to somewhat casually as the 'global community' would have to be conceived of as a global system of status and prestige with at least two basic features. The first of these is a globally valid value principle, in this case the neo-liberal norms of global business success. The ideal path to global business success is paved with criteria formulated in the language of economics and combines a high level of currency stability, moderate wage increases and low strike rates with a minimalist state, which in turn limits itself to creating appropriate competitive and social conditions, while shifting a large amount of responsibility onto individuals and entrepreneurs. These values of economic freedom are accompanied by values of political freedom, that is, the worldwide enforcement of norms in respect of human rights and democracy. Both taken together – the implied non-divisibility of economic and political freedoms on a global scale – form the 'core value' which, when put into practice globally and furnished with the corresponding capacity to apply global business and military sanctions, leads to a global social hierarchy of prestige, at the top end of which are the '*good* states', the Western '*overdog* states', and at whose lower end are the '*bad* states', the *global underdogs*, or, to use a term taken from American foreign policy, the '*rogue* states'.

The second basic feature of strategies of preventive dominance are as follows. The prerequisites for implementing a global hierarchy of prestige are many and varied. As I have said, appropriate sanctions need to be available. In other words, conformity to global business priorities must be rewarded and deviation from them penalized. This mechanism works by way of the actual, real intervention, or rather non-intervention, of global investors, or again through IMF and World Bank policies, and so on, as well as via a policy of 'military humanism' which threatens, to great effect, to place the systematic violation of human rights above the dictates of autonomy entailed by international law and to take military action in the name of the 'international community' against 'ethnic cleansing' and genocide.

The objectified and institutionalized value criteria implied by the global business profile of success signify good conduct and thereby steer capital flows in certain directions. Even where this does not occur, the discursive hegemony of neo-liberal discourse – which, as we have shown, draws its power not least from the way it dissolves boundaries between reality and possibility – facilitates an awareness of the 'not yet', something which provides a spur to economically conformist action. In other words, the worldwide equation of basic values with economics, and of life with successful performance, is implemented through the actual or expected punishment meted out by global business in the case of non-conformity, a punishment that makes use of the power of sanctions exerted by global business actors and global economic organizations.

The influence of these global-level neo-liberal value imperatives is complemented and reinforced by various mechanisms and procedures. Thus, for example, even conflicts over the exclusion of rogue states ultimately have the effect of reinforcing rather than weakening global business value, as one might first think. Or rather, they do so if and when such conflicts facilitate collective agreement about the basic values of economics and freedom on which it (the conflict) is based. Similarly, radical inequalities in prestige between different countries do not necessarily call the integration of the global community into question, but rather enhance the possibilities for applying sanctions, as candidates for relegation can be presented with models of upward mobility. It is therefore beneficial to make a special feature out of 'country trajectories' and to promote them and celebrate them, as occurred with the East Asian 'tiger states'.

Tiger states are thus not only the counter-model to rogue states. They also give low-status countries on the periphery a dynamic, middle-income point of reference and have a reaffirming impact on the global economic system of values in both an upward and a downward direction. They prove to those below them that 'you can make it' – the message being that you are ultimately responsible for your own failure, for your own status as a loser. To those above them, they convey the shocking message: you'll drop down if you don't fulfil the criteria for global business success! In either case, then, there need to be ways of documenting and demonstrating mobility in different directions so that economic values can develop their cohesive influence everywhere. This rules out two possibilities: first, acceptance of a *static* global order of prestige in which there are *eternal* winners and losers among states and world regions, *regardless* of success. Second, it also rules out the suggestion that a country's status in the global order of prestige is allocated *independently* of the politics of the states concerned, either on account of historical or cultural background (the violent history of the colonies, or imperialism) or on account of the monopoly position of global business actors – despite the proactive neo-liberalism of politics.

This strategy of preventive dominance, which I have called a 'rogue state strategy', leads to a strange paradox. On the one hand, concepts such as 'global market' and 'global society' seem to be so complex that even the word 'complexity' itself is a coarse simplification. On the other hand, life in the integrated global market society is apparently similar to life in Springfield, Minnesota. Here, the world is still in perfect working order. Here, everybody knows that there are good people and bad people, and that you can tell them apart: the goodness of the good people shows (and is affirmed) in the fact that they get angry about the badness of the bad people and that they exclude them – with all the goodness and badness they can muster. And so, in a tacit show of unity between the good and the bad, the system of norms they both share is reinforced. To the extent that such a self-definition holds sway (even if it is only in the form of an ideology), it does indeed become possible – let's by all means put it this way – to 'allow' state policies to develop that are *preventive*, that conform to global business priorities and are simultaneously autonomous, *without* any direct intervention on the part of global business actors.

Strategies aimed at the neo-liberalization of the state

These strategies attempt to eliminate the qualitative difference and substantial contradictions between the state and the global market by changing the state into a *global market* state. In other words, the state is conceived of as the extended arm of the global market, as a continuation of global market politics by state political means. This is exactly what the *political* rather than the economic programme of neo-liberalism seeks to achieve.

What it involves, first of all, is a paradoxical acknowledgement that government, the state and politics are indispensable and irreplaceable. In their dual role as both home and host to global business actors and companies, governments play a *crucial, indeed an increasingly important*, role in enforcing global business interests. This is the *sole* reason why it is necessary to translate neo-liberal orthodoxy into neo-liberal reform politics, a politics of the neo-liberal state. Only in this way can the state change its role from tamer and opponent of global business to fellow team player.

Accordingly, the period since the 1970s has seen the development of a neo-liberal theory of politics and society based on competition between locations, one that translates the neo-liberal creed into a theory of the 'business state' – the 'competition state' – and its corresponding image of the 'business society' – 'enterprise culture'. In this theory, political actors – of the state or the city – are depicted as *accumulation actors*. Taking the neo-liberal imperative as a given, the concept of politics is tailored and reduced to its new minimal existence as a local agent for global business policy, within which context the new coordinates of foreign and domestic policy (whose boundaries no longer apply as such), labour market and education policy, social policy, and so on, are worked through in meticulous detail. If the managers of global business were to write a wish list to Father Christmas, it would probably end up looking much like the theory of the global business-oriented competition state.

This political and state theory of anticipatory neo-liberal obedience is certainly backed up by a number of observable trends. One issue that is becoming increasingly important – in terms of states' own self-interest, of course – is how to find ways into the global market and secure a share of it. The old bilateral diplomacy between states is being progressively replaced by multilateral diplomacy, in which global market actors acquire a key role in enforcing the state's objectives. One manifestation of this trend is the emergence and proliferation of a new layer of transnational political arenas, represented by institutions such as the WTO, the OECD and the G-8 countries. It is essentially here, rather than in national arenas, public spheres or organizations, that the rules of the meta-power game of global politics are being negotiated, written and rewritten, rules which then change national politics and societies fundamentally. One indication that this is the case is that the classic fields of nation-state domestic policy – such as education, transport, energy, domestic security and finance – are increasingly being understood and redefined according to the premises of international competition on the global market.

Since the end of the 1970s, a neo-liberal consensus has emerged between the states and organizations whose decisions and politics play a large role in shaping the global economy (the US government, G-8 countries, OECD, IMF, World Bank and so forth). This consensus is that it is necessary as well as desirable for nation-state institutions to be reformed on the premise of a '*dual freedom*', that is, in line with the principles of *political* freedom (democracy, human rights) and *global business* freedom. If we see these as the key principles of a politics of the 'Third Way', then this political programme can be said to ensure that nation-state political premises and institutions are reorganized in conformity with the global market. The politics of the Third Way sees itself as the key 'modern' definition of a new 'common good' for the era of globalization and thus becomes a *politics of preventive dominance on the part of global business actors*. Ultimately, the criteria of rationality associated with transnational business – and with the global financial markets in particular – become a point of orientation; much more, indeed, they become the criterion of rationality for a politics that seeks its salvation in integration into the global economy. People have long been debating the end of ideology and, more recently, the end of politics as well. In its loyalty to the global market, this variety of politics has virtually made the end of ideology *and* the end of politics its trademark.

However, this strategy is based on a grave mistake – contrary to its self-perception as realistic and moral. The need for states to adjust in order to cope with competition in the global market is wrongly equated with a *lack of alternatives* to a 'politics' that would rush ahead to implement what are implied as being 'the laws of the global market'. What this amounts to is an *economistic self-misunderstanding* on the part of politics, with politics and the state being seen as secondary to the *exclusive* primacy of global business priorities, something that is ultimately equivalent to the self-curtailment, self-denial and eventual self-disempowerment of politics and political theory with regard to global market conformity – loyalty to the party line.

However, this critique is fundamentally ambiguous, as it can be misunderstood from the position of political science realism. The latter assumes that the state, and in particular the nation-state, can *never* be reduced to economic policy, but rather that it always pursues geopolitical and military objectives and interests in its role as defender of the monopoly on violence. Therefore, the equation 'state + neo-liberal state + competition state' really does amount to a form of disempowerment. If this equation were correct, politics would be robbed of its core by being denied the continuous possibility of military intervention; and, as has so often been the case throughout history, such a denial would be grounded in an over-eager pacifism, this time given a global business rationale. However, since conservative political and state theory provides no answers to the challenges posed by the global market, it usually restricts itself to dismissing the questions and consequences thrown up by economic globalization as 'all talk' or 'pure ideology', while referring to a lack of empirical evidence; it also declines to explore the possibility of a parallel globalization, or a *transnationalization of the state and politics* – and in this it coincides with strategies aimed at the neo-liberalization of the state.

In both instances, the gap in power between politics bound to a specific territory and deterritorialized global business is set in stone *analytically*. The possibility and necessity of reinventing politics for the age of globalization is ruled out categorically. There is a failure to recognize the alternatives available to politics under global market conditions because it is still completely caught up in the conflict with a conservative nation-state theory of realism and, as a logical consequence, in the attempt to make political and state theory more responsive to the new global politics of the world market. Not a word is spoken about the need to define and distribute global market risks and global unpredictability – *the* task of politics in an age of market liberalization. It falls victim to an optimism that has not been acquired by thinking through or rehearsing possible disasters, but which stems from the nonchalant motto: what I don't know can't hurt me.

Ultimately, the failure to recognize the historical contradiction emerging today stems from a habit of thinking located within the terms of the national outlook. The supposed contradiction between global business and national politics is being set in stone once and for all. The possibility of a transnational politics – an understanding of politics, the state and the nation that has been opened up and changed by cosmopolitanism, for example – is not even taken into consideration. And this in spite of the fact that the obvious thing to do (and this has now been argued by many people in great detail) would be to rethink and redesign the concept of democracy – which began as a city-state and which, in its national guise today, appears to have assumed its final historical form as a state-organized parliamentary democracy – for the *post*-national, *trans*national constellation (Held 2000: 91ff.).

Incidentally, to *imply* that there is no alternative to conformity, to say that it is the only answer to the global economy and one that broadens the scope of politics, amounts to a remarkable willingness to renounce strategies of state power that might otherwise be used in actively shaping events. Accordingly, any alternative theories of the state would have to begin from the following starting points.

- They would have to expose the false alternative between neo-liberal strategies of deregulation and national or neo-nationalistic strategies of intervention and protectionism.
- They would have to mobilize the political resource of political regulation of conflicts and markets.
- In doing so, they could take up those issues that have been subject to criminal neglect by the politics of neo-liberal self-conformity. These include, for one, the disparities and conflicts resulting from the endemic destruction of nature and the environment, and, for another, the well-regulated and well-suppressed but politically explosive issue of *precarious* full employment (and whether or not it can be achieved at all). Both sets of issues have by now entered into public consciousness to the extent that they have become a major concern to the very section of society that is so hotly contested politically, namely the centre.
- Thus, rather than dressing up the facts and thereby subjugating oneself to the normative dictates of the global economy, the thing to do would be to exploit the *politically productive force of pessimism*, that is, the power of a dramaturgy of conflict and risk.

The mere act of proposing new, international market regulations is capable of turning the tables and forcing business to recognize the reclaimed primacy of politics. Only by introducing new regulations concerning rights and responsibilities in the entire global economic system (as a complement to collective agreements and welfare-state measures) can a new consensus be created between the power of business and political power on the one hand and democracy on the other.

Existing transnational institutions responsible for coordinating global business are also pursuing a politics of reform along these lines. Organizations such as the IMF, the World Bank, the OECD and the G-8 countries certainly cannot be reduced to a single common denominator. Each one does politics in its own way, and yet it is the strategy of preventive global business dominance that predominates in each case. This could be successively replaced by alternative reform projects that add a proactive, cosmopolitan project to economistic defeatism.

A crucial part of this would be to develop a new way of dealing with the incalculable risks of unregulated global business. The starting point for this is the realization that public awareness of such risks spells not the end but rather the very beginning of politics. A political renaissance may – to exaggerate the issue – transform these sources of risk into resources for political renewal if – and this 'if' is crucial – if it is possible to open up national barriers and to refashion the globality of threats into a *trans*national renewal of politics. There would also be a need to think about new, transnational bodies capable of discussing how to deal with emergency situations in the economy, the dynamics of national capital markets and public investment priorities and expenditure structures, and capable of negotiating proposals for appropriate political responses.

A transnational revival of politics and development of democracy of the sort described here does not have to begin at the same time in every place throughout the world; nor does it have to be understood as an affront to or a renewal of imperialistic claims by that majority of countries and states which still see themselves even today as being exploited by and dependent on the 'centres'. This self-renewal of politics and democracy in the second modernity could begin in key regions and key sectors with the aim of bringing about greater transparency and responsibility in the global centres of economic decision-making. Since these are – as we have seen – mini-global societies, these experiments would have to be negotiated, agreed and undertaken independently of the old – and now false – distinction between centre and periphery.

5

State Strategies between Renationalization and Transnationalization

This chapter will address the following question: how can politics and the state move towards a cosmopolitan self-transformation?[1] The aim here is not merely to observe and describe the way governments bemoan the so-called global exigencies of the world market while simultaneously instrumentalizing them in order to outmanoeuvre their own domestic opposition. Instead, the issue is how the democratic-republican exercise of power might be reinfused with self-creative legitimacy. In other words, how can the broader environment within which states act be changed in such a way that it becomes possible to work at reducing global problems 'glocally'? What form of democratic legitimation is already emerging, or what kind might be created, that has an affinity with the globalization of business and the transnationalization of social movements and experiential spaces? Before moving on to consider what forms the renaissance of politics in the global age might take, we need to note that the *very question* itself is obscured by four escapist approaches:

(1) Justified criticism of 'state-centredness' tends to promote the *grand illusion that a world without economic or cultural barriers will be characterized by a new, non-political spirit of peace.* Contrary to this view, we need to be clear that the taming of high-risk capitalism by civil society is *not an option*; it is a dangerous expression of naïvety. And global business pretensions to 'imperial sovereignty' cannot be democratically tamed by the New Internationale of non-governmental organizations or by the new magic words 'self-organization', 'social responsibility' and 'self-legitimation' applied to global business. Without overcoming the national orthodoxy of the state and politics, that is, without developing the reality and theory of the state further, such a move cannot succeed, indeed it cannot even be conceptualized.

(2) *New International Political Economy*: The argument here is based on the premise that economics establishes a 'sound barrier' that politics *cannot*

break through because it is and always will be the handmaiden of economics. However, this ignores the *political* character of the meta-power game: it may be the case that global business breaks out from the national repositories of power that house the state and the economy, that it makes the first move into the arena of transnational power and forces boundaries to be opened up, and so on. However, it is completely wrong to think of this in terms of *determinism*, of the state becoming a colony of global business authority.

The representatives of the New Political Economy are caught up in a curious paradox, because it is precisely the neo-Marxist critics of global capitalism, of all people, who have become the unwilling prophets of the state's neo-liberalization ('competition state', 'market state', and so on.). They, too, can see that the state is engaged in a kind of self-transformation, but they analyse this exclusively in terms of the conformity of state politics to the maxims of neo-liberal global market governance. As a result, the question as to what transnationalization strategies are available to the state is rejected out of hand without having even been posed. This theoretical and research perspective also entails a kind of meta-game, one that is ultimately always decided in advance: capital wins, the state and politics lose. But let it be stressed once again: the outcome of the meta-power game is open-ended. The situation is unclear and calls for an explanation. Old questions crop up once again and require new frames of reference in order to be answered politically and analysed scientifically.

(3) *Governance without government*: Globalization forces us to search for a new narrative of the democratization of global politics. The much-used term '*global governance*', however, exudes an aura that suggests a legitimatory vacuum. It has the whiff of a monitoring regime *without* democratic legitimacy, which then leads to the false option of *either* defending the nation-state *or* appealing for governance without government. One key question that falls by the wayside in the process is this: how can the state become – or be made into – the agent of its own transformation from nation-state to cosmopolitan state?

(4) *The self-obstruction of politics*: The distinction between the national and the cosmopolitan outlook is crucial. It is not a question of the downfall of the nation-state or of its recovery (whether it gets smaller or bigger, or in which areas of politics it has greater or lesser influence). Rather, it is a question of opening up a new perspective on the entire field of power play. The weakness in the globalization debate up until now has been that it has remained captive to the old distinctions implied by methodological nationalism, meaning that all the explanations put forward by critics and defenders alike have proved inadequate. It is only once a change in perspective has taken place that it becomes possible to perceive new constellations of power,

new moves and new possibilities of global governance in multilayered networks, none of which the national outlook enables us to see. State capacity depends not only – and perhaps not even crucially – on the dictates of economic globalization; it depends rather on how states define themselves during the course of the meta-power game. Globalization has opened up once and for all the great political game about fundamental change in politics and the state, in which the question of how statehood might develop further in the cosmopolitan era has become the key in relation to the distribution of power. The self-definition of state capacity has thus become a strategic variable in the meta-power game.

If the goal of capital is to merge with law in order to access resources for self-legitimation, then the state ought to be looking to merge with global civil society in order to acquire transnational capacity along with new sources of global legitimacy and power. State strategies therefore need to be distinguished according to how far they unquestioningly take on the apparent nation-state *a priori* of politics and how far they loosen the obstructive influence of the nation on the state and overcome the latter's subjugation to the primacy of economics – that is, to what extent their goal is a cosmopolitan redefinition of the state and a repoliticization of politics.

New state strategies need, therefore, to break away from the *false alternative* of either neo-liberalizing or neo-nationalizing the state. It is necessary instead to develop strategies for *repoliticizing* politics and the state, strategies that draw their power from the project of a *different* globalization and a *different* modernity. Nation-states embody the deep-frozen condition that politics is in, a condition that can be overcome by developing reflexive strategies for the self-revival and redefinition of the political sphere. States certainly do have the power and the possibility to renew themselves. Once the state is no longer equated with the nation-state, once states discover, try out and nurture the political power of *cooperative transnationality and trans-sovereignty* available to them – beyond the bounds of sovereignty and autonomy – then it becomes possible to access this potential.

As we have seen, the strategies of capital are aimed at reversing the historical differentiation of politics, limiting wherever possible the indispensable functions of the state, preventing state monopolizations and ensuring that global business actors have the most comprehensive authority possible to exert control over events – and all this by way of politics as a side-effect. The 'ideal' here would be to have a state that can be easily replaced and interchanged at will, one that is fully immersed in competition with the greatest number of similar states, and one that operates both autonomously and in conformity with the world market in fulfilling a set of tasks largely cleansed of their independent decision-making, control and legitimatory functions and trimmed back in 'minimalist' fashion.

Table 5.1 State strategies

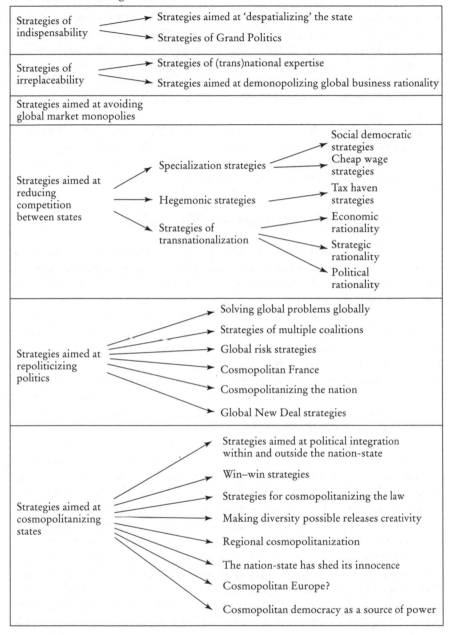

Strategies of indispensability	→ Strategies aimed at 'despatializing' the state → Strategies of Grand Politics
Strategies of irreplaceability	→ Strategies of (trans)national expertise → Strategies aimed at demonopolizing global business rationality
Strategies aimed at avoiding global market monopolies	
Strategies aimed at reducing competition between states	→ Specialization strategies → Social democratic strategies / Cheap wage strategies → Hegemonic strategies → Tax haven strategies → Strategies of transnationalization → Economic rationality / Strategic rationality / Political rationality
Strategies aimed at repoliticizing politics	→ Solving global problems globally → Strategies of multiple coalitions → Global risk strategies → Cosmopolitan France → Cosmopolitanizing the nation → Global New Deal strategies
Strategies aimed at cosmopolitanizing states	→ Strategies aimed at political integration within and outside the nation-state → Win–win strategies → Strategies for cosmopolitanizing the law → Making diversity possible releases creativity → Regional cosmopolitanization → The nation-state has shed its innocence → Cosmopolitan Europe? → Cosmopolitan democracy as a source of power

Accordingly, states must seek to avoid a situation

- that makes any single state, or state policy as a whole, dispensable and replaceable: strategies of *indispensability* and *irreplaceability*;
- that exposes them to global monopolies *without any alternatives*: strategies aimed at *avoiding global market monopolies*;
- that maximizes interchangeability and competition between states: *strategies of cooperation* and *strategies aimed at reducing competition between states*;
- that perpetuates the equation between the state and the nation-state; strategies aimed at *transnationalizing and repoliticizing politics*; or
- that prevents the political sphere from being developed beyond the nationality trap: strategies aimed at *cosmopolitanizing states*.

5.1   Strategies of indispensability

The aim of state strategies of indispensability is to win back the primacy of politics in the age of globalization – not by making the state and politics into the extended arm of global business, but just the opposite, by renewing the *difference* between politics and the world of business and celebrating the monopoly politics has on collectively binding decisions, democratic legitimation and the organization of the legal system. This implies a need to dust off and modernize the 'state instruments of torture' used in relation to global business, by freeing them from their nation-bound inadequacy. There is a need to demonstrate, not only to global business but also to a global public intimidated by neo-liberalism, that no amount of concentrated economic power, global monopolies or even 'successful' state privatizations can *ever* replace, let alone obtain, the consent of citizens or of consumers.

The conditions needed to pursue global business activities, namely a peaceful society and the fundamental consent of citizens, cannot be bought. The production and reproduction of agreement and consent requires an *independent sphere of politics, culture, democracy and state*, that can never be subjugated to the logic of economics – unless, of course, global business wants to dig its own grave. Strategies of indispensability therefore attempt to counter the politics of neo-liberal defeatism by reviving people's faith in the creed: *nothing can be achieved without politics*. This is the goal of strategies aimed at remonopolizing the political sphere. They also attempt to show that, in spite of all the power gains made by self-globalizing capital, it is ultimately the *self*-denial and *self*-disempowerment of politics – rather than the power of capital – that is the decisive factor in the depoliticization of politics. In other words, the end of politics can only be brought about by politics itself and not by capital or anybody else.

Having said this, there is a world of difference between affirming the primacy of politics in relation to the self-globalizing world of business and putting it into practice. It is not simply a matter of proclaiming the autonomy of politics and staging its return through mass media representations; rather, it is about redefining, demarcating and remonopolizing the political sphere in opposition to global business. This is what strategies of indispensability aim to achieve. They demonstrate

(a)   the fact that all attempts on the part of global business actors to achieve as much autarchy as possible for the state and politics are completely illusory, and the reasons why this is so; that is, they demonstrate, conversely, that

(b)   the autonomy and inherent logic of a state policy that is not subordinate to the primacy of business fulfils tasks and performs functions *without* which 'autarchic' global business would necessarily fail.

To focus on just one example, there is much talk nowadays of the new, 'unbounded' nature of capital markets and commodity flows. However, only in an ideal scenario are state boundaries irrelevant – they still exist in practice, certainly for people, but also for business transactions. Open boundaries presuppose that the state is continuously opting for *non*-intervention. The state has to accept, establish and guarantee the lack of boundaries. Unboundedness is *one* of several state strategies pursued in the context of global capitalism. For example, the terrorist attacks of 11 September made it clear in a flash how quickly an apparent lack of boundaries can be brought to an end and new controls introduced (for the movement of goods and capital as well as people), and that it is the perception of risk that provides legitimation for renewing boundaries. At the same time it has become clear (in the search for the sources of terrorist funding, for example) that establishing and monitoring boundaries is not a national task, but rather a transnational one that can no longer be fulfilled by individual nations acting in isolation.

If it is correct that politics is constrained on account of its one-sided subordination to the primacy of global business, then a two-phase movement may enable politics to be renewed and remonopolized.

First, politics must free itself from the paradox of its neo-liberal self-destruction and win back its decision-making options and its power by becoming open to multiple coalitions. Second, a 'modern' economic policy would be one that powerfully reaffirms the simple ABC of the relationship between politics and global business – namely, the fact that wealth brings with it demands for rights and justice – and makes the powerful responsible. A politics that goes in the opposite direction and seeks to radicalize social inequalities and dismantle rights not only stirs up endemic conflicts but also hurtles headlong, eyes wide open, into a wall of non-consent. Moreover, the move away from neo-liberal orthodoxy and towards an opening up of politics represents a renewal of politics and the state not only in terms of concrete concerns but also in *strategic power* terms for those frustrated and threatened by globalization, for globalization's losers. To put it another way, the remonopolization of politics presupposes a renewal of the *substance* of politics.

It may be that imagining concrete political objectives in an age of globalization is desirable and, indeed, an absolute must from an ethical and political point of view. However, something that is possibly more crucial needs to be said about this: *renewing the substance of politics is the best way of renewing the power of politics.* Thus, *idealism* can be more than just idealistic; it can also be about *strategies of power.* Even the most cynical Machiavellian – so the theory goes – has to become a convert to idealism in pursuing his power-optimizing political strategies. Winning back power and winning back utopia are two sides of the same coin. Thus, strategies of state power are not initially about a utopian utopianism but about a *utopianism based on strategies of power.* Similarly, to look at it from the other side, the point is to criticize the neo-liberal utopia not only in moral and political terms alone, but also from the point of view of strategies of power. The political ban on utopia, executed only too eagerly by politics itself, commits politics to the premises of territorial, nation-state politics; this in turn restricts the political imagination itself to the parameters of the national and puts a seal on the self-disempowerment of politics in the face of the worldwide expansion of global business actors' power.

It is not (only) a question of whether trade unions, churches, NGOs or anyone else is willing or powerful enough to confront today's turbo-capitalism with the *necessities* of social justice. Perhaps these necessities exist, perhaps they do not. But even if there were no justice and no turbo-capitalism intent on treating all notions of social justice with disdain, they would have to be invented, precisely in order to regain and redefine the political aspect of politics. The more petty politics is and the more it makes itself an accomplice of its own conformity to purported global market laws, the more powerless it becomes, until it finally finishes itself off and attends its own funeral. The converse is also true: the more imaginative, infectious, grand and credible is politics' drive to shape events – that is, the more convincingly it delivers itself from its neo-liberal self-sacrifice – the more powerful it becomes, reactivating and remonopolizing its internal logic and autonomy in relation to the autarchic strategies of global business. The task facing politics therefore consists in *making the problem into the source of its own solution* – but doing so, as already mentioned, in order to renew itself through the twin forces of idealism and strategies of power.

In order to examine the extent to which state strategies are capable of counteracting the strategic power of capital, it is helpful to introduce a distinction between *potential* and *current* power. *Potential state power* arises out of the sum of the strategies available to the state and to politics when they break through the dual self-imposed obstructions of neo-liberalism and nationalism and when the *deterritorialized* and *denationalized* state gains access to new, *trans*national opportunities for exercising power and shaping events.

Current state strategies in relation to global business, on the other hand, restrict the negotiating power of individual states and their capacity to shape events to the – *relative* – *lack of options at the national level.* States bar their own access to the spectrum of options available – strategies of deterritorialization, strategies of denationalization, strategies of political self-renewal. Those who refuse to countenance anything other than an empirical approach, and who see the issue solely in terms of current state power strategies, automatically restrict themselves and others to producing *intra*national responses to the dictates of global capital. Thus, 'current' state strategies are, *eo ipso*, *nation*-state strategies that follow from having control over one's own territory. This certainly includes the manipulation of internal markets, of which labour markets, with their corresponding educational requirements and social security systems, are a part, but it excludes transnationalization and strategies of cooperation.

The distinction between *potential* 'despatialized' state strategies and *current nation*-state strategies is so important because it does two things at once. On the one hand, it reveals an element of 'emancipation' on the part of the state and of politics, which follow the lead of their global business opponents by freeing themselves from their national and territorial 'parochialisms'. On the other hand, it also shows clearly what it is that prevents political actors – that is, governments and political parties – from seizing these opportunities and putting them into practice, namely, the *false a priori of the indissolubility of nation and state*, of politics and territory, of political influence and national sovereignty.

Strategies aimed at 'despatializing the state'

The discrepancy between the territorially defined arena of the state and the deterritorially and transnationally defined arena of the global market can ultimately be countered – from the point of view of states – *only* by extending the state's activities beyond its territorial borders. As it becomes possible to develop ideas towards a '*despatialization*' of the state and politics and to embark upon such a path, so political answers will be found in response to the newly emerging economic geography. Only in this way can the 'fate' of state politics – from having been the driving force behind globalization to being driven along by it – be turned around to provide a new boost for politics. This becomes possible by means of transnationalization in the sense of *inter-state cooperation*.

When governments negotiate agreements that are binding under international law, or when – as in the European Union – they join together in new, transnational cooperative executives, each government is effectively acting within a 'transnational arena', because the commitments they have entered into demand a binding commitment from all parties. In this way, 'state-based cooperative, transnational' organizations emerge, spaces of 'cooperative sovereignty', which are more than capable of defying global private business corporations and creating a new operational environment for them.

However, this gain in transnational state power needs to be paid for down to the last penny, using the currency of national autonomy. In other words, the transnationalization of state power and the despatialization of politics go hand in hand with a gradual self-denationalization of the state and its hotly contested 'sovereignty'. It is not a matter of relinquishing sovereignty, which is an oft-heard lament; rather, it is a matter of the loss of *national* sovereignty, which is definitely more than compensated for by an expansion of transnational cooperative sovereignty. This step outside the national arena and into the apparent void of the transnational is an almost inconceivable and certainly very painful one for many nations, national politicians and nation-state theorists, but it is a consequence of the problems and regulatory necessities that confront us at every turn in the global age. Thus, the solo efforts of individual states are doomed to ineffectuality in almost every sphere of politics – whether it be law, crime, further education, technological development or preventive measures against incalculable risks, especially in environmental politics. The *only* possibility of finding solutions to the burning issues that we face lies in seeking transnational approaches and, as their prerequisite, the deterritorialization of politics and of the state in the form of cooperative alliances and international regimes. One final point is crucial here: relinquishing national rights of sovereignty by no means equates with a loss of capacity for solving national problems. Rather, just the opposite is the case: the *only* way of solving the burning issues at a *national* level is to *trans-nationalize* the activities of the state and of government.

There is one essential, basic insight regarding the state and politics in the second modernity: *the only way to revive national politics is to denationalize it*. An internal connection exists between a loss of national sovereignty and a gain in transnational sovereignty – that is, the development of national sovereignty regained through cooperation and essentially used for tackling the 'national issues' of a politics oriented towards problem-solving.

These ways of extending nation-state policy options come with one problematic consequence, however: they are incapable of obtaining direct democratic legitimation. At least, this is the case as long as the arenas of parliamentary democracy coincide with nation-state borders and as long as the transnationalization of politics is not linked with a transnationalization of democracy. Viewed in this light, if nation-state politics manages – unlike the proverbial leopard – to change its national sovereignty spots (which are fading more and more in any case), it can even make gains in *national* power in a way that places the latter beyond the control of the parliamentary opposition and the national public sphere.

To put it in Machiavellian terms: the transnational empowerment of national politics is a dual one. It extends across national borders *and* is effective at national level because it is capable of circumventing democratic control. Thus, transnationalization opens up a new option for national politics: it becomes possible to neutralize one's own opposition via Europe or the WHO or the World Bank, and in the process enforce collectively binding decisions nationally via the transnational route. For example, governments that take their first transnational steps are in a position to limit the policy options of successor governments.

The German government coalition between the Greens and the Social Democrats found out the hard way how this can lead to tensions with regard to a change in electoral opinion when it attempted to push through a legal ban on nuclear reprocessing within Germany. It soon discovered that its hands were largely tied due to the existence of intergovernmental agreements that had been established between its predecessor government and the nuclear power-friendly governments of France and Britain. The conservative–liberal coalition government had garnered foreign support in order to be in a better position to protect a programme which they suspected would generate domestic controversy and political resistance. (Wolf 1999: 18)

Strategies of Grand Politics

In order to argue convincingly for the indispensability of the state in relation to a form of global business that colonizes the political sphere, it is necessary to break the hegemony of neo-liberal discourse and replace it with a discourse about the themes of Grand Politics. Note, I am speaking here of *strategies*, whereby these can never be equated with their realization. To reject these strategies of Grand Politics because it appears utopian to put them into practice at the present moment in history would mean preventively rejecting a key strategy of political power. What we are talking about in this context, then, are political themes within a strategic power calculation. The fact that this is ultimately possible only if the themes themselves are convincing and are able to enthuse and mobilize people can certainly be regarded as part of the strategic calculation. It is worth noting that neo-liberal globalism does *not* possess this inspirational power. Neo-liberal globalism is the ideology of a technocratic elite and not an ideology capable of motivating the masses into action. This is the message the new neo-liberal crusaders preach: be lean, downsize, becoming more flexible, and if you then hook up to the Internet, the future is yours for the taking. But this is not exactly how to create a new sense of mutual belonging, solidarity, or a new identity. In fact, the very opposite is the case: the free global market ideology undermines pre-existing traditions and democratic cultures by radicalizing social inequalities and endangering the principles of political freedom, social justice and security.

Those who would counter the discourse of neo-liberalism, which has enjoyed extraordinary political success worldwide, need emphatically to demonstrate the indispensability of the political sphere. This is the objective, first, of *strategies aimed at delegitimizing* global business activities, followed by strategies of *conflict and crisis* and, finally, strategies of *utopia*, which spell out the transnational renaissance of the political sphere in the form of a programme of self-reflexive politics.

One of the ways of vividly highlighting the indispensability of politics and bringing its influence to bear is to redefine the *monopoly on legitimation* of democratic states in its confrontation with global business. Business needs a transnational political framework in which to operate, otherwise global business actors face a loss of public acceptance and, with it, declining power. The emergence of translegal domination needs to be matched by a new 'translegal politics'. Since all power relies on consent, the concentration of power within global business is in a *precarious legitimatory position*. In fact, we might even say that, as power increases, so too does its precariousness, which then both enter the public consciousness. The often-mentioned crisis of confidence in global business bears witness to this.

One objection to this could be that business is neither elected by the people nor relies on their consent. However, in striving for global economic autarchy over against politics and society, it demonstrates one of its ideological Achilles heels. It is precisely transnational business that lives off *borrowed* political legitimacy, or *infusions of state legitimacy*, as it were, which can be administered without a single word but can also be withdrawn at any time. Political and state apparatuses, for example, have to underpin and justify the economic, social and ecological consequences of private capital flows and investment decisions – including the collapse of entire countries and world regions, unemployment and environmental destruction. This is why governments are forced to anticipate the negative aspects of private investment decisions *and to justify them without* being able to exert any direct influence on the decisions themselves.

Moreover, even capital, which plays a powerful role in the legitimation-free arena of translegality, is *in itself* extremely susceptible to crises of legitimation. When corporate profits are calculated on a global scale but with minimal margins on individual products, consumer protests can act like stray sparks in a parched summer forest, setting off wildfires in this legitimation-free space and bringing global market constructs to the point of collapse. In this respect, it has something of the quality of whistling nervously in a dark forest when anti-globalization protests are dismissed in the boardrooms of corporate management as the reaction of '*globophobes*' and of unrepresentative, non-legitimate 'pressure groups' that are ultimately out to prevent the very economic growth that benefits the world's poor.

It may be that such protest groups have little political or economic power in the conventional sense. But they are very good at embodying a 'global conscience' and putting it to use against the 'overwhelming power of the corporations', as people throughout the world view it. Moreover, these transnational protest movements, which now also operate in a deterritorialized way, are as strong as the concentration of global business power is fragile, given the shaky legitimatory ground on which it stands. In spite of – or even on account of – maximizing their economic power, global corporations themselves can withstand *conflict* only if others are willing to lend them legitimatory support and, if necessary, defend their market position using state means of violence. In cases of public conflict, dependencies are turned around the other way: the powerlessness of corporations in terms of legitimation becomes just as apparent as the indispensability of state politics with its monopoly on legitimation. The 'worst case scenario' for global business power, then, is when transnational conflicts flare up. Both imminent and actual conflicts disempower global business actors and empower governments. It is crucial to recognize this, as the capacity of politics to deal with transnational conflicts is a major source of its self-renewal.

Thus, the old question as to the 'power of the multinationals' presents itself in a new light: perhaps global corporations' autarchic strategies do work, after all, according to the old Marxist logic which says that their very success is what threatens their legitimatory foundations. How will global corporations react in a world in which countless thousands take to the streets in Seattle, Davos and Washington to express their fear of globalization, and in which the social and political consequences of growing corporate dominance meet with more and more public resistance all over the world in the form of alliances made up of colourful coalitions of large and small political groupings?

The counter-pressure from NGOs and a broad array of social and consumer movements is greater than ever before and has certainly had some impact: the OECD's all too company-friendly 'Multilateral Agreement on Investment' (MAI) has failed; powerful biotechnology companies in Europe have had to climb down (for the time being, at least); and even in the USA, the country that invented the apologetics of unwavering belief in progress, bio-tech corporations have gone on the defensive, while more and more influential voices are drawing attention not only to the opportunities but also to the uncontrollable risks posed by biotechnology, information technology and robotic technology. Even the WTO seems to be in a state of paralysis since the Seattle riots. These are the signs of a collapse in legitimacy that globalization's elites – much like those who held power in the former East Germany – like casually to dismiss. But just like those who held power in the GDR, they may suddenly find themselves standing before the ruins of their fake autarchic power constructs, made ever more precarious by the withdrawal of consent.

If state politics is concerned to revive its fortunes in the transnational arena and in relation to global business, then it should undo the cast-iron coalition between the nation-state and business interests; it should be capable of dealing with conflicts and be keen to do so; and it should *join in a coalition with NGOs and consumer movements to become an advocate for a newly defined 'public welfare'*, which is systematically violated by the short-term interests of capital. Politics makes gains as soon as it puts the legitimation of global business onto the public agenda. Legitimation crises prove that global business is not autarchic and that it is vulnerable on the issue of legitimation – and they prove that politics is indispensable. It might just be possible to turn the tables, to clear politics worldwide of the charge of neo-liberalism and to uncover those endemic deficits in legitimacy that only grow bigger as power increases; if this can be done, then a revitalized politics may even break up the neo-liberal discursive hegemony and replace it with a discourse of political self-renewal.

In relation to global business, this means demanding accountability, responsibility and transparency. In relation to the public and the electorate, it means transforming rhetorical soundbites and empty promises, along with the principles of justice and law that have already become binding through the United Nations (human rights, standards of dignified working conditions, environmental protection), into executive and legislative initiatives, at both national and international level. However, this will only be possible if parties and governments are prepared to do a u-turn, following the creed: *abandoning utopia means giving up power*. A professed lack of utopianism is not only a sickness of the human spirit, it also represents a blank cheque for politicians to give up on politics. Only those capable of enthusing others will win consent and power. The best way to escape from the self-induced passivity – and powerlessness – of nation-state politics in the second modernity is ultimately to rediscover Grand Politics.

Conversely, for a politics that renews the national sphere rather than overcoming it, a dramatic gap opens up between political goals and situations demanding intervention on the one hand, and a growing incapacity to act on the other. While globally networked economies are able to operate in a temporal context of simultaneity and continuity, a political approach that is limited to the national sphere remains embroiled in a local minus-sum game. This involves nation-states having to pay for their 'obligingness' – further deregulation of the national market, for example – with social and political costs which in the long term put social cohesion at risk. In this sense, a politics whose programme consists of nothing but 'save, save, save!' endangers not only voter consent but also itself.

Both the politics of deregulation *and* the politics of preserving power are mutually exclusive in the long term. Nobody willingly agrees to their own demise. And yet the strategy of political neo-liberalization prepares the ground for politics to be completely drained of power. The elites of neo-liberal globalization seem not yet to have understood that the world has become democratic. This is why the confrontation between capital and politics with respect to political power is intensifying. The former Spanish prime minister Felipe Gonzáles put his finger on this very point: 'We (social democrats) may be in government throughout almost the entire European Union, but we are not in power.'

On the other hand, the challenges facing political action and political imagination are steadily mounting, a situation that is perhaps comparable – if at all – only with that at the start of the industrial revolution 150 years ago. Back then it was a matter of 'building' nation-states, parliaments, governments and constitutions, and creating the corresponding education systems, transport structures, and so forth. The reforms required today are, if anything, of a magnitude that is even more intimidating: the task today is to reformulate and reimplement the democratic and social achievements of the nation-state in line with the demands of the transnational era. This is why the key institutions of parliamentary democracy, conceived along nation-state lines, need to be opened up to the transnational context just as much as the social welfare state does. A number of issues need to be resolved in the process, such as how people might be enabled to anticipate and so live with the new precariousness of work, and how to deal with what are largely still unresolved issues around rampant global environmental destruction and the as yet utterly incalculable risks of new technologies that are advancing ever more rapidly upon us.

All these issues have at least one global dimension to them as well, so that the dilemma facing national politics at the start of the twenty-first century presents itself in the following way: while opportunities for shaping events are becoming fewer and fewer due to the self-paralysis of national political institutions and the concentration of global business power, the scale of existing political challenges is increasing beyond measure.

This is the dilemma addressed by the strategy of the self-renewal of state power and its concrete concerns. Politicians and governments cannot expect others – the will of the people, the public sphere, global business, the mass media, NGOs, and so forth – to create majorities for them and to put the big questions onto the negotiating table. They can and must put these big issues at the centre of a renewal that encompasses the concrete concerns of politics itself and of political power. This can only be achieved by transcending the borders of individual nation-states – in other words, if politics is capable, in small steps and larger leaps, of divesting itself of its national parochialism, breaking up the neo-liberal discursive hegemony, and winning over public opinion to the various projects entailed by a cosmopolitan political renewal.[2]

5.2 Strategies of irreplaceability

Both strategies of indispensability and strategies of irreplaceability refer to the relationship between the state and business (and not to the state-to-state or business-to-business relationship). Whereas strategies of indispensability renew the monopoly which politics has over against global business (and in this respect they are in exact opposition to global business strategies of autarchy), strategies of irreplaceability counteract corporate technological and organizational strategies of monopolization: *the strategy of transnational expertise.* These strategies are also directed against the monopolization of rationality by global business. Thus, in the latter case, they are aimed at limiting, or rather reversing, the transfer of state functions from the public arena to the private sphere of global business actors: *strategies aimed at demonopolizing global business rationality.*

Strategies of transnational expertise

In order to attract foreign capital, states need to establish a legal and organizational environment that is cost-effective in comparison with other states. In addition, however, the nature of this environment needs to be such that it enables states to face corporations as equals when negotiating conditions, by possessing the relevant know-how and organizational and legal expertise. For example, they need to be capable of enforcing and monitoring agreements in the face of corporate interests that come armed with highly paid experts. If states do not have at their disposal the relevant specialists, or laws, or institutions, or (tax) experts adept at dealing with international corporations, their negotiating power is limited accordingly, and this only makes their confrontation with the concentrated power of corporate legal and technical experts, who are thoroughly initiated in transnational affairs, more fraught.

State strategies of irreplaceability are therefore aimed at creating stricter legal frameworks in the host countries. For example, the possibility of actually levying agreed taxes presupposes the existence of suitable monitoring institutions and well-versed legal experts, as well as relevant administrative and managerial specialists who are also familiar with the transnational meta-power game and cannot be checkmated after two moves. The situation of individual states in relation to global corporations can also be improved if each state pursues a policy of cooperation, helping to establish comparable conditions of production between host countries and 'host cartels' formed on the basis of similar interests. One aim would be to exchange relevant information with one another, and another would be to limit the risk of being played off against one another.

Conversely, corporate negotiating power increases if

(a)   the technological complexity of the planned investment regime is larger or grows more quickly than host countries' transnational administrative and knowledge-based capabilities or their ability to learn; and/or

(b) the size of the planned enterprise as a whole exceeds a state's existing administrative and monitoring capabilities in terms of project-related knowledge and legal procedures.

While both sets of conditions exist in part and in relation to specific projects in the states of the centre, they are present especially in the countries of the so-called Third World.

Strategies aimed at demonopolizing business rationality

The worldwide triumphant success of the rationality of the market coincided with the collapse of the Soviet Union. This not only signalled the departure of a military bloc from world history and the emergence of a multi-polar world; it also signalled the emergence of a *global monopoly on economic efficiency and rationality*. Because of the bankruptcy of the communist planned economy, and in particular of the ideas behind it, the division of labour and of rationality that underpinned the Western idea of the social welfare state also disintegrated. Here, too, the state possessed a quasi-economic monopoly on rationality in relation to those sovereign economic activities that were under state management – the military, the police, the judiciary, but also the service and industrial sectors.

There is no doubt that state (economic) activities come to be *replaceable* once business (and thereby, in the medium and long term, global business) succeeds in extending its monopoly on rationality to *all* economically relevant activities and is thus able to reorganize more and more state and public affairs to its own advantage, in line with the principles of profit maximization.

This process is now in full swing throughout the world. One of the crucial questions for the future clash between political and business power is: where does the privatization of state functions end? Can schools and universities be completely or predominantly privatized? If so, why? Does the same go for courts and parliaments? If not, why not? Can international commercial law alone be privatized but not national commercial law? And what about the police and the military? In other words, in a context of neo-liberal discursive hegemony, certain trends are thoroughly conceivable that would involve state monopolies with economic significance being dismantled step by step and delegated to the rationality of private enterprise. Perhaps it is only the officers and higher level civil servant jobs that need to be organized by the state, while the lower grades in the military and administration can be 'much more efficiently' entrusted to the business management rationality of private companies. This is exactly where state strategies of *re-regulation* and *deprivatization* come into effect. These latter are aimed at breaking down the global business monopoly on efficient management that has come into being and at reappropriating those state functions that had been transferred over to private (global) business. As privatization advances and its problematic consequences – which in some cases are catastrophic – become apparent, they provide the raw material for developing corresponding state strategies of indispensability.

The wave of liberalization washed over Britain relatively early on, so that its problematic consequences are by now very much in evidence. Here, all casual talk of the 'higher rationality' of privatized companies merely elicits ironic laughter, if not worse. Anybody who is forced to travel regularly on the British railways has to struggle through what, to a foreigner, is an impenetrable jungle of timetables; this is because different sections of the railway network are operated by different private companies and have so far failed to be coordinated as part of a single system. Moreover, passengers have to be prepared for chronic delays and perfectly normal train cancellations. Repairs are never brought to completion, and are a permanent source of apologetic announcements – rather like the weather. In Britain, where, as we all know, it rarely rains, 'unpredictable rainfall' can bring whole regions of the rail network to a complete standstill. Worst of all, though, is the catalogue of accidents – even genuine disasters are no longer a rare occurrence, and subsequent inquiries usually highlight dramatic safety deficiencies. One outcome of this has been that Prime Minister Tony Blair, who continues to fly the flag of privatization, has had to cope with a dramatic decline in electoral support in relation to this issue. All the harping on about the superior rationality of private enterprise must sound like a very bad joke in train passengers' ears. And now, with the privatization of the Deutsche Bahn, Germany is going through its own 'Britainization'.

There are thoroughly systematic reasons for all this. One of them is that economic rationality clashes with safety considerations, and this clash takes place not only in extreme contexts – in relation, say, to issues regarding the technical safety of nuclear power stations or standards governing the installation of track systems and their technical safety architectures – but also in the grey areas where specialists with long-term contracts are replaced by semi-skilled workers with part-time contracts or employment arrangements that can easily be terminated. Critical observers may well wonder whether it is only through being set up and maintained by third-party – i.e. state – funding that a railway network can operate as a privately run, profit-oriented concern, since investments of this magnitude generally run counter to the profit calculations made by private business.

This assumption certainly has the benefit of empirical evidence on its side. In many areas of public life, the privatization of social services has not only raised costs but also increased levels of inefficiency. Health provision in the USA, for example, costs twice as much as in Europe and is chronically poor in quality. And this is not even to mention a whole set of other deficiencies:

privatization replaces public administrations – which were at least subject to democratic control – with private bureaucracies that are unaccountable and lack transparency for outsiders.

In addition, there is one crucial disadvantage to privatization: it does not replace public waste and maladministration with private enterprise efficiency – as legend would have it – but rather public monopolies with *private monopolies*, which are a breeding ground for mismanagement and rising costs. Note, this is by no means true of states in the Third World alone, but also of the major centres in the West.

It is important for political strategies of deprivatization and re-regulation to turn the tables in the following respect: if neo-liberals have been concerned with the 'contradictions of the state', a new breed of politicians needs to be concerned with the *'contradictions of privatization'*. Surely the growing number of accidents and serious disasters on the railways, for example, point to endemic safety deficiencies which can be attributed at least in part to the desire to cut costs by employing fewer skilled workers and informally relaxing safety standards? Surely there is a link between efficiency and accountability, between profitability and responsibility, between quality service and democracy? And if this is the case, do we not perhaps need a different concept of 'business rationality' and 'business efficiency', one that encompasses both standards of transparency and those of social justice and public accountability? In sum, it seems more than likely that enormous efforts are being made to set up new monopolies under the guise of privatization which then lead to forms of private sector mismanagement.

Similar cases exist that speak volumes in favour of a transnational *politics of re-regulation*. Over the past few years, industries subject to large amounts of regulation have been liberalized, telecommunications being the main example, others being energy, food and finance. The worldwide competition unleashed in this way has brought national standards authorities into conflict with one another, and the free movement of goods has made the problem into a global one. Yet all this is only the beginning. Even today it is clear that further sources of conflict lurk on the horizon – including global environmental norms and labour market standards, and so on. Negotiation is urgently needed in areas where regulations are even more important and more difficult to establish on account of being highly sensitive politically.

This, too, is an area where neo-liberal politics reveals its flip side, one that can be made the subject of political renewal. The first wave of national deregulation makes a second wave of transnational re-regulation necessary. This process entails granting enhanced status to those areas that were pushed to the sidelines during the 1980s, namely the state and politics. What is required is the exact opposite of neo-liberal deconstruction: strong cooperative states capable of enforcing transnational market regulations both within and beyond individual countries.

5.3   Strategies aimed at avoiding global market monopolies

States can improve their position of power insofar as they are able to increase competition between global business actors and reduce competition among themselves. *Strategies aimed at avoiding global market monopolies* are directed at achieving the former while *strategies aimed at reducing competition between states* are directed at the latter.

The nature and extent of competition between multinational or transnational companies over investment opportunities in a certain country is an essential factor in how much negotiating power host countries have at their disposal. If certain corporations have a monopoly in terms of the specific package on offer in a certain country, there will be a lack of competition between investors, which places the country concerned in a much weaker position. Equally, the converse is true: the more corporations compete with one another over a country that has an attractive host profile, and the greater the differences and 'national origins' of these corporations are, the greater the power of the host state concerned.

Thus, from the point of view of extending the range of national and transnational options available to states, one might say: let a thousand multinational corporations bloom! State strategies for increasing competition between global business actors can be developed in two directions, namely in relation to conditions both inside and outside a given state. Strategies related to the domestic sphere emphasize the attractiveness of the country for investors and underline its unique features; they attempt to create a plus-sum game that enables domestic, national critics and contradictions to be countered by facilitating greater opportunities and participation for different groups. Competition between corporations might be expected to grow, therefore, in instances where potential host states are able to supply urgently needed resources (oil) and cheap labour – or else urgently needed, well-qualified specialists who are hard to find – as well as mediating (export) institutions that allow investors to operate in both domestic and foreign markets.

When these kinds of structural advantages and provisions are insufficient or non-existent, competition between investors is reduced, while the likelihood grows that the power of the state concerned will seep away in a monopolistic relationship with a single foreign investor.

The range of options open to individual states within their own borders are very limited and generally always amount to governments taking the neoliberal ideal of the state as a blueprint for their 'reform policies'. However, power relations shift in favour of states when *external, transnational* options come into consideration. For countries and states in the so-called Third World in particular, the leap from a position of monopolistic dependency to having a choice between several willing foreign investors is extremely important, as it is only this opportunity to choose between different investors that enables such states to free themselves from their traditional, often postcolonial and imperialist, dependency on dominant Western countries. This enables them, in turn, and with the aid of diversified and pluralized trade relations, to assert their relative autonomy in both domestic and foreign spheres.

During the 1950s and 1960s there was hardly any competition – and in some cases none at all – between foreign investors, so that the power of Third World states in relation to the global economic power blocs of Western states was reduced to almost zero. From the point of view of postcolonial countries and states struggling for their autonomy and for ways of moving forward, 'imperialism' is the perceived enemy to be combated, but there is always an element of global market strategy to this as well. This *'imperialist constellation'*, as we might call it, consists in the following features which, as already mentioned, existed in the 1950s:

(a) maximum competition between states, generated by the availability of alternative sources of raw materials and the existence of cheap labour, which minimized the negotiating power of individual states;
(b) a predominance of American corporations on the global market so that national and military dominance was allied to global market monopolies.

Both these factors sealed the almost hopeless situation of dependency in which the group of states concerned found itself.

In the meantime, however, this situation has been changed on both counts. In the international oil industry, for example, countries with oil resources have succeeded in establishing competition between the multinationals in order to increase their share of oil production. Also, 'Japanese' corporations have now set up operations in Latin America, as an alternative to 'US American' companies, just as 'American' and 'German' corporations are cropping up more and more frequently as an alternative to 'French' companies in Africa.

Having said this, old imperialistic constellations have remained intact while new ones are emerging. For example, the situation in the particularly attractive sectors of manufacturing, new technologies (including information and communication, biotechnology and genetics, robotics and artificial intelligence) and service initiatives is generally characterized by the creation of new monopolies and the involvement of privileged states. These new super technologies, which are set to change the world in every respect, require huge amounts of investment and can therefore only be developed with the support of the rich states, which subsidize this activity not least through investments in military technology. Nonetheless, the debate in Germany over 'green cards' for IT and high-tech specialists from India demonstrates that the new computer technologies have now penetrated into the so-called Third World economies, and this with no little success, something that may bring about new varieties of dependency even for the so-called highly developed countries.

In terms of the position of power occupied by states and countries struggling for access to the world market and for the 'prospects of promotion' this brings with it, the crucial issue is the extent to which they actually manage to activate their *potential* power and bring it to bear against global market actors (Tarzi 2000: 162 f.). The extent to which states succeed in putting their power options into practice can be measured, among other things, by their respective governments' willingness and ability to deal with conflict.

Foreign investors are the trigger to a multitude of domestic political conflicts. They induce conflicts that can either be ironed out or may become the key to opening negotiations with investors and the states that support and protect them. As host countries succeed in breaking up the imperialist constellation – that is, in reducing competition between states and improving their own range of management skills in dealing with transnational corporations – so their chances of bringing the dynamics of conflict within their own country to bear in negotiations and reaping the resultant benefits improve. Thus, as the population – students, workers, local and national companies, and even the administrative staff in state authorities – becomes mobilized around the issue of conditions *within* national markets, as well as in relation to promotional opportunities within the education system, citizens' rights, the transport system, and so on, so the intensity of conflict at the national level over foreign investments and the conditions attached to them increases.

Thus, a key question for weak states in particular is to what extent their governments are able – given a situation that has been structurally improved by means of agreements and multiple, diversified international trading relations – to raise the price for settling current or potential social conflicts and thereby, step by step, to become part of globalization's winning team of organizers rather than remaining among its passive losers.

One point clearly reinforced by this is that conflicts do not worsen the position of states in relation to global business; instead, they *improve* it. The opposite interpretation, disseminated through neo-liberalism's political correctness, stems ultimately from the latter's calculation of power, which entails weakening the position of states – especially those struggling for their own advancement – in relation to the dominant global market actors.

The verdict that state authority must be minimalized – which is also included among the creeds and ideological postulates of an *economistic* development of power – points in the same direction. It is precisely developing countries and regions that depend most on having *strong* states which, in turn, are then in a position to build up a relative degree of strength in relation to the overbearing power of Western monopolistic strategies. This is why state-critical discourse in regions with weak states amounts to a barely disguised call to unconditional capitulation in the face of organized global market monopolies.

Conversely, while one would think that corporate power is exclusively economic in nature, corporations can certainly use their power to serve the goal of democratization within countries. Why should it not be possible, for example, for an alliance of transnational corporations to establish standards for the political and moral environment in which they have to operate and to make them binding, so that the silent force of the economy can be used to generate pressure to implement human rights and social justice?

The reason why the question arises at all is that multinational corporations themselves deliberately develop cooperative strategies among themselves in order to minimize or disable the negotiating power of states. In order to minimize the political risks associated with their investments in particular, transnational corporations build *transnational alliances*, which pass almost all of the potential costs of political instability on to the host states and thereby improve – if not dictate – conditions for the investment project to their own advantage. Such multinational economic cooperatives and alliances often mobilize the political, financial and diplomatic power of states to their own advantage, under whose ensign they are nonetheless happy to sail whenever the possibility of receiving support for such projects comes up. Third World governments' dealings with the pharmaceuticals and automobile industries, for example, demonstrate the way in which this kind of global corporate network of alliances is capable of reducing the power of host states and possibly even crushing it altogether.

A similar point is that multinational corporations, by multiplying their practical options, also exert influence over transnational political actors such as the World Bank, the IMF and others. They do this not only in individual cases but also in structural terms, by setting specific benchmarks, in order to improve their position in relation to host states. The opportunities for doing so are growing because the trading interests of transnational companies have a neo-liberal profile that is much closer to the interests and politics of those international organizations, while political 'loyalty' – the existence of interests that run parallel to those of international business executives – is not (necessarily) given among national governments and non-international companies.

The policies and crisis management of international institutions thus acquire crucial significance in relation to weak states' efforts to improve their power status and their position in the global market. On the one hand, they certainly *could* counter the creation of monopolies by transnational corporations and even prevent them altogether by means of targeted interventions and regulations. On the other hand, their failure to implement such a policy raises the question: is the purpose of the transnational organizations set up to regulate the global economy – the World Bank, the IMF, OECD, the G-8 countries, and so on – to *protect monopolies* and to ensure that the global market is controlled by the dominant, transnational oligopolies? Is the rhetoric of the free market simply a masquerade aimed *de facto* at favouring and furthering a perverse politics of protectionism, namely a *'monopoly protectionism'* for global business actors?

5.4   Strategies aimed at reducing competition between states

The problem of competition between states has been addressed in a variety of ways. This competition is created and sustained when more or less all states become competitors to one another in and via the global market, rather than individual states being 'autarchic' and organizing their economic interests exclusively in national markets.

This 'more or less' entails quite a number of relativizations. For example, the significance of a country's position in the global market depends on the size of a state's domestic market (which, in countries such as the USA, China and Russia, is considerable). We also need to ask to what extent the influences of global market actors limit the impact of nationally based global market companies within different 'national' economic arenas, to what extent the latter squeeze out the former or vice versa. Are economically powerful states pursuing a *politics of double standards* with respect to the market economy by insisting that the principles of the free market should apply to every other country while they themselves act in a protectionist manner to shield their own domestic markets from 'hostile takeovers'? This is indeed the case with large nation-state economies, which, in doing so, are promoting a hierarchy of inequality with their protectionist policies. They denounce all protectionist tendencies in other states but think that protectionist egotism is the most natural thing in the world when applied to themselves.

At a global level, this schizophrenia is most clearly institutionalized along the dividing line between capital and labour. While capital and the owners of capital are able to move freely throughout the world, it is considered the most 'natural' thing in the world to limit that right for workers worldwide through an international alliance of national protectionism. The fact that every border is wide open to capital and its owners is nowadays seen as completely normal and natural, while workers who wish to utilize their labour and educational capital in other countries – who want to try their 'investment luck' – are usually seen as 'asylum seekers' or 'economic refugees', who are criminalized and prevented by police or military action from freely utilizing their human capital. This schizophrenia is heightened when countries that lack workers with a specific qualification issue 'green cards', or when 'experience abroad' is stipulated as one of the requirements for securing a higher position.

This fundamental *asymmetry between capital and labour* is indeed remarkable. Nobody talks about 'investment asylum seekers'. There are no calls for investors to be rounded up in detention camps at airports and queried about their motivations, just as little as embassies or foreign ministries are urged to compile a list of criteria for deciding from which countries a certain number of 'legitimate' capital asylum seekers may be accepted. Has any debate erupted to date over the issue of how well or badly multinational corporations have become integrated into the national and local culture of their host country? This may be the case here and there. But what is astonishing is the extent to which we all of us around the globe quite unquestioningly live with a divided consciousness: we talk about globalization when we actually mean *only* the globalization of capital. Meanwhile, the globalization of labour is turned into a criminal act, so that people are forced to take up this (refused) right by giving themselves over to unscrupulous people smugglers. This new trade in human beings has now become a global business growth sector. When fifty-eight poor souls are found suffocated to death in a refrigerated container, the public outcry is considerable. Yet the only ones to be called to account are those who seek to profit from the racist difference between migration and mobility, rather than those who keep a careful watch on the asymmetry between the mobility of capital and the immobility of labour.

At this point, it becomes clear that if the demand for unhindered mobility on the part of labour were applied in a generalized way *it would actually change the nation-state face of the world beyond recognition*. It is this global schizophrenia of a free, liberal market economy imposed *exclusively* for the benefit of capital which is above all responsible for maintaining the territorial premises and façades of nation-state politics and society.

If competition between states is established in this form by the world market, albeit in a thoroughly selective and limited way, it is no less important to make a distinction between this inter-state *global market competition* and national *rivalry* among states. The latter is based on the notion of a national threat and presupposes the need to safeguard the greatest amount of national autonomy possible in relation to other states. National rivals or enemies help one another when they mutually issue military threats. In contrast to this, states in competition with one another in the global market mutually support one another by limiting that competition through cooperative arrangements that are mutually beneficial. This is exactly what strategies aimed at reducing competition between states do. States can achieve the goal of a reduction in competition in three ways:

1 through specialization strategies and
2 through hegemonic strategies. These strategies are available to state actors in the national context, albeit under vastly unequal conditions, and are to be distinguished from

3   strategies of transnationalization. These can only be pursued by states if they succeed in maximizing the benefits of cooperation in order to compensate for the costs generated by a loss of their so sacredly held 'national sovereignty'.

Strategies of state specialization

'Specialization' is a strategy aimed at reducing competition among states in the global market and may be explained by analogy with the professions. If 'professions' are seen as training packages, or as 'proprietary brands' of the commodity 'labour' that can be acquired in the education system and traded on the labour market, then the 'acquisition' of a certain profession means that competition is reduced and channelled for its 'owner'. Nurses are in competition with all other nurses, but not with accountants, and the competition among nurses is that much greater for being played out in a limited sphere protected by clear-cut areas of expertise.

Of course, this example from the world of the professions can only be applied with certain caveats to the relationship between states on the global market, but the same applies here as well: states can develop particular 'proprietary brand profiles' which are not only anchored in terms of technical functionality, but also need to be seen in a political and cultural light. States with the same or a similar brand profile face stiffer competition from one another, while competition between states with different kinds of specialization profiles is reduced.

It is possible to identify two ways of classifying such strategies of state specialization. First, it can be done by limiting them to *rigidly economic* considerations. This leads us – with Manuel Castells – to identify new patterns in the national division of labour that are characteristic of the 'new, global economy', consisting of *'high quality' producers* of the new forms of work based on information and knowledge, *labour-intensive producers* of low-skill work involving precarious contracts and flexible organization, the groups that process raw materials, and so forth.[3] The advantage of these sorts of specialization profiles is that they address foreseeable future differentiations, but their disadvantage is that they do this using a taken-for-granted technocratic approach. In other words, they fail to recognize the strategic political character of the global division of labour and they also obscure the fact that the division of labour between states can *never* be comprehended in a rigidly functional, technical way, but only in terms of a comprehensive profile in which technical, economic and functional aspects are embedded in cultural and political traditions and fictions.

Focusing on this last factor, it is possible to identify four 'proprietary brand strategies', or specialization strategies, available to states, namely

(a)   the social democratic strategy of the protective state,
(b)   the downwardly mobile strategy of low-wage states,
(c)   the parasitic strategy of tax haven states, and
(d)   the Anglo-American strategy of neo-liberal depoliticization, of divesting the state of its functions qua state.[4]

Strategies of state specialization are aimed at creating and exploiting economic and cultural as well as political specificities and strengths – 'proprietary brands'; in doing so, they steer clear of the politics set forth in the neo-liberal blueprint of Americanization, the main message of which is: learning from the USA means learning to win in the global market. The argument held against this approach is that, if every state becomes a 'baker', then the entire international community of states will collapse, and this for at least two reasons. The first is that bread and cake end up being everybody's downfall because the rules of specialization according to which differences and diversities are rewarded have been flouted. The second reason is that, as states become more interchangeable, so the competition between them increases, rather than being reduced or channelled. This in turn means that the power of states is minimized while the power of global business is maximized, that is, fresh confrontation between capital and politics becomes inevitable on account of the primacy of capital.

On the other hand, specialization strategies – that is, becoming a particular proprietary brand in the world market – involve neither ruling out competition nor increasing it to the extent that every state becomes interchangeable with every other state; instead, they involve *channelling* competition. Competition grows within the same state models of modernity ('proprietary brands'), whereas it is kept to a minimum between states with different profiles and models of modernity.

Thus, the theory of a global market without borders can be set against the theory of *partial global markets*. The latter assumes that there *is no single* best way within global capitalism, but rather many ways, *alternative modernities* in which the demands of the global market are variously combined with cultural logics, dominant institutional structures and actors as well as political projects ('how do we want to live?').

Nonetheless, all the common proprietary brand strategies of state specialization are at risk of being eroded by neo-liberalism. The question is to what extent these responses, all of which have been developed and struggled for during the phase of the first, nation-state modernity, can be applied in the second, transnational modernity, and to what extent all strategies characterized by the national, territorial approach will have to be revised, reformed and possibly even reinvented in new forms. In this respect, the distinction introduced above between the current (nationally defined) and potential (transnational) power of states is crucial in the context of specialization strategies as well. The need for states to adapt to competitive conditions in the global market should not be erroneously equated with the lack of options that characterizes a variety of politics intent on conforming to the global market and acting in accordance with its rules. To do this would be to rule out the strategic alternative – the transnationalization of politics – which presents itself in the process of the state being freed from its spatial limitations. In other words, it is important not to confuse the transformation and reformation of the state with the dismantling and decline of the same.

(a)   Social democratic strategies of consensus

The social democratic strategy of the welfare state has gone very much on the defensive over the past few years on account of the hegemony of neo-liberal discourse. Generally, this is attributable not only to the false standards set by the 'one and only' capitalism minted in the Anglo-American, neo-liberalist tradition. Much more than this, there has been a failure to recognize that the social democratic strategy of consensus (of which, as Esping-Andersen emphasized in 1991, there are different European versions and trajectories) represents a historically specific political package of responses in which the strategy of selectively opening up towards the global market is combined with specific protective and niche-market strategies, as well as with ideas of equality and solidarity rooted in the political culture. Both Katzenstein (1985) and Palan and Abbott (1999) stress that the crucial specificity – the 'ploy', as it were – of these strategies of the 'protective state' 'is a selective integration into world economy – what we refer to as economic dualism' (1999: 103). 'Economic dualism', however, is a semantic euphemism for the fact that the social democratic strategy of global market specialization is based on *institutionalized double standards in relation to the free market*. It combines a comparably radical openness to the global market (more radical in comparison with many other countries) with protectionist and isolationist policies in many other sectors. This institutionalized contradiction achieves several things all at once, in relation to constituencies both within and outside the country concerned (cf. Palan and Abbott 1999).

- Towards the outside world, welfare states based on the principles of social democracy and consensus can create a positive image of themselves as pioneers of global market liberalization and thereby maximize their export opportunities as well.
- In relation to the domestic scene, they are in a position to protect their own national companies, commodity markets and labour markets by setting up or maintaining national barriers against the 'harmful' impacts of global market competition.
- These double standards are usually justified in the national sphere by reference to strategic security interests as well as the preservation of com-

munity and culture. This is where the strategic significance of communitarianism in the European context becomes apparent. Invoking traditional community values can often provide a cover for doing things that are otherwise hard to defend in public, namely, excluding foreigners and renewing old hierarchies (say, between men and women).

- Nonetheless, the institutionalized double standards of social democratic welfare states have made it possible to realize a form of *welfare-state individualization*, based on income and social safety nets. This 'institutionalized individualism' has led, as is most frequently stressed, to a crumbling of traditional hierarchies and accommodative attitudes in everyday family life, sexuality and marriage, as well as in social clubs and organizations and among traditional party voters. In turn, it has raised the burning question of how the spirit of individualism can be recaptured and corked in the institutionalized 'collective bottles' of parties, trade unions and churches. However, it has also generated a consciousness and a self-awareness that has overcome national as well as class barriers and parochialisms to combine specialist, local identities with cosmopolitan attitudes. This willingness to define oneself not merely as a victim of globalization, but also as a participant in shaping it, is crucial for states' capacity to specialize and to assert their position in the world market in the future.

- Social democratic welfare environments, however, are based on certain key assumptions that are now becoming questionable. On the one hand, they are based on a (relatively) *homogeneous self-image* that is problematic in an age of cultural and ethnic globalization. On the other hand, they nurture the self-image of (relative) *egalitarian solidarity*. This political culture has so far protected social democratic states in continental Europe from the new social diseases of crime, poverty, exclusion, drugs and disintegration in public life, which are much more dramatically in evidence elsewhere, such as the United States and Britain.

Furthermore, let us not forget that the welfare-state culture and politics of egalitarian solidarity is *the* response to the disasters of the twentieth century, to the human devastation wrought by fascism and the forced collectivization of state-organized communism. It was Polanyi in particular, in *The Great Transformation* (1944), who demonstrated that economic openness can and must be linked to a vision of state politics that protects humanity from a return to fascism. What this means when applied to the situation at the start of the twenty-first century is that a 'new deal' is needed, one that establishes a new balance between political and economic power and forces international capital to accept the new rules of cultural and political engagement, along with the existence of transnational states revitalized through mutual cooperation. If this fails, there is a danger that modernized, neo-fascist versions of regression and dehumanization may rear their ugly heads once again. Cultures that emerged in the welfare environment and are dedicated to freedom and a form of individualism based on solidarity can ensure that this does not happen.

At the same time, the situation is ripe for revisiting issues concerning democratic solidarity and spelling them out anew in relation to the transnational constellation. This applies principally to Europe, although even here the barriers of *national protectionism* are already in evidence. The reason for them, first, is that the nation-state consensus only came about in the context of a clear 'us–them' distinction and has only been capable of being maintained on this basis. Homogeneity had to be established domestically between those deemed to be 'the same', and among whom welfare-state solidarity has been institutionalized. This could only be done, however, by drawing a clear dividing line in relation to 'foreigners'. Both moves presuppose a high degree of homogeneity in the population and in its ethnic self-perception, and this has been achieved by marginalizing linguistic, ethnic and religious differences and conflicts.

By the same token, global market success is based on a *national closure* which Habermas has characterized, in Germany's case, as 'Deutschmark nationalism'. This strategy of closure could more generally be characterized as *'prosperity nationalism'*. The two elements on which the national, social democratic state is based – cultural homogeneity and nationalism rooted in prosperity – become sizeable barriers to modernization in the global era, culturally, socially and politically. They prevent the societies that apply double standards in relation to the global market from attaining a self-critical awareness of their role as globalization's selective *winners*, whose welfare niches are safeguarded precisely by *excluding others*.

They also dramatize *costs* of transnationalization in the public perception by playing on national egotistical sentiments. The image of relentless decline that haunts Europe in tandem with the spectre of neo-liberalism has not really been countered as yet by the alternative that is within reach, namely a transnational renewal of democracy, social justice and security, and of ecological thinking and action *outside the bounds of* nation-state exclusivity.

Transnationalization presupposes a society that has become open to cosmopolitanism. Perhaps it is important to recognize in this context that opening up to the global market can happen in different ways. It is possible to compare and contrast the neo-liberalization of capital and labour embarked upon in Britain, for example (where its impacts have been softened by social democracy), with a renewal of culture and society as introduced through the policies of the former French prime minister Lionel Jospin. Beneath the headline 'The new desire for revolution', the German weekly broadsheet *Die Zeit* stated: 'France's governing elites are avoiding painful structural reforms; they are happier to go beserk on social policy instead.'[5] French society is being opened up to the challenges of the global era from the inside, by reverting to its traditions of liberty, equality and fraternity.

The crux of this approach consists in two reform projects, which are directed not so much at the labour market in the first instance as at something that is preserved in the more traditional understanding of 'nation', namely 'natural' inequalities and constraints that conflict with the liberty and equality of citizens. The renewal of the socio-political revolutionary impulse is being used to open up an experimental space of 'life politics' (Giddens). Almost unanimously, the left and the right have,

after much lively debate, passed two laws with laudable intentions and unforeseeable consequences: *'pacs'* and *'parité'*. The one creates a new form of legally regulated co-habitation both for homosexuals and for unmarried heterosexuals. The other aims to increase the proportion of women in political life from a very low level to one that reflects their natural numerical standing in society as half of the population. The *pacte civil de solidarité – pacs* for short – has been in force since December 1999. It creates a legal status for partnerships between two adults who are not married, or 'pacsed', with their partner. Upon signature of a contract, both partners can draw housing benefit and other social benefits normally available to married couples only. After three years of certified co-habitation, they are allowed to submit a joint tax declaration. If one of them dies, the surviving partner has to pay a small amount of inheritance tax – albeit more than a married partner . . .

The second law, which is highly symbolic and whose repercussions are as yet unclear, aims at reorganizing not only private but also public life. The law regarding *'parité'* obliges French political parties, as of 6 June 2000, to put forward an equal number of women and men. In direct elections, such as those for the national assembly, a mechanism involving financial penalties comes into effect if half the candidates throughout the country are not female. The vote on this was once again a lesson in political correctness: only the bourgeois member of parliament Christine Boutin, who had already held her own against everyone else in respect of pacs, voted against. (*Die Zeit*, 21 June 2000)

What is remarkable here is not only that the political implementation of such essentially controversial socio-political reforms managed to bulldoze what were surely a large number of opponents using a strategy of political correctness. Equally remarkable is the way in which the values of liberty and solidarity – ultra-traditional values of (French) modernity – have thereby been released from certain essentialist constraints, in this case the equation of 'natural' sexuality and the marriage bond with heterosexuality and officially sanctioned marriage. In the second case, the contradiction between women's equality in education and the world of work – achieved thanks to the successes of the women's movement – and their continued exclusion from politics and public life (something that applies to almost every continental European state) have been challenged politically.

The striking thing to note is how the *contradictions between retraditionalization and emancipation from tradition* are being played with in this strategy of politicization. To put the issue somewhat pointedly, retradition-alization and the appeal to national traditions of liberty and equality are being used to get rid of outmoded social structures that pose a historical limitation to this emancipatory tradition. This politicizing *tradition-counter-tradition strategy* is one to pay heed to, because, although its starting point is in the national context, it simultaneously detraditionalizes the latter and thus opens it up transnationally.

As far as the issues themselves are concerned, however, politics is merely following a trend that has become part of the population's dominant self-image. For example, whereas in 1981 49 per cent of French people believed that same-sex love was 'never justified', this had fallen in 1999 to only 23 per cent. Naturally, the usual concerns emerge: will the equality of women in politics actually be realized through *parité* – or is this just a dangerous quota in misleading packaging after all? Can the new definition of the 'citoyen', now being spelt in its female form, be extended to dealing with ethnic minorities – in other words, will the quota ruling for women on election lists be followed by a quota ruling for blacks in television? These questions illustrate where the opportunities for such a politics involving apparently small socio-political changes with widespread repercussions may lie: they *repoliticize* society and thereby open up the social and political arena for transnational renewal from the inside.

(b)   Cheap wage strategies

Many states, including those in the so-called Third World in particular, attempt to acquire a distinctive profile in the global market and to attract long-term foreign capital investment by trading with the proprietary brand of *low costs and few controls*. In other words, they either relax or abolish laws to do with health and safety, the environment and state taxes. This may be either a permanent feature or one that is limited temporally and/or locally – the latter is much more common. Unlegislated export zones – or export enclaves – are created, within which certain rules of exemption apply; these include the rule whereby the entire set of legislation which normally applies as a matter of course outside these zones does *not* apply within them. The 'cheap wage' specialization profile is thus manifested above all in a contradictory system of rules and exemptions.

While the welfare state strategy can be thought of in terms of *a minimum dose* of the bitter neo-liberal medicine, which states prescribe for themselves and proceed to swallow, the strategy of downward mobility is more akin to the state taking an '*overdose*' and thereby putting itself at risk. It is important to stress, nonetheless, that the act of taking this or that dose does not stem from a decision taken freely by the 'patient' concerned. Rather, it is an act dictated largely by prior historical conditions and trajectories, such as the circumstance of being located either at the centre or at the periphery. In this sense, there is no doubt whatsoever that taking the minimum welfare-state dose of neo-liberal medicine presupposes a degree of prosperity that one is seeking to safeguard and renew in this way. In contrast to this, the strategy of downward mobility is dictated by need and involves an attempt to make a market out of it. It is no coincidence that, in countries which guarantee unlegislated zones for foreign capital, brothers even offer their sisters to Western tourists for prostitution. *Both* actions stem from the same dictates of poverty.

Cheap labour carried out under inhumane conditions and ecologically disastrous forms of production were certainly not invented by these states. However, that is a different issue from whether such elements are combined to form a state's specialization profile. When this happens, a *global labour market sector for unlegislated work and production*, associated with particular states, comes into being on a global scale and leads to a kind of 'state *proletarianization*' and 'state *prostitution*'.

There is a dual meaning contained in the notion of strategies of 'downward mobility'. Firstly, downward mobility becomes a specialization profile in inter-state relations, a proprietary brand used by these states to open themselves up to foreign capital in the global market. Secondly, this strategy can also be used to force *downwardly mobile states into competition with one another* so that they undercut one another, making downward mobility turn into exclusion.

This specialization in downward mobility poses a risk to itself insofar as it makes a gap in the inter-state system the basis of the state's economic survival. In other words, the strategy of downward mobility not only stirs up competition among states themselves, it is also in open conflict with the interests of rich nation-states, whose economic and cultural existence and political values are called into question by the creation of unlegislated zones for capital investment. If governments, too, were to become 'global players', these conflicts between rich and poor would intensify on a global scale. If norms of social justice, dignified forms of work and the peaceful use of natural resources are to become more widespread, the first prerequisite is an international consensus. Only if such consensus exists can effective sanctions be applied against those who violate the rules. So far it is not clear whether or how this would even be feasible in the transnational context. At any rate, the route *towards* becoming a welfare state, where this consensus already exists, cannot be applied straightforwardly to the transnational level.

(c) Tax haven strategies

A number of states attempt to gain access to the global market and maintain their position in it by making themselves into a 'tax haven' for foreign investors. If we compare this strategy with the one discussed above, what is immediately striking is that regulatory gaps in international relations enable states to develop a distinct global market image for themselves, not only through the strategy of downward mobility but also through that of upward mobility. To be more precise, states attempt to transform downward mobility into upward mobility. As a result, there are a large number of states using the principle of bank confidentiality to give globalization's winners a place to hide, in the hope that they themselves might also become a winner from globalization: more than forty states worldwide currently secure themselves a parasitical existence in the global market in this way.

The questions that arise from this are similar to those in the strategy discussed above: what will become of these state-organized tax havens when the community of states wishes to create a new, transnational architecture for financial markets – as it certainly will? The 'Tobin tax', for example, which is to be levied on international financial transactions, presupposes that the possibilities and preconditions for creating tax havens are abolished. Here, too, it is the case that norms of welfare and justice can only be applied at transnational level if these state-guaranteed, unlegislated arenas for profit maximization are dismantled. That, however, requires the consent of the loser states – the tax haven states – who are hardly likely to agree to their own demise. The only way to go about this, therefore, will be to tackle such structural obstacles in a politically direct way, by opening up new development prospects to such states within a demonopolized global economic order.

Hegemonic strategies

Remaining for a moment within the national context, states can reduce competition among themselves not only through specialization strategies but also through *hegemonic strategies*. In other words, they can force cooperation to occur by situating this hegemony within the national context on the one hand and yet making it exceed this same context on the other, that is, by dictating to other states a form of international 'cooperation' based on national presuppositions. Once one begins to search through the international debate from this perspective, one finds all kinds of peculiarities. On one side there is the 'hegemony obsession' with which political science neo-realists conjure up the dangers that threaten the world if the *pax americana* – American hegemony – were to collapse. The central premise here, albeit usually a tacit one, is that the double anarchy of nation-states *and* global capitalisms can only survive if there is a hegemonic structure in place. On the other side one encounters the furious voices of a critique rooted in desperation, coming in particular from countries of the so-called Third World and denouncing globalization as a continuation of imperialism by more sophisticated means. For analytical purposes, then, it is necessary to define the hegemonic strategy of competition reduction in terms that are as precise as possible.

It makes sense, initially, to distinguish between *global* hegemonic strategies and *regional* hegemonic strategies. While these are not mutually exclusive, they are based on different mechanisms of power that entail different
kinds of contradictions. For global hegemonies there is only one candidate
so far, the USA – although there has been a remarkable turnaround in the
literature on political science and political economy over the past few years.
State-centred theories are no longer preoccupied with the potential rise or
fall of the big powers or with the issue of whether US hegemony is in the
process of decline in view of the ascendancy of powers in East Asia and
Europe. On the contrary, the view that is becoming more and more widespread is that after the end of the Cold War the USA entered a period of
renewed, indeed open, hegemony, both economically and politically. The
indicators presented as evidence of this are the following: neo-liberalism, as
the ideological spearhead of Americanization, is unchallenged in dominating
the so-called reform debates around the globe. Direct American hegemony
has been replaced by a multilateral Americanization in which, for example,
apparently transnational institutions such as the World Trade Organization,
the G-8 countries, the World Bank, and so on put American hegemonic
claims into practice under their own auspices. However, the US government
is also prepared to roll up its sleeves in exercising its 'world leadership role'.
It pushes through its national trading interests in relation to other states and
continents using undisguised directness and the open threat of trade wars.
Several observers believe that it is the USA's hegemonic position of power
that has given it an almost unbelievable degree of robust, steady economic
growth over such a long period of time.

One point seems to me to be crucial, though, and it is one that is often
absent in these debates: *only* the USA – and not its potential rivals in Europe
or Asia – has the *monopoly of a global vision*. This vision is one of *dual
freedom*, where political freedom and market freedom not only do not contradict one another but actually form an indivisible unity. This American
vision says: by implementing capitalism and democracy universally, we are
not only bringing peace to the planet, we are also creating a global society
worthy of human dignity, in which equal rights and therefore justice for all
have become a thoroughly attainable utopia. It is this *visionary monopoly* in
particular that the USA in its hegemonic position confirms. Along with all
the ingredients that go to make up hegemony at the dawn of the twenty-first
century – a creative and powerful domestic economy, dominance of the
global market, military strength, integration of allies and beneficiaries, and
so forth – it is above all *Grand Politics* with a cosmopolitan goal that makes
this hegemonic position possible.

Nonetheless, the problematic consequences and the costs of such a global
strategy of hegemony should not be underestimated. Establishing and maintaining hegemony entails having permanently to mobilize the population not
only of one's *own* state but also of allied states – and this in the context of a

global economy that is chaotic and anarchistic and increasingly evades *all* national attempts to monitor and control it. The willingness and capacity to interfere politically and militarily in other countries' affairs is not only extremely cost-intensive, it also establishes the constant expectation that one will always and everywhere be present and involved in events, something that goes beyond the bounds of any government's management capabilities and places it under permanent stress, no matter how competent it may be.

Thus, the vision of permanent hegemonic control that is often portrayed as such by its opponents can easily turn into a nightmare for those seeking to assume such an arrogant position in the global age of contingency and complexity. Indeed the question even arises: to what extent can a hegemonic state actually turn its overwhelming power into economic gains in the global market? Is it not the case, conversely, that the costs of hegemony sooner or later turn into considerable competitive disadvantages in the global market? Perhaps such a state might even be able to develop highly cunning strategies for transferring the burden of the costs of hegemony onto other states, in order to squeeze them out of global market competition? Is the strategy of hegemony possibly the exact opposite, even, namely, an indirect strategy for *suppressing* competition from rival states?

If we stop seeing hegemony in its old guise as an imperialistic strategy backed up by military might, then the question arises: what would global market hegemony look like if its main aim were to reduce competition in the global market? Global big business itself is capable of doing this only to a limited extent, as it would entail getting serious about political autarchy and creating a kind of global state fashioned around private enterprise. The dictatorship of the proletariat would become transformed, as far as its objectives are concerned, into a management dictatorship of global proportions, which would have completely internalized state power.

This is an utterly absurd idea, which again raises the question of what a strategy of hegemony appropriate to the global market might look like or how it might be understood. In this sense it bears asking to what extent the essence of a hegemonic strategy applied to the global market might not lie in a kind of 'politics of politics', which rewrites the rules of the meta-power game of global politics? To put it in a simplified way, hegemony is a 'power multiplier' (Palan and Abbott 1999). The corresponding strategy is aimed at *bringing together different elements in order to multiply power.*

To find out which elements become meshed with one another in such a scenario, we only have to look at the regional hegemony that Germany enjoys in the European Union. First, with a population of over 80 million, Germany is the most powerful country economically and has a highly developed export and domestic economy. At the same time, thanks to its alliance with France as well as the new development opportunities it has acquired in relation to the states of Central and Eastern Europe and Russia, it has a special mediating role concerning issues of global economic integration and those of political representation within the European Union. If we add to this Germany's important position as a European ally of the USA, what emerges is a multiplicity of elements of power that might very well provide grounds for the existence of a hegemonic position. In this instance, too, we can see that the image people have of hegemony – the way they judge it – is subject to extreme fluctuations, dependent only to some extent on one's position within this web of power. The main reason why the same phenomenon is subject to different perceptions of it lies in whether one continues to see hegemony in terms of the national calculation of power (as in political science realism), or whether it is viewed from a cosmopolitan perspective. Hegemony as a 'power multiplier' *could* – without any false idealism – be recast as a prerequisite for national politics to open out into the transnational arena. (The fact that neo-realist political theory would view this as nothing other than a more sophisticated way of pursuing national interests under the pretext of transnationalist goals – and 'expose' it as such – is another story.)

Strategies of transnationalization

Strategies of specialization in the global market and hegemonic strategies are not the only ones available to states: strategies of *cooperation* between governments and states are aimed at reducing national rivalries and inter-state competition in relation to global business actors by means of treaties, regimes or other legally binding regulatory instruments. Transnational – that is, regionally limited – inter-state strategies of cooperation are multilayered, multifaceted and multifunctional state strategies which stand out from the ones named above by the fact that they enable states to transcend the range of national options available and to initiate the transnational power game in relation to global business actors.

Mobile business enterprises that operate within a global network are in a position to play individual states off against one another and thereby weaken them. The more the *national point of view* predominates in people's and governments' thinking and acting, the easier it becomes to consolidate deterritorial, translegal domination. When national rivalries, egotisms and competitive instincts are stirred up, the international community of states becomes divided and is no longer able to discover and develop the powerful force inherent in cooperation between states; as a consequence, global business is able to play isolated nation-states off against one another, according to the principle of divide and rule. In this respect, a global market–nation-state constellation that is historically redundant is blocking the transnational renewal of politics *and* the taming of global business.

This cat-and-mouse game between global business and the nation-state can really only be countered by states following the lead of 'dis-located' companies and extending their state activities beyond their own national borders.

This can happen either under the primacy of national politics, in which case it is known as conquest or hegemony, or else in the form of inter-state co-operation – in which case the seemingly 'natural' unity of state and nation would need to be systematically and progressively undone.

Alliances between states are based on the reciprocal insight that internationally binding treaties and regimes of this sort help to avoid a situation that is damaging for all parties, namely when states attempt to outbid or undercut each other. Transnational strategies of cooperation thus serve two goals, that of increasing competition between global business actors and that of reducing competition between different states.

This strategy has its price, however. The acquisition of new opportunities for governance in terms of exercising sovereign influence – that is, the expansion of sovereignty – has to be paid for with active self-denationalization, with a reduction in *national* autonomy.

In the circumstances of economic globalization, then, states find themselves caught to a certain extent in a *denationalization trap*. If they cling to the sovereignty postulate of nation-state politics, then two things increase: both competition for investment between states *and* the danger of monopolies emerging on the global market that in turn disempower state actors. If, on the other hand, in order to strengthen their position in relation to global business, they reduce competition among themselves by forming alliances that are binding for all involved, then they need to reduce the scope of their national sovereignty.

This paradox makes manifest one of the main features of the postnational constellation: those elements that had been bound together with one another within the national paradigm – the independence of the state, national self-determination and the role of politics in executing important state tasks (welfare, law and order, security) – become autonomous in relation to one another while simultaneously becoming recombined in a new way. In order to push ahead with executing important national tasks, governments have to relinquish the independence of the state and allow their hands to be tied in cooperative agreements, as it were, by mutual arrangement with other states; in this way, they also acquire new possibilities for concrete action, not only internationally but also *intra*nationally, in relation to the political opposition and the public sphere.

Strategies of transnationalization demand a new boundary politics. On the one hand, strategies of cooperation loosen the territorial focus of state action by making the borders of cooperating states open to one another. On the other hand, however, state territoriality is not abolished but rather extended, its new limits being established through regional state alliances. The main examples of this are the European Union and NAFTA, but smaller cooperative alliances, such as the one entered into by China and Hong Kong, also bear the informal imprint of 'transnationalization'. The alliances mentioned here are regional state alliances which, through complex, legally binding treaties and corresponding institutions, serve to expand the range of options available to the states concerned, while simultaneously limiting them transnationally. The experience on which such alliances are based is that the state's adherence to a national agenda and to national parochialism poses an *obstacle* to inventing politics along transnational lines and to enabling state-hood to evolve in an age of economic globalization.

At this stage, we have reached a turning point in the argument. In the state strategies described so far, the situation at the beginning of the twenty-first century is assumed to be fixed, with a transformed and revolutionized business constituency caught in the transition from a nation-based economy to a global economy on the one hand, and territorially based politics still caught up in its nation-state *a prioris* on the other. Once strategies of transnationalization come into play, however, something new occurs. 'Cooperation states' work together to influence events in networks consisting of inter-state agreements, doing so on the principle that the loss of individual state capacity can be compensated for only by combining and extending inter-state competencies.

In other words, *politics is beginning to break through the 'national sound barrier'*. Indeed, it is only by getting rid of national parochialism that it becomes possible to revive politics in the national arena. *Transnational states* are 'both/and states', ones that have been revived and reformed transnationally so that they are no longer '*only* nation-states' but '*also* nation-states'. They are on their way towards a '*cosmopolitan nationality*', in which national traditions are exposed to cosmopolitanism and thereby broken open, expanded *and* given a new lease of life.

As long as states are equated with territorial states, and territorial states with nation-states, and these in turn viewed as monopolistic actors in international politics, the issue of transnational autonomy and a transnational *expansion of national political sovereignty* will not even arise. Political autonomy is equated with national sovereignty and applied solely to the sphere of inter-state relations. These 'national spectacles' also determine the way people see relations of international cooperation. International cooperation can be conceived of and developed as cooperation only *between* nations rather than as '*trans*national' cooperation.

International cooperation can certainly make sense within the terms of reference of the national outlook: it can make strategic sense by strengthening the position of the nation state in relation to its rivals (in the world market). Thinking and acting within the national paradigm, then, by no means rules out cooperation *per se*, although the likelihood of such cooperation actually occurring decreases in line with the extent to which national sovereignty is impaired or disabled by it. The more nation-states commit themselves within the context of cooperative strategies and institutions, the less likely it is that such cooperative strategies and structures will be accepted by the nation-state orthodoxy. The central mechanism at work here only becomes apparent within the frame of reference of a *cosmopolitan* vision: when politics restricts itself to the national context, it simultaneously creates the preconditions for its transnational, and therefore also national, renewal.

The key historical example of this is the creation of the *European Union*. Here, too, small states cooperate with large states, and powerful states with less powerful states. In this respect, it would be an obvious move to view the creation of the European Union in terms of the theory of imperialism, which says that the restrictions dictated by geography and population can only be overcome if nations set about accumulating foreign territories and populations. However, this does not apply to the second phase of European integration, which began with the creation of a common European market. For the first time in history, this strategy of cooperation has been seized upon and implemented within a transnational community of states whose external boundaries are delimited regionally and whose internal, national boundaries have been opened, in order to create the conditions within which cooperating states can collectively renew and expand their economic and political power.

One of the things that becomes clear from this is that the impact of the strategy of cooperation in terms of reducing competition essentially depends on the *size* of the market formed by the cooperating states. Indeed, it might even be said that, in principle, the strategy of cooperation amounts to a strategy of size. The larger the market thus developed, and the more numerous and powerful the cooperating states involved, the greater is the global market power of the state bloc, of the transnational network of sovereignty and cooperation formed in this way.

Transnationality is nothing if not ambiguous and multivalent. It can be differentiated not only in terms of space (size) but also in terms of contractual organization, whether this consists in inter-state agreements, international regimes, or alliances involving cooperating states. As a result, state forms and state treaties of this kind can be designed with a view to global market priorities on the one hand and to overcoming national rivalries on the other. This latter aspect becomes clearer if we compare the political architecture of transnationality with that of (national) federalism. Both demand a highly differentiated, balanced power structure – in the case of federalism, within a state, and in the case of transnationality, between different states. Since states display many different sub-characteristics, it is conceivable that in-between forms might emerge – a *transnational federal architecture* – which, in steps both large and small, successively abolish the apparently steadfast unity between the nation and the state through federal transnationalizations (following the example of the European Union), *without* thereby generating an institutional power vacuum or making states unviable.

Whereas so far there has been a choice only between *either* national (and therefore state) self-determination *or* integration (subordination) into national (and therefore majority-dominated) state apparatuses of domination, we are now seeing new options of transnational federalism emerge. In an ideal scenario, these make it possible – national claims to dominance notwithstanding – to have one's cake *and* eat it, as it were. In other words, it becomes possible to exploit the advantages of a transnational extension of sovereignty without suffering the disadvantages entailed when one would-be nation has to subordinate itself to the other. Especially in the case of long-term, ongoing conflicts between nationalities and neighbours, as well as imminent annexations – as in the case of Taiwan and Hong Kong by China, or of Montenegro by Serbia – the blueprint of a transnational state federalism could offer a way out of the politics of false choices. This is because it represents a new *strategy of pacification in relation to entrenched conflicts based on nationality and imperial dependency*. It forges a connection between a reduction in the significance of the national arena on the one hand and a cooperative expansion of politics and sovereignty, along with greater openness to the global market, on the other.

Furthermore, transnationalization also makes it possible for state structures as well as belongings and identities to become *despatialized* and to overlap with one another, so that they are no longer mutually exclusive, like the hierarchies of sovereignty in the Middle Ages. Instead of imagining nationality in *exclusive* terms, it now becomes possible to imagine *inclusive nationalities*. A transnational China, for example, could reincorporate the rich and influential 'foreign Chinese' who live on different continents and within different national subcultures in the Chinese diaspora, only this time not on the basis of a national bond, but rather within a new 'transnational sovereignty'. A flexible, transnational form of state citizenship would fit with this vision (Ong).

Transnationality not only weaves an economic and political rag rug, it also generates corresponding cultural and political patterns of living and identity in which people and places intermingle and overlap with one another in the mix of global cultures and world politics. In this respect, transnationality not only brings out the absurdity of the nightmare envisioned by the world-view based on national premises, namely, that beyond the national sphere there is just plain nothing, a power vacuum, total chaos and all-encompassing war – it turns it into its exact opposite. To put it in more general terms, the transnationalization and despatialization of states brings with it a broader mechanism for ordering political affairs, which is capable of both intensifying and defusing the conflicts arising from overlapping side-effects, political identities and responsibilities.

But what might encourage national population groups and elites to set out on this path and try out transnational strategies of cooperation? The question gets turned around the other way once the multifunctionality and multirationality of inter-state cooperation has been examined and understood: how is it actually possible for the expansion of political and state power facilitated by committing the nation to strategies of cooperation *not* to be pursued and put into practice? This form of *'power multiplying' cooperation* can be elucidated in three dimensions (which may appear to be mutually exclusive but in fact complement one another): (a) economic rationality, (b) strategic rationality and (c) political rationality.

(a)   Economic rationality

The rationality of inter-state cooperation can be explained in the first instance in the context of neo-classical economics. The latter favours the creation of large markets, albeit on condition that they open up new spheres of opportunity for industry and the service sector; these in turn improve the conditions in which member states operate, and therefore also stimulate investment. In other words, one of the most common explanations for the creation of large markets lies in the assumption that this is how the 'national economies' of member states can be expanded, something that is impossible if individual states remain isolated from one another. It enables both domestic and foreign trade between sectors and countries to be intensified within and outside the market concerned. At the same time, the capacity of the economic zone as a whole increases in terms of the ability to finance more and more scientific-technological innovations and, accordingly, exploit them both within and outside individual states' borders as an element in consolidating power. As early as 1950, Jacob Viner effectively formulated a postulate that is still seen even today as a kind of orthodoxy in the theory of international trade and political economy, namely: *the size of a market and its degree of integration either create or are at least favourable to both economic growth and economic diversity.*[6]

However, this type of economic rationality can only be used as an explanation for corresponding political action if – as suggested by such different theoretical perspectives as neo-classical economics and Marxist political economy – the 'rationality' of political action is erroneously equated with economic rationality, or if politics is understood as a continuation of economics by other means. Thus, to point out that the strategy of cooperation amounts to an economic calculation is no answer to the question as to why this calculation becomes the basis for political decision-making and for political motivations and objectives. This applies even more so when attempts to enforce economic principles are confronted with considerable resistance and protest at the national level – protests and conflicts which are dismissed and mistaken as being 'irrational' in economic thinking. While it remains a mystery as to why politicians, parties and governments appropriate the economic calculation for their own purposes, the political rhetoric of economic rationality can conversely provide an autonomous, political strategy and a façade for *rationalizing* in retrospect the adapted strategy of broadening out transnational activities.

The notion of the primacy of the economy in relation to politics – a view widespread in the public sphere as well – is informed by a simplistic image of politics being controlled by powerful business interests. As Edgar Grande (1995), among others, demonstrated using the example of governance in the European media system, a community of cooperating states has to deal with multiple other states and interested parties, which in the end enables governments to play powerful lobbyists off against one another. Thus, the complex, pluralized world of multiple levels and purposes actually *empowers* states in relation to particular influential parties, and therefore also in relation to business. Convoluted decision-making processes and complex, formal and informal structures of responsibility make it hard for external actors wishing to exert influence to get a clear picture of the situation; moreover, there is no longer any single 'main address' that needs to be cultivated and won over when it comes to pushing through one's own interests. Edgar Grande speaks of a 'paradoxical weakness', by which he means that, while states lose autonomy in the multilayered European system, they can also expect to make considerable *gains* in autonomy, precisely because they are strengthened in relation to the plural addressees and interested parties of political decisions. Here again, it becomes clear that deliberate denationalization of a nation's own political sphere – that is, letting go of national axioms – by no means signals the end of politics, as is often claimed, but rather can be understood and pursued as a strategy of the *self-autonomization* of politics.

(b) Strategic rationality

Neo-classical rationality equates regional cooperation between states with economic growth. In contrast to this, strategic rationality works with the notion that, when states join together in cooperation, it consolidates their position in the global market by enabling two things to happen at once: competition between states is reduced, while political power is developed in relation to global economic actors. This cooperative expansion of state power enables transnational states not only to take up a position in opposition to global business but also to establish a political framework within which the latter must operate. Unlike the neo-classical calculation, then, the strategic calculation of cooperation is based primarily on political ambition and relies on the (partial) autonomy of politics and the state in relation to the economy.

Viewed from this perspective, sovereignty is not eliminated by inter-state cooperation, but rather extended and given a new rationale. This becomes apparent if transnational strategies of cooperation between states are no longer seen solely as strategies designed to provide support for their member states in the global market or in their dealings with national rivals (as political science realism implies). Rather, strategies of cooperation also open up *domestic political* policy options to governments via the roundabout route of the transnational arena. As Klaus-Dieter Wolf argues, states that rely on cooperation are able to gain advantages on several different fronts at once.

Internationalizing governance by pooling individual states' problem-solving resources can help states to fulfil their socially authorized role as public regulator with renewed effectiveness; but as a means of entering into mutually binding commitments, it can also serve either to maintain or to regain a degree of autonomy in relation to civil society's demands for a role in political decision-making. Using the instrument they created to restrain the power of the market, governments can also free themselves from the constricting embrace of their social taskmasters. The outcome of this is de-democratization through intergovernmental mechanisms of self-commitment. (Wolf 2000: 61)

In this sense, transnational cooperation – in addition to strengthening the position of individual states in the global market – opens up policy options in the national arena for tackling the pressing 'issues of the future' more effectively, such as unemployment, falling economic growth, crime, migration and military security. The paradox that emerges here can perhaps be demonstrated best by looking at the transnationalization of the military as an example.

On the one hand, the *inter*nationalization of weapons *production* is becoming a very important strategy of rationalization – not least for reasons of cost savings, but also in order to produce better weapons more efficiently. Within Europe, transnational collaboration, co-development and co-production have become crucial ways of damping down the exploding costs of weapons manufacturing. While this 'cooperative pacification' of military production is still utterly consonant with a commercial logic that seemingly conflicts with the primacy of national security, transnational military politics clearly demonstrates that politically, as well, national security can only be guaranteed within the arena of transnational cooperation. The European Union cannot be used as an example of this, since it does not (yet) have its own military force; NATO, however, has not only rendered the postulate of national sovereignty in issues of defence invalid, it has also provided answers to national security questions in a transnationally organized form. As a result of this development, NATO is not unlike multinational corporations in that it has become a *polyethnic microcosm* in terms of its staff and administration, where people from very different backgrounds with many different mother tongues have simultaneously denationalized and transnationalized issues of national security and thereby renationalized them through cooperation.

This illustrates the fact that the common conceptual scheme which would understand transnational cooperation as a negation of the national dimension completely fails to recognize the complexity of the situation. The transnational domain can and must be deciphered in a much more sophisticated way, as a virtual battlefield on which national and local battles are fought out, having been removed from their original temporal and spatial locations. Transnationalization enables national actors to break open the 'power repositories' of the nation-state and of national society both *from inside and from outside the nation's borders*. Transnational cooperation does away with old boundaries and makes it possible to establish new boundary divisions *within* and between local and national power structures. To put it differently again: transnationalization needs to be understood as a strategy for revolutionizing the national arena of power *from the inside*. External, transnational alliances can be forged in order to redistribute national power.

It is precisely this insight that renders comprehensible where the temptation lies for politics and politicians to choose to break through the barrier posed by national *a prioris*. The cunning aspect of this strategy consists not least in the fact that it enables states involved in transnational cooperation to swear allegiance to the flag of national politics, even though their own actions point in a different direction. In this way, two courses of action become possible that otherwise appear to be mutually exclusive, namely, keeping globalization's *losers* onside with national slogans while simultaneously appropriating a range of new transnational political options with the aid of professions of neo-liberal faith. This contradictory strategy of 'Haider–Berlusconi capitalism' has its limits, although this does not necessarily mean that it will not permanently change the political landscape – both in Europe and elsewhere.

(c) Political rationality

Finally, the multifunctional nature of the strategy of transnationalization can be identified in particular by the fact that – as already mentioned – it gives rise to a paradoxical link between relinquishing and expanding state autonomy. In the transnational context, *politics experiences and reinforces its own interest in itself*. This self-interest that politics has in extending and consolidating its practical policy options either goes unrecognized or is underestimated within the terms of the economic calculation and of strategic rationality. 'When we speak of the "state's interest in itself"', argues Claus Offe, 'what we mean is its interest in finding and maintaining a system for organizing social life *at all* that is free of contradiction and is capable of standing firm in the long term. State activity consists in doing nothing other than pursuing this interest of the state in itself (as a collection of organizational forms and resources that has always existed), its interest in being free of contradiction and in continuing to exist' (1975: 13).

Although Offe sees 'securing the state's continued existence' as being a 'transcendental' interest of the state and politics in themselves, this can also be reinterpreted in a more dynamic way as the self-transformation of politics and the state for the purpose of expanding their practical options. As paradoxical as this may sound, global society affords numerous opportunities for providing a new, more grand rationale for politics. However, the concept of 'politics' and 'state' referred to here is not one reduced along economic or nationalistic lines, with politics being confused with economics and nation-state anarchy considered the *non plus ultra* of world history – as is implied in the paradigm of neo-classical economics, in Marxist theory and in political science realism. Rather, politics develops within the complexity and contingency of global society as politics' interest in politics, something that should certainly be regarded as ambiguous. In order to counter any premature optimism that with greater danger comes a greater prospect of rescue, it is important to keep the following in mind: this kind of self-autonomization of politics in the transnational institutional jungle is based not least on the fact that the new process of state development may be accompanied by – and is fed by – a *de*-democratization and *re*nationalization of politics and society.

The 'dis-location' of politics also means, in that case, that the nation-state locations of politics – the parliament and the public sphere – become less central. They become one 'interest group' among others, so to speak, and – much like transnational capital – have to be *instrumentalized* in the course of making full use of the new options for political power and influence. As Michael Zürn (1998a) shows, intergovernmental governance provides individual states with fresh problem-solving capacity. This new capacity, however, is based on the fact that democratic co-determination and control do *not* grow to match the changed political modus operandi, although it is precisely this impulse for technocratic power which, given the widely diagnosed need for democratic states to reform and their inability to do so, may paradoxically contribute towards their legitimation. If the façades of democratic procedure can be successfully preserved, that is, if commitments established in the transnational arena can be given the nod by national parliaments, then states can do two things at once: they can formally adhere to the democratic rules *and* keep the electorate onside with more impressive reforms.

The axioms of nation-state democracy claim that it is *only* in nation-states, with all that these presuppose and entail, that democracy is possible; clinging to these axioms, however, has the effect of intensifying the de-democratizing impact of a transnationally renewed politics. This ends only at the point where the territorial understanding of democracy is replaced by a deterritorialized understanding of democracy. In this latter view, it is not the central nation-state locations of democracy that guarantee democracy, but rather a broader set of other instruments and institutions of democratic control (such as sub- and transnational voting models).

If transnational strategies of cooperation are paid for domestically with a spectacular loss of democracy, the image they project to the outside is one of a *cartel of rich states* that only makes the situation of so-called Third and

Fourth World countries worse. Thus, when states within certain geographic zones form cartels that are closed off to the outside, this may contribute towards the exclusion of the so-called failing states, which already face considerable obstacles in developing and implementing effective competitive strategies in the global market.

Thus, it would be naïve in the extreme to assume that the 'transnational renewal' of the political sphere automatically gives rise to a transnational civilizing of politics and to greater democratization. It is obviously quite wrong to believe that the political forces released in the transnational arena point in one direction only. Many parties and actors are deeply illiberal, antidem-ocratic or ademocratic and are busy pursuing a policy of re-ethnification of the state. Their activities may have a self-destructive effect in that, for example, they weaken the state monopoly on violence and blur not only the boundaries of organized crime but also the ever narrower dividing line between criminal and social violence. The *democratic* expansion of transnational politics is only *one* objective among many competing ones (see p. 263ff. in this volume). It undertakes the attempt to bind together the productive force, or creative power, of politics – which grows through cooperation – in such a way that the high-risk, global irrationality of economics can be tamed in the transnational arena by means of a cosmopolitan project.

5.5 Strategies aimed at repoliticizing politics

So far we have attempted to outline how the social and political control systems of nation-state first modernity are undermined by business becoming global, and how state strategies that first comprehend and then overcome national *a prioris* by transnational means are able to defy this 'emancipation' of capital. We can conclude from this that any theory seeking to give a realistic account of this global condition and to show plausible ways in which it might develop needs to be political in a twofold sense. On the one hand, it must describe the power confrontation between global capital and national politics as a power game involving strategic power; on the other hand, though, it has to develop *concrete political perspectives* for the self-activation of politics as it rids itself of its national parochialism and discovers the range of concrete options available to it in the transnational sphere. The idea that links these approaches with one another is this: *cosmopolitan renewal of the concrete concerns of politics is a crucial power resource.* To put it differently, *abandoning utopia means abandoning power.* Only those who are able to instil enthusiasm in others will win consent and power. The rediscovery of grand objectives, of Grand Politics, serves both to reinvigorate politics in terms of substance and to empower it. Both taken together coalesce in a strategy for *repoliticizing politics.*

The political project that can be set against transnational capital and its strategy of privileging the state must itself be a transnational one, namely the project of a *different* globalization and a *different* modernity. This project is supported by a vision of 'cosmopolitan reason' that takes in the entire globe. States most certainly have strategies at their disposal for changing the direction and the character of economic globalization, although this is not true of every nation-state. It is only through the model of cooperative transnational states that politics can regain its visionary energy and use it as a global force for order.

Solving global problems globally

Some of the goals of cosmopolitan politics have since turned into rhetorical models in certain national and transnational political circles. In declarations signed amid great ceremony, for example, the heads of state of the G-8 countries and centre-left governments repeatedly call for today's 'turbocapitalism' to be brought to heel politically and reconciled with the principles of political freedom and social justice. The 'social justice' talked about in this context is no longer one restricted to the familiar nation-state context; rather, it is seen in a new transnational – indeed, possibly global – perspective, although its contours here remain extremely blurred. Accordingly, almost no tangible proposals whatever have been tabled for putting this rhetoric of the 'politics of global justice' into practice in the international and the national arena via legislative initiatives and an institutional architecture of transnational politics. At present, the general nature – i.e. the wooliness – of politicians' rhetorical pronouncements at global level is twinned with a conspicuously defensive attitude when it comes to putting them into practice.

Let us take as an example the *Progress Report on Business and Human Rights*, which was published by the United Nations at the start of the year 2000. This report sets out nine central principles relating to labour standards, human rights and environmental standards to which global business should adhere, on which agreement had already been reached in international documents and under the auspices of the United Nations. However, the United Nations has no teeth. Ultimately, all that Secretary-General Kofi Annan can do is 'call upon' the business community to put these norms and treaties into practice themselves, on a *voluntary* basis. Some of the 'morally reputable' transnational corporations (a characteristic acquired through being economically astute), such as Shell and BP, have signalled their intention to sign these declarations. But the majority of global business actors will politely ignore the documents.

What is equally true, however, is that there is a growing sensitivity among ordinary people and consumers around the world (and their associated social movements), who are articulating their rights clearly and exercising them with a great deal of political skill. These people are also pressing for the decision-making elites in politics and business to account for what they are doing to contribute to the implementation of civil rights and consumer rights. If it is correct that power is increasingly being exercised in the global private sector, then the pressure both from the public and from national and transnational politicians will increase for business elites to become involved in a cosmopolitan project whose aims include civilizing and humanizing the financial markets. If this does not happen, however, the transnationalization of government policy can carve its connective project out of this deficiency by opening out the political ideals of the first modernity – social stability and justice – to the transnational era and spelling out how the objectives of a dialectic of global–local politics can apply to concrete tasks. Such a policy might be thought of as a practical response to the insight that international capitalism must accept and implement the new rules of political engagement – and fast.

Strategies of multiple coalitions

The Secretary-General of the United Nations is increasingly placing his hopes in multiple coalitions. By forming partnerships with non-governmental organizations, civil society, companies and universities, he is attempting to gain a little autonomy for the UN's global policies. Annan sees in these new forms of cooperation both untapped potential for overcoming global problems such as poverty, environmental pollution and population growth, and a way of removing, so he hopes, the internal obstacles that hinder the United Nations in its work. 'This approach has brought with it a new dynamic, a new kind of political creativity that we have not seen before now.' He mentions by way of an example an agreement that has been struck with five pharmaceutical companies to enable anti-AIDS drugs to be sold to the countries of the periphery most severely affected by this catastrophe at a price that is 90 per cent lower than it otherwise would be. In addition, he is holding negotiations with multinational corporations to try to encourage them to sign up to and implement his 'global deal'. This includes standards of social justice and labour norms, such as the prohibition of forced labour and the worst forms of child labour. Annan is publicly posing the question as to private companies' political responsibility in the age of globalization; that is, he is addressing them as 'global, political actors' and attempting to get them involved in a positive way within their own sphere of power. This means corporations not only having opportunities to influence events transnationally and politically through their worldwide investment policies, but also themselves becoming advocates of a global politics in opposition to obstinate governments and states stuck in their nation-based egotisms.

In this way, Annan is opening up a new, multinational and multidimensional game of politics, in which states lose their monopoly on politics and become one partner – or competitor – among others, albeit a very important strategic one. What emerges from this are multiple coalitions and a corresponding force field in which even alliances between non-governmental organizations and transnational corporations can be forged in matters of human rights or health and safety policy against governments wedded to the national *a prioris*. In response to the question of whether, in doing all this, he is not actually undermining the foundations of the United Nations, which started out as a collaborative project between states and governments, Annan replies by referring to the United Nations charter, which states that it has been written on behalf of all people, and by pointing out that in any case governments on their own cannot fulfil the promises of the UN constitution. That, he says, requires transnational and multidimensional coalitions instead. In other words, the UN charter is being freed from its nation-state tunnel vision and being opened up to cosmopolitan expansion and renewal.

Global risk strategies

Alongside the global economy and its incalculable risks for the world, global environmental risks and global technological developments have become the main themes to which politicians nowadays pay special lip service. The decoding of the (human) genome was greeted with worldwide celebration in summer 2000. The US president, Bill Clinton, enthused that we now held a new 'map' in our hands, undoubtedly the most important, most wonderful map ever drawn by humankind, and far more important than the map of America. The scientists joined their political patrons in heralding this triumph of the human spirit of discovery, which had succeeded in deciphering the letters that make up the language of human genetic material – albeit nobody yet knows how to read or speak this language. In a press conference held simultaneously throughout the world, the message was sent out across the continents that this was a historic moment in the 100,000-year history of humanity.

The grand objectives brought nearer by this technological leap were once again highlighted in grandiose terms: the possibility of extending a person's lifetime by an average of 150 years, the availability of cures for Alzheimer's, Parkinson's, diabetes and cancer. Life, it was said, will get better – for all the world's citizens, not just for the privileged. This, the US president warned, is why politicians must ensure that the information acquired is used to transform medicine, and not abused to develop new weapons or 'to make man his own creator'. All these noble sentiments are brought together in the chorus: this cannot be done by nations going it alone; it can only be achieved through grand, global politics. Clinton called upon the world to tackle the social, juridical and ethical problems together, regardless of different political constitutions and social moralities.

One can either dismiss this as a risible outburst of 'American naïvety' or else praise it as admirable. Looked at more soberly, only two options remain: either this technology develops 'without limits' in two senses, transcending the boundaries of both nation-states and ethical systems; or else it does indeed become possible to implement global regulations for dealing with this menacing paradise of human genetics. If the latter task is tackled, it can succeed only as a global political endeavour. Only in this way, and not through the gung-ho politics espoused by the apologists of technology or the reluctance of national decision-making bodies, can the necessary sharp boundary be drawn that separates research into serious diseases and the development of cures from genetic quality control of humans, born and unborn. Only at a global level is it possible to prevent a situation in which human embryos are made – with the most moral objectives in the world – into research material. This is ultimately the only way to ensure that the worldwide ban on surgical intervention in human stem cells, a commitment that is currently being reaffirmed, does indeed remain in place. But here, as we have already said, the same logic prevails: foreseeable moral disasters can only be prevented through global politics and its transnational empowerment.

Cosmopolitanizing the nation

The silent, internal revolution going on in French society today reflects a model of civilization in which seemingly contradictory elements – cosmopolitanism and nationalism – are brought together in a creative way, with the result that French society is, as it were, reinventing itself in the global context. Here is one example: the intellectuals who thirty years ago struggled against the state, the army and consumer society up and down the country, from Paris to Larzac, have turned their hand to farming. Not only are they utterly at ease driving a tractor, they also know exactly how to use the media to mobilize the masses against globalization, be it in Seattle or Davos. The trial of the nation's new hero, José Bové – who, in a deliberate act of provocation, demolished his local McDonald's as a symbol of globalization – turned into an opportunity to hold a huge street party in the small town of Millau, with at least 50,000 people singing and dancing away until the early hours and eating bread with Rocquefort cheese – a significant choice, as Rocquefort is a symbol of local producers' pride as well as of French gastronomic culture, whose essence and existence are threatened by global uniformity.

When a country's culinary culture and lifestyle are defended in this way, not by lobbyists but by smart transnational political coalitions with cheery and appealing publicity campaigns, the whole country is all for it, from the extreme right to the extreme left, regardless of political allegiance – even if it involves having to take on board deliberate contraventions of the law. Several things are achieved at once by this kind of approach. National allegiances are defused by regionalist sentiments on the one hand, even as they enter into new alliances on the other, having been broadened and given fresh impetus by cosmopolitan influences; as such, the national impetus develops into a force well nigh capable of commanding a majority, with its battle cry against globalizing uniformity. In this way, a 'glocal' France is able to portray and fête itself as the cosmopolitan master of ceremonies for worldwide resistance to excessive economic deregulation, cheese has its status elevated to object (and subject?) of a cosmopolitan act of resistance – and all the colourful cosmopolitan diversity of the world in the postcolonial age is sworn to the red, white and blue of the *tricolore*.

In other words, there is not a hint here of the cosmopolitan and the national fundamentally contradicting one another. Far from it: they encounter one another in a creative and explosive ideological mix that involves a political chemistry potent enough to enable a notorious nay-sayer in political negotiations – France – to stop sulking in the corner of the world's cultures and instead to present itself to its amazed neighbours and to global observers alike as a nation purified in the crucible of cosmopolitanism.

Global New Deal strategies

'Certainly, cosmopolitanism is a fine idea', argues Avishai Margalit, 'that speaks to the good inside us. But is the idea itself good?'

Humanity is not a society; the individuals who make up the aggregate we call 'humanity' do not interact systematically enough to be a society with state-like institutions. To be sure, comprehensive international relations exist, as do expanding, transnational relations and democratic organizations; but cosmopolitan realities and organizations do not. To put the question the right way round: should we transform humanity into a society with fully formed global institutions? Should we set out on the path towards a world society? (Margalit 2000: 80)

We can respond to this (as Kant did) in the following way: cosmopolitanism does *not* think of the world society as an enlarged national society or strive towards a world state that is an enlarged nation-state. Cosmopolitanism means – figuratively speaking – that the Ptolemaic system of the nation-state world is opened up to a Copernican revolution; it means that the distinction between one nation and another, between periphery and centre, domestic policy and foreign policy, economy and state all lose their model function and have to be spelt out anew for the second modernity, particularly with respect to the distinctions (or, rather, the non-distinguishability) of global–local and universal–particular.

Any cosmopolitan project, accordingly, needs a transnational political architecture that must be founded on a global version of the New Deal. Such an architecture would consist of transnational courts of law with the power to impose sanctions, as well as new transnational parties, world citizen parties, that address cosmopolitan issues *within* nation-state public spheres and political arenas as well as beyond nation-state borders (i.e. transnationally), while attending to them in national contexts. Perhaps it is indeed appropriate, in that case, to speak of an 'international community' or a 'global public sphere' – a perspective that may then make it possible for citizens' rights and human rights to be represented effectively at a transnational level, in other words, both globally *and* within individual nation-state political arenas.

These cosmopolitan institutions would need to be given political substance by means of new, flexible *transnational civil rights*. This *earthed cosmopolitanism*, which puts down roots in specific locations and in their traditions, should not be confused with the old, elitist, bourgeois-imperialist cosmopolitanism that once elevated the European norm to the status of global norm. It is based instead on the principle and the value of a *radical conception of diversity*, that is, on a recognition of the otherness of others.

But what does this mean with regard to the cosmopolitanization of the state?

5.6 Strategies aimed at cosmopolitanizing states

Cosmopolitan states, as we have variously argued, are ones that emerge from a process of merger with global civil society. This means that, where there was once the particular universalism of the nation(s) and of national homogeneity, there is now the question of how politics – democratically legitimated, political decision-making – can function in conditions of cultural diversity. How can a state-organized, cosmopolitan countervailing power be constructed and exercised in opposition to the levelling power of the neo-liberal regime? How can an alternative cosmopolitan programme of governance be developed in the global age that is capable of breaking through the dual dominance of the neo-liberalization and neo-nationalization of the state and of arming the latter realistically and powerfully, ready for a revival of democratic republicanism at the beginning of the twenty-first century?

Strategies aimed at political integration within and outside the nation-state

The cosmopolitan state is one that has internalized the cosmopolitan outlook institutionally, that is, it has relinquished its adherence to the national outlook and has thereby gained access to the options opened up by the breached boundaries of economics and culture and by the detachment of politics and the law from state entities and actors. In concrete terms, this means that the cosmopolitan capacity of the state needs to be grasped conceptually and developed politically, 'independently of prior notions of sovereignty and autonomy'. 'The focus of analysis would then no longer be on the "sovereignty" or the "autonomy" of the state, but rather on *state capacity* in the widest sense', that is, the ability of states to contribute towards solving global problems (Grande and Risse 2000: 253). To put the issue in even more concrete terms: having regained state capacity by cosmopolitanism means, the state's options for intervention are *expanded* both domestically *and* abroad by acting and governing in transnational networks that include other states, as well as NGOs, supranational institutions and transnational corporations. Thus, unencumbered by any scruples about sovereignty, the cosmopolitan state makes use of the unpaid work of other governments, non-governmental organizations and global business corporations for solving 'national' problems, that is, for solving transnational problems that are a high priority within the national arena.

Cosmopolitan state capacity can therefore no longer be derived from the institutional capacities of national governments, as this would be the equivalent of a nation-based misapprehension. The 'theory of governance' derived from methodological nationalism is wrong, because it brackets off the co-governance of transnational actors in the national political arena and does not have the wherewithal to conceptualize 'national' governance as a busy 'shunting yard', as the unpaid 'push-me-pull-you' work of multinational actors. Even nation-state capacity only becomes apparent to the cosmopolitan outlook through the worldwide networks into which governance in the global age has to integrate actively and creatively if it wants to be successful. Cosmopolitan state capacity, to put it in terms of a quasi-mathematical formula, is the *sum* of the capacity of national governmental organizations and bureaucracies *plus* the targeted use of cooperative capacities of transnational political networks. These latter encompass NGOs, supranational organizations, transnational corporations, and so forth. It is the sum of these and not the nation's resources alone that constitutes the capacity available to integrated cosmopolitan states in their efforts to meet national and international challenges (cf. Katzenstein 1978; Weiss 1998). Thus, it is 'foreign' resources in particular which the cosmopolitan state builds up and exploits in order to develop credible responses to 'its own' as well as 'foreign' issues of a national, transnational or global nature.

One consequence of this theory is that the reduction in state capacity in modern welfare states, via 'political integration' (Scharpf) and public–private systems of negotiation, must *not* be confused with the *trans*nationalization of state activities. If *domestic* political integration leads to a loss of state autonomy in the dominance of the national outlook, this by no means applies necessarily to the cosmopolitanization of the state. On the contrary: as cosmopolitan governments succeed in acquiring credibility in transnational action networks, the radius of their activities will most likely *widen* with respect to both the domestic and the non-domestic arena. It then becomes possible to formulate a *hypothesis of asymmetry between political integration within and outside the nation-state*. Whereas the state's power to shape events within cooperative networks *runs aground* domestically, state capacity is expanded and revived (under certain conditions) by playing a creative role in *external* political networks. This makes it clear once again that the loss of state sovereignty and autonomy must be 'strictly distinguished from a loss of capacity to lead, to act or to solve problems'. 'It is thoroughly conceivable that the days of the hierarchically structured nation state are numbered, while the organization of political domination in network-like contexts in which nation states "are abolished" opens up new options in a globalized economy and culture' (Grande and Risse 2000: 253; cf. Elkins 1995; Albrow 1996; Beck 1998a; Zürn 1998a; Grande 1999).

In this respect, the integration of domestic and foreign 'cosmopolitics' – especially the expansion of domestic state policy options via their instrumental integration into 'foreign' transnational issues and practical contexts – has to play a major role in any future post-national, cosmopolitan theory of governance. In a reference to the very recent history of the nation-state, Krasner speaks of sovereignty as 'organized hypocrisy'. The full significance of this judgement will only unfold once the state becomes cosmopolitanized.

It is certainly true that plus-sum games in which everybody is a winner are not the only thing set in train by this kind of active self-networking of state politics. This would be wrong-headed idealism. It also gives rise to new, dramatic lines of conflict, relationships based on exclusion and uncompromising either/or situations. You cannot confiscate rebel weapons with NATO in Macedonia and at the same time want to decide, as a sovereign nation, whether or not to do so. The process of deciding whether or not to call a state of emergency – the classic criterion of nation-state sovereignty – is one that starts to unravel in the transnational arena. It is hard to establish exactly where such decisions are ultimately made. However, this much is for sure: they are not made in the parliaments of the countries involved, *or by any single government on its own*, but rather 'somewhere' in an ademocratic 'in-between' place. However, once taken by 'NATO', such decisions develop a momentum towards consensus that individual parliaments and governments are hard put to resist.

This actively networked 'foreign-domestic' and 'domestic-foreign' politics removes the element of hierarchy from state politics and makes it more fluid; it renews the trans-state capacity of state actors both within and beyond national borders. A further advantage of this kind of politics is that it exists within the consensus that it has itself helped to generate, and is thus able to regain credibility, even in relation to its critics, either by chipping away gradually at both the small and large global problems of concern to people on a daily basis, or else by preventing them from occurring in the first place.

The cosmopolitan state is also in a position *preventively* to nip those problems in the bud which in any case only emerge out of the nation-state orthodoxy of borders, homogeneity and sovereignty to begin with – problems such as tax avoidance, migration, military security, technological risks and environmental threats. Everybody has to have their own army and make their own mistakes. It is an unbelievably expensive undertaking to establish and maintain national homogeneity and sovereignty. In this respect, one can say that the cosmopolitanization of the state is perhaps the greatest possible rationalization measure in any state's civil service, since it relativizes – or rather overcomes – national axioms, which are an inexhaustible source of problems and costs. The choice to pursue certain policies would surely reap benefits: promoting global justice would mean not having to fear any raids on the national social welfare coffers; struggling resolutely to solve environmental problems would save on health spending; work on implementing a global regulatory framework for technological risks would mean not having to spend huge amounts of money reinforcing the stable door of political confidence and remedial research once the horse has bolted; and urging the scientific community to acknowledge the consequences of their research early on would mean not having to pay compensation once these consequences have come upon us. Almost all the key problems have one aspect that opens out to the global dimension: they can adequately be addressed only in global agreements and institutions, and in the context of global public political debate and reflexivity.

National politics finds itself in a *de*legitimation trap. On the one hand, it contributes to the production and reproduction of these kinds of global problems through its focus on 'national' concerns while, on the other, it can do little to help deal with them effectively for exactly the same reason. This is the very trap from which the state can break free through its cosmopolitan self-transformation: cosmopolitanization can contribute towards reducing or avoiding the (global) problems that arise from national isolation and cannot be tackled because of it.

A number of substantial issues are linked to the formation of transnational political communities. If the consequences of national decisions are transnational or global – as is the case with nuclear energy, climate change, and so forth – then duties towards others cannot be restricted merely to duties towards one's national fellow citizens. In circumstances such as these, democracies have not only a specific obligation to include fellow citizens and foreigners alike as co-legislators in an extended political community; it is also in their national self-interest to do so. It thus becomes possible, on the basis of risk definitions that transcend any one nation's borders, to create political communities of risk in which cosmopolitan rights of participation are institutionalized. To illustrate this by reference to the everyday consequences of climate change: humanity is increasingly plagued by weather-related disasters that are no longer considered 'natural' but are seen to be a result of human action; moreover, vivid images and commentaries in the mass media attribute these disasters to decisions emanating from the modern risk society – to 'inappropriate action'. As a result of this, there is growing pressure on the various states to implement relevant agreements both nationally and globally in the national interest. Every new disaster – too much rain here, too much sun there – raises the question, 'what is the rain and the heat telling us?', thereby either contributing to the litany of political failures or else becoming the source of transnational political renewal.

Win–win strategies

This applies not only to 'natural' and technological risks but also to large-scale economic risks. The recent history of global economic crises shows clearly what the crux of the issue is. In 1982, for example, Argentina, Brazil and Mexico and a number of other developing countries were no longer able to service their debts. A decade later, the debt burden of developing countries more than doubled again. In 1989, the inflation-driven 'economic bubble' of the Japanese economy burst. In 1997, the Asian crisis erupted, resulting in whole population groups sinking into poverty. Since 2001, the Argentine economy has been in a state of collapse, and its neighbouring countries are not alone in fearing that the 'killer virus' will spread throughout the whole of Latin America, given the crisis in the US economy and near-zero economic growth in Europe. One way of building a firewall against these threatening financial crises and catastrophes would be to construct and consolidate cosmopolitan states – even if the words 'government' and 'state' are like a red rag to a bull to neo-liberal advocates of the unbounded economy.

One particular insight is crucial in this context: national governments are in any case bound to take on the role of global fire brigade and put out the wildfires sparked by global financial risks and their destructive impacts. But nobody has taken the trouble to work out what global casino-capitalism's adventure spree is costing the 'general taxpayer'. Cosmopolitan states and governments, on the other hand, can act in a *preventive* way and not only minimize the extent of public and private capital's destructive impacts but also try to turn a highly negative, crisis-riddled situation around.

Global financial markets and financial flows endanger not only entire groups of countries and cultures but also burden investors themselves with enormous risks. Equally big is national governments' fear of the consequences of unregulated, global mobility applied to capital and corporations, which – and this is the crucial point – operate within rule systems involving minus-sum games, in which *win–lose* or *lose–lose* strategies predominate. Corporations and supranational financial organizations try to play states off against one another while at the same time passing on the risks of their investment decisions to these states. Cosmopolitan state capacity would be the extent to which states were able, on the basis of alternative theories, to transform these minus-sum games into *plus*-sum games – into *win–win* strategies – by pooling and sharing sovereignty in the form of global agreements.

In other words, the national outlook forces its adherents into accepting the lose–lose games of laissez-faire global market politics and putting a positive gloss on them. The cosmopolitan outlook, by contrast, looks for alternatives that allow these predominantly minus-sum games of global politics to be carried over into win–win rules, that is, to find or create new cosmopolitan regulations and institutions that enable all those concerned – states, corporations and nature itself – to emerge as winners (as has occurred through the institutionalization of environmental standards in the European Union, for example).

Cut-throat globalization generalizes the *role of the victim*. The universalization of the market destroys health and safety standards and workers' rights to co-determination; environmental regulations are dismantled or undermined and natural resources exploited. Even powerful corporations can become the potential victims of restructuring, of hostile takeovers and of global financial risks. If states were to empower themselves through a cosmopolitan approach, they might succeed in squaring the circle in exactly the opposite way, in a strategy aimed at reining in the self-destructive tendencies of a capitalism divested of its national fetters, and *thereby* opening up the sources of cosmopolitan legitimacy to state politics.

Strategies aimed at cosmopolitanizing the law

The cosmopolitan state is the answer to the critique of nation-based metaphysics. The latter is based on the subordination of legal sovereignty to the sovereignty that resides in power. National sovereignty connects law to the actual exercise of violence, as in the words of Mephistopheles: 'Since might is yours, you'll have the right.' The nation became the source of law, while its claim to universalism was either dropped or, worse still, delegated to the national community. The cosmopolitan state, by contrast, can be defined as a power structure in which the state exercises *divided* legal sovereignty over a certain population in order to protect their rights as world citizens and to safeguard democracy. Legal rights of self-determination presuppose an open attitude towards others and their rights of self-determination within and outside the national context. In other words, state closure requires that trans-state, international dialogue, both within the national context and beyond it, be institutionalized.

It was Bodin who, in this context, argued for a *divided* sovereignty. His conception of sovereignty involved the provision that state sovereignty, in which all military command functions are ultimately concentrated, should be linked back into a restraining 'cosmic' legal order to which *everyone* is subject. However, in his way of thinking there is no authority capable of enforcing this universal legal claim against the sovereign's monopoly on violence. In the end, all that remained of the metaphysics of natural law was a moral appeal to the ruler to comply with the universal norms of natural law, in spite of his autonomous hold on power in reality.

The cosmopolitan regime comes into its own when the legal autonomy of the state is subordinated to the human rights regime. In this respect, the situation desired by many in which global citizens' rights prevail calls into question the independence of cosmopolitan states. 'Direct membership in an association of world citizens would protect the state citizen from the despotism of his or her own government. The most important outcome of a body of law that has precedence over the sovereignty of states is, as the Pinochet case has shown, the ability to hold state officials personally liable for the crimes they have committed while serving the state or the military' (Habermas 1998). Thus, the cosmopolitanization of the law includes the expectation that states will support those standards, legal forms and organizations which guarantee democracy, human rights, civil liberties and cultural diversity, both within and beyond national borders.

Realistically, different states will face quite different challenges as a result of this cosmopolitanization of the law. For example, it is plausible to assume that states which have more of an authoritarian structure will feel perfectly happy to put their signature to human rights conventions because they can keep the consequences in check with a strong hand inside their own national borders, whereas those states that already have an extensive system of autonomous laws and courts will barely be able to keep the consequences under control. On this basis, one could formulate a *paradox of transition* from the nation-state to the cosmopolitan state: *non*-genuine, instrumental and symbolic forms of cosmopolitanization of the law can most readily be expected where states are *least* able to satisfy cosmopolitan legal expectations (this would be one way of understanding the African Union, which has so far been founded on paper only; on this, see pp. 226–7 below). By contrast, in those states that are already pursuing a domestic cosmopolitanization of their legal systems, resistance to a genuine cosmopolitanization of the law may be expected to grow. It follows from this that we should not allow the rapid spread of cosmopolitan political rhetoric to deceive us about the considerable adversity faced by a cosmopolitan *realpolitik*.

Creativity is unleashed when the state enables diversity to flourish

In the national point of view, insurmountable obstacles rear up at every turn. Doubts are raised, for example, as to whether a transnational legal pacifism can be enforced at all in opposition to nation-state sovereignty. Also, to what extent does a thoroughgoing legalization of international relations presuppose transnational procedures for conflict resolution? To what extent can these sorts of juridically tamed procedures for dealing with state violations of human rights be brought about without resort to the monopoly on violence of a global state and without a global government? To what extent is the world security council an appropriate instrument in this context – should it not be complemented by additional institutions, such as the binding judgements of an international criminal court or a kind of representative general assembly of global citizens?

When institutions are consolidated at the *supra*-state level, the precondition for this is ultimately always *nation*-state autonomy; *the possibility of cosmopolitanizing the state is not even taken into consideration*. The cosmopolitanization of the state *relieves the strain on* the supranational level in this sense. Politics and democracy are shifted back to the level of the networked, 'glocally' integrated state, which draws its legitimacy from enabling diversity to flourish. Cosmopolitanization – as we have argued – means the constitutional recognition of difference. The state can only fulfil this social ordering function if it distances itself from its identification with a homogeneous national community bound together by the state (*Staatsvolk*). Just as the cosmopolitan state needs to be constitutionally tolerant towards the different religions for which it guarantees equal conditions, it must also provide cultural and political forms of participation for different nations and different ethnic identities within its sovereign domain. Indeed the state acquires its identity and legitimacy precisely from this cosmopolitan 'civilizing' of ethnic-national differences, oppositions and enmities. It is not a matter of the state setting up and watching over a politically impotent leisure park of cultural differences, but rather of facilitating cultural diversity *as* political diversity. In this sense, the cosmopolitan state is a pedagogical state. It creates opportunities for experiencing constitutional tolerance, where diversity can be both de-essentialized and lived as a new source of creativity. Like early Christianity, it takes the essentialist poison out of the national fixation on ethnicity and arouses the desire for diversity. With a combination of cosmopolitan art, public holidays, festivals, prosperity, education, consumption, democracy, and so on, it might just be possible to enable people to experience the positive aspects of the cosmopolitan conflict of ethnic and/or national diversity and its unavoidable political contradictions.

Global cities are the actually existing laboratory of cosmopolitan civilization in microcosm. 'The global city', as Arnold Toynbee argues, 'is an image of the wide world on a small scale, its walls encompassing every class, every nation and every language' (Toynbee 1958: 243). Capital cities are the birth-places of nationalism, while global cities are and can – could – be made into birthplaces of cosmopolitanism. It is in global cities that the issue will be decided as to how far cultural and political diversity can be merged into a cosmopolitan openness and public sphere that is at once locally rooted *and* inspiring.

Regional cosmopolitanization

Cosmopolitanization has little chance of success as a strategy pursued in isolation by individual states; instead, it presupposes that different nation-states, with their respective historical backgrounds and a shared definition of 'risk community', are constituted as collective state actors in the grand meta-game of global politics. The self-definition of the state as a cosmopolitan actor can therefore only come about collectively in the form of regional state alliances, something that realistically involves new trans-national boundary constructions and exclusions. The European Union provides the historical model for this, although it simultaneously shows that such alliances are favoured by certain historical preconditions. In this case, they include the traumatic experience of two world wars and the Holocaust, as well as the 'economic miracle' after the Second World War and the triumph of demo-cratic ideals in the sense of the accountability and electability of a ruling elite. This new cooperative of transnational states is still extremely fragile and con-tested, even in Europe, and is disrupted time and again by renationalizations (as in Italy and Austria). Does this not mean that – if it is possible at all – cosmopolitanization as an evolutionary opportunity is restricted to the OECD world of developed democratic welfare states? Is it yet another example of Europe as the great physician, supposedly curing all the world's ills?

What are the complementary prospects for the non-OECD states, for the majority of the world's states and its population? Is it not the case that the cosmopolitanization of states quite simply presupposes the existence of the state, a *Western* assumption that does *not* apply to large sections of global society? And if this is indeed the case, are the prospects for transnational governance not a good deal *more negative*, given that in many regions of the world there are not even any states identifiable as such to provide the nec-essary precondition for forming cosmopolitan alliances of transnational gov-ernance? And would this in turn not mean that ultimately whole regions of the world – measured against the new global standards and values of cos-mopolitanization – end up being normatively and politically sidelined?

The fact that this need not be so is demonstrated by Africa, a con-tinent portrayed in the Western mass media as a symbol of the decline of civilization. In summer 2002, heads of state and government leaders gathered at a congress in Durban to bring the *African Union* into being, based on the model of the European Union. The aim of the member countries in this confederation of states is to develop the politically productive forces of transnational cooperation. By overcoming national egotisms in this way, they hope to play a bigger role and take greater responsibility in tackling the central problems of the continent – war and starvation – for the benefit of all. 'Today Africa has taken a gigantic step forwards', said the South African president, Thabo Mbeki, in his opening speech at the event. 'This is a moment full of hope for the continent and its peoples', he continued, in front of more than forty African heads of state: the time had come for Africa to take its 'rightful place' in the world. Prior to the ceremonial founding event, the member countries agreed on a transnational regime, that is, on procedures aimed at guaranteeing cooperation between the most important organizations of the African confederation (assembly of heads of state and government, executive council, permanent committee of representatives, AU commission, AU peace and security council). More negotiations were due to take place the following year over further institutions, such as a pan-African parliament, a law court and the founding of an African central bank.

It would be naïve to expect this step into the transnational era to lead automatically to overcoming the African malaise. And yet certain essential preconditions for doing so may be established as a result, as this is how the problem-solving and regulatory potential of strategies of cosmopolitanization can be exploited in the medium and long term. These strategies enable Africa to engage in a process of modernization that transcends individual countries' borders, as provided for in the economic programme 'New Partnership for African Development'. For the first time, there will even be African peacekeeping troops and a security council, in order to eliminate Africa's most deep-seated problem, namely ongoing conflict and war. To achieve this, the principal doctrine of the nation-state era – the previously unassailable principle of non-intervention in the internal affairs of other states – has even been replaced by the counter-principle of a transnational responsibility for peace.

'A dead dream' (Hove 2002) might be one objection to this. 'One has only to think of the war between Ethiopia and Eritrea over a barren strip of border territory. So many deaths, so much destruction over the simple question of who that tree there belongs to. Given these sorts of circumstances, a functioning African Union is inconceivable for the next one hundred years.' As insistent as this voice of despair is, it still remains wedded to the national perspective. While corrupt African rulers, in an extreme case of *non*-genuine cosmopolitanization, may approach such an initiative in a cynical way, the transnational game of politics can fashion it into a precondition for aid and reconstruction funding set down by the UN, the EU, donor countries and investors. Thus, the AU is a *trans*national institutional expression of African hope. Post- and transnational state strategies are concerned with the institutional architecture of cosmopolitan *perspectives*, as regards both political action and political science. Even the lack of cosmopolitan options would never be able to justify a flawed methodological nationalism for Africa, Asia, Latin America, and so on. Here, too, we can derive two principles from this that enable us to describe and assess the cosmopolitanization of states.

On the one hand, cosmopolitanism – unlike universalism – means recognizing difference in relations between states and world regions, meaning more specifically that others' history and Europe's own involvement in it need to be acknowledged and reconstructed. This is the cosmopolitan change in perspective demanded and practised by New Critical Theory in particular, *not least* in terms of relations between states. As a result, European states need to recognize and acknowledge the extent to which Africa's past and present are part of Europe's past and present; they need to recognize the fact that European colonialism and imperialism, as the instruments by which the peoples of Africa were enslaved, needs to become – like the Holocaust – the benchmark for European restitution payments, or at least appropriate levels of economic aid.

On the other hand, recognizing the otherness of others also means asking to what extent certain contexts contain the historical roots of and concrete historical preconditions for cosmopolitanization. Are there divergent and yet concordant traditions of a cosmopolitanism that may be rooted in local circumstances?

On this point, Sakamoto Yoshikazu has developed a number of perspectives regarding a *cosmopolitanization of East Asian states* (to put it in my terms). According to Yoshikazu, globalization fulfils a dual function here:

First, there is the historical dimension. While the penetration of the logic of the market can be beneficial in sweeping away cronyism and corruption rooted in the traditional regime and culture, it has led to the breakdown of social linkages and fragmentation of the emerging civil society. It seems, therefore, that a critical reconstruction of the traditional culture of the people is also necessary in various social contexts as a way of addressing the problem of how to strengthen a public sphere of citizens' cooperation and solidarity. (Yoshikazu 2000: 110)

Countries that are late-comers to industrialization find themselves confronted with *all* the contradictions of developed modernization; in other words, they have to cope with the radical non-simultaneity of (a) 'premodern' conditions and (b) the models of the first national industrial modernity, in the face of (c) the turmoils and contradictions of the globalized second modernity, all of which elements are interconnected and in a process of reciprocal acceleration.

This can be illustrated by looking at the contradictions faced by East Asian countries. While they have been highly successful in building up national economies, they were integrated into the capitalist global economy after the Second World War without going through *any* intermediate regional integration comparable to that of the European Union. These states were incorporated into processes of globalization almost exclusively through the mediating role of the United States as their largest export market and by a currency system that tied them to the US dollar as the major currency. To put it in a nutshell: these states experienced an *asymmetrical bilateralism* with the United States, but no horizontal-regional multilateralism. For this reason, the countries of East Asia have to perform different kinds of tasks at the same time: they have to preserve the limited autonomy of their national economies while also building up new regional frames of reference for multilateral cooperation. Equally, however, they have to cope with the consequences of economic globalization, not least in order to regulate global capital flows, with the aim of defending and extending the democratic rights and legitimate expectations of their citizens.

Thus the East Asian countries are confronting a *common historical challenge*. They must define their present position while dealing simultaneously with the two dimensions of 'past and present' and 'state, region and world'. If countries find themselves facing common historical issues, it is desirable that common agents be created to deal with those issues. And the presence of common historical tasks suggests the existence of shared conditions for a common response . . . The first task concerns the issue of how to create agents for regional cooperation in East Asia. The recent currency and financial crisis in Asia has brought to the surface the reality that the region already is, despite the diversity of the conditions of respective countries, in a state of economic interdependence, and, in a sense, has already in practice created an 'economic community' with a common destiny. On the other hand, the fact that the current situation was something that no one had predicted ruthlessly exposed the reality that a conscious, proactive, political framework for regional cooperation has been decisively lacking. So, how might we begin looking for an agent to promote a regime for East Asian regional cooperation that would impose public regulation on the unrestrained globalization of the market? (Yoshikazu 2000: 111)

Yoshikazu thus uses all the state strategies that have been expounded in this chapter:

- the historical starting point in which the advent of the global economy pulverizes fossilized traditional structures on the one hand, while forcing countries critically to reconstruct and to revitalize binding traditions on the other;
- the experience of being part of an economic community of risk, which facilitates, indeed forcibly creates, a *single* definition of the situation that exists in the arena of global power; and
- regional regulatory responses that have to be developed on the basis of analysis of this monetary and financial South-East Asian crisis (the estab-

lishment of a regional Asian currency fund in order to be capable of reacting quickly and appropriately to crises and in order to limit currency speculation, systematic observation and monitoring of speculative fast track investments, and so on).

Also included here is something that Yoshikazu calls the 'civic state' and that has similarities with my concept of the 'cosmopolitan state'; that is, the obligation of the regional confederation of states to enforce the human rights regime both within and beyond individual states' borders and, emerging from this, cooperation with non-governmental organizations and transnational and supranational corporations and organizations (2000: 114ff.).

Here, too, it becomes clear that strategies for the cosmopolitan self-transformation of states cannot be practised successfully by individual sovereign states, but are realistic only in the form of a regional, inter-state strategy of cooperation. The degree to which these prospects for Asian (or African or Latin American) cosmopolitanization can actually be realized will simultaneously give an indication of the extent to which different historical and regional 'cosmopolitanisms' will be capable of being developed and realized in the second modernity.

Nationalism has shed its innocence

Nation-states are 'paranoid monsters' – these are the radical terms in which Edgar Morin sums up critique of the national context.

They deal with one other in a mad, bloodthirsty way. They recognize no law higher than their own barbaric will. Treaties are only ever a scrap of paper that gets torn up whenever there is a shift in power relations. They are incapable of loving and they lack a conscience. And we individuals, as well as humanity as a whole, are utterly at the mercy of the drunken rage and the atrocities committed by these Uranian monsters. The destiny of the planet is in their hands. It is indeed nation-states that pose the greatest threat to individuals as individuals (totalitarian alienation) and to humanity as humanity (total annihilation). (Quoted in Coulmas 1990: 477f.)

The negativity of modernity and that of its consciousness is no empty gesture, no mere ideology of the tragic. It is the historical consciousness of nation-based modernity which, without mercy or consideration for its own self-destruction, has given rise to the moral, political, economic and technological seeds of catastrophe and turned real life into a laboratory experiment with horror. The mass graves of the twentieth century – those from the world wars, the Holocaust and the atomic bombs of Hiroshima and Nagasaki – all bear witness to this, and the list of absolute evil is never-ending. It is not worth shedding a single tear over the end of *this* modernity. Those fond of nostalgia for the national orthodoxy suppress the moral and political invalidation of the same, which has acquired a globally binding symbol in the transnational commemoration of the Holocaust (Levy and Sznaider 2001).

The victory of nationalism in the eighteenth and nineteenth centuries meant that the particular (a single group) was elevated to the status of the universal, one's own nation was equated with humanity. Many particular humanities generalized the particular into a norm of political solidarity and thereby created something that was apparently insuperable historically – the universalism of the national, or particular universalism. In this sense, what is beginning today is – depending on one's standpoint – either a cosmopolitan counter-revolution or a process of overcoming the lie of the national age that says: basic rights can be divided by nation, they can be granted to those who are like us – members of this nation – and denied to everybody else.

In a certain sense cosmopolitanism brings feminism to completion. The feminist movement demanded and won basic rights for the non-male part of humanity, while cosmopolitanism seeks to do the same for the non-national part of humanity. In this respect, one could argue that the theoretical and political development of the cosmopolitan state puts an end to the brief but bloody eternity of the national counter-revolution against the origins of the cosmopolitan modernity.

Cosmopolitan Europe?

Nation-based politics remains committed to the prospects for the self-preservation and possibly the expansion of its sphere of power. To the extent that they are conceived of at all, global visions can only be imperialist visions in this context. This lack of visionary globality, of an ability to locate one's own nation within the broader context of global social cooperation and thereby generate more political options, also exists in respect of what has, up until now, been the only original transnational political unit that there is, namely, Europe. Given the way it has so far emerged and developed in the interstices between nation-states, and given how it is being shaped, Europe is a hybrid between a market and a bureaucracy, but it is no political entity with visionary powers, either in terms of how to shape Europe as a group of states, or with regard to Europe's position in relation to other global regions. Do the Europeans want to integrate or 'Latin-Americanize' Russia? Does Europe want to put its colonial, or quasi-colonial, tradition in its relations with Africa and the Arab world behind it? How will Europe respond to the modernization plans self-confidently embarked upon by other cultures, particularly in Asia? Will it abandon its monopolistic claim on modernity and open itself up to the challenges posed by multiple modernities, including that of self-criticism, as is demanded of both European modernity and its critics? Is 'Europe' more than just a cartographic designation with fuzzy boundaries, more than just a market-fixated vision concerned only with how the wheels of economic growth are turning? What prospects is Europe developing for the mass of the poor worldwide who are doubly dis-advantaged by their powerlessness and lack of a public voice in the global power game? What is Europe's attitude towards the transnational class of modernizers who feel just as much at home in Jakarta or Moscow as they do in London, São Paolo or New York; and what is its attitude towards the immense number of all those who experience cultural and economic global-ization first and foremost as vehicles of dispossession? How will a Europe that has potentially undergone political renewal behave towards a commu-nity of states whose political hopes, if anything, are focused on national poli-tical projects, but who are now turning in disappointment to ethnic or religious militancy because these hopes have been ground down by cor-ruption and continuing imperialism? The questions could go on and on, but the message is clear: Europe to date has possessed only a provincial soul. The profound consequence of this is that Europe is *not* a cosmopolitan actor. Paradoxically, this deficiency is highlighted precisely by concerns con-centrating on what the normative political consequences of the federal structure of European states and of a 'European' constitution will be within Europe itself.

Cosmopolitanism as a power multiplier

Let us return to the question posed at the start of this book: who are the cos-mopolitan renewers of the political sphere? The nation-state is not trans-formed into a cosmopolitan constellation by an invisible hand. It is not an invisible hand that moves populations and governments to delegate their autonomy to a 'cosmopolitan sovereignty' and to experiment with a new balance between cosmopolitan and national ethics, between respect for those who are culturally different and adherence to national egotism.

We began by claiming that the question of whether one opens up to the cosmopolitan perspective and its dialogic ethics is not one of morality or enlightenment, but is more to do with acquiring strategic power. The central question of this book – can the political community be renewed in such a way that both respect for and curiosity about cultural difference are awak-ened and become a permanent feature of its make-up? – can be answered with a resounding 'yes'. So, to summarize the outline of New Critical Theory with cosmopolitan intent presented here, what are the ways in which the cos-mopolitan regime might make its power and presence felt?[7] Here are five answers:

1   Those who think only in national terms are losers. Only those who learn
    to see the world through cosmopolitan eyes will be able, on the one hand,

to avoid the costs of decline and, on the other, to discover, try out and acquire for themselves the newly available options and opportunities for power. The greater sense of power that arises from overcoming national barriers is what – potentially – awakens enthusiasm for all things cosmopolitan.

2   The new interactive power of the political, denationalized and decoupled from state structures, is manifested in the fact that sovereignty is experienced, facilitated and developed no longer through homogeneity and isolation but rather through diversity and joint collaboration. It is this expansion of the arena of power – this is the crucial point – that opens up new game moves and power resources to the skilful cosmopolitan in *national* political arenas. Cosmopolitan players therefore hold a few trump cards over their merely national opponents. In playing this multi-level game of the political, in skilfully staging two plays at once while remaining well aware of the distinction between symbolic politics alone and symbolic politics aimed at pushing through cosmopolitan projects, they demonstrate just who are the experienced cosmopolitan 'lions' and who the national 'foxes'.

3   Global problems bring ennoblement. One would have more or less to invent the challenges of cosmopolitan politics if one wanted to acquire opportunities to outgrow every other player politically and thereby gain access to the rare wellspring of democratic assent and exploit it to the full.

4   The cosmopolitan shift in perspective opens up the transnational arena of political action and domination. This is the only way in which realistic answers can be found to the global problems of concern to people on a daily basis, the only way of renewing trust in the creativity of the state and politics.

5   Cosmopolitan action means action in a world of permeable borders. Not only is it possible to get involved in another country's domestic affairs, other countries can also get involved in one's own domestic affairs. Doubtless this in turn depends on the cosmopolitan hierarchy of power. But even those who would prefer to shield themselves from constant invasion by others have to do so interactively and with a cosmopolitan eye for what is possible in reality, if they are to be successful. In other words, even those who have been steamrollered need cosmopolitan vision in order to turn their vulnerability, step by step, into strength.

Human rights as a strategy

Let us add one further important argument to this list of cosmopolitanism's strategic benefits in terms of power: *human rights are a source of cosmopolitan power*. There is one overriding consequence that emerges clearly from the meta-power theory advanced in this book. Transnationality generates a *spectacular lack of legitimacy* on *both* sides – that is, not only on the side of capital, but also on the side of a redefined state power and politics. Consent becomes the most urgently needed and most scarce resource worldwide. It follows from this that states which make the human rights regime the basis of their politics, in terms of both policies and institutions, gain access to completely new sources of legitimation. Regardless of whether the policy-based and institutional marriage between the state and civil society – the cosmopolitan state, the civil society-based state – is morally reprehensible or desirable, this combination at any rate places state action on a new power footing. This is hard for the old, national Machiavellians to grasp: *morality, rather than violence, is the source of power, of global power in the global age.* The situation today is this: *if you have morality, the morality of human rights, then you have the right to exercise military power – anywhere in the world.*

The universalistic reach of the law has been forgotten in the metaphysics of the national, or else – worse still – has been subordinated to the norms of ethnic community. In contrast to this, the cosmopolitan constellation and the cosmopolitan state decouple legal sovereignty, at least partially, from the sovereignty of violence to which it has been subordinated. What does 'cosmopolitan' mean in this context? 'In the first instance, cosmopolitanism stands for those basic values that set standards or limits, which no actor, regardless of whether he represents a government, a state or a civil association, may contravene' (Held, unpublished essay). One minimum principle of the cosmopolitan state, then, is expressed in the fact that legal sovereignty is divided and linked into certain *cosmopolitan minima moralia* – constitutional moral principles which, if need be, are subjected to military, supranational control. No matter how this global human rights morality may be justified, it becomes the basis of power from which state action springs in two ways.

- For one thing, the 'human rights check' becomes the key indicator – possibly even the criterion for inclusion or exclusion – for foreign investment. Only those states and countries that have internalized the human rights regime both institutionally and ideologically send out the right signals of trustworthiness that are capable of attracting highly mobile and highly sensitive investors and financial flows.
- For another thing, the clear conscience of (Western) states in matters of human rights makes the rest of the world open to a situation in which the (no longer purely domestic) affairs of foreign countries are constantly subject to external governance. The human rights regime provides a moral justification for the arena of power filled by a global domestic politics that reaches through and across every border. To turn the old Clausewitz statement around the other way, this allows – or perhaps even makes it necessary for – military violence to be deployed everywhere as a continuation of the *morality of human rights* by other means.

The nation-state is an unfinished state, a state that structurally negates its moral responsibility towards the rights of minorities and foreigners. Hegel speaks of the 'rational state', referring to the core idea that the state embodies – and should bring to bear – the ethical responsibility of mediating between the different loyalties, convictions, identities and confessions in a society. This is exactly what nation-states *negate*. They represent a threat to their own domestic diversity, to the multiple loyalties associated with the flows and exchanges that take place within their borders. Nation-states embody a denial of diversity. Nation-states stand for violence against minorities and foreigners. Nation-states tolerate war as a legitimate expression of state sovereignty. Nation-states embody tolerance towards the violence that is at their sole disposal both within and outside their borders. Nation-states imply that they and they alone are the exclusive subject of international law.

Cosmopolitanism contradicts nations' right to self-determination, understood as the right to close oneself off towards the rest of the world, and it stresses the necessity of combining internal sovereignty with responsibility for others, for foreigners both within and outside national borders. It is not a matter of negating or even condemning self-determination – on the contrary, it is a matter of liberating it from national narrow-mindedness and linking it with a cosmopolitan openness towards the concerns of the world, of finding a new balance between its duties towards fellow citizens and its duties towards other fellow citizens of the world. In this respect, the Kantian principle that all people should be treated as ends in themselves must necessarily come into conflict with the betrayal of this principle at national borders. Why do we have to accept a special moral obligation towards people just because they happen to have the same nationality as ourselves? Why should we be free of any moral obligation towards our fellow human beings for the sole reason that they were born and brought up on the other side of the national garden fence?

The cosmopolitan state does not cancel out our moral obligation towards humanity; instead, it cancels out the fundamentally dubious notion that a person's obligations within a national border are total and that their release from all obligations beyond this border is also total. Cosmopolitan civil rights *link* the condition of belonging to a nation or a state with the recognition and acknowledgement of other nations and other states. Those who claim the right to collective self-determination for themselves while denying it to the others with whom they live side by side deprive themselves of that same right. This means that, wherever different cultures, affinities and loyalties mingle and live together within a relatively small space, the recognition of one's own right to cultural self-determination must be combined with a recognition of the right to self-determination of those who are culturally different. However, this reciprocal right to self-determination and its dialogic acknowledgement can only be guaranteed by a state that remains neutral and indifferent towards different groups' right to self-determination: the cosmopolitan state. The critical question that constitutes the litmus test for any bond of loyalty is this: what kind of difference does it construct and exclude, and how does it behave towards those whose designation as culturally different it has generated (cf. Connolly 1995)?

It is the way in which moral, economic and military power and legitimacy mutually reinforce and overlap, or merge, with one another that opens up new kinds of capacity to the cosmopolitan state in the transnational sphere and makes it superior to the old version of the nation-state. If, by way of a thought experiment, one mentally walks through this real space of possibilities that is cosmopolitan regime building, and assesses its parameters, the main thing that catches the eye is the multiple plus-sum game that is made possible by it: morality and economics and the military all complement and reinforce one another to become a Grand Politics of boundaries and of conscience – so much so, in fact, that it could just about give you the jitters.

6

Strategies of Civil Society Movements

The strategies of capital and the strategies of the state, as we have argued, are an expression of *translegal domination*. We have defined this extension of Max Weber's typology as a form of domination that is *neither illegal nor legitimate* – a double negation that by no means adds up to an unambiguous affirmation. In other words – and this element is crucial in what follows – it is an intermediate form between illegal and legal domination, in which one feature in particular stands out, namely, the *asymmetry between legitimation and domination*: a great deal of power together with legitimation under threat are lined up opposite power under threat and a high level of legitimation.[1]

To put it another way, building and consolidating on domination in the transnational arena – and this applies to global business as much as to states – is accompanied by a reduction in (democratic) legitimation. This decline in legitimation is of a radical nature. On the one hand, breaking away from the nation-state shell means breaking away from institutionalized forms of legitimate domination. This applies above all to global business actors, but it also applies to the strategies of states and governments. At the same time, there is a parallel increase in the demands and claims made on the legitimation of domination. One might almost say that, just as the transformation from the first to the second modernity takes place within the shadow of old categories and hollowed-out institutions, this transformation of modernity is accompanied by spaces of power formation in which legitimation is absent, and where the effectiveness of economic and political action is bought with forms of non-legitimated (which is not the same as non-legitimate) power concentration. The result of this is the *delegitimization of domination*, the key trend in the transition from the first to the second modernity. This delegitimization occurs in relation to the translegal domination of global business and it includes the privatization of state tasks and the transfer of state functions to global business. Meanwhile, the transnationalization of states gives rise to strategies and forms of cooperation between states as well as to international regimes: governance without government.

This is the context in which the public awareness-raising strategies of advocatory movements come into their own in terms of both opportunities and power. The denationalization, delocalization and transnationalization of business and the state generate and intensify both the legitimatory decline of domination and the dilemma of democracy in the global age. While democratic legitimation is tied to the nation-state in its parliamentary constitution on the one hand, the new meta-power game of global politics necessarily creates a new definition of domination and politics in the transnational arena on the other, in business and in politics alike. As the central actors of the emerging global society migrate out of the national arena of democratic legitimation, domination becomes de-democratized, which in turn means that collectively binding decisions are ultimately made and executed in the transnational arena *without* the consent of the sovereign. In contrast to this, the self-determination and participation of thinking and acting people worldwide assume an increasingly important role. The *dismantling* of democracy and the *claims* made on democracy grow and contradict one another more and more openly, thereby mutually reinforcing and accelerating the legitimatory decline of domination.

Neither solitary individual states nor global business 'egotists' are capable of mobilizing global public opinion. Strategies of global public awareness-raising constitute the polyvalent monopoly of networks of actors in the environmental, women's, human rights and consumer movements – albeit this monopoly is limited in terms of its power resources.

What constitutes the basis of the counter-power of global civil society advocates in contrast to capital, which is self-empowering and self-legitimating? NGOs – as varied, uncoordinated and internally contradictory as they may be – certainly have a very smart, global, civil 'weapon' at their disposal, to the extent that they are able to strike at the corporations using their own weapons. The cold logic of abstract markets has many actors. They include not only owners (that is, shareholders), nor only managers, banks and supranational financial organizations. They include not least the *global customer*, and this customer has an increasing amount of power at their disposal. Much like capital, the global customer possesses the *global power of refusal*, of non-purchase. Much like capital, the political consumer can enact this policy of refusal as a *calculated side-effect* of economic action; such a strategy cannot be monitored or controlled, and neither does it involve much cost to the consumer themselves. In short, the 'consumer strike' is a means of counter-power *that cannot be countered by power*. Capital is largely at the mercy of the politicized global customer. In a certain sense, the political consumer avenges the state: just as transnational capital breaks the power of territorialized states through a politics of refusal, so the political consumer breaks the power of transnational capital by buying this product instead of that product.

The weapon of non-purchase is weakened in its impact, however, by the difficulty of organizing the non-purchase of non-members (this is what consumers are) on a permanent basis. This would require the existence of information systems, work in awareness raising, use of the media as an instrument of symbolic politics, factual information, and so on and so forth. Moreover, consumer resistance – when consumers purposefully deselect the new management princes and their worldwide capital policies using the ballot paper of non-purchase – collapses as soon as media attention turns to some other issue.

But the very thing that makes this weapon so fragile also gives it a powerful influence that extends across all national borders and all continents: non-members – once they have been organized and given information via networks – can strike *anywhere* and everywhere in the world, and can thereby counteract the transnational power of the corporations.

NGOs, too, are certainly in a position to challenge the corporate emperors' new clothes, their new sources of legitimation. Economic activity generates global side-effects that threaten humanity's basic resources for survival and, by the same token, the legitimatory foundations of 'autonomous' investment decisions.

In this sense, the advocatory movements of global civil society are the originators, advocates and judges of global values and norms. The way they create and hone this everyday, local and global awareness of values is by sparking public outrage and generating global public indignation over spectacular norm violations. This they do by focusing on individual cases, whether it be environmental scandals, where corporations are 'caught in the act' and found guilty of wrongdoing, or the pain-filled biographies of victims of torture that arouse the world's conscience. They establish the perpetrators' guilt by (ideally) disseminating truthful information and thereby effectively staging a global public trial where they are the prosecutor, global public – consumers – and judge rolled into one. As judge, they can and should execute their judgement directly with the boundless ease of non-purchase. However, there are two other problems (besides those already mentioned) faced by these counter-movements of resistance. For one thing, there is no clear enemy around whom conflicts can be organized and, for another, there is no single unambiguous language of conflict available, but rather a Babel-like confusion of many different languages of conflict – of ecology, human rights, feminism, religion, nationalism, trade unionism and xenophobia. In other words, there is *no cosmopolitan language of conflict*. Is this internal plurality of advocatory counter-power a strategic disadvantage or an advantage? It is probably an advantage, as it makes any form of external, centralist instrumentalization harder to achieve.

The 'power of public awareness' that advocatory movements have is *specific* because it publicly mobilizes and highlights legitimatory resources: it *generates the production, distribution and strategic use of information*. Note, it is not the use of information as such, but rather the *creation of global public awareness* of that information which constitutes the particular parameters of advocatory movements' power, their particular power resource. In other words, it is the way advocatory movements deliberately and strategically link information and legitimation as a strategy of global public awareness that determines their position in the power triad alongside the strategies of capital and those of the state. To put it another way: the 'power' of information as a legitimatory resource is measured not in relation to information itself, but rather in relation to the *decline in legitimation of translegal domination* – that of global business in particular, but also that of states. Thus, the strategies of public awareness deployed by advocatory movements make use of a politics of informational pinpricks to dramatize and display for public effect the startling contradiction between the maximization and delegitimization of translegal domination.

These features of transnational movements' power, which is based solely on information and legitimation, may appear insignificant in the face of the economic, political and military power resources commanded by other global actors. And, indeed, advocatory movements do *not* exercise translegal domination; they 'merely' instrumentalize its contradictions. Thus, advocatory movements *cannot* practise a politics of *faits accomplis*, they *cannot* make any collectively binding decisions, either in the national or in the global arena. They have neither economic nor political power. In fact, their own legitimation itself always remains fragile. They are not elected or appointed as such; rather, they assume the role of self-appointed advocates who themselves have repeatedly to generate legitimation for their informational activities through these very activities themselves, to reaffirm and safeguard it under public cross-examination.

It is precisely this tension between the self-authorization and delegitimation of state and global business actors and the self-legitimation of their own advocatory practice that defines the inner contradictions and consequent limits of advocatory strategies of public awareness. This in turn illustrates the fact that the power of global public actors and of strategies of global public awareness emerges not out of these strategies themselves – or at least only partially so – but rather from the legitimatory vacuum in which global and indeed 'collectively' binding decisions are made at the start of the second modernity. Given this fact, we shall now ask what forms the *basis* of advocatory movements' power. In doing so, we need to identify

1   their *legitimatory capital*, along with three types of strategies:
2   *strategies of risk dramaturgy,*
3   *strategies of democratization,*
4   *strategies of cosmopolitanization* aimed at creating a transnational or even a global public sphere.

6.1   Legitimatory capital and its non-convertibility

One crucial source of power for advocatory strategies of public awareness-raising lies in the fact that they are organized in the form of transnational networks of actors. As such, advocatory movements are participants and, in certain respects, virtuosi of the new, transnational power game. On the one hand, they are in a position to play their opponents in the global political meta-power game – states and corporations – off against one another, by forging issue-based coalitions and orchestrating provocative confrontations. On the other hand, they have a power resource at their disposal which, from the point of view of classical international politics, isn't one at all: rather than having state power or market power, they possess *legitimatory power*. Global consumer movements and boycott campaigns, for example, have greater opportunities for power under the following conditions.

- When the legitimation of markets is fragile: markets presuppose trust – the trust of the public and of consumers (two categories that cannot easily be kept separated); in this respect they are dependent on perceptions and therefore also on legitimation.
- Since company profit margins are based not only on the globalization of production but also on the globalization of consumption – that is, on the safeguarding and monitoring of global markets – the fragility of legitimation is *the* Achilles heel of global corporate power in global markets.
- This is even more the case insofar as legitimation *cannot* be bought.

Pierre Bourdieu distinguishes between economic capital, educational capital and social capital. His central thesis is that economic capital can be translated into educational and social capital (and vice versa). As far as I am aware, Bourdieu does not refer to the concept of 'legitimatory capital', which I introduce here in relation to the meta-power game between the state, capital and social movements. In the case of legitimatory capital, the opposite principle applies from that of Bourdieu's theory, namely the *non*-convertibility of economic capital into legitimatory capital. At first sight, the size of global corporate media advertising budgets would seem to contradict this. But the widespread assumption that public trust and consumer confidence is won with whole-page glossy advertisements in daily newspapers, or with TV ads, and then lost when risks are highlighted in the news ('Poison of the week'), is one of the more naïve approaches within the industry and one long since identified as such by the initiated. Advertising campaigns can sometimes even trigger the very opposite reaction to the one intended, the general sentiment being: anyone who advertises must have something to hide!

It is this legitimatory capital that enables advocatory networks to make the most strategically of factual information and even to establish new concerns and categories in opposition to much more powerful organizations and governments. In this sense, advocatory strategies and networks not only influence the outcomes of decisions, but also transform the concepts and perceptual frameworks of public controversies. Networks can thus be described not only as *'moral* entrepreneurs' but also as *'categorical* entrepreneurs': something that had once been inconceivable comes to be taken for granted (as illustrated, for example, by the 'rags-to-riches' trajectory of environmental critique). Nonetheless, it is often the case that, once certain principles have *gained acceptance, a standard is automatically set by which they may fail.* To give an example of this, one of the outstanding successes of the Rio de Janeiro conference in 1992 was the 'precautionary principle'. Principle 15 of the Rio Declaration of June 1992 states: 'Where there are threats of serious or irreversible damage, lack of full scientific certainty shall not be used as a reason for postponing cost-effective measures to prevent environmental degradation.' However, when this statement is set as a standard alongside the policies that have since ensued, as, say, in the area of genetically modified foods, one has to acknowledge that advocatory movements have failed almost completely.

To put the matter another way, transnational advocatory networks and strategies need to be understood as a self-created political space in which differently positioned actors acquire and apply their (ever threatened) 'legitimatory capital' in opposition to state and global market actors.

Furthermore, the power of networks, being based *solely* on legitimation, arises from the opposing principle to that of (inter)national sovereignty. The actions of advocatory movements are based on the principle of the *non-*sovereignty of states (or corporations) in the key issues facing humanity: environmental degradation, large-scale technological and global business risks, human rights, civil rights, global poverty, and so forth. The assumption is: it is legitimate and necessary for states and non-state actors to become involved in the so-called domestic affairs of other states.

In other words, legitimatory capital acquired through specific campaigns but also brought to bear to oppose egotistical national and global business interests presupposes a *vision of cosmopolitan responsibility* that both transcends and undermines national borders.

It sometimes seems as though states refuse cooperation with advocatory networks in order to put other states under pressure in issues of human rights and environmental destruction. But this is by no means – or at least not exclusively – the case. Interestingly enough, advocatory movements often manage to forge *strategies of cooperation* with and between states in order to put other states under pressure (just as they are able to use coalitions with global corporations to put legitimatory pressure on the activities of other states). For example, a group may intervene at national level and have this intervention blocked at national level, yet this group may still be successful if it manages to construct a transnational coalition of activists, states and corporations to break this national resistance. By forging coalitions and staging confrontations beyond the boundaries of states and corporations, the powerlessness of a strategy based solely on the resource of legitimation may be transformed into a powerful force capable of achieving its objectives.

Ultimately, the legitimatory capital of advocatory movements, and therefore their power, is based on the extent to which they are able to make *truthfulness* as such into a political issue. Providing information and uncovering facts does not, in and of itself, constitute political action. On the contrary, those who *use* facts politically, those who dramatize facts in order to achieve certain political goals, lay themselves open to the suspicion that they are merely one interested party among others. However, when advocatory movements bring facts out into the open, such as the violation of human rights in a country, or the danger of certain forms of production or contaminated foods, and so on, their power springs not from the work they do with these facts, but conversely from a situation in which these facts are systematically suppressed and denied by those in power – be they states or corporations. In a world where it is nothing out of the ordinary to play fast and loose with facts, even a simple fact can pose a threat to those in power.

So it is the art of propaganda practised by translegal domination that turns uncovering facts and making them public into a politically loaded and powerful activity. When lies are the order of the day rather than an occasional occurrence, those who call a spade a spade become something of a menace. The state of today's world risk society gives us reason to assume that *power lies*: states and corporations engage in a strategic use of the truth, meaning that they hush up the facts that can hurt them and propagate those they hope will give them a strategic advantage.

In this respect NGOs can provide both states and international organizations and corporations with *more reliable information* – information that threatens the position of certain other states and corporations. Their legitimatory capital is thus based *on their long-term credibility as producers of reliable information*. They endanger themselves if they use facts instrumentally – like their opponents – in order to force through their own interests over against those of specific corporations or states, or to boost their funding by attracting donations and members.

Ultimately, the role of advocatory movements as independent reporters uncovering buried facts is what gives them legitimation. Whenever they turn into routinized, professionalized 'promulgators of facts', into moral 'fact entrepreneurs', feigning harmony between their own interests and the truth, their legitimatory capital is frittered away.

Herein lies a tricky contradiction for advocatory movements: on the one hand they are forced into dramatizing information, while on the other they thereby place a question mark over the seriousness of their own work with factual information, the very element that constitutes their legitimatory foundation. In this regard, uncovering facts and presenting them in advocatory fashion to national and international publics is a *balancing act* in which the very foundations of advocatory networks themselves become open to challenge.

6.2 Strategies of risk dramaturgy

Conversely, advocatory strategies are based, as we have said, on the collective experience of states' and corporations' lack of credibility, or rather that of their information policies. It is the gap between reality and self-presentation that makes the strategy of delegitimation into a powerful advocatory tool. Accordingly, advocatory campaigns are most successful in those countries where liberal discourse has been internalized to the extent that social movements are able to investigate the discrepancy between claims and reality and make an issue of it.

This is what *strategies of risk dramaturgy* aim to do in the first instance. The 'advocatory methodology' – generating a willingness to change by bringing certain facts to public awareness – is extremely effective in uncovering and illuminating the discrepancy between the safety pronouncements of corporations (and governments) and the perceived risks, uncertainties and fears harboured by consumers. As we have said, though, the countervailing power of advocatory movements comes about not least as a result of the market resonance of suppressed and revealed consumer risks. By revealing the uncontrollability of global risks, risk strategies also give rise to the *uncontrollability of global markets*. In this way they give the legitimatory deficiencies of global business actors an *economic* twist, thereby hitting them where it hurts most: their need to safeguard their global sales in order to make a profit.

The worldwide conflict over the risks associated with genetically modified foods – Frankenstein food, as it has commonly become known in Britain – offers a prime example of why, in conditions of incalculable uncertainty, even powerful genetic technology manufacturers have had to make a (temporary) withdrawal, first in Europe and then in the USA. Neither the technology's proponents nor its critics know for sure what its consequences will be. The victory of genetic technology forces everybody into making impossible decisions that may influence our very survival, while being *completely unable* to ground these decisions in knowledge. In fact, what we are dealing with here is not (calculable) risk but (incalculable) uncertainty. We are dealing with a dynamic in which more scientific knowledge, rather than leading to greater certainty, leads instead to an increase in cognitive uncertainty and normative insecurity. The biotechnology revolution opens up more and more options which immediately provoke new constellations of decision-making and risk. This is because every new technology that extends our access to nature both outside and inside human bodies puts unresolved cognitive and normative problems onto the agenda. The fact that this also applies to genetically modified foods, a subject of great controversy, can be demonstrated by means of a banal, pragmatic indicator. The answer to the question of whether genetically modified food industries are (adequately) privately insured is a plain and simple 'no'. While the corporations and their experts say: 'there is no risk to the public', the private insurance industry, which would have to put its own capital on the line to back up this 'zero risk' scenario, says: it's too risky, we can't insure you (not cheaply, anyway)!

Corporations often make defamatory comments about consumers' awareness of risk, probably not least because they have no 'antidote' at their disposal to deal with advocatory strategies of risk – unless they *really were* to operate a transparent information policy (rather than merely claiming to do so). One reason why the strategy of risk is so successful is that it calls for the implementation of one basic right: the thinking consumer's right to information. When consumers ask questions concerning risks, they are effectively demanding to have a say in issues regarding technological and industrial production and the products that are consumed. This is how advocatory movements, using the example of genetically modified foods, succeed in raising the question: who governs our lives?

Genetically modified foods are a global business, and people all over the world are troubled by concerns over their unknown consequences for the planet. It is the globality of this phenomenon, however, that explains why corporations rely on their global muscle to get their way and why this very approach brings them face to face with the dilemmas posed by risk strategies. No country on its own can prohibit genetically modified foods and products without coming into conflict with the global system of open markets. If a government delays the introduction of genetically modified foods, it is confronted with the opposition of the major food companies, who want uniform standards implemented throughout the world – as long as they work in their favour; but it also comes into conflict with the World Trade Organization and similar bodies. Yet this apparently all-powerful global coalition of corporations, the WTO and governments provides the backdrop for concerned consumers – certainly in Europe, but now in the USA as well – to be sensitized to risks and uncontrollable factors that are being systematically ignored.

6.3   Strategies of democratization

Another option for advocatory movements is to throw light on an increasingly glaring contradiction. Since the end of the East–West conflict, *every* state has stated its commitment to the norms of democracy, and yet globalization entails a dramatic 'de-democratization' of the process of making collectively binding decisions, in both economic and political spheres. While risk strategies address the discrepancy between claims of control and uncontrollability, strategies of democratization tackle the conspicuous contradiction between universal professions of commitment to democracy and the sharp decline in actual democracy.

Surprisingly enough, these kinds of strategies generally emerge at the point where attempts to mobilize mass support have *failed*. To put it another way, strategies of democratization take a diffuse collection of basic norms and convictions – such as the defence of human rights – and turn them into a willingness to act. What constitutes the particularity of advocatory strategies and movements, then, is the difficulty – classical political theorists would call it an 'improbability' or 'impossibility' – of translating general and non-binding consent into specific acts. Consequently, they succeed only when the relevant conditions, coalitions and options for action are linked together in a particular way.

Advocatory strategies of this sort have to be based on reliable information, on hard facts that inevitably need to prove their veracity in the course of the conflict triggered when they are made public. But facts and figures on their own are not enough. The figures have to be given a voice, a face and a story, and that story needs to be told in public by people whose lives have been damaged. Thus, a large number of strategies aimed at motivating people into action are based on a connection between facts and life stories that arouse universal compassion.

Such symbolically mediated compassion cannot be 'generated' in accordance with standards of universal reason. It has to coincide with basic convictions concerning *human dignity*, convictions very much alive in the different contexts and cultures that have emerged from different traditions. While the notion of individual (universal) and indivisible human rights by no means enjoys the same elevated status among all people throughout the world, a related belief in human dignity *does* exist everywhere. This means that violations of human rights are usually in conflict with existing notions of human dignity. Because of this, people who bear testimony to the destruction of their body through state oppression and torture are capable of arousing compassion among people from very different cultural contexts, regardless of whether such compassion derives from a commitment to the upholding of human rights or of human dignity. Thus, in order to generate an appropriate response transnationally, it is important not only to document the violation of norms in general but also to bring facts and figures to life through personal narratives.

To put it in sociological (that is, in cynical) terms: advocatory movements ought to take a leaf out of the book of medieval European beggars' guilds, for example, which had the self-stylization of the body down to a fine art for the purpose of turning rich Christians' compassion into hard cash.

The shortest route to uncovering a nation's human rights violations and mobilizing political resistance is often one that takes in other states along the way. International contacts and coordinated action, for example, can help to overcome national authorities' and governments' refusal to acknowledge certain human rights violations by increasing the volume of voices protesting against them. This approach becomes even more effective as the costs to national governments arising from these connections become more and more obvious – that is, the costs of ignoring violations of freedom, democracy and human dignity. In this sense, advocatory strategies work towards redefining the 'national interest' by raising the costs of blindness regarding human rights issues.

All this presupposes that the principle of national sovereignty is deliberately relativized and undermined both by advocatory movements themselves and by their international coalition partners. The effect of this may be to make the globality of values and networks that have been activated by the actors of advocatory movements into a kind of self-fulfilling prophesy.

6.4   Strategies of cosmopolitanization

Advocatory networks and movements have variably been thought of as executive organs of a global culture of common values, comparable with the International Olympic Committee and the Red Cross. However, this appraisal fails to do justice to the role they play, because advocatory movements actually do not execute pre-given, global values at all. What they do is reinterpret, create and reinforce international norms and rules at the same time as they attempt to put them into practice in concrete political contexts and campaigns.

The theory of world culture, as formulated by John Meyer, John Boli and George Thomas among others, implies that an international society emerges as very different actors disseminate global norms worldwide. According to the authors, these include national governments, international agreements and non-governmental organizations, which, for them, consist of the classical NGOs and transnational corporations. All these actors agree on the (often unseen) consequences of their actions: they strengthen and reinforce the process whereby a 'world culture' becomes institutionalized in accordance with the principles of universalism, individualism, rationalism and global citizens' rights. According to this view there is *no* meaningful distinction between different transnational actors and strategies that reinforce or challenge the domination of nation-states and transnational corporations.

Contrary to this view, it is clear that different actors certainly do occupy different positions within the emerging structure of domination of global society and therefore have very different kinds of strategic possibilities at their disposal. In addition, they pursue very different aims and purposes. This is why it is necessary to distinguish between different categories of national and transnational actors, although of course the 'logics' of transnational advocatory movements must not be confused with the aims and purposes pursued, say, by technical institutes for safety, the World Trade Organization and corporations.

In this sense, the theorists of world culture *fail to recognize* the particularity of advocatory strategies. These latter draw attention to and instrumentalize the rapid decline in legitimation afflicting state and global business domination, contributing to the creation and contours of the emerging cosmopolitan regime in so doing. Beneath the active gaze of advocatory strategies, the walls and boundaries of the national repositories of state and society dissolve and are opened up to cosmopolitan responsibility and power. However, while these movements and their strategies are able to open up the national framework, they are not able to eliminate it entirely.

The cosmopolitan question to which advocatory movements give voice is still aimed at *state addressees*. They are the ones, rather than transnational actors *per se* or some ominous world state, whose moral and legal foundations should be receptive to cosmopolitan values. The guiding assumption is this: *human rights can only ever be enforced and guaranteed in a grand coalition of states (and perhaps of corporations within the domain of states as well).* Individuals who rebel against the violation of their human and civil rights have to be supported both transnationally and transculturally in their resistance to the state to which they belong. The cosmopolitan society can be awakened within the state and can exercise pressure from outside the state. But the actors with political responsibility remain states.

It is precisely because advocatory movements are so successful in creating values, institutions and politics that observers are forced to cast a realistic eye on their internal contradictions and inherent limitations. Global civil society actors are caught in a twofold dilemma: on the one hand they rely on states to implement their goals, while on the other they are the main opponents of states and corporations. In order to be successful, they have to make states into willing converts, as it were, to the values of civil society – human rights, environmental protection, and so forth; on the other hand, their successes render them superfluous and they are squeezed within the cooperative embrace of states and corporations. Usually, both scenarios apply.

Accordingly, the issue of sovereignty is viewed in highly contrasting ways among the different factions of global civil society, depending on whether the actors are based in the North or in the South. Generally speaking, activists in the North regard the erosion of sovereignty as a good thing, while activists in the South view it as a bad thing. These contradictory perceptions and assessments are a reflection of very different historical situations. While activists and theorists in the North base their actions and assessments on a historically entrenched state system, the representatives of the South are often confronted with situations in which the very word 'democracy' has a derisory ring to it and the word 'state' remains an unrealistic utopia. As the notion of a 'cosmopolitan society' becomes more realistic, so the conflict over what its structures, values, concepts and institutions mean – and for whom – comes to be more bitterly contested.

7

Who Wins? On the Transformation of Concepts and Forms of the State and of Politics in the Second Modernity

The argument I have elaborated in the preceding chapters is this: what we are witnessing in the global age is not the end of politics, but rather its migration elsewhere. A transformation of political concepts and forms is occurring before our very eyes and at our own hands, although until now we have been prevented from perceiving it and researching it on account of a lack of historically appropriate categories and perspectives, a deficit this book seeks to help rectify.[1] The structuring of opportunities for political action is no longer defined by the national/international dualism but is now located in the 'glocal' arena. Global politics has turned into global domestic politics, which robs national politics of its boundaries and foundations. What is new in this is not the fact that the strategies of capital are putting pressure on states or making them follow their lead – this is exactly what political economy has been about from the very beginning – but rather *how* this is being done. In particular, it is about the way in which global political economic power instrumentalizes the threat of disinvestment and thereby triumphs over a politics paralysed by its ties to 'terra patria'. Global business actors are not fundamentally more powerful than states – but they *have* managed to break free from the parochial confines of the national orthodoxy: *that* is what is new.

Consequently, anyone who expects to see a return of politics in the form of the nation-state will inevitably join the choir of those lamenting the end of politics. One of the errors committed by methodological nationalism is that it has blinded large parts of political theory and political science to the transformation of politics in the second, cosmopolitan modernity. As a result, a number of things have been missed along the way, such as the political reflexivity of a society and a history open to the future; the fundamental experience of historicity, of double contingency, of change towards an open future characterized by a different kind of society, statehood and politics. Globalization makes global politics a necessity. But how can the role of politics be defined in the new global political economy? How can politics seize its opportunities? Who will decide on strategy? Who will win?

These are the questions to be explored in this chapter. They will be discussed in six stages:

1   the meta-power game revisited: the end of the end of politics;
2   perceived threats to humanity from the self-generated risks of technologized civilization as a source of legitimation for global domination: Thomas Hobbes revised for the world risk society;
3   the concepts and forms of statehood transformed: a typology of the state for the second modernity;
4   the idea of the neo-liberal state demystified;
5   the concepts and forms of the political transformed: a typology of politics for the second modernity;
6   what this means for the concept of politics and for the concept of theory: a typology of critique.

7.1   The end of the end of politics

The diagnosis of the end of politics may be true for the national outlook, but it does not hold for the cosmopolitan outlook. The contrast between the national and cosmopolitan perspectives could hardly be more dramatic: while the national perspective makes it appear as though politics was virtually *devoid of all contingency*, the cosmopolitan perspective paints a picture depicting the *globalization of contingency*. In the latter scenario, contingency no longer takes place within the rigid, preordained ordering frameworks of domestic and foreign, national and international politics. Instead, this seemingly cast-iron, eternal ordering of the political realm has been replaced by a double game of contingency. The game of classical industrial society carries on, but, as it does so, many of the players are calling for the system of rules to be turned upside down and are indeed beginning to do just that, although it is thoroughly unclear whether the game to be played in future (figuratively speaking) is snap, snakes and ladders or football. Rule-governed politics and rule-changing politics are overlapping, mixing and intersecting with one another.

The distinction between the rules of the game and the game itself, between background and foreground, institutional framework and contingent action, no longer holds. What distinguishes the world of the national outlook from that of the cosmopolitan outlook is the *difference of contingency*: while this difference strives to reach zero in the national outlook, the cosmopolitan outlook opens up a contingent sphere of action full of opportunities and potential disasters to which the national outlook is oblivious. In other words, the strategic space that begins *beyond* nation-state self-reproduction – and includes, for example, strategies of Grand Politics, strategies of the despatialization of the state, strategies of transnationalization, strategies of multiple state coalitions, global risk strategies, strategies of domestic and foreign political integration, win–win strategies, strategies of the cosmopolitaniza-tion of law, strategies of regional cosmopolitanization – can be constituted only through the cosmopolitan outlook. The critical potential of New Critical Theory is grounded in precisely this difference, which we might con-ceptualize in quasi-mathematical terms as follows: *critique + the difference between the number, range and quality of state strategies opened up by the cosmopolitan perspective and closed off by the national perspective.* What, then, is the main point of New Critical Theory? This can be answered by three observations. First, as long as political actors follow the logic of the national outlook, it makes no difference who is in power. The cosmopolitan outlook tells us that the national outlook leads to a political dead end. Second, the differences between political parties are rapidly disappearing. This much is confirmed by current research in political science, although its analytical trajectory is quite a different one, affirming and amplifying the theory of the end of politics. This stands in stark contrast to the global con-tingency of politics diagnosed by the cosmopolitan outlook. Third, New Critical Theory teaches us that parties *could* make a difference if they opened themselves up to the range of options available for shaping global domestic politics, which has entered a state of flux.

The theory of the 'end of politics' maintains that the end of *nation-state* politics has been reached. This means that the prospects for a cosmopolitan change in orientation are very good. The end of national politics signals the start of transnational politics, and this in turn can be transformed into a cos-mopolitan state. The refusal to acknowledge such insights and possibilities is what constitutes the failure of all politics and political science based on the national outlook.

However, there can be no going it alone in breaking away from the national paradigm, as isolated strategies fall far short of their goal. The same goes for capital as for civil society: without the state, there can be no collec-tively binding decisions, no legitimation. Yet the converse is also true: there can be no fundamental reform of state politics without the existence of alliances between political parties and governments on the one hand and global civil society and sections of capital on the other. The transformation from the national to a cosmopolitan paradigm of statehood can only succeed through a process of programmatic and organizational networking between politics, the state and transnational subpolitics, with its global business and civil society power networks.

The critical potential of New Critical Theory consists less in moralistic finger wagging or the orienting power of cosmopolitanism than in switch-ing reality and possibility around. Theories concerning the range of oppor-tunities open to state strategies will be read as a critique of political action if the possible – cosmopolitanization – is granted priority over the real – nation-state orthodoxy. What we have here is a variety of the speculators' bear market: it is not acceptance of some superior morality but rather the hunger and desire for power – the crux of politics, according to Max Weber – that provides the incentive to put the idea of a cosmopolitan regime and a cosmopolitan state to the test. The political and intellectual dance on the pinhead of national politics is coming to an end, to be replaced by curiosity and the desire to explore and experiment with the unfamiliar landscapes, delights, contradictions and dilemmas of cosmopolitan political strategies.

7.2   *Man is a wolf to man*: Thomas Hobbes revised for the world risk society

This still fails to provide an answer, however, to the key question of how to escape the nationality trap. What might persuade self-confident nations to share their national sovereignty with other nations or to surrender it entirely? The theory to be explored in this section of the book is that *the perceived threat to humanity from the self-generated risks of technologized civilization* releases the national outlook from its blinkered state while simultaneously turning it into a source of new, global political dangers. This theory of self-generated risks lies at the heart of the political theory of the second modernity; in what follows, I shall explain its fundamental features by translating two authors – Fritz W. Scharpf and Thomas Hobbes – from the national into the cosmopolitan perspective.

Scharpf distinguishes between democracy and legitimation and links this to the supposition that modern states and governments need something other than just democracy on which to ground the legitimacy of their domination – after all, they have at their disposal the sources of both 'input-legitimation' (which Scharpf also calls 'domination *by* the people [*Volk*]') and 'output-legitimation', which is measured by how effectively they are able to solve problems (and which Scharpf calls 'domination *for* the people'). The notion of '*Volk*', as well as terms such as 'input' and 'output', presuppose the national outlook. Scharpf distinguishes additionally between participation and consensus. Here, too, the idea is that consensus is not tied to participation. The efficiency with which political solutions are devised is an important source of legitimation for nation-state domination.

In the national context, or outlook, domination for and by the people – that is, through participation and efficiency – can and should be both capable of legitimation and legitimated. In a multilevel system of political action such as the European Union, however, these two sources of legitimation become separated – as Fritz Scharpf shows by referring to a number of case studies. In order to answer the question of how the blinkered national perspective can be opened out, we need to extend the sources of legitimacy for political domination. Alongside democracy and efficiency, the *perceived threat to humanity from the self-generated risks of technologized civilization* enters the picture. This complements both legitimation through democracy, which is tied to the nation-state context, and legitimation through efficiency, which is not tied solely to the national context and is ademocratic. However, it also calls into question the entire nation-state order of legitimacy.

The advent of the world risk society brings with it an autonomous source of global political legitimation for domination. This occurs when actors – not only states, but advocatory movements from civil society and, not least, corporations as well – are able to claim that they are working to avert or counter the risks facing humanity from technologized civilization. Legitimatory power possesses an entirely different dimension here, in terms of both its origins and the scope of its impact. This is because it is based on countering a danger that threatens the survival not just of individuals, groups and nations, but of *everybody*, of humanity as a whole.

Humanity's foremost priority is the timeless principle of self-preservation. Death is the first among all evils. At an individual level, it cannot be avoided, but not so at the level of humanity. The death of humanity, the self-destruction of humans as a possibility of human action, is the new thing brought into the world by a highly technologized civilization. The shock triggered by this realization is capable of creating a global consensus that in turn creates global power. It is in the nature of politics that the power of this consensus, translated into legitimate global domination aimed at averting the threats to humanity, is highly ambiguous in its consequences.

Humanity's potential suicide can never be a voluntary death, as when an individual takes their own life (out of desperation, pain or loneliness). It is necessarily the involuntary 'murder' of all – collective murder as an unintended side-effect of scientific, technological, military and political action; a 'murder' that originates nonetheless in individual acts and in a system of acts that has become autonomous. It is not a present occurrence but a future one, not an actual occurrence but a potential one. The *perception* of the impending suicide of the human race opens up access to globalized legitimacy and sources of power based on consensus. These sources of legitimation of global domination are, firstly, ademocratic, as they elude all democratic procedures simply on the basis on their globality – albeit they are dependent on global perceptions and global acknowledgement of risks, that is, on mass media representations. Secondly, they are potentially anti-democratic as well because, as the perceived danger to humanity grows, so too does people's willingness to cast off the fetters of democracy.

Thomas Hobbes's political theory of sovereignty is based on the formula *homo homini lupus*, man is a wolf to man. The political theory of the risk society, by contrast, takes an adapted version of this principle as its starting point: *humanity is a wolf to humanity*. The 'predatory character' referred to by Hobbes is attributed here not to individual people but to humanity as a whole. Humanity is at once the subject and object of its own endangerment. It is not a nation-based 'faith in the community' (Max Weber) that creates legitimacy, but rather a *belief that the risks facing humanity can be averted* by political action taken *on behalf of* endangered humanity. In this sense, the fundamental relations of human co-existence, including the nation-state order itself, become subject to the primacy of changeability, the existence of alternatives, and contingency.

The sentence 'humanity is a wolf to humanity', as a principle of cosmopolitan theory, displays a fundamental ambiguity. The possibility of species suicide – the threat of an end to human life on earth – creates the chance for a new beginning. We might even ask: is there any kind of power at all that has the scope and impact necessary for protecting humanity from itself? One thing is certain – such power is beyond all the 'saviours' brought forth by history and by the history of political theory: the proletariat, the poorest of the poor in the global age, the Enlightenment, the global capital profit-mongers, party leaders and heads of government, even a 'good dictator' of global society. If anything at all, it is only the perceived risks facing humanity – which can be neither denied nor externalized – that are capable of awakening the energies necessary for creating a global community of common destiny, one that will demolish the walls of nation-state borders and egotisms – at least for a global moment in time.

Precisely because it has to do with perception, this political legitimatory power of the global perception of global risk is not tied to the objectivity of risks. Its omnipresence needs to be implanted into people's hearts and minds through global information and global symbols, regardless of such objectivity. This dialectic of breakdown and new beginnings is crucial: the central point at which the national order breaks down – namely the perceived threat to humanity – is also the point at which a transnational order emerges, along with the highly ambiguous alternatives that thereby enter the realm of political feasibility. Perception also means *anticipation*. Once people perceive the dangers facing humanity, those things that governed the past, such as the dominance of boundaries and traditions, become politically irrelevant and are replaced by the things that govern the future, in which the uncertainties surrounding risk take a firmer hold. This means the coordinates of time and space are rearranged. Experiential spheres and horizons of expectation become separated from one another. What emerges is a global arena of domination in which the features of negative and positive integration, which obey the logic of the national outlook, become grouped together in new ways.

This occurs as follows. *First*: Elements of positive and negative integration *become merged*. It is 'positive' in the sense that the perception of risk creates political reflexivity concerning globality; the 'negative' aspect of this consensus-creating power of global risk perception is that the barriers of national closure are removed at a single stroke, both intranationally and internationally.

Second: The democratic consent of this or that nation is replaced by the consent of humanity – albeit the latter *lacks* democratic legitimation, indeed it lacks even the possibility of democratic legitimation. The shock globalized by the horrific television images from New York on 11 September 2001 *seemed* to amount to a kind of global ballot. When the shockwaves of danger struck, the most powerful nation on earth, militarily and economically, was authorized by the overwhelming majority of people – *without* a ballot – to avert this danger, this threat to the moral and physical existence of humanity. Perceived threats to the species become transformed into resources for a *global populism of defence against risk*, which at once authorizes and legitimizes radical action – including military intervention in other states. Threats to humanity create public awareness and situations that demand action, in comparison to which voting procedures seem like relics from a petty-minded idyll in which people still nit-picked over such trifling democratic concerns.

Third: This type of legitimation is tied neither to the objectivity of risk nor to the *effectiveness* of its elimination. Ineffective action does nothing to diminish the formation of this counter-power, precisely because the immediacy of the threat to the human race mobilizes global political action to counter it. Less effectiveness means greater danger, which in turn brings with it more problems for humanity collectively. The paradoxical consequence of this is that a wrong response can cleanse itself of its wrongdoing in the waters of the problems to which it has contributed. As the mistakes that multiply people's woes increase, so too does threatened humanity's willingness to forgive those mistakes.

Fourth: Thomas Hobbes's 'state of nature' describes a condition *pre*-civilization that is overcome by the power of the sovereign. In the perceived threat to humanity, however, this relationship gets turned around the other way. The order of nation-state sovereignty in technologized civilization is rendered invalid by the 'predatory quality' of a humanity that has turned on itself. Rather than the absence of an ordering power that forces people to pursue their interests by socially acceptable means, it is the continued existence of the nation-state order itself that constitutes the source of universal threat, or at least an obstacle to averting that threat. The danger lies not in questioning the order of the sovereign, but rather in *not* questioning it.

Fifth: A further paradox is rooted in the fact that the Hobbesian solution – power delegation, the construction of the Leviathan – is an impossibility for 'humanity'. The mandate to save humanity is therefore assumed by states and state federations, as well as by global civil society actors and transnational corporations that take up the cause of saving the environment or defending human rights. Perhaps it is even true to say that the 'threat to humanity', as a factor shaping global relations of domination, is the key to understanding transnational politics.

Sixth: The legitimatory principle of nation-state order breaks down in the face of the perceived threat to humanity. Since the national sovereign is unable to guarantee internal and external security or to protect the lives of his citizens any longer, the citizens' duty of obedience *becomes null and void*.

The consequence (according to Hobbes) is that civilized humanity reverts to a state of nature in which everyone is his own master and is responsible for defending his natural rights. Global perception of the dangers facing humanity threatens to bring about a global delegitimization of the nation-state order – unless endangered nation-states set about rebuilding themselves into transnational states, into cosmopolitan states. The social contract can no longer be grounded in the anarchy of separate, individual states. Instead, it needs to create an inter-state order that draws its cosmopolitan legitimacy from preventively combating the threat to humanity.

Fritz Scharpf has pointed out with regard to Europe that the need to achieve consensus by no means automatically improves the chances of reaching collectively binding decisions. In fact, if anything, the opposite is the case: as the need to achieve consensus grows – that is, as more people (have to) join in to reach a decision – so too do the difficulties surrounding cooperation, and thus the more likely it is that *no* decision will be made. The crucial question, according to Scharpf, is what rule for decision-making applies when everybody *doesn't* participate. The unanimity rule means that there is an increase in pressure to achieve consensus as well as a greater likelihood that no decision will be reached. This situation gives rise to a 'consensus gap', which widens as the institutionalized need for consensus becomes greater than the political pressure exerted by the individual states to reach a joint, consensus-based decision. Such asymmetry makes it more difficult to reach agreement. This is how Scharpf explains the paradox that it is precisely the increased need for consensus that leads to a lack of decisions. In the national arena, the majority principle applies, which means there is less need for consensus; as a result, states potentially have *more* options available to them here than in the international arena, where the pressure to reach consensus comes up against the unanimity rule. The consequence to be drawn from this is that transnationalization succeeds when the majority principle is introduced on the one hand and the need for consensus reduced on the other.

What this argument and the conclusion drawn from it fail to take into consideration, however, is something that the cosmopolitan shift in perspective brings into view, namely, the fact that the perceived threat to humanity generates a situation in which the pressure to reach consensus closes the gap between the need for consensus and political decision-making. The result is that, in spite of the principle of unanimity and the involvement of *all* states, whose interests manifestly conflict with one another, decisions do come about that are binding at a global political level. The reason this is so is that global public reflection concerning global threats closes the consensus gap. And the way this occurs is through risk *perception*. It is this – and not the objectivity of ecological, economic or terrorist threats – that opens up a range of options for the transnationalization of financial markets, climate protection measures and, not least, the transnationalization of police forces, military authorities, secret services and political competencies for combating terrorism.[2] However, while the global legitimation of domination based on a global perception of threat may have these sorts of profound political effects, the price to be paid for them is their short-term impact. Since everything depends on the way threats are perceived through the mass media, the legitimatory power of global political action based on global risks lasts only as long as the attention span prompted by mass media representations of them.

Thus, political action in the age of globalization is made possible *by the perceived globality of risk*, which melts down the seemingly cast-iron system of international and national politics and makes it open to change, at least for one historic moment in time. In this sense, the political reflexivity of the world risk society generates quasi-revolutionary opportunities for action, which may, however, be exploited in very different ways.

7.3 Forms of the state in the second modernity

The starting point for systematically identifying and defining different forms and concepts of the state is the realization that *there is no turning back*! Every actor in the meta-power game of global politics undergoes a radical change – not least because their roles, resources and opportunities for power change in line with the way they locate and define themselves in this 'game' over the power rules of global politics. Edgar Grande (2000) helpfully distinguishes between statehood – as a basic *principle* of modernity – and forms or concepts of the state – in the sense of different basic *institutions* of modernity that lend concrete shape to the principle of statehood in different periods of the first and second modernity.[3]

This approach makes it possible to free states from a false reification and to understand and research them instead as contingent, changeable entities. By discarding the national oulook, in which the state has become an *empty* category, we are able to trace the ways in which statehood has been transformed in terms of cultural identity, economic and military foundations, democracy and legitimation.

It is important first to shift awareness to something that to a certain extent is presupposed in table 7.1: national (and international) 'business-as-usual' is not an option. Those who think, act and research within the national framework will find themselves thrown completely off balance and the world itself turned upside down. In other words: *every* form of state will change completely and, with it, manifestations of 'statehood'. Statehood refers to the institutional-conceptual form required for operationally creating, organizing and reproducing political opportunities for power.

Table 7.1 State typology for the second modernity

		Global interdependencies (economic, cultural, military, political, ecological)	
		Isolationist/ protectionist	Open/ cosmopolitan
Sovereignty	National/autonomous	Ethnic state	Neo-liberal state
	Transnational/cooperative	Transnational surveillance and citadel state	Cosmopolitan state; cosmopolitan regime

The ethnic state

A clear distinction needs to be made between (ethnic) nationalism in the first and in the second modernity. Ethnic nationalism in the second modernity is the *postmodern* return to origins and, in this respect, is both illusionary and highly perilous politically. The cosmopolitan outlook in particular cannot underestimate the significance of nationalism for the global age. However, the crucial difference in contrast to affirmative methodological nationalism is that *today's (ethnic) nationalism is different*. The unity of people, state, democracy and nation, the implied ideal image, has been shattered by the globalization of national spaces. It is also the case, however, that globalization and ethnic identity are not mutually exclusive but rather mutually inclusive (Miller and Slater 2000). The new systems of mass communication – radio, television, video, computer, mobile phone – are being used for the purpose of networking and activating ethnic communities at a transnational level, in order to oppose both the nation-state *and* the elites of a cosmopolitan culture. This could lead to the paradoxical phenomenon of an anti-global ethnocentric internationalism, whose motto might be: xenophobes of the world, unite! Or else it could lead to the 'utopia' of an ethnocentric, transnational alliance of citadel states against, for example, terrorists and rogue states.

Anthony D. Smith (1995) argues that, in this sense, the nation and nationalism have been neither depoliticized nor demilitarized, let alone normalized. To suggest that the ethnic-national state has become a peaceable entity in the alliance created between the global market and global culture, willing to be stuffed and exhibited in the museum of political forms like a dinosaur from early modernity, runs completely counter to current trends, according to Smith. Economic and cultural globalization endanger the very existence of polyethnic states, as it gives rise to conflicts that have a centrifugal impact. To this extent, we cannot rule out the possibility that the ethnic state may emerge as the *victor* from the current race to transform states and establish new ones, and that in future the civic nationalism of nation-states and the ethnic nationalism of ethnic states may co-exist in productive tension or may mutually reinforce one another in the course of virtually intractable conflicts.[4]

In order to understand these trends and to unravel their contradictions, it is necessary to distinguish between nationalism and ethnicism (Tamás 1996). If *nationalism* is geared towards the outside world – towards conquering and assimilating the foreigner – then *ethnicism* is based on exclusion, non-coexistence with those who are culturally different, no expansion and no universalism. This is because the ethnic state does not recognize minorities. Those who are culturally different are not integrated into a 'national' identity, always conceived in universal terms, but rather are faced with the alternative of either leaving or being killed. The ethnic state cuts back its universalist roots and becomes oriented towards the interests and identities of whichever ethnic group is dominant in each area of the state apparatus (education, police, military, law, foreign policy). The ethnic state is a *depoliticized* state – in the sense, at any rate, that no lively public exchange or use of national civil rights and civil liberties takes place within its borders.

Since globalization weakens the nation-state, a paradoxical alliance evolves between ethnicists and globalizers for opening up access to the delegitimized and depoliticized powerhouse of the nation-state for ethnic groups. The denationalization of the state creates favourable conditions for its re-ethnicization.

The conventional categories of political polarization can no longer be applied here: the ethnic conquest of the state is neither fascist nor democratic, but a bit of both at the same time. In an environment of emerging ethnic states (in Central and Eastern Europe, the Middle East, Africa, India and Pakistan, and South-East Asia, among others) even the old nation-state seems like a barely realistic utopia. The contradictions of the ethnic state are plain to see: threatened or actual human rights violations make it a ready candidate for pariah status and lay it open to international, including military, intervention. Indeed, in an unbounded and unrestrained world of growing economic, military and cultural interdependencies, how are boundaries to be shored up and cemented in such a way that insular ethnicity is even a possibility? How can 'foreign' investors, with their 'foreign' economic power, be tempted into the country if 'foreigners' are to be excluded?

The ethnic state is part of a *modern atavistic dynamic* from which it benefits and which it establishes and maintains, but which brings about a situation in which the basic *principles* of modernity are violated or fall into disuse.[5] In a certain sense, it is even a euphemism to say that the ethnic state is a *xenophobic* state in which hatred of foreigners is raised to the status of a principle, because to put the issue in terms of 'foreigners' conceals the principal feature of this dynamic of decline.

1   Ethnic states stage, or, rather, they execute, the real-life tragedy of how neighbours turn into *enemies*. In other words, what is involved is not hatred of 'foreigners', but rather hatred of 'citizens', hatred of 'neighbours', because fellow citizens have to be made into enemies using the bloody force of definition, with methods whereby they are singled out or wiped out.

2   The distinction between wars involving different states and wars involving a state's citizens – 'civil' war – is therefore rendered invalid. What emerges instead is war involving both states and citizens – states fighting against citizens and citizens fighting against states – as a way of establishing ethnic difference using atavistic state and non-state means of violence. The rampant nihilism that gives rise to suicide attacks shatters the normal, everyday trust of 'civil society', whose citizens they target, while states execute 'terrorists' without trial, and this is seen as 'right'.

3   The cycle in which state ethnicization becomes caught up can be called 'atavistic' because it involves a dynamic in which hatred and violence stir one another up in such a way that not only basic institutions but also the basic principles of modernity – such as human rights, which are accorded even to one's 'enemies' and are upheld in relation to them – are allowed to fall into decline. These trends are 'modern' as well, because they involve the use of the latest modern technology, the exploitation of rights and transnational networks, as well as the internationalization of experiential spaces. Even more horrifying for the outside observer is the way in which this decline in civilization is accelerated not only by the competition between ethnic groups but also by the overarching impact exerted on it by religious belief.

4   This dynamic of decline, in which those who profit from ethnic states and those who accelerate their formation come into their own, has global impacts. Global public outrage turns nation-states, whether they be national or cosmopolitan in orientation, into ones that *tolerate* and thereby *participate* in a barbaric conflict that violates the sense of values and responsibility of observer states. This means, however, that they are caught in the dilemma of complicity. Observer states face accusation, whatever they do: if they don't intervene, their non-intervention becomes the source of their undoing; and if they decide to deploy military forces, their intervention likewise becomes the source of their undoing. As an example of where this political dilemma can be observed, the Middle East conflict is not an isolated case. It is happening under the spotlight of global public attention only because there are key Western interests at stake. The way the ethnicization of state violence leads into the atavism trap can also be observed in the state-organized genocides that occur inside Africa – albeit with the not inconsiderable difference that, in the African cases, the global public stands accused of *not* taking a concerned interest.

The neo-liberal state

While the god of the nation-state may be mortal, it certainly doesn't mean that the state itself will die (as the national outlook would have us believe). If anything, the situation is more like that in the legend where the hero cuts off the head of the dragon, only to see several new heads grow in its place. A second form into which the model of the old nation-state is transformed in the cosmopolitan constellation is the *neo-liberal state*. The neo-liberal state is the competition state, the market state, the state figuration in which politics follows the logic of capital. This form of the state bears the 'IMF-tested' stamp of approval, as it were. The probability that the nation-state will be transformed into a neo-liberal state grows in parallel with the process of states' disciplining in line with the demands of the global economy, something forced upon them by the IMF as a result, in particular, of the carrot-or-stick policy consisting of either the threat of loan withdrawal or the offer of loans. In this sense, a worldwide 'Panopticon system' (Patomäki 2001: 101) exists in which agencies that establish creditworthiness probe and judge states, corporations and municipal communities according to whether they follow the rules of 'good', that is, neo-liberal, budgeting. As the twenty-first century begins, the IMF is monitoring the economic policies of at least every third 'sovereign' state on the planet.

Interestingly, the neo-liberal state is an outstanding example of the *internationalization* of the nation-state. The 'reformers' and the 'modernizers' who feel committed to the neo-liberal creed are not only engaged in redesigning or dismantling the welfare state – they are also performing the self-internationalization of the nation-state without relinquishing the 'national' label. Nation-state autism is the very prerequisite that allows the form of the state to undergo its necessary – 'realistic' – adaptation to the prevailing 'Washington consensus': the trinity of deregulation, liberalization and privatization. This form of the nation-state, with its conformity to the demands of the global market, illustrates the way in which, even today, behind the hollowed-out façades of the 'nation-state', the latter is being radically reconstructed.

In this case, too, the contradictions have become more than apparent: what we have here is a textbook model for the active self-dismantling of nation-state power, politics and democracy – although the notion that there are no alternatives to this transformation of the state in line with the logic of capital *has* been refuted in this book.

The transformational forms of statehood presented here are ideal types: even if they can be clearly distinguished conceptually and appear to be mutually exclusive logically, in reality they can easily be combined with one another, rather like parts of a state Meccano set. This leads to the emergence of states that have, as it were, been 'cobbled together', and in which set pieces from the neo-liberal state are combined with set pieces from the ethnic state.

This also applies even when barely intractable 'contradictions' become the criterion of goodness for an emerging or desired form of the state. As German fascism teaches us, it can take as many as twelve bitter years of a 'Thousand-year Reich' before this kind of anti-civilization experiment with reality collapses from its own internal and external contradictions.

Transnational states

General agreement exists on the fact that the new forms of statehood identified above – the neo-liberal and the ethnic state – differ from the following two forms of the state – the *transnational surveillance state* and the *cosmopolitan state* – in at least one respect: they do not make use of the power opportunities opened up by cooperative transnational sovereignty. Contingency, including that of the state, is a multilayered, multifaceted phenomenon. It can seem like (or be staged as) a threat or a trap, as well as an opportunity and a promise. It can be conceived of as an end point and as decline, or alternatively as a positive reassessment of contingency; it can be used as an opportunity for a beginning (Hannah Arendt), as the source of something genuinely new that feeds into fresh initiatives.

In the meta-power game, states are structurally disadvantaged in comparison to global business actors. They have to struggle with a double disadvantage. First, they have to deal with taking the second turn – in other words, global business makes its move first and states then make theirs. At the same time, states have to work to build up this counter-power against the new mobility of global business power. What is more, global business actors (with the exception of the politics of the IMF) exercise their global political power as a *side-effect* of economic rationality. In a partial break with the self-conception of the nation and its taboos, 'states' (and everything that goes with them: parties, associations, populations, traditions, religions, regions, and not least parliaments, publics and the mass media) have to undergo a historic transformation within the timescale of the electoral cycle and in the face of a chronic lack of legitimation, growing numbers of floating voters and chronic budgetary deficits, and all this beneath the watchful eyes of the critical media.

This double disadvantage experienced by state actors arises both from the fact that their starting position is a defensive one, isolated as they are from one another by state egotism, and from institutionalized immobility. It raises a number of questions, such as who can and should seize the initiative. If individual states attempt to escape the stranglehold of global business actors, will they not be automatically punished through being spurned by highly mobile and highly sensitive investors? How is it even possible to start off in a transnational direction when howls of 'impossible' and 'out of the question' abound? Surely the inter-state consensus to be created needs to exist already in order to enforce even elementary measures, such as the prevention of tax evasion, against those states that profit from it?

This makes it all the more interesting to consider how individual egotistical states are learning that the very specific problems they face can be solved only in transnational cooperation with other states. The view used to be held that foreign policy was a question of choice, not of necessity. Nowadays, a new kind of 'both/and' approach prevails: foreign and domestic policy, national security and international cooperation are inextricably linked. The only way of achieving national security in the face of impending globalized terrorism – but also of financial risks, climate change and contaminated foods, etc. – is by engaging in transnational cooperation.

At the same time, the way in which politicians deal with terrorism shows that the dazzling realization of the superiority of transnational cooperation can open doors to very different kinds of worlds. The discovery and development of cooperative state power that transcends national borders is being used, on the one hand, for the purpose of fortress-building along the lines of a *transnational surveillance state* à la Orwell; this can be interpreted either in a more *global-unilateral* way (USA) or in a *cooperative-multilateral* way (Europe). It can also be used, on the other hand, for the purpose of acknowledging and facilitating diversity, in the form of a *cosmopolitan state*. As the United States' reaction to transnational terrorism shows, however, the protectionist use of transnational cooperative power has gained a clear power advantage over the cosmopolitan use of it.

This conceptualization of state architectures (outlined only roughly here), this description of the fissured landscape of power opportunities available at the start of the twenty-first century, represents a setting aside of the national outlook (in politics and research alike), and becomes apparent only within the cosmopolitan perspective of New Critical Theory. As such, it is evidence of the greater access to reality that this perspective opens up ('positive problem shift', Lakatos 1970).

The pluralization of states

This typology of states could also be developed and discussed from the point of view of the relationship between particularism and universalism in the different state forms. Thus, one might ask which element predominates within what kind of compromise formula and involving what kinds of contradictions. It makes no sense fundamentally to see the national and the cosmopolitan outlook as an incompatible set of opposites, because the national outlook, both historically and in terms of the development of concepts, has always contained at least some complementary elements of the cosmopolitan outlook. As far as modern political action and modern political theory is concerned, the problem from the very beginning has been how to link universalism with particularism and how to safeguard the possibility of universality *within* national particularity.

In methodological nationalism, for example, the assumption is that nations see general human rights and ethnic-cultural and political membership roles as being related to one another in particular ways. However, this no longer applies to the ethnic state, while the contradiction of a 'transnational ethnicity', the political reality and explosiveness of which can be studied in Central and Eastern Europe, is built into the model of the transnational citadel state.

Many political theorists early on gave conceptual expression to their belief and their hope that the particular state, as a type, might be understood as a universal one once the contradictions within the *system* of particular states, even if they cannot be resolved, are at least historically laid to rest. It was the role of the international relations theorists to remind us of this. However, a whole set of questions regarding the *meta-transformation of statehood* have not even been asked yet, let alone answered. For example, how might *different* types of state exist alongside and in opposition to one another, not just temporarily but permanently? What might a world look like in which the nation-state model no longer has a monopoly and in which the *pluralization* of states has led to a 'system' of mutually contradictory conceptions of the state? Moreover, how might such a world be kept stable?

As far as inter-state relations are concerned, there is one essential difference between the first modernity of nation-states and the second modernity of plural states. Whereas the first modernity assumed the existence of a globally valid 'nation-state' model that was fundamentally homogeneous, in the second modernity statehood becomes differentiated, so that it is necessary to regulate the competition between contrasting forms and conceptions of the state. This occurs, for example, when ethnic states come to a completely different understanding and assessment of boundaries, sovereignty, human rights and the associated norms and definitions of 'international law' compared with that of cosmopolitan states. Such a situation exists today in the relationship between the USA and Europe in matters of climate change, for example, and the establishment of an international court of law. In both cases, Europe takes a rather more cosmopolitan stance, while the USA clings to the model of the hegemonic nation-state. Whereas in the first modernity the instability of the international system was rooted in the anarchic relations between nation-states – albeit these could be regulated on the basis of a homogeneous conception of statehood – this 'anarchy among equals' has now been replaced by something that is much harder to tame, namely an 'anarchy of unequal conceptions of the state'.

In other words, in the sphere of statehood something is happening which we have already rehearsed in other areas of the social sciences. The singular

model of the 'normal family', for example, has been replaced by an acknowledged plurality of forms of family life; the monopoly of the model of 'normal
work' has been replaced by the (still disputed) pluralization of forms of paid
work. Nonetheless, the problem of how stability and security can be guaranteed in a world of plural statehood remains utterly unresolved and has so
far been neither acknowledged nor dealt with.

Of course, it would be completely wrong to assume that *all* states and
populations around the world have an *equal* opportunity to choose between
differently valued alternatives of statehood in the second modernity. (It
would be just as wrong to neglect or deny relations of exclusion on the one
hand, and the side-effects and contradictions between different individual
strategies and groups of strategies on the other.) Instead, the crucial thing
will be to explore systematically the issue of *conflicts of opportunity*. Thus,
how is it possible, on the one hand, to create state confederations that open
up possibilities for cosmopolitan action and, on the other, to forge coalitions
with the strategies of capital, which then, of course, have to be tamed once
again within the cosmopolitan state? How is it possible to pursue the ethnicization of the state while at the same time surviving in the world market,
when ethnic protectionism is targeted for criticism in the global media by
actors from global civil society? How is it possible to gain political support
for cosmopolitan legislation in election campaigns if this leads to global
inequalities being delegitimized?

Perhaps we need to distinguish states' strategic power opportunities
according to how far individual states and groups of states are able to intervene *actively* in the meta-power game of global politics and how far they can
be labelled *passively* as victims and losers of globalization by others' decisions. What gradual succession of strategies will allow the poor victim states
to advance to a position where they actively participate in shaping global
politics, a role that would simultaneously enable them to use this global
involvement to help solve their national problems? To what extent does the
power and control exerted by supranational organizations, such as the IMF,
conflict with individual states' chances of taking a lead in countering the neo-
liberalization and commercialization of the world? How can multilateral
global political campaigns be organized once the dominant states – the USA
in particular – have committed themselves to neo-liberalizing the state
system? If powerful interests put a stop to state strategies of transnationalization and cosmopolitanization, does this not make the latter politically
inadmissible, even if they are possible in principle? Perhaps it will be the next
disaster (and it will surely come) that opens people's eyes, hearts and hands
to a cosmopolitan reorientation. Or is the exact opposite the case, that the
global consequences of a global catastrophe will remove any prospects for a
cosmopolitan shift in perspective and instead make it possible for the ethnic
state or the transnational citadel state to become established?

How ought we to assess the gap between intentions and outcomes in the different global political scenarios? After all, the aim of renewing politics to enable cosmopolitan states and a cosmopolitan democracy to become established can very quickly turn out to have the opposite effect, giving fresh impetus to movements and parties intent on establishing ethnic isolationism. To whom does it fall to take the lead in arguing for the cosmopolitan outlook – to those in the centre, once again, or perhaps only to those on the periphery, or perhaps to both? What role can be played by the Asian tiger economies who, given the fact of global interdependency, are engaged in overcoming their historical conflicts and taboos and are forging ahead to create new, regional, multinational models of the state? Or is it perhaps the unbounded and unrestrained violence of the Israeli–Palestinian conflict that provides the dominant model for the future? Or a multi-ethnic, multinational, cosmopolitan Europe that elaborates its global political role with self-confidence? Perhaps the poor G-77 states, in spite of their heterogeneity, might seize the initiative for a cosmopolitan transformation, following their Geneva summit in July 2000 when they committed themselves to working for the introduction of the Tobin tax. Or would the non-Western states that became involved in such an initiative become targets for some form of punishment, merely serving to accelerate the process of economic decline and social implosion and the rise in political violence?

7.4   The perception of global risks robs the utopia of the neo-liberal state of its persuasive power

In the search for a countervailing power capable of counteracting the hegemonic power of neo-liberalism – embodied, for example, in the policies of the USA and the IMF – a whole range of actants come up for consideration but are usually rejected: the global civil society groups and networks within anti-globalization movements, the states of the European Union, and even the poor states of the southern hemisphere that have lost out as a result of globalization. However, what is normally lost from view is the global political momentum associated with the perception of risks generated by technologized civilization and attempts to avert them. Nowhere can the political force entailed in this be studied in such exemplary manner as in the impact exerted on the Bush administration by the perception of the terrorist threat: while it had come to Washington steeped in ultra-liberal convictions, the process of conversion that followed was remarkable. Under the impact of the terrorist threat, the US government had Congress approve a supplementary budget that was a mockery of the neo-liberal creed with which it took power. Asked by a journalist whether this spending policy stood in stark contrast to the Bush administration's neo-liberal conception of the state, its press spokesman replied tersely: 'National security has priority here.'

Whereas the common maxim before 11 September 2001 was '*roll back* the state', this has changed since 11 September into its very opposite: '*bring back the state*' – and this has occurred worldwide. At a single stroke, the utopia of the neo-liberal state has become politically obsolete. Indeed, in the USA, public perception of and reflection on the terrorist threat has broken the spell of the economy as a multi-purpose panacea. All over the world, 11 September is leading to a rediscovery of the primacy of the state.

The global outbreak of terrorism amounts to a Chernobyl of globalization. In that instance, the blessings of nuclear energy were forever laid to rest, while in this instance the same fate has befallen the promises of salvation proclaimed by the neo-liberal state. The suicide attackers and mass murderers have not only revealed the vulnerability of Western civilization, they have also offered a foretaste of the kind of conflicts engendered by the neo-liberal misunderstanding of globalization. In a world of global risks, the neo-liberal project of replacing politics and the state with business and finance is rapidly losing its persuasive power.

As this realization becomes established, so the hegemonic power acquired by neo-liberalism over the past few years, in both conceptual and practical terms, begins to fade dramatically. And in this sense, the horrific images from New York contain an as yet undeciphered message: a state or a country is perfectly capable of neo-liberalizing itself to death. What is remarkable is that under the impact of the terrorist threat, which shook the public to its core, Congress forced the Bush administration to declare its neo-liberal bankruptcy by *nationalizing* aviation security!

In times of crisis brought on by the global perception of threat, neo-liberalism apparently has no political answers to offer whatsoever. The therapy of radicalizing the dose of bitter medicine when total collapse threatens is a dangerous illusion for which the penalty is now being paid. The terrorist threat makes us aware once again of the elementary truth which the triumphal march of neo-liberalism had suppressed: those who preach the decoupling of global business from politics put everybody at risk – including the very foundations of global business. In this respect, it is little wonder that the counter-principle to the neo-liberal state – the necessary expansion of the state – is suddenly present again everywhere in its oldest Hobbesian form: the guarantee of security. Who would have thought it possible, before 11 September, that a European arrest warrant could be issued that effectively disregards sacrosanct national sovereignties and questions of law and enforcement – yet it has become a reality. And that is just one example among many. Perhaps we will soon be seeing a similar joint effort when the world is shocked by the global perception of the threats posed by *global business*. In this sense, 11 September certainly doesn't spell the end of the neo-liberal state, but it does spell the end of the political power of persuasion exerted by its utopia.

7.5   Both right and left: on the transformation of the concepts and forms of politics in the second modernity

Our efforts at classifying the meta-game of global politics in terms of its contingency and thereby identifying different ideal types of statehood in the second modernity necessarily result in the realization that, under these conditions, politics and political action inevitably have to be conceived of as the medium through which these conflicts, contradictions and ambiguities come together and are organized and through which they are handled. That is, in the context of different political programmes they are intensified, glossed over, or merged together with the old conflicts that took place in the national and international arena. As to the question of *who wins* the meta-power game of global politics, who decides on the choice of state strategies, how cosmopolitan governance is possible in view of the disparity of opportunities in global politics and the programmatic competition between ethnic, neo-liberal and transnational citadel statehood and cosmopolitan statehood – there is evidently no answer (so far).

Nevertheless, we can develop some initial ideas about how this field of possibilities may be given conceptual shape and, in particular, which alternative(s) need(s) to be ruled out. At this point, we need to distinguish between two interpretations of the relationship between the national and the cosmopolitan outlook, namely the *either/or* approach and the *both/and* approach. According to the either/or scenario, the institutions and parties of the national and the cosmopolitan outlooks exist in *exclusive* opposition to one another, and the logic of the cosmopolitan outlook *replaces* the logic of the national outlook. This notion of *radical* discontinuity ultimately remains wedded to the linear mode of thought and fails to recognize the real-life hybrid forms in which the newness of the cosmopolitan era is manifested.

Instead, the cosmopolitan era needs to be conceptualized according to the both/and principle. This means that two registers of political thought and action (of political institutions) exist alongside each other, absorbing, combining with and marginalizing each other: national and transnational approaches, established and alternative approaches, closed-in and opening-out approaches. Thus, the cosmopolitan outlook *doesn't replace* the national outlook; rather, the logics of both *co-exist*, conflict, overlap, combine and function in separate spaces and worlds without being connected.

These configurations of the *contaminated* newness of the cosmopolitan era can and must be named conceptually within political parties, governments, bureaucracies, confederations, and so forth; they need to be empirically explored, researched, confirmed or refuted. New Critical Theory claims that the opening up of contingencies to the cosmopolitan dimension remains a *fundamentally ambiguous* undertaking in many respects. There is the 'objective possibility' (Max Weber) of openness. 'A politicization characterized by openness and conducted according to the *"and"* principle rules nothing out – not even the established forms of politics' (Palonen 1998: 328). In other words, the break between the first and second modernity, the notion of discontinuity, is given more precise expression. The globalization of contingency includes the possibility that the new perspectives and conceptual apparatuses will be *absorbed* by the patterns of established politics. However, it is also likely that the global state of tension existing between the opposing force fields of nationalism and cosmopolitanism will give rise to new contradictions and programmatic political alliances within and between established organizations and institutions.

The metaphor of the double theatrical performance emphasizes the fact that contingency at the meta-level 'demands that in political terms one must be able to master at least two kinds of game and choose between them in any given situation. The choice of game doesn't consist in choosing between unequivocal opposites. On offer, instead, are the competing options of established and alternative politics, rule-bound and rule-changing politics, and a field of sub-politics' (Palonen 1998: 328). We might add that these newly forming fields of power play and lines of conflict also subsume the distinction between policy and polity.

National world citizens' parties

For the cosmopolitan outlook to become a force to be reckoned with politically, a new political subject needs to be established – national parties of world citizens, or *'world parties'* (Beck 1998b: 43). These *new* cosmopolitan parties represent transnational concerns transnationally, only within the nation-state political arenas. Thus, in terms of both their programmes and their organizational forms, they are possible only in the plural – as national-global movements, as world citizens' parties. They compete with national parties for consent and power in the issues and conflicts that only *seem* to be national ones. There are three senses in which they can be called 'world parties'. Firstly, their values and goals are not national but cosmopolitan in the sense that they appeal to the values and traditions of humanity in every culture and religion and feel committed to the planet as a whole – unlike national parties, which appeal to national values, traditions and solidarities.

Secondly, they are world parties because they make issues of globality the focus of their political imagination and political action; in doing so, they contradict the fixed, bogged-down priorities of national politics both programmatically and institutionally by means of a politics of concrete alternatives.

And finally, they are world parties because they can only come into being as multinational parties. In other words, there need to be world citizens' movements and parties of French, North American, Polish, German, Japanese, Chinese and South African provenance, which struggle together in the various nooks and crannies of global society to gain acceptance for cosmopolitan values and institutions. Inside the world parties, then, *beats the Babylonian heart of cosmopolitanism.*

Pluralization of left and right

In contrast to this, the second scenario starts out from the 'political paradox of globalization' (Grande and Kriesi 2002: 775), namely, that initially and principally the new cosmopolitan dynamics of conflict 'can only be dealt with within the national framework and within national political processes.' The change of tack required to open up access, for example, to transnational and cosmopolitan state strategies and the opportunities for power they offer must first be struggled over and undertaken *within* the established party spectrum and within existing governments or government coalitions. While the spectrum of different possible state transformations – from the nation-state to the ethnic state, the neo-liberal state, the transnational citadel state or the cosmopolitan state – has to be dealt with in the frame of reference of global economic, cultural, military and ecological interdependencies, it will initially be a subject of conflict within established political organizations and institutions. Once it becomes apparent and it is publically acknowledged that this pattern of established political organizations *is incapable* of handling the challenges posed by a cosmopolitan modernity, the struggle for *explicitly* new parties might begin. It is precisely *because* the national outlook prevails – that is, the failure of national political axioms is *not* acknowledged – that we can assume in all probability that the programmatic conflicts of cosmopolitan modernity will be dealt with in the dispute over cosmopolitanism within more or less hollow organizations and will go by the same names as they did before.

These distinctions between different 'programmatic packages' make one thing in particular clear: any attempt to absorb global political conflicts within the political nation-state arithmetic of the first modernity changes the established opposition of left and right *beyond recognition*. The fact that the elements depicted below have been divided into two tables (7.2 and 7.3)

Table 7.2 Political typology for the second modernity: pluralization of the left

		Protectionist	*Open to the world*
Sovereignty/ identity	*National/autonomous*	Protectionist left	Neo-liberal left; 'Third Way'
	Transnational/cooperative	Transnational citadel left	Cosmopolitan left

Table 7.3 Political typology for the second modernity: pluralization of the right

		Protectionist	*Open to the world*
Sovereignty/ identity	*National/autonomous*	Ethnic right; xenophobic	Neo-liberal right; 'right-wing Third Way'
	Transnational/cooperative	Transnational citadel right	Cosmopolitan right

should not be interpreted as a reinstatement of the left–right polarization. On the contrary, this form of representation of the internal pluralization of 'reft' and 'light' serves the goal of illustrating the ways in which they intersect and merge with one another.

The *protectionist left* defends the nation-state model of politics above all in the belief that this is the necessary precondition for the two central achievements of the first European modernity, namely, parliamentary democracy and the welfare state. Bound together in this belief in the nation-state are such diverse and contrasting positions as the social democratic defenders of the welfare state, communists and environmentalists. This position has also enjoyed widespread sympathy among the post-war generation of political scientists because, as an antidote to totalitarianism, it has provided society with a scientifically grounded belief in the nation-state as an indissoluble unity of nation, democracy and social welfare.

The *neo-liberal left* takes on board the challenges of globalization that are, as it were, 'preventively' denied by the protectionist left. This involves devising a new synthesis between the nation-state and the global market, one that has been described in detail in the form of the political programme of the '*Third Way*', particularly in New Labour. In the words of Giddens (1998: 26), what is involved is a new 'framework of thinking and policy-making that seeks to adapt social democracy to a world which has changed fundamentally over the past two or three decades.' This objective is pursued through two programmatic changes: first, in the form of a reconceptualization of the concepts of community, nation and citizenship in a globalizing world; and, second, in the attempt at advancing the process of the internationalization of the nation-state by means of its integration into global business contexts and supranational organizations.

The political programme of a *transnational citadel left* is less clearly discernible. It becomes manifest, though, at those points in the construction and reorganization of Europe where the principle of the social state is more or less linked necessarily to the exclusion of those who are culturally different (migration policies), as in the notion of 'Fortress Europe'. The *cosmopolitan left* argues powerfully for implementing the cosmopolitan point of view *within* nation-state policy contexts. Here, belief in the nation-state is replaced by belief in the possibility of expanding democracy along cosmopolitan lines, and national community-building is replaced by the idea of building cosmopolitan identities and networks. At the centre of such a programme is the goal of a *different kind* of globalization, which results in a twofold conflict. One is rejecting, on the one hand, the hegemony of neo-liberal political ideas and, on the other, right-wing populist and xenophobic anti-globalization movements and parties. This is expressed, for example, in the struggle for the Tobin tax and the upholding of human rights. The aim is to democratize supranational organizations in terms of both their programmes and their politics. Among the central concerns of the cosmopolitan left is the need to address inequalities beyond the limits of the national outlook, along with the related issues of 'global justice and freedom', spelt out in global economic and development priorities and programmes.

The power of the cosmopolitan movement essentially depends on the extent to which it succeeds in forging North–South alliances for political activity – a challenge that not only faces considerable obstacles in terms of transcultural communication and coordination, but which also involves taking a leading role in global political debates. When the world of social inequalities and democratic institutions is shaped according to the cosmopolitan rather than the national outlook, and when this leads to the possibility of corresponding transnational networks of organizations and action, the conflicts present in the world break out *within* political movements. There are no longer any Big Answers, just attempts at doing politics in the in-between, here-*and*-there places. The cosmopolitan outlook *de*legitimizes global inequalities – and therein lies a tremendous source of conflict. The cosmopolitan left fully accepts the consequences of its position and makes itself open to the ambiguities present in the world. The model for this is a power-engendering process of regulating and organizing diversity and difference on the basis of their acknowledgement, one that acquires its distinctiveness and fascination in contrast to the fundamentalist tendencies expressed in the new wave of certainties. The characteristic feature of the new cosmopolitan left, then, is that it establishes itself programmatically and organizationally across the board in political parties (in the Greens, but also in caucuses in other parties) and in transnational alliances involving a wide range of civil society movements and groups, transcending all manner of borders and boundaries.

The *ethnic right* responds to global interdependencies with a move involving a dual exclusion, namely *economic* and *cultural* protectionism. Xenophobic ideologies and practices predominate here, whether open or hidden. The guiding principle is the ethnic state, which perfects the isolation and exclusion of those who are culturally different.

In contrast to this, the *neo-liberal right* champions a policy in which economic openness (neo-liberalism) is combined with cultural exclusion (xenophobia). In the case of the *transnational citadel right*, this policy is pursued not at national but at transnational level, as in Europe, for example. As a result, it is extremely hard to draw a boundary between 'left' and 'right' at transnational level. Given the internal pluralization and division of left-wing and right-wing positions, it becomes increasingly difficult to work out which elements are trading under the labels of 'left' and 'right'.

One might think that the *cosmopolitan right* is somewhat akin to a black albino – that it is logically impossible. However, as a glance at the history of the European Union shows, this is empirically wrong. The founding fathers of Europe were, after all, *cosmopolitan conservatives* who shared the same political philosophy and experience: Robert Schuman, Konrad Adenauer, Charles de Gaulle and Alcide de Gaspari were practising Catholics and European patriots who grew up in the experiential space of a divided nationality and were profoundly marked by the moral self-destruction of European nation-state modernity in the madness of the Second World War and the Holocaust. They were the ones who designed and built the supranational federal architecture of a 'Vatican Europe' as an act of liberation from Europe's belligerent history and as a means of insurance against its repetition. Catholicism creates a link between conservatism with cosmopolitan elements in two ways. First, Christianity – at least at the level of ideals – renders invalid the essentialism of ethnic and national distinctions and conflicts by conceiving of the essence of human beings and of human co-existence as being defined by Christian faith. The future of the pre-, post- and transnational community (and political action) is created through *baptism*, not through a past represented by ethnic origins or through biological-social characteristics (e.g. of age or sex). As history has shown, however, what this introduces in place of ethnic distinctions between 'us' and 'them', between the civilized and the barbarian, is the bloody distinction between baptized and unbaptized. Second, Catholic social teaching gave rise to the *principle of subsidiarity*, which provided an orienting framework for the structure of European institutions from the time of the Schuman plan onwards. The purpose of this principle is the creation of a social order in which pluralism – of traditions, regions and nations – is a fundamental principle. Nonetheless, this combination of Catholic-tinted, limited cosmopolitanism and the continued existence of nationalism, as expressed in the phrase 'Europe of the fatherlands', leads to the illusion that underpins the founding of Europe, namely, that it is possible both to pursue the creation of Europe *and* to have the continued existence of nation-states – a contradiction that is becoming more and more obvious and politically sensitive as European capitalism is freed up within a common market and currency union is introduced in the form of the euro. The cosmopolitan question has consequently become an issue once again even within conservative parties.

This internal pluralization of left and right marks out the spectrum of conflicting political positions within which the programmatic battles of the twenty-first century will take place. Characteristic of this situation is that – in line with 'both/and logic' – the boundaries between different political positions are blurred, so that they often have to be redrawn and rationalized all over again in an ad hoc, random way, relative to the specific issue under discussion. In particular, however, it gives rise to certain dynamics of conflict that render the boundaries invalid. This can be illustrated by examining the way in which the politics of the neo-liberal left turns into a politics of the neo-liberal right.

The neo-liberal left strikes up an alliance between state politics and capital in which politicians create a society that conforms to the demands of the market while at the same time having to compensate for the problems that result (growing social inequalities, unemployment, exclusion). This left-wing politics of the 'Third Way' spells not less but more government involvement, albeit more for guaranteeing the interests of capital and less for guaranteeing the interests of the people and civil society. Since the neo-liberal left at least accepts a politics of power redistribution in favour of capital, even if it doesn't actively pursue one, there is a growth in poverty and insecurity and, with it, growing potential for dissatisfaction and conflict. This in turn makes it necessary to enforce law and order. In this sense, the politics of the neo-liberal left, which confers a central role on business in the meta-power game, turns into a politics of law-and-order associated more with the neo-liberal right; this form of politics in turn channels increased resources towards the police and the military and intervenes in more and more domains of society in order to advance the neo-liberalization of the economy, society and the state. A previously latent contradiction emerges in this (unintentional) interplay between the neo-liberal left and the neo-liberal right, namely that between democracy and globalized capitalism – 'freedom or capitalism' (Beck and Willms 2003). This is true of both domestic and foreign state relations.

In foreign state relations, the nation-state principle 'legitimizes' growing global inequalities. It represents a regime of exclusion which, viewed on a global scale, privileges the minority and discriminates against the majority. Capital uses the machinery of the nation-state in two ways: on the one hand, to guarantee its capacity to access resources; and, on the other, to 'legitimize' the resulting global inequalities between rich and poor by treating them as irrelevant and unreal.[6]

The counter-power of the cosmopolitan left

As far as the prospects of success for the cosmopolitan left are concerned, two theories can be drawn from the foregoing argument.

First, the question of who will win is, in principle, *undecided*. This undecidability is the essential characteristic of the second modernity.

Second, the successes achieved to date by the cosmopolitan left tell us that such success can *only* be achieved in *alliances* – with and against states, with and against sections of capital. Only by expanding the concept of politics to include the actors and arenas of global and national subpolitics does it become possible to analyse adequately the dynamics and polarizations of politics from a political science perspective.

So far, only anecdotal evidence exists to support this theory. For example, cosmopolitan movements and groups apparently slowed down the unrestrained acceleration of deregulated globalization during the early 1990s (Broad and Cavanagh 2000: 197ff.). Pressure exerted by US American people's movements to get the language of health and safety and environmental protection integrated into trade agreements has meant that it has become considerably more difficult to achieve consensus in the US Congress on enforcing new trade agreements. This is why President Clinton in November 1997 was unable to fend off this pressure from the people's movement, when the majority of Congress denied him fast-track negotiating authority on trade agreements. Another case points in the same direction. At the end of 1995 the governments of the North attempted to expand the power of the World Trade Organization through a 'multilateral agreement on investment' (MAI). A people's movement in the South had initiated opposition to the agreement, which was eventually blocked by an initiative based in the North, whose power derived not least from the fact that it included governments from the South and was thus able to mobilize a broad-based transnational coalition. The conditions favouring the success of the cosmopolitan left can also be examined by looking at how it has managed, at least in some circumstances, to anchor the rights of workers and the environment in voluntary codes for business and in general trade agreements. 'Working with allies in the U.S. Congress and in unions, human rights groups, and relevant Third World countries, the International Labor Rights Fund and other groups helped craft U.S. legislation to link U.S. trade and investment privileges to other countries' respect for these basic workers' rights' (Broad and Cavanagh 2000: 202) – even in opposition to the determined resistance of the industry involved. Basing our considerations on the theory outlined in the preceding chapters, we can identify a few ways in which the counter-power of the cosmopolitan left might be strengthened.

1   *Diversity as a unifying strength*: One essential condition for success almost certainly consists in the fact that the cosmopolitan left manages to constitute itself both domestically and in foreign affairs as a national and global player in the meta-game of global politics. 'The' cosmopolitan left doesn't really exist as such, as it divides up into a million initiatives or, invisible to the outside, acts in the form of individuals behind the familiar party political brands – unless, that is, the cosmopolitan left constitutes and defines itself as such. The internal diversity of programmatic

aims, languages and individual concerns as well as political tactics and strategies seems to pose an insurmountable obstacle to this kind of reflexive self-definition. But it doesn't have to be this way. The programmatic key to it all – acknowledgement of diversity – can also be understood and interpreted as organizational 'unity', although, for this to be so, diversity must no longer be seen as a flaw, but must instead be affirmed and practised as a characteristic of the essence and identity of the new cosmopolitanism. In this sense, the cosmopolitan left itself should first practise the values of the cosmopolitan society for which it argues politically.

2   *Alliances and oppositions*: The extent to which the cosmopolitan left succeeds in gaining a distinct profile and political influence will depend on its ability to gain access to the transnational spaces where where it can act and exert power. This means, for example, that even small movements ('small' when measured against their fellow actors in the national context) can mobilize considerable international awareness when they form networks that transcend the boundaries of nation-states, production sectors and cooperative actors, which enables them to maximize their chances of success. At the same time, it is necessary to locate this transnational power in the conflict and cooperation that exist between different political forces. Thus, a movement that ultimately portrays itself in isolation as an extra-parliamentary and extra-state initiative is condemned to frittering away the power it has. Pure and undiluted 'anti-movements' against the state and capital are condemned to powerlessness. On the other hand, as the different groups of state actors or capital have their eyes opened to the potential of the cosmopolitan outlook, the cosmopolitan left acquires greater visibility and muscle. The only successful strategy is one that includes rather than excludes the state and capital.

3   *Self-critique*: The cosmopolitan left cannot preach any ideology, neither can it preach the general idea of love for humanity. It has to disarm others by presenting all the arguments, and this is precisely where its persuasive power might lie. If a person presents the arguments both for and against what they are arguing for, they will provoke curiosity and elicit people's trust, while also making them aware of the lived contradictions that constitute the fascination of the cosmopolitan outlook.

7.6   Searching for a lost imagination

In order to elucidate the meaning of New *Critical* Theory with cosmopolitan intent on which this book is based, it is necessary to distinguish between two forms of critique and self-critique: negative (self-)critique and positive (self-)critique. *Negative critique* refers to criticism of the national outlook and the nation-based axioms of both political science and political action.

Positive critique, by contrast, is about developing and providing grounds for, or legitimating, the cosmopolitan outlook, that is, cosmopolitan polity and policy. With regard to this change of perspective, a distinction also needs to be made between the level of political science and that of political action. Thus, we have two complementary stages: critique of the national outlook + *negative* critique; and providing grounds for and developing the cosmopolitan outlook + *positive* critique.

Complementarity is a euphemism for a certain kind of dependency: positive critique presupposes negative critique. However, it is also true that both are initially inspired by the cosmopolitan imagination – negative and positive critique, as well as the self-critique undertaken by politicians and political scientists. From a social science perspective, both kinds of critique are justified first of all by the fact that they eliminate the fictions of the national outlook, that the cosmopolitan outlook is a closer approximation of reality and that there are associated benefits for the actors involved. As we have shown, the cosmopolitan outlook opens up a range of practical options for states that the national outlook closes off. Politically, of course, this is judged in a completely different light, because the change in orientation forces a radical shift in interests and patterns of conflict.

The meaning of the 'self-critique' of New Critical Theory in this context can be illustrated using the example of negative critique. As the latter begins to gain influence, the key justifications for the national paradigm are undermined. This then raises the question as to the *political costs* of negative critique – for example: who decides on the desirability, direction and moment for 'transnational reform' of the existing national order? National parties?

Table 7.4 Varieties of critique and self-critique of New Critical Theory with cosmopolitan intent

	Negative: critique of the national outlook	*Positive: providing grounds for and developing the cosmopolitan outlook*
Political science	Critique of methodological nationalism[7]	Development of methodological cosmopolitanism; exploration of the dilemmas of cosmopolitanism[8]
Political action	Analysis of the self-disempowerment of national politics; the issue of the political costs of critique of national politics;[9] critique of the alternatives to the nation-state (ethnic, neo-liberal and transnational surveillance state)[10]	Opportunities for a cosmopolitan renewal of statehood;[11] exploration of the dark sides of cosmopolitanism[12]

National parliaments? The IMF? The European Commission? The UN General Assembly? The G-7 states? Why do particular governments bow to certain trends? Is there a latent consensus of leading states to which all must bow? Are there corresponding hegemonic mechanisms? Or does this all happen according to the model of 'meta-change', behind the actors' backs, as an unintended consequence of the strategic interdependency of their actions? Do all these possibilities have some measure of validity, perhaps? In other words, Critical Theory, with its self-critical orientation, explores the disruptions and dangers that accompany successful critique of the national outlook.

Which concept of politics is intended?

Politics is understood – to overstate the point somewhat – neither as applied ideology or the art of muddling through, nor as something that plays a merely 'academic' or ornamental role in theory. On the contrary, politics, political theory and concepts of politics are more or less constitutively related to one another. This is as true of the national as it is of the cosmopolitan outlook, albeit with the opposite effect: just as the national outlook – and not so-called structural constraints, for example – closes off access to global political opportunities for power, the cosmopolitan outlook opens the door to the same.

Indeed, the following formulation could function as a basic principle for the new politics and political theory: *a changed reality presupposes a changed perspective*. Politics emerges from and consists in the way it itself interprets given situations historically. Cosmopolitan social science, if it practises this shift in horizons methodologically, is perfectly capable of playing the role of the political eye-opener.

What, then, is meant by the concept of theory?

Critical Theory's understanding of theory is a reaction to a change in intellectual climate. In *The Sociological Imagination* (1959), Charles Wright Mills wrote a polemic against '*Grand Theory*' (Parsons) and '*mindless empiricism*' (Lazarsfeld) in contemporary sociology. It was and remains an unusual attack, criticizing as it did the proud achievements of the up-and-coming science of sociology in the name of a lost imagination – not better science!

The notion of the 'cosmopolitan outlook' takes up this critique while also giving it a characteristic turn: it is the *nation-state imagination* that should be subjected to creative destruction, so that a *cosmopolitan imagination* can come into being. Without this painful, conflict-ridden shift in perspective, there is a danger that the science of crisis and change, of all sciences, with all the professionalism and sophistication it has acquired, may become blind to the radical nature of the changes that are shaking the world to its foundations.[13] Or, to quote Max Weber: a self-critical New Critical Theory with cosmopolitan intent is needed in order to win back the *'eternal youth'* of the social sciences.

The cultural problems that move people appear in ever new shapes and forms, so that the spectrum of what is meaningful and significant to us, of what emerges as 'historically specific' out of that constantly endless flow of individual occurrences, remains fluid. The contexts of thought in which it is regarded and scientifically recorded are subject to change. Therefore, the starting points of the cultural sciences will remain changeable into the boundless future ahead, as long as no Chinese paralysis of the intellectual life robs people of the habit of asking new questions of a constantly inexhaustible life. (Weber 1988: 184)

'There are sciences that are granted the gift of eternal youth, namely, all the *historical* disciplines, all those which the eternally advancing flow of culture presents with ever new problems. The transitoriness of *all* constructions, as well as the inevitability of ever *new* ideal type constructions, lies in the essence of their task' (ibid.: 206).

Is Grand Theory making a comeback in the wake of New Critical Theory? No. But the latter is also directed against the *anti-theory fashion*, which in a generalized postmodernity avoids generalizations like the plague. At the same time, it criticizes the structuralist objectivism (of Talcott Parsons, for example) that delimits and denies contingency. The striking feature of such objectivism is that it marginalizes contingency, which becomes tailored to a suitable shape and size to fit *within* pre-given categories. Methodological cosmopolitanism issues an unequivocal rejection of such totalizing concepts of society and social theory with nation-state intent – and appeals to Max Weber in doing so: 'For Weber, history issues a harder lesson. It is never simply a story about ourselves, but rather a record of differences, contingencies, unanticipated consequences and paradoxical meanings' (Scaff 1989: 63).

A Brief Funeral Oration at the Cradle of the Cosmopolitan Age

The big ideas of European modernity – nationalism, communism and socialism, as well as neo-liberalism – are a spent force. The next big idea could be a *self-critical cosmopolitanism*, depending on whether this ancient tradition of modernity can be opened up to the challenges of the twenty-first century.[1]

If this is to succeed, the dream of the cosmopolitan renewal of politics and statehood must be elaborated in relation to its corresponding nightmare, which surely also lies dormant within it. Berthold Brecht once wrote, with reference to the twentieth century, that poetry had become a crime because it involved remaining silent about so much evil. After such a century, surely the angry, iniquitous and utterly wrong-headed statement 'To speak of "humanity" is a lie' must be turned into a methodological tool for examining the unintended side-effects of the cosmopolitan regime *before* it comes to realization.

In an age of side-effects, there can be no gung-ho justification for anything, only the arduous route of critique, the most profound critique possible of one's own claims. This is how the New Self-Critical Theory has to operate. By way of conclusion, then, we shall apply this methodological principle in the following way.

The first step consists in protecting the idea of cosmopolitanism from the more crude sources of its misunderstanding by locating it in relation to competing descriptions (globalism, universalism, multiculturalism).

The second step involves turning Europe's ontological pessimism around to produce the surprising hypothesis of a positive dialectic of the Enlightenment at the turn of the global age: the unreliable, roaming spirit of cosmopolitanism, which eliminates and blurs every boundary, emerges triumphant in the face of enemy attack, doing so using the power with which it cancels out all distinctions.

Then, in a third step, the very opposite of currently prevailing assumptions, namely the *victory* of the cosmopolitan regime (that is, the acknowledgement of diversity, human rights, civil society and everything else that is good and beautiful), will be examined in terms of its dark sides. In effect, we shall be thinking through a modified version of Jean-Paul Sartre's famous phrase – 'Hell is us' – for the cosmopolitan age. The aim is fully to immerse ourselves and our thoughts in what is for most people an utterly utopian, non-realistic, cosmopolitan world-view and breathe in its *air empesté*, in order to hold – as already announced – a *brief funeral oration at the cradle of the cosmopolitan age*.

8.1 Roots with wings: cosmopolitanism in relation to competing distinctions

Is there any more apt and more improbable Cinderella story of the history of philosophy than the following one? Cosmopolitanism, a philosophy that dates back to the very beginnings of civilization and is as old as political thought itself, is destined to emerge victorious from the Babylonian confusion of political concepts and conditions that marks the beginning of the third millennium. Never before was the sentence 'I know that I know nothing' as fitting a diagnosis of the times as today.

Consider all the many things cosmopolitans have been blamed for, all the things they have been accused of! All the mockery and scorn they have had to endure! 'Those for whom all is well at home, or those who no longer like being at home or who have no homeland, let them become a cosmopolitan – whoever they may be, may they never come anywhere near my fatherland! The Everyman-citizen is like the Everyman-friend, in other words, nobody's friend.' The nation-based exclusion of the other was held to be a universal model for friendship! Those who have no 'national' feeling are 'as cold as snow'. Their morality is rootlessness, they have elevated betrayal of their heritage to a moral principle. This is how Ernst Moritz Arndt (1845: 376) denigrated the nationlessness [*Volklosigkeit*] of the cosmopolitans:

'They will become a commonplace nation, a commonplace people. They may have been given the ostentatious name of cosmopolitans; but with such a confusion and dilution of their uniqueness they are well on the way to becoming such commonplace people known as slaves and Jews.'

And Joseph de Maistre remarks, not very astutely: 'There are *no men* in the world. In the course of my life I have seen Frenchmen, Italians and Russians; and I even know, thanks to Montesquieu, that it is possible to be Persian; but as far as man is concerned, I declare that I have never encountered one in my life.' 'It is solely for the sake of paradox', writes Ferdinand Brunetière (1895: 636) by way of caricaturing this hooligan-like outburst from a would-be *grand seigneur*, 'that the very Catholic De Maistre has forgotten, on this of all days', that 'Rome knows only Christians' and 'not Italians and French, Chinese and Annamites.'[2]

The images evoked in people's minds by the terms 'cosmopolitan' and 'cosmopolitanism' are, accordingly, the *enemy* images that an emerging nationalism has shaped and imprinted on people's imaginations. That is why it is important to take up the following question: what distinguishes the notion of cosmopolitanism from the often barely distinguishable notions of *Americanization, neo-liberal globalism, universalism* and *multiculturalism*?

Universalism and cosmopolitanism

The cosmopolitan question is: what is your attitude towards *the otherness of others* [*die Andersheit der Anderen*]? The answer appears obvious: cosmopolitanism acknowledges it, Americanization and neo-liberal globalism deny it. However, this hasty answer calls for some explanation. All over the world we are seeing a surge of critique aimed at Western modernization. The critics, above all postcolonial voices, are revealing the fact that built into European universalism are a variety of constructions of how 'Europeans' behave 'towards those who are culturally different from them'. This goes back a long way. The discovery of 'humanity' as an empirically useful social unit coincided historically with the discovery of the 'barbarian'. Hardly had advances in navigation and the possibility of worldwide trade promised to give us the *res publica mundana* (Bodin), than the *genus humanum* – humanity – was being divided up according to the same/equal and different/inferior antithesis. As Teivo Teivainen (1999: 84–116) shows, a parallel can be drawn between the conference of Valladolid in 1550, where the question was debated concerning what degree of difference existed between 'Indians' (to use the term of the time) and Europeans and therefore how inferior the former were to the latter, and the politics of the present-day IMF.

At that time, there were two opposing positions, embodied by the Aristotelian philosopher Juan Ginés de Sepúlveda and the Dominican priest Bartolomé de las Casas. The Aristotelian philosopher assumed that humanity's natural condition was hierarchy, while the Dominican priest assumed it was equality. Consequently, the philosopher placed great emphasis on the differences between the Spanish and the Indians. To him, the decisive issue was that the Indians walked around naked, offered up human sacrifices, and knew nothing of the use of horses and donkeys, or of money, or of the Christian religion. The philosopher separated the human race into people who populated the earth at the same time and existed in different stages of culture. To him, difference was synonymous with inferiority. And from this he drew the following conclusion: first, when we look from civilized Europe across to barbaric America, we see that man is a god to man. Second, it follows from this that subjugation and exploitation are a pedagogical obligation.

The Dominican priest defended the rights of the Indians. He argued that they were surprisingly similar to Europeans. They fulfilled the ideals of the Christian religion, which knows no distinction of skin colour or background. The Indians were extremely friendly and modest, they respected norms of human interaction, family values and their traditions, and in this respect were better prepared than many other nations of the world to hear the word of God and to practise his truth. For the Christian priest, the essence of the Indians was not different and therefore not inferior compared with the essence of European civilization.

Commentators have frequently highlighted the progressiveness of the Dominican and criticized the early racism of the Aristotelian. However, the cosmopolitan perspective highlights something that both positions have *in common*. What is actually interesting here, it says, is that none of the early antitheses held at the cradle of European civilization allowed for the Indians to be both different *and* equal. Furthermore, both positions implied a universal standard that transformed differences with compelling logic into superiority and inferiority. Even the good las Casas, the Christian, accepted the equality of the Indians only because in his eyes they were capable of recognizing the universal truth of Christianity. The barbarian can be baptized and can share in the universal truth of Christianity. To formulate the issue in modern terms: 'developing countries', or 'traditional societies', can be 'modernized', they can attain the salvation of Western universalism through the baptism of the market and democracy.

Two forms of domination can be observed here. As history shows, the universalism of difference and inferiority and the universalism of sameness and equality have *both* been used in the end to justify physical violence. The Christian notions of conversion and the Western mission are still present in the concepts of 'modernization' and 'development policy' and continue to be used to justify domination by reference to *pedagogical* goals. It was just this pedagogical dimension of domination that Gramsci had in mind when he wrote that every relation of hegemony necessarily requires an educational dimension for its justification, and that this is true not only within but also between nations and civilizations. Michel Foucault calls this the 'rituals of truth'. They arise from the obligation to normalize truth, to deny difference and to make others into *converts* of universal truth, which is in the possession of Europe and the USA, in other words, the West.

It is also worth noting that both positions – the notion that humanity is divided into hierarchies of different and inferior 'more-or-less-humans', as well as the opposing notion that all people are the same by nature – are examples of metaphysical realism: both images of the human being are assumed to be timeless, valid for the past and for every possible future to come.

The claim made in this book is that cosmopolitanism essentially means the acknowledgement of difference. This can be made more specific against the background just described. What is meant is something ruled out by *both* positions, namely, the *affirmation* of others as both different *and* equal. Two positions are rejected in this move: *racism* and *universalism* (in its various manifestations). Cosmopolitanism entails challenging the seemingly timeless nature of racism and its future viability and claiming the future for itself. But it also means: representing the West's ethnocentric universalism as an anachronism that can be overcome, without getting caught in the snare of relativism.[3] Cosmopolitanism is an antidote to ethnocentrism and nationalism of both right-wing and left-wing varieties. By gaining subtle insight into the ugly global community of ethnocentrism and xenophobia, we can take an initial, realistic step towards a cosmopolitan *common sense*.

Multiculturalism and cosmopolitanism

Can all this not be expressed just as well using the familiar concept of 'multiculturalism'? Someone once said that multiculturalism refers to the aesthetic vision of dog, cat and mouse all eating from the same food bowl. Indeed, it is true that multiculturalism implies – even if in very attenuated form – an essentialist identity and rivalry between cultures. In the universities of the USA in particular, the politics of multiculturalism often leads to a compulsory but empty form of representation of minorities for representation's sake, a universalistic particularism for the sake of the particular.

Cosmopolitanism, on the other hand, presupposes the existence of *individualization*, and reinforces and affirms it. The individual, by virtue of their personal identity, their marriage, their family of origin, their work life and their political views and ambitions, is a member of different communities at the same time, ones that are often territorially exclusive. Within the space of a single lifetime, a person may live different lives, histories and memories that are separated nationally and territorially. In such 'borderline' cases, global society happens in the microcosm of a person's own experiential space. The term 'multiculturalism' presupposes collective categories. It is oriented towards more or less homogeneous groups which are conceived of as being either different or the same, but in any event separated off from one another, and which incorporate individual people. In this sense, multiculturalism is an opponent of individualization. If multiculturalism is to be believed, the individual doesn't actually exist. He or she is a mere epiphenomenon of their culture and society.

In this respect, there is a line that extends from the duality that is Europe versus its barbaric others, via imperialism, colonialism, ethnocentrist universalism, the distinction between tradition and modernity, through to multiculturalism and 'global dialogue': the individual can be conceived of only in terms of hierarchical and political units based on territory and ethnicity, which then enter into 'cross-border dialogue' with one another. Such social predetermination of the individual also shapes large parts of classical sociology, but is dismissed by the cosmopolitan outlook. Individuals are not determined by the different kinds of claims and expectations entailed by their identities; instead, they are set free by them in a process involving considerable conflict, one that forces them to undertake acts of bridging and translation as they practise the art of survival. There is no doubt that there are radically unequal resources available for this task, but this by no means entails a belief in cosmopolitan progress: any nasty person could get into power and all sorts of political orientations could be promoted.

Thus, cosmopolitanism (unlike globalism) does *not* entail a timeless levelling or elimination of all differences, but rather exactly the opposite – the radical rediscovery and acknowledgement of the other. Taken to its logical conclusion, this implies five fundamentally different dimensions:

- acknowledging the otherness of those who are *culturally different* (other civilizations and other modernities);
- acknowledging the otherness of the *future*;
- acknowledging the otherness of *nature*;
- acknowledging the otherness of the *object*; and
- acknowledging the otherness of other *rationalities*.

The variety of themes implied here as part of an invigorating self-critique of Western modernity (of Critical Theory with cosmopolitan intent) has been taken up and elaborated only very selectively in this book, primarily with respect to the first dimension – acknowledging the otherness of those who are culturally different.

This brings me to the second question in this chapter: what grounds are there for supposing that this soft and rather vague idea of cosmopolitanism, of all things, might be a successor to the big ideas of the twentieth century? I would like to mention four paradoxes of victory in my funeral speech at the cradle of cosmopolitanism.

1 Resistance to globalization accelerates and legitimizes the same.
2 Globalization advances by virtue of a paradoxical alliance of its opponents.
3 Global risks take the place of democracy.
4 Self-justification rules out the possibility of democracy.

8.2 Resistance to globalization accelerates and legitimizes the same

On 30 January 1996 the Zapatista Army of National Liberation in Chiapas, Mexico, called for 'a world assembly against neo-liberalism and for humanity' to be convened.[4] What they proposed was a series of intercontinental congresses at which opponents of globalization could consult with one another on strategy. The call referred to the fact that all around the world the power of money serves merely to trample on people's dignity, insult their honesty and kill off their hopes. 'Neo-liberalism', went the argument, 'is the latest in a history of crimes aimed at accumulating privileges and riches and democratizing misery and hopelessness. The word globalization stands for the modern war being waged by capital, a war which both destroys and forgets. Instead of humanity, neo-liberalism offers us share market value indexes, instead of dignity, it offers us the globalization of misery, instead of hope it offers us emptiness, and instead of life, it offers us the internationale of terror.' To counter this 'internationale of terror', it was necessary to mobilize 'the internationale of hope'.

Thus, globalization generates its own colourful variety of opposition, made up of a confusing array of wildly contrasting groups including anarchists, trade unionists, neo-nationalists, environmental activists, those who set fire to hostels housing refugees and asylum seekers, small businesses, teachers, priests, Catholic bishops, the pope, communists, fascists, feminists, the ultra-orthodox, Islamic fundamentalists, bird lovers and lovebirds. All of them – whether intentionally or unintentionally, whether consciously or unconsciously – act according to the motto of the Zapatista movement: globalization has to be combated – with globalization! The globalization of terror has to be countered with the globalization of hope.

To put it another way, resistance to globalization makes globalization complete using the instruments of resistance. What we need to grasp is that globalization denotes a strangely circular process driven forwards in two radically opposing ways: either you are for it or you are against it. To put it in a nutshell: resistance speeds things up! Richard Falk describes the process in terms of resistance to globalization from above via globalization from below.

The peculiar inevitability about being able to practise and justify resistance to globalization only under the banner of a different kind of globalization – namely a good and true one – is manifested in a number of ways. Those who go on the streets to protest against globalization are not '*opponents* of globalization' – what a misnomer! They are opponents of the pro-globalization lobby [*Globalisierungsbefürwortungsgegner*], or *propponents* [*sic*] of globalization, who are seeking to establish different global norms in the global arena of power in opposition to other *propponents* of globalization. First one and then the other group of *propponents* gets ahead in the race to globalize, thereby driving on the process of globalization ever farther and faster using the whip of resistance and contradiction.

All 'opponents of globalization' not only share global communications media with their 'opponents' (thereby increasing the ways in which these media can be put to use by transnational protest movements in their efforts to organize). They also operate on the basis of global markets, the global division of labour and global rights. This is the only way they can potentially and actually achieve their border-transcending omnipresence. They also think and act in global categories, for which they create global publicity through their actions and which they thereby seek to realize globally. The aim of their struggle is to tame the financial markets, and so they appeal for global treaties and organizations to monitor them. The globalized economy can be regulated properly only at a global level, and only those who fight for this globally have any chance of success whatsoever. In turn, the globalization of protest acquires the dynamic of a self-fulfilling prophecy of success.

Let us take the example of trade union rights: the right to organize to enforce labour rights that often exist on paper alone is a long way from being a global reality. Unlike violations of the WTO's trade rules, violations of existing UN conventions on trade union freedoms or the prohibition of child labour are not punished with sanctions. This is why many thousands of activists in the USA have joined campaigns to protest against the unbridled exploitation of workers in textile factories in Mexico, Nicaragua and Indonesia, where seamstresses produce expensive brand-name jeans for a few cents an hour and every attempt at self-organization is put down by violent police action. It is this direct connection between the culture of protest in the metropolitan centres and trade unionists in developing countries that lends the movement of globalization's *propponents* its global clout. It is important to grasp this curious principle: resistance to the speeding up of globalization accelerates the speeding up of the same.

Even if it is the case that globalization ultimately wins through using the power of its enemies, this certainly doesn't mean that it all amounts to the same thing in the end. What drives protest forward is not the global freedom of capital but the global captivity of globalization's victims. Resistance to the neo-liberal agenda of globalization inevitably gives rise to a cosmopolitan agenda of globalization. All the crises, conflicts and collapses generated by globalization have one and the same effect: they reinforce the appeal to a cosmopolitan regime and open up (whether intentionally or unintentionally) the space for a global order of power and a global legal system. Conflicts over globalization globalize cosmopolitan horizons of thought and expectation, they globalize the realization that there is a need to civilize national attacking instincts. This circularity – that the conflicts and crises entailed by globalization serve to globalize globalization – can be demonstrated in a number of ways. Because the *propponents* of globalization organize their summit protests transnationally, the corresponding police response likewise has to be transnationalized. Police forces from different nations have to overcome their focus on the national context and denationalize and transnationalize themselves. In other words, supranational protest requires a supranational police force, a corresponding supranational information system, supranational legal systems, and so forth.

The global arena of power seems like a self-confirming prophecy of the cosmopolitanization of the world. Nietzsche once argued: 'A thousand goals have there been so far, for there have been a thousand peoples . . . the one goal is lacking. Humanity still has no goal. But tell me, my brothers, if humanity still lacks a goal – is humanity itself not still lacking too?' (Nietzsche 1966: 2.323f.). In fact, just the opposite is true: taking the cosmopolitan view of the actual unity of humanity becomes a precondition for dismantling, step by step, the discrepancy between appeals to globalization and its realization. A fictitious reality of globalization is constructed in order to realize its fictions; postulating the attainment of the goal of 'humanity' becomes the means by which that goal is achieved.

When proponents and opponents merge into variations of globalization's *propponents*, it is difficult to work out who is on whose side. The *propponents* on the street may contradict the *propponents* in government, but both sides constantly outdo one another in paying lip service to global norms and regulations, so that in the end one might well ask whether the street-protesting *propponents* wouldn't ultimately make better heads of government and the governing *propponents* better protesters. Then again, why can't all of globalization's *propponents* form a gigantic worldwide coalition with all other *propponents*, in order to make the cosmopolitan regime into an opposition that embraces all the different fronts?

Let us take the example of *tax evasion*: tax havens such as the British Cayman Islands, the Dutch Antilles and Liechtenstein are increasingly turning into a black hole for the global economy. According to estimates undertaken by the International Monetary Fund, personal fortunes valued at more than $5 trillion in total are registered in places such as these, enabling their owners to pocket the returns tax-free. The German tax authorities alone lose out on at least €10 billion every year in this way. But all initiatives to put a stop to so-called offshore financing have failed because governments cannot muster the strength to challenge this privilege of the rich. The *propponents* on the streets agitate for the *propponents* in government to take the necessary steps.

8.3   Globalization advances by virtue of a paradoxical alliance of its opponents

There is one rule that applies equally to all the different groups of players and their strategies in the meta-power game: no single actor – neither capital nor advocatory movements nor states – can achieve their goals in the meta-power game *on their own*. They are *all* dependent on forming coalitions if they want to see their goals realized. This leads to a dynamic of integration through which the boundaries between 'pro' and 'contra' become blurred and interwoven and the general *propposition* [*sic*] is brought to completion.

It takes the authority of states to achieve the NGOs' goal of establishing a world order based on civil society, for they are the ones who can give this order a legally and politically binding shape. A plural global order is inconceivable without the existence of strong, active states. Even strategies of capital that are only pursuing their economic interests remain ultimately dependent both on states and on civil society's moral pronouncements – this is the only way the cultural and political preconditions for the investment freedom they enjoy can be guaranteed. The gap between the *propponents* of the different camps is indeed closing in this general mêlée of mutual instrumentalization.

Corporations have taken on the role of NGOs, committing themselves to fighting worldwide for human rights and raising a loud voice when President Bush, allegedly speaking on their behalf, withdrew from the Kyoto Treaty on global climate change. In 1998, as a result of a campaign led by global environmental groups, the OECD states rejected the multilateral agreement on investment (MAI), which would have fulfilled global capital's most cherished desires regarding investment freedom. Why? Have governments suddenly changed camps and joined the non-governmental organizations? Well, yes and no. By carrying out their protests, non-governmental organizations were effectively representing the state interests of an 'ideal umbrella government' against parochial national government interests. Once those in government came to realize (with the help of civil society protest) that the agreement desired by global business interests on safeguarding global investment freedom really did go against elementary state interests, they sided with the non-governmental organizations.

There are countless examples of this game of swapping sides. It is this *paradoxical alliance of opponents* that drives the cosmopolitan regime onwards. For example, environmental protest groups, including Greenpeace, along with Attac and the German aid agency Welthungerhilfe have all called for the cancellation of the poorest countries' debt and a radical change of course in climate policy. But the German chancellor, for example, is calling for the same thing, in concert with other heads of government, albeit the gap between policy pronouncements and *realpolitik* is often a huge one. Of all the grandiose promises issued in communiqués after government summit meetings, very few of them, if any at all, are actually carried out. But this merely goes to show that non-governmental organizations represent the *clear conscience* of governments and might even make the better governments; the aim of their protest is to spur governments on to do what they allegedly already do, namely, govern. For example, one proposal that is currently enjoying renewed popularity among non-parliamentary *propponents* in the USA and Europe is that put forward at the beginning of the 1970s by the economist James Tobin. The idea is that a general tax on all foreign currency transactions, the so-called Tobin tax, should be levied to throw a spanner in the works of speculative dealing while simultaneously filling state coffers. Calculations indicate that, even with a low tax rate of 0.2 per cent, this would yield more than €100 billion – money that could be reinvested in expanding supranational aid organizations or used to establish a basic social safety net for everyone in the world. In supporting this proposal, which is proving more and more convincing to Europe's political establishment, non-governmental organizations are representing the interests of states and governments against these very same states and governments; or, to be more precise, they are representing the interests of an anticipated transnational, cosmopolitan state against its (still) existing national parochialism. It can only be a matter of time until those in government shake off the self-imposed stasis of their national and neo-liberal captivity and stand shoulder to shoulder with non-governmental organizations in order to advance their own best interests.

However, the principle that comes to light here is an extremely strange one and requires closer analysis: power and counter-power are moments – one might even say accomplices – in the process of bringing the cosmopolitan regime into existence.

The absolutist immanence of a cosmopolitanism that comes into being despite all manner of resistance – indeed through the power of the same – can be interpreted in two ways. The cosmopolitan regime is a *regime of enemies without enemies*, in other words, a regime in which opponents are integrated through a process of inclusive reproduction. In this way, the cosmopolitan regime is capable of generating and renewing the dissent-consensus that protects its own power space. *Implementing* the cosmopolitan regime and *criticizing* the cosmopolitan regime are two sides of the same coin. Any attempt at averting it or overcoming it becomes a part of the driving force behind its implementation.

However, this doesn't mean that cosmopolitanism meets with consent on all sides or that there is no one struggling against it. On the contrary, the absolutist power of definition possessed by the cosmopolitan regime is manifested not least in the fact that it does away with key distinctions, undermining them, merging and recombining them. Everyone is a *'propponent'*, everyone is in the *'both/and'* category. This 'both/and' category is personified in the figure of the professional speculator George Soros, who embodies both *untrammelled capital* and the *radical counter-movement*. He is both an expert speculator and one of its most radical critics. On the one hand he forces whole countries on to the defensive with his casino investments, while loudly declaring on the other that financial markets harbour the danger of self-destructive development. As a prevailing principle, there is something totalitarian about this 'both/and', which devours both actors and counter-actors in its huge belly and even feeds off resistance: it cuts the ground from under the feet of resisters by eliminating the principle of opposition. What would be the *conceivable Other*, the *Afterwards* or the *Beyond* of the cosmopolitan principle? This is a question that leads us nowhere. Elimination of opposites, which cosmopolitanism elevates to the level of a principle, absolutizes immanence.

One way this is made clear is that all attempts aimed at continuing to play the old national and welfare-state game are successively being undermined. No doubt there are – and in the future increasingly will be – powerful, reactionary counter-movements that will try to channel the storms of protest against globalization into their own sails so as to win momentum and influence in political arenas. There will be those who voice regret over the decline of the old order and who appeal for past values to be restored – those of religion, culture, the nation, national solidarity, the working class, or whatever. Much of current thinking on both left and right is hopelessly infected by the virus of nostalgia. This is equally true of the backwards-looking visions of various communitarianisms, which conjure up for future use the political mythology of a Golden Age that has always only just come to an end. Indeed, even today there are signs that perverse policy combinations are being pursued, such as open markets on the one hand and state-propagated xenophobia on the other. On the outside, in relation to the global markets, governments act as though they are adaptable, while on the inside, at home, they act with authoritarian rigour. Neo-liberalism takes care of globalization's winners, while fear of foreigners is whipped up and the poison of re-ethnicization administered in careful doses to its losers.

But this too makes it clear that a modernized fascism – even if it were feasible – would not be able to escape the inevitability of oppositional immanence. It too would have to go with the flow of globalization and reflect this not by seeking to prevent globalization from occurring, but possibly by speeding it up. Classical fascism did exactly the same thing: it too was a modernization movement which spoke of blood and soil on the one hand while propelling modernization forwards using totalitarian power on the other.

Of course, this doesn't mean that the party political landscape will not be forced to change radically by cosmopolitanization. A plausible prognosis for an increasingly right-wing populist Europe is that the centre right will be ground down into an extreme right forced to labour over the contradictions of combining globalization with a closed, homogeneous national society. Meanwhile another part of the centre right will be absorbed by a cosmopolitan centre which, sensing that its economic and political chances lie in escaping towards the future, proceeds to do so.

The contradictions involved in resisting the cosmopolitan regime can be illustrated by looking at the potential resistance of workers. Workers would have to turn against themselves, against their own tradition of internationalism (which was a form of anti-nationalism), if they wanted to struggle against the cosmopolitan regime. The internationalism of the workers' movement was a struggle *against* the nation-state and *for* the creation of transnational solidarity, justice and the 'unity of the people'.[5] Paradoxically enough, the victory of global capitalism over Soviet Marxism opened up the power space for a new 'workers' internationalism – without the workers'. It would be a perverse historical twist if globalization's detraditionalized losers, the workers, gathered beneath the banner of national protectionism, of all things.

The totalitarian government of the 'both/and' principle, which drives the cosmopolitan regime forwards, is also manifested in the fictions created by a conservatism that produces some very strange effects. The intellectual spacelessness of opposition is expressed not least in the helplessness with which counter-prescriptions are propagated. There are those, for example, who support a protectionist economic system in which everyone produces goods in their own country and exports at most a small proportion of these goods to other countries. Given what have by now become generally accepted facts, such people merely confirm the suspicion that they have lost their grip on reality, something that is nowadays enough to have a person committed to psychiatric care. Those who call for radical strategies of national isolationism – import barriers for capital and commodities from other countries – will meet with the determined resistance of the poorest countries, in spite of having appointed themselves as their spokespersons. Word has got around that national protectionism does more harm than good in the long term. This is precisely why states in Africa, Central Asia and Latin America are pressing for the WTO's so-called Millennium Round to be reconvened – the liberalization round that was brought to a halt by the Seattle protesters.

In a situation where opponents and proponents are inextricably bound together in perpetual opposition, opting out of globalization is no longer an option. Of course, immanent conflicts of interest remain and will become more acute. The degree of hatred with which these conflicts of interest are fought out will increase, possibly even *because* of the growing realization that conflicts of interest do not conflict. The neo-liberal and the cosmopolitan, civil society agendas contradict one another in terms of their key principles and visions for the future. Also, none of the conflicts between men and women, North and South, West and East, old and young, Jews and Arabs, and no plea for or against the unlimited use of human genetics will be solved by the cosmopolitan regime. On the contrary: once the cosmopolitan regime is brought to bear, the contours defining people's perception of social inequality, which had served to exclude the suffering of foreigners from the national field of view and action, will begin to fade. The perilous chasm that opens up between the prosperous countries and the rest of the world can no longer be ignored and erupts into the political arena. Thus, the closer Kant's 'eternal peace' comes, the more it turns into 'eternal strife'. Neither is anybody denying that the effects of such differences are most keenly felt at the micro-level: the difference between living under a liberal or a tyrannical government remains a vital one even under a cosmopolitan regime.

But – and this 'but' cannot be stressed enough – all these strands of resistance, conflict and difference remain *within* the horizon of the cosmopolitan regime, thus making one key point abundantly clear: the notion of a counterpart to the cosmopolitan regime that might call the latter into question from the outside is neither conceivable nor foreseeable. This totalitarian dark side of cosmopolitanism comes to the fore when cosmopolitanism itself comes into existence.

8.4   Cosmopolitan despotism: humanity's threat to humanity takes the
place of democracy

When one considers the global political events that followed on from the terrorist attacks of 11 September 2001, the obvious conclusion to be drawn is
that the idea of cosmopolitanism should *not* be so readily entrusted to the
state – the cosmopolitan opportunities for action that accrue to the state will
only be used to strengthen its own position of hegemony and consolidate
the transnational presence of surveillance states. Arguments based on the
perception of threat open the way to a global political fundamentalism of
risk prevention. Cosmopolitan despotism refers to the danger that global
political instrumentalization of cosmopolitan risks may take us back to a
time before modernity, by allowing the baby to be thrown out with the
bathwater. In other words, if the basic *institution* of the first modernity –
nation-state democracy – is done away with, then the basic *principle* of
modernity – the centrality of *democracy per se* – will not be far behind. A
variety of reflexive fundamentalisms are springing up, including a global,
anti-democratic populism around protection against threats, as well as forms
of self-justification based on efficiency and human rights, which simultaneously undermine the procedures of democratic legitimation and exceed its
capabilities. One of the fundamental ambiguities with regard to cosmopolitan risks is the way in which they are used secretly to legitimize the revoca-
tion of democracy underneath the alluring guise of democracy itself. In order
to understand the force with which this occurs, it is necessary to unravel the
fascinating concept of risk itself.

Global risks throw humanity's survival into doubt and *thereby* open up
global opportunities for action. The prognosis that suggests itself is this: the
century of potential planetary self-destruction will become a century of planetary unity – 'one world'. The knowledge that the tragedies of our time are
all global in terms of their origin and scope gives rise to a cosmopolitan experiential context and to cosmopolitan expectations. There is a growing realization that we are living in a global context of responsibility from which no
one can steal away. In this sense, 11 September made publicly visible (for the
first time in fifty years) the fact that peace and security in the West can no
longer be reconciled with the existence of trouble hotspots in other areas of
the world or with the situations that give rise to them. It is this transnational
aspect that necessitates cooperation across national borders in order to solve
one's 'own' problems. Granted, the collapse of global financial markets on
the one hand and climate change on the other entail quite different consequences for different parts of the world. But this alters nothing about the
fact that everyone is affected and that each person will potentially be very
much more seriously affected in the future. This is why the global perception of global risks ultimately creates a common national-global interest in
every country. It is not difficult to predict that the battles over defining these

titanic problems will trigger new kinds of conflict. But it is just as important to recognize that these very conflicts also display an *integrative* function, because they make it abundantly clear to everyone that global solutions have to be found and that they are ultimately to be found not through war but through negotiation and treaties.

In the 1970s a generation of hippies coined the slogan 'make love, not war!'. What might the slogan be for an emerging civilization of risk at the start of the twenty-first century? Perhaps 'make *law*, not war!' (Kaldor).

The appropriate response to the terrorist threat, then, is cosmopolitanism – to say that every one of us, whoever and wherever we are, has the right to live, to love, to dream and to long for a world in which everyone has these rights. It will be a world in which the scourge of terrorism, along with the scourge of poverty, ethnic persecution, illiteracy, injustice, sickness and human insecurities, is combated, a world where terrorism is prevented from putting down roots or yielding any fruit. The insidious thing about it is that this nice idea can be turned around and used to achieve the exact opposite.

A strange kind of discourse has developed in the USA, in which the shameful concept of 'empire' is being recast as one that has positive value. Viewed in these terms, 11 September provided proof of the inadequacy of America's involvement and presence in the world. The solution deemed to be the right one is to establish American values – the 'American way of life' – in a more determined and effective fashion all over the world. The idea appears to be that it is necessary to turn everyone into Americans, so that Americans are able to live in safety in a world without borders.

As a result of the terrorist threat, the cultural nerves of the USA have been severely shattered and a storm of patriotism unleashed. Given the demands of domestic politics, the US government has thrown itself into a frenzy of foreign policy activity aimed at eradicating its domestic enemies outside the country – the suddenly omnipresent terrorist threat. The terrorist attacks have enabled the US military and US foreign policy to resurrect a much missed enemy image, one that enables them to construct a clear focus around which consent and support can be mobilized both domestically and abroad, beyond the boundaries and the different camps of parties and states. Moreover, by highlighting military considerations, this coalition can be steered out of the hazy mists of general consent (or critique) and into the clear waters of an 'either/or' decision. This creates opportunities for forging new coalitions between countries that had traditionally been enemies, such as Russia and China, who have been integrated into an 'alliance against terrorism'. This has been all the more successful given that both countries have thereby been granted a licence they have long had to do without, namely to take ruthless action against their *own* terrorists, without fear of foreign accusations over human rights abuses.

In order to reach a realistic assessment of the opportunities for self-empowerment suddenly presented to states by the terrorist threat, it is important to distinguish between, on the one hand, conventional enemy images among states and, on the other, transnational terrorist enemy images, which are aimed primarily not at states but at groups, networks and individuals. It is precisely this transnationality – that is, the delocalization, destandardization, lack of state ties and potential omnipresence – of terrorist networks, along with corresponding 'enemy images' based on a range of places and groups – that facilitates the strengthening and renewal of powerful states' hegemonic position. The key question is: who gets to decide who is a 'transnational terrorist' and who isn't, and what are the relevant criteria?

As things stand, this task falls neither to judges nor to international courts, but to powerful governments and states. This is the way they empower themselves – by deciding, without any form of checks or controls, who is *their* terrorist, *their* bin Laden. This is how President George W. Bush comes to decide that Iraq, Iran and North Korea form an 'axis of evil' and that their governments must either be rejected or else robbed of their capability to build weapons whose potential for mass destruction poses a threat to the USA and other countries. At the same time, he declares that al-Qaeda camps and networks exist 'in at least a dozen countries', and that 'tens of thousands of potential terrorists must be eliminated'. This often includes all those groups or individuals who have some connection or other with members of al-Qaeda. 'We will not allow the most dangerous governments and regimes in the world to threaten us with the most dangerous weapons in the world', says Bush.

He thus demonstrates how it is possible, with the help of politically constructed terrorist risks, to mobilize the American nation on a permanent basis and at the same time to justify an enormous increase in military expenditure. The alarmist rhetoric of the US president captures the anonymity of the enemy in somewhat metaphysical terms: the enemy is 'evil' rather than, more concretely, a group of terrorists and the governments that support them. However, universalizing the terrorist threat means simultaneously accepting the paradox that results: that terrorist groups thereby receive from the hands of their enemies the very seal of recognition of their global power that they so keenly desire. When the various possibilities and impossibilities of terrorist attacks are explored in detail time and again in the media, and when a terrified public is told again and again how little it takes – using modest resources put to clever use – to put us all in danger, and how tiny the chances are that the state can do anything about it, the global perception of risk becomes a normal, everyday part of life.

All these activities have a similar effect: *they globalize the culture of fear.* No longer do we anticipate domestic social reforms or the next big invention; instead, we fear – in a sense, pre-emptively – the new risks that these introduce into the world. In risk societies that have lost the 'pre-given' securities of nature and tradition, fear creates a new, fragile community bond. What we are seeing emerge are the emotionalities and irrationalities of communities of fear, which may very well provide fertile soil for radical groups committed to violence as well as isolationist movements. Political and military definitions of the terrorist threat channel and focus these fears in such a way that there is always a surge of support available for a war against someone or other within or outside one's own borders. People who are scared are generally prepared to accept interference in the fundamental aspects of their everyday lives without asking questions and without offering resistance, where previously it would have been unthinkable even to call for such a thing.

Nearly 250 years ago Benjamin Franklin warned that those who 'give up essential liberties in order to obtain a little temporary safety deserve neither liberty nor safety.' This sentence sounds quaintly wooden in a globalized culture of fear in which people are increasingly prepared to pay for lost safety with the hard currency of liberty.

The policies introduced following 11 September 2001 have furnished proof of the fact that fundamental liberties are blithely being sacrificed at the altar of the terrorist threat. The USA has passed into law a 'Patriot Act' – meant not in the least ironically – which, among other things, intensifies high-tech surveillance. If this trend continues, there will soon be no unbugged telephones in the country that hosts the Statue of Liberty. Police forces are also being allowed to monitor e-mails and Internet connections. Uncle Sam wants to find out who are the *goodies* and who are the *baddies*. No wonder countries around the world are following this example and extending the powers of electronic surveillance. All this is being carried out and justified in the name of anti-terrorism, and yet the expansion of power involved can be used for all kinds of purposes.

There is good reason to doubt that the world has indeed become a safer place since these anti-terrorism measures were put in place. There is also reason to question whether a perfected surveillance state really will be able to seek out those who are determined to act underground across country borders. Terrorists are hardly likely to be smuggled into the country as illegal immigrants. They will travel using all legal means and will hold a passport. We know we cannot stop them entering the country and that we are hardly likely to discover them and reveal their true identities when they are here. We also know that it is not businesses, friendships and family relationships alone that are bound together across different continents and integrated into networks of social proximity by the Internet and all the other communications media. Every time an additional million Internet access points are set up, it becomes less necessary to meet in certain places to arrange activities. These conspiratorial meetings become dissolved in the new communication flows of 'liquid modernity' (Bauman).

Yet despite all this, the control argument is being used to establish an Orwellian surveillance state transnationally. Washington insists that the threat is immense, that mobilization must be placed on a permanent footing, that the military budget be dramatically increased, that civil liberties be curtailed and that critics who protest against this be intimidated and excluded as being 'unpatriotic'. Who will protect people from these precursors of a cosmopolitan despotism intent on dismantling the fundamental values of modernity in order to protect them?

8.5 Self-justification rules out the possibility of democracy

'The soil doesn't lie', according to the doctrine of national modernity. ('La terre, elle ne ment pas', said Pétain when the Germans marched into France, in order to mobilize the French against the fascist invasion.) The doctrine of cosmopolitan modernity is: 'Human rights don't lie'.

The rule of human rights is self-legitimating and knows no limits. It follows the logic of ahistoric self-justification – it is based not on voting but on consent, not on conquest but on non-conquest, not on democracy but on reason. The human rights regime posits a universal, transcendental law that simultaneously establishes power. This law is no longer rooted in the territoriality of nations or states but in the fabricated immediacy of individual and globality, something not subject to any democratic controls. This gives rise to a space of expectation directed towards a global military power charged with establishing and keeping order; such a space is constituted wherever calls for the defence of human rights – the source of legitimacy for global power – are combined with the expectation that current cross-border conflicts which pose a threat to the order of human rights should be regulated.

The silent compulsion that leads to knowledge and understanding of what is good – the power of self-legitimation – takes the place of democratic legitimation. In the value principles of the cosmopolitan order, which no longer recognizes any standpoint apart from itself, self-legitimation replaces democratic legitimation. However, the triumphal march of cosmopolitanism conjures up the danger of a cosmopolitan regime *without* democracy. The phrase 'cosmopolitan democracy' would merely be a fig leaf used to conceal the undemocratic, moral and metaphysical self-justification of ademocracy (not 'anti-democracy') in the diverse cosmopolitan society.

What makes the cosmopolitan regime, exemplified by the human rights regime, legitimate and/or legal? Is it even possible to speak of an illegal or illegitimate human rights regime? Or is the concept of an illegal, illegitimate human rights regime a straightforward contradiction in terms? Who or what decides on the legitimacy or legality of the human rights regime? How does the cosmopolitan human rights regime respond to national constitutions and laws, or to the practices of (either democratically or non-democratically legitimated) governments? What decides whether and in what circumstances human rights violations that are considered *legal* within a certain state are so serious for the community of (which?) states that they warrant military humanitarian intervention?

Who determines how the relevant armed forces should be structured? To what extent does the act of setting up transnational alliance armed forces and equipping them for the military option of humanitarian intervention in other regions of the world constitute a threat to foreign states, or to what extent is it a necessity brought about by the need to validate the cosmopolitan human rights regime in the face of national claims to sovereignty?

What gives those members of the international community who feel committed to the human rights regime the authority to intervene in the domestic affairs of other states, regardless of whether or not the governments of those states request such intervention? In other words, who is responsible in concrete situations – given the existence of divergent economic, moral and military options and interests – for setting out the principles and norms of the cosmopolitan regime *in opposition to* the old nation-state order in such a binding way, both legally and militarily, that the question of which sources of legitimacy apply in this case – the old nation-state ones or cosmopolitan ones – is itself considered by the different observers, participants and those affected to be 'legitimate'?

The more binding the cosmopolitan regime becomes, and the greater the degree of interdependency between states, global business corporations and organizations as well as global civil society actors, the more likely it is that questions of this sort will lead to some crucial tests, because at the point of change from the national to the cosmopolitan outlook the *sources of certainty* are also interchanged – entailing a radical change in reality.

One thing is clear: the legitimacy and legality of the cosmopolitan regime cannot be achieved 'from the bottom up' – by seeking democratic agreement and consent among the different states. Instead, it has to be justified 'from the top down', that is, deductively, from the evident universality of its principles and basic premises, and on the basis of the consequences both for humanity and for each individual.

'Inductive', democratic justification of a cosmopolitan regime is based on the analogy between the role of individual states as members of the international community and the role of individuals as members of national societies. However, this overlooks the fact that states are collective actors and, no less importantly, that hegemonic states which benefit from the economic and political inequalities within the international community have obvious interests in authorizing only those systems of norms and rules that safeguard and legitimize their hegemonic position.[6]

Furthermore, the range of actors and organizations whose practices are recognized and standardized by the order of the cosmopolitan regime is

Table 8.1 Transformation of the legitimacy of global politics

	First modernity National outlook	Second modernity Cosmopolitan outlook
Frame of reference *Level/scope*	National/international International society of nation-states; legal sovereignty	Transnational/cosmopolitan Transnational actors; government without governance, supranational financial organizations, NGOs, transnational corporations
Subject	Nation-state, international law	Individuals, states, human rights
Source of legitimation	Voting; democracy	Consent: self-legitimation; threats to humanity
Nature of justification	Inductive contract theory: from the bottom up	Human rights and domination: deductive, from the top down

wider and more diverse than the old concept of 'international community of states' suggests. The cosmopolitan regime includes, in its regulating capacity, those collective actors who exercise power *alongside* states in the global arena, namely transnational corporations, supranational organizations, non-governmental organizations and, in particular, individual actors in their relationships with states. It is the human rights regime that effectively constitutes such individual actors as such in the first place, with their own rights in relation to collective actors.

In this sense, it is virtually impossible (at least under given institutional conditions) to legitimize the cosmopolitan human rights regime *from below* (in the form, say, of a vote in the United Nations plenum, that is, via nation-states) – unless one were to create the institution of a world citizens' parliament which decided democratically, as a sovereign global body, on the conditions that are to hold in the global order. But this is neither planned nor is it a practicable option, as it would constitute a *post hoc* vote that merely confirms and puts into practice the self-legitimating consent that already exists. Indeed, to put the question once again, would it even be conceivable for a world citizens' parliament *legitimately* to *reject* the human rights order? Surely not.

Several key examples suggest that the moral, political, legal and strategic significance of the human rights regime develops *independently* of whether it is ratified by those states most affected by its influence. Indeed, one could almost say that the human rights regime *corrodes* national legitimacy in precisely those cases where states refuse (for good reason) to consent to its implementation.

Take the universal declaration of human rights, which was signed in 1948 as part of the UN Charter, not least in response to the experience of the Holocaust. It was immediately labelled by many as a 'soft' power strategy in the Cold War, though it subsequently turned out to be extremely effective. Granted, it is hard to assess how big a part it played in the collapse of the Soviet Empire. However, there *is* evidence suggesting not only that the institutional arthritis of Soviet Marxism was delegitimated by its denial and violation of human rights, but also that its refusal to uphold human rights lent strength and encouragement to the civil protest movements of the former Eastern bloc, something that has become historically evident since the Berlin Wall came down. A similar trend can be observed in Amnesty International's success story.

This non-governmental organization has made the self-legitimacy of human rights into a form of self-authorization, in that it works for the implementation of the human rights regime within state arenas, as a 'private' non-governmental organization. Amnesty International has appointed itself global prosecutor of human rights violations everywhere in the world before a global court consisting of the global public. Rather like a self-fulfilling prophecy, this global court has been created, among other things, by an information policy based solely on facts and case studies.

This example of a global, proactive human rights conscience being successfully constituted both socially and politically recalls the figure of *self-legitimation* and illustrates the kind of active, organizational form this can take. The task that Amnesty International set itself was, by raising awareness about the violation of universal rights, to make them a tangible reality, to show that there are grounds for them and, by thus triggering a call for sanctions, to make them effective. With its transnational form of organization, it became an independent voice and a point of authority for transnational law, one which made the violations of universal law visible and subject to sanctions, bypassing the boundaries and walls of state law based on violence. Having the character of a *non*-governmental organization lent this voice moral credibility in contrast to government posturing based on the abundant resources of state power and legal structures. By concentrating on individual cases, that is, cases involving an individual against the state, Amnesty achieved two things at the same time. First, the emotional impact of the individual victim's situation meant that human rights – by their very nature individual – acquired visibility and credibility in relation to the sovereign rights of states. Second, the practice of confronting states about their human rights violations in the glare of world publicity lent the claim to universality of the human rights regime – specifically, equality between states on the one hand, and between the individual and the state on the other – a credible binding character.

All this has helped bring about a situation in which, since the end of the Cold War, it has become more difficult strategically to instrumentalize the human rights regime. In this respect, our distinction between genuine and non-genuine cosmopolitanism has, as far as the issue of human rights is concerned, been shifted noticeably in favour of a genuine cosmopolitanism. Given the existence of a global public sensitive to human rights issues, it has become more difficult to misuse the human rights charter for purposes of expanding nation-state power. The cosmopolitan regime of human rights has established worldwide a normative horizon of expectation that has not only undermined the reality of the old national–international system of rules in strategic terms but has also rendered it morally bankrupt. However, such a situation simultaneously generates a political and military vacuum that calls for new military, political and economic structures and institutions.

Given the foregoing comments, it is clear that the following two philosophical and political positions are historically incorrect: first, the *Marxist* position that maintains that all notions of rights are ultimately bourgeois institutions, and that it is therefore politically and morally reprehensible to make the universalism of human rights the foundation and goal of political action. This Marxist idea is plainly wrong, because it fails to recognize the mutually reinforcing and confirming moral, political and strategic significance of universal human rights. What is more, this approach stands in stark contradiction to the tradition of internationalism in the workers' movement.

Second, the *postmodern* position also loses something of its persuasive power when it asserts that human rights are a late offspring of the Enlightenment; the Enlightenment, in turn, has proved to be one big mistake with devastating imperial consequences and so in this respect has refuted its own claims. The internal imperialism of the universality of the human rights regime – so postmodern theorists are forced to argue – stands in open contradiction to a world full of cultural differences. These differences not only hinder communication, they rule it out completely, along with the common context supposedly created by 'universal' human rights. In postmodern thought, the notion that the cosmopolitan regime of human rights creates a general, normative horizon of expectation that is binding for all concerned provokes the worst suspicions. This way of seeing things, it is held, can be nothing other than a vehicle for repression and the domination of one set of cultural claims against a different, excluded one. The notion that human rights and the cosmopolitan regime in general establishes and sanctions precisely this right to be different stands in open contradiction to postmodernism and places a big question mark over dogmatic postmodern relativism.

Jürgen Habermas has reason to celebrate: both Marxist and postmodern resistance to the human rights regime is collapsing, or, to be more precise, is becoming limited to immanent controversies. These tend to be about historical peculiarities and the cultural diversity of conceptions of human rights, or else critiques of narrow, deductive, naïve interpretations of human rights, ones based solely on morals rather than on power strategies. However, as soon as pleas for difference and plurality to be acknowledged begin to be voiced, it becomes apparent that this is a case of the different *propponents* of the cosmopolitan regime lining up to face one another full of rage and anticipatory consent.

As the cosmopolitan regime loses its enemies, or absorbs and converts them, its internal conflicts and contradictions become heightened, people become aware of them, they shape the political arena and struggle for institutional forms of expression. David Held, for example, proposes a kind of 'ten commandments' consisting, albeit, of seven cosmopolitan 'principles', which should be shared universally and should form a basis for establishing which rights and obligations of individuals should be protected, and in what way, and how people can be put in a position to influence the institutions that govern their lives: '(1) equal worth and dignity; (2) active agency; (3) personal responsibility and accountability; (4) consent; (5) reflexive deliberation and collective decision-making through voting procedures; (6) inclusiveness and subsidiarity; (7) avoidance of serious harm and the amelioration of urgent need' (Held 2002: 24).

To develop these principles of the cosmopolitan regime in detail – as David Held has convincingly done in very nuanced fashion – would go beyond the bounds of the present discussion. Our aim instead is to point out that this approach opens up the prospect of a new set of contradictions. These will influence the way in which political structures and organizations emerge in the national, international and transnational arenas *within* the cosmopolitan regime. Even today these sorts of contradictions and controversies are very much in evidence as they seek political and institutional forms of expression. This occurs, for example, in arguments over the extent to which human rights should be accorded priority over trading interests, or again in debates over the relationship between efforts at protecting the environment and boosting economic growth *within* a particular group of countries and efforts aimed at expanding trade *between* countries and creating supranational initiatives and authorities aimed at protecting and improving the quality of the environment within different countries.

Can the principles of a cosmopolitan environmental regime be applied straightforwardly to rich and poor countries, highly developed and industrializing countries alike? Is it necessary and legitimate to push through measures for the protection of the ozone layer or the global climate system *against* countries that manufacture products and use resources central to the development of the industrialized countries, which have essentially generated the hole in the ozone layer along with all its risks?

Of course, one can argue that it is necessary to insist on the upholding of human rights in countries such as China and Russia, come hell or high water, even if this means threatening their prospects for economic development and integration into the global economy and thereby damaging the trading interests of Western states. Yet arguments of this sort sometimes seem rather unworldly and are only honoured *post hoc*, once democratic governments have won the day.

What is the best way of translating human rights into a reality? Some say: economic growth and the prosperity it brings make people open to the notion of human rights. Others argue the other way around: democratization and human rights guarantees within a country are preconditions for a thriving economy.

In accordance with the rules it would doubtless be right, in the interests of protecting and maintaining biological diversity, to persuade countries such as Brazil, Indonesia and Malaysia to renounce strategies of economic growth, which their respective governments deem to be absolutely necessary. And no doubt it would be advisable to link free trade regimes with environmental and human rights regimes. But how?

Would it be legitimate, for example, to exclude countries within a free trade zone that contravene the rules of democracy and the human rights charter? Can it be made a condition that member states of a free trade zone should uphold the norms of the environmental regime? Who decides? Can decisions about exports and imports to and from other countries be made dependent on the extent to which human rights and environmental norms are upheld in these countries? Can such decisions be left to individual states for whom environmental standards play a major part in their value system? Can states take it upon themselves to introduce restrictions in order to protect themselves against other countries' products and practices that they feel are completely unacceptable? Or are such trade restrictions an 'illegitimate', 'illegal' instrument? Who decides the issue, and on what legal and legitimatory basis? Who will fight for its acceptance in the face of resistance from powerful states?

The main focus of the human rights regime is against the abuse of political power by states. But surely it is equally necessary to place limits on economic power. One objective, therefore, ought to be to impose the binding norms of the cosmopolitan regime on corporations, or even to make them its executive bodies – to commit them to the implementation of human rights as well as environmental norms and so on. But what exactly does the 'cosmopolitan regime' – the all encompassing, earthly word of God – have to say about such controversial issues and conflicts over interpretation? Or, to be more specific: *who* says what the cosmopolitan regime says? Perhaps we will see the emergence of a cosmopolitan elite, much like the priestly exegetes of the Qur'an or the Bible, whose job it will be to give a more or less binding interpretation, geared towards specific cultures and treating specific themes, of the internal contradictions and hermeneutical entanglements of the cosmopolitan regime's more or less formalized, codified and legalized value principles. There will probably be cosmopolitan mullahs who will investigate and supervise international *as well as* national legal and judicial systems in terms of the 'purity' of the cosmopolitan 'word' and its wisdom.

It is when the cosmopolitan horizon of possibilities has been made binding that the conflicting differences between one set of *propponents* and another come radically into view, and it is more than likely that these conflicts will be addressed in quite bitter and passionate terms because the element of conflict has been taken out of them.

To repeat the question: can there be such a thing as legitimate resistance to the human rights regime? Will there not always be just one line of resistance to *this* interpretation in favour of a *different* interpretation of human rights? Must rejecting the principle of environmental protection not involve at least verbally paying tribute to the need to protect the environment? Democracy will be abolished in order to save it!

On what is the legitimacy of the cosmopolitan regime based, though, if it is legitimated neither by the state nor by democratic procedure? Does cosmopolitan sovereignty – the possibility of establishing a set of laws that are both transnational and valid for every possible actor, including individuals – require an *imperial* form of sovereignty?

We can identify three possible sources of cosmopolitan sovereignty: *rational law*, *legal positivism* and *pragmatism*. All three conceptions vary the figure of self-justification. Moreover, they are by no means mutually exclusive, but rather complement and reinforce one another.

In the Kantian tradition, the cosmopolitan regime is conceptualized as an evident kind of self-justification, made concrete in forms of legal constitutionalism. In this sense, cosmopolitan principles, as norms of the '*ideal speech situation*', are present and justified in every conceivable instance of communication (Habermas). This mute inner compulsion to possess the better argument can always be assumed by all participants to exist in every speech situation, and is in itself transparent and obvious to all participants; it is what gives cosmopolitan principles their universal binding character.

Legal positivism, on the other hand, operates from the standpoint that legal norms can never include justifications based on principles, leading to the conclusion that the validity of, say, the cosmopolitan regime can be read from the degree to which it is *empirically effective*. At this point, self-justification based on principles dissolves into *empirical self-justification*, which is dependent on circumstances, but might also be backed up by circumstances. To put it more straightforwardly: as the cosmopolitan regime wins acceptance and succeeds in its goals, so it becomes self-justifying.

This view can be seamlessly reconciled with that of *pragmatism*, in which the validity of the cosmopolitan regime is measured against the extent to which global problems are tackled successfully with its help at a global level (and therefore at a national and local level as well). The ontological and metaphysical status of the cosmopolitan regime is transposed at this point into a form of *pragmatic self-justification*. As the cosmopolitan regime *proves its worth*, so it acquires legitimacy. As it succeeds and proves itself in practice, so the wellsprings of legitimacy begin to overflow.

What is remarkable is that the mutual interaction of these three modes of possible self-justification of the cosmopolitan regime reinforce its unassail-ability and absolutist immanence. This is because all three modes follow the logic of postulation, which justifies itself ethically *and* empirically *and* prag-matically. The specificity of this self-legitimation through postulation comes to the fore when one compares this 'axiomatization' of the cosmopolitan regime with political-democratic legitimation: postulations that are self-justifying in whatever way *refuse* democracy.

If, as is the case with the cosmopolitan regime, the aim is to establish a fundamental order of morality for everybody, for the new humanity without borders, then by definition the legitimacy of this order cannot be derived from the legitimatory sources of a bounded, territorial nation-state order. It requires its own sources of legitimacy, as this is what enables a moral and legal order to be set up in the first place as a prospective reality for *every-body*, that is, for each individual, and therefore *in opposition to* nation-state actors and legitimatory principles. The revolutionary act of getting beyond the nation-state order is conceivable only in the form of a *cosmopolitan pos-tulation*, which enacts its self-justification ethically, pragmatically and poli-tically in the form of a self-fulfilling prophecy.

In this respect, the self-justifying postulation is at the same time a princi-ple of *nominalistic* reason or of *rational* nominalism. In other words, the transcendentality of self-justification is at once realized *and* withdrawn nom-inalistically and is thus unassailable.

In the end, then, what we have in the cosmopolitan order of values is a kind of conceptual definition of what counts in a generally binding way as 'good'. This definition is contingent, in other words it could certainly turn out differently. But conceptual definitions can be neither true nor false. In particular, it makes no sense whatsoever to hold a vote on them. They do not become 'more true' or 'more false' through being accepted or rejected. We can argue over conceptual definitions – and do so, exhaustively – but the argument can only be settled *pragmatically*, namely in the *conclusions* that can be derived from them and examined empirically and politically. In this way, by virtue of its at once rational and nominalistic 'being', the cos-mopolitan regime softens the blow of every critique. Interestingly enough, this rational-nominalistic form of self-justification enacted by the cos-mopolitan regime acquires greater persuasive power once reason is demys-tified. *In fact, it is that 'reason' which acquires validity after the end of reason.* At precisely the point where nothing holds any more in and of itself, this postmodern, rational, pragmatic nominalism is able to develop its irresistible, unchallenged omnipotence. As studies by John Meyer and others show, this pragmatic-postmodern 'postulational reason' can by all means be trans-formed into a *'working hypothesis'* capable of being 'made hard' – made into 'reality' – using the language of global empirical social research, that is, mass data.

I want, in conclusion, to point to two consequences that arise out of this. First, self-justification applies *across all time*. It has a 'before', but no 'after'. As it acquires binding character, so too do the 'metaphysics of the eternal present' (Cwerner 2000: 335). Once established, cosmopolitanism becomes a regime with a long past but no otherness of the future – it is timeless and eternal.

At the same time, the logical figure of self-justification comes to take the place of the non-logical figure of democracy. The place of voting comes to be taken by . . . *understanding*. Whoever (still) fails to see and understand the 'good' in the cosmopolitan order at any given stage of pragmatic self-justification doesn't *want* to see it, and this reflects back onto them. But those who lack such understanding *must* be excluded. This 'must' has to be, because good facilitates understanding of good out of its own goodness: lack of understanding is, understandably, the fault of those individuals, countries, ethnic or religious groups, parties, and governments themselves who lack this understanding. To this extent, all critique of the cosmopolitan regime is permanently open to the accusation that it is exercised by those who deliberately lack understanding, by wicked people who are out to destroy the order of good.

And so the circle is completed. The cosmopolitan regime can be understood – and used politically – as 'good' *per se*, all opposition to which is no longer possible. It is the figure of self-generated risk and self-justification which, given a political turn and thought through to its radical conclusion, not so much abolishes democracy, but gradually thins it out and makes it superfluous amid the silent inevitability of understanding. Cosmopolitanism's good world order and value system knows no alternatives, it is self-justifying, and it is no longer dependent on elections and ballots that are always arbitrary. As we have said, the cosmopolitan regime has only *propponents*.

Accordingly, the game of power and counter-power, government and opposition comes to an end in the absolute immanence of cosmopolitanism. This doesn't mean that democracy is abolished under the cosmopolitan regime. But it does come to be secondary, derived, limited, cherished and kept by for certain occasions – and is then celebrated all the more enthusiastically. Democracy becomes the religion of a *past* age. People still practise it – on Sundays and at 'Christmas', under the 'Christmas tree' of the election ballot box. But hardly anyone still really believes in it. It is the dead God of the first modernity who lives on. Secularized cosmopolitanism keeps up its feast-days-only faith through the holy sacraments of democracy.

This is the point at which I pause, somewhat breathlessly, to ask myself and the reader: for all my good intentions of justifying my argument through self-critique, have I not overshot my target? Has the time not come to remind myself, in the form of a critique of critique, that I have myself promulgated the second modernity as being open-ended and ambiguous, so that the fatalism with which the cosmopolitan regime has been revealed as an ademocratic regime clearly contradicts the very premises of this book? Is there not, after all, light at the end of the tunnel – or at least a tunnel at the end of the light? The cosmopolitan outlook itself is anything but lacking in contradiction; still, surely it is at least contradictory in the sense that it contains a glimmer of hope. *How*, then, can the danger of a Western de-democratizing fundamentalism based on good intentions be countered systematically in thought and action?

The answer is: in two (closely connected) ways that follow from the logic of self-critique. One is for democracy and human rights *not* to be decoupled (that, as we have shown, is the path that leads directly towards the hell of good) but instead to be *connected* and *merged together* (both conceptually and institutionally). The other is for the cosmopolitan regime to drive forward this process of merger between democracy and human rights at the global political level, and thereby to refute the fears set out above through appropriate deeds and facts. In other words, it is the cosmopolitan regime itself, understood as the *reform* of global politics with regard to both *ideas* and *practice*, that provides the grounds for proof of its own legitimacy – or not, as the case may be.[7] Such 'reasonable outcomes' (Habermas) would be (to put them in unsystematic and incomplete terms):

- a strengthening of existing *transnational organizations* or the *founding of new ones* capable of acting as a counter-power to transnational corporations and banks and creating a normative framework of rules, guidelines for conduct and codes of conduct, not only for governments but also for global business actors and private companies. In this way, cosmopolitan actors with the power to negotiate effectively on issues concerning the non-economic dimensions of the global market – ecology, climate, disease, poverty, exclusion, as well as living with contradictions – would testify as to whether the cosmopolitan regime has become a reality or is mere ideology.
- successful *reform of the IMF and World Bank*, to replace lack of transparency with transparency and to introduce new forms of democratic representation, particularly on the part of the poor target countries (e.g. the one country, one vote principle); also to ensure that issues impacting on global fairness and global justice are systematically taken into account in IMF policies; that there is more recruitment of specialist staff and directors from non-Western countries; and, not least, that regulation of nation-states is matched by regulation of global business.
- *state democracy*: Even the rich and powerful states must see themselves as addressees of the cosmopolitan regime; they must acknowledge its

existence and work with others on expanding and strengthening it. Thus, the foundations of the cosmopolitan regime – such as the International Criminal Court, the Kyoto Protocol on climate change, the conventions on arms control, which range from the prohibition of biological and chemical weapons through to nuclear weapons – ought to be ratified also by the weapons-producing countries of the West, especially the USA. 'Cosmopolitan regime' means that *all states are equal before the rule of law*. This aspect of state democracy, in which *all* states, even the most powerful ones, submit themselves to the law of a jointly approved regime, would be a convincing criterion for distinguishing between the light breeze of ideology and the heavy winds of cosmopolitan reality.

- *human rights policy*: How are human rights applied in concrete situations? Are there democratic decision-making procedures? To what extent are these transparent? To what extent and in what way can operational distinctions be made between democratically legitimated and democratically non-legitimated 'humanitarian intervention'? Human rights exist as ideology, they exist as national policy (e.g. of the USA), and they exist in a cosmopolitan regime in close association with an institutional democratic infrastructure. So self-governance and human rights need not be a contradiction; in fact they may form an integrated whole, as when human rights follow from the idea of formally constituted co-existence.

- *global (citizens') parliament*: A prime example of the merging of self-governance and human rights would be the founding and grounding of a global parliament, even if realistically such an initiative on the part of cosmopolitan-minded governments included only a fraction of existing states initially, and even if this cosmopolitan parliament had access initially only to the levers of symbolic political power. This would doubtless create a global public location where global problems, including human rights violations, could be dealt with transnationally to great effect.

- another link connecting self-governance and human rights – the creation or strengthening of institutions that enable individuals to *enforce attested global citizens' rights against their own states*.

- *substructure of intermediary institutions*: To what extent have existing institutions such as the UN General Assembly, the World Security Council and the G-8 states been reformed accordingly or else complemented by newly created institutions? To what extent is there an integration of continental regimes at transnational level? In other words, in what ways are the big players – the USA, the EU, China, Asia, Africa, South America – linked back to democratic institutions? Are there new forms of connecting and networking between them? To what extent do they obey the principles of transparency and accountability?

- *legitimation through self-fulfilling prophecy*: Flagrant abuses of human rights, or, to put it more generally, violations of the cosmopolitan regime, could create a global public sphere in which a common cosmopolitan consciousness becomes impressed on people's minds. This is most likely to happen if these violations are perceived as a contravention of one's *own* principles. Perhaps the cosmopolitan regime will generate integrative conflicts and effects for a global public sphere – albeit *critical*, rather than positive, instances of solidarity. In fact, the whole point is precisely that a global politics and global society, constituted in accordance with the cosmopolitan regime, requires such critical – rather than positive – integration.
- *conflict mediation*: How can decisions be made in a sea of conflict? Will we see the emergence of preventive and real infrastructures for dealing with mutually exclusive certainties? What are the consequences of this for law and education?

This is where we can see that the cosmopolitan perspective – the transnational level – does *not* entail any new principle. Democracy and human rights are among the basic principles of modernity, but they are principles that need to be embodied in different kinds of institutional and conceptual forms in the first, nation-state modernity and in the second modernity respectively. The key is either to find or to invent a different kind of architecture for linking democracy with human rights in the cosmopolitan modernity, and to make it a concrete reality through specific stages of reform.

Thus concludes, with this critique of critique, my 'brief funeral oration at the cradle of the cosmopolitan age'. As it turns out, it has actually become a eulogy for *democracy* at the cradle of cosmopolitanism. But, without democracy, cosmopolitanism has died before it had even begun to live; without democracy, humanity's dream of cosmopolitanism is *nothing* – or else it has long since turned into an actually existing nightmare.

We are speaking (still, for now) in a global situation in which the hope – that is, the non-reality – of the cosmopolitan regime motivates and mobilizes actors. This *project* of cosmopolitanism needs to be clearly distinguished from *actually existing* cosmopolitanism, which is ruled and tyrannized by its unwanted, unseen side-effects. The earthly religion of the nation could be replaced by that of cosmopolitanism. Unlike the national order, however, cosmopolitanism no longer has any 'others' or any 'outside'. Ultimately, cosmopolitanism is the secularized divine order after the divine order has come to an end.

Having come to the end of this treatise on cosmopolitan Machiavellianism almost without drawing breath, it seems only right to finish resolutely with the words 'and yet' (not only is it both customary and polite to do so, it has become almost a necessity and will surely do both reader and author good). This liberating 'and yet' is hovering impatiently in the wings, waiting to be spoken aloud at long last: is it not consoling to know that the cosmopolitan regime that we have struggled towards in this book and whose side-effects we unveiled in pre-emptive fashion in its last chapter is still a long way from becoming a reality? Or does not even this count as a consolation any more?

Notes

Preface

1 There are two closely related terms in German that approximate to the English term 'power'. These are *Macht* and *Herrschaft*. The former refers to an open-ended, sociologically amorphous form of power, while the latter refers to institutionalized forms of power aimed at achieving some expedient objective and translated in Max Weber's *Wirtschaft und Gesellschaft* as 'domination'. Throughout the following, *Macht* will be rendered as 'power' and *Herrschaft* as 'domination' [Trans.].

Chapter 1   Introduction

1 In this chapter I have drawn on the following literature: Nietzsche 1966; Kant 1964; Marx and Engels 1982; Weber 1972; Cerny 2000; Habermas 1998, 2005; Grande and Risse 2000; Cheah and Robbins 1998; Hardt and Negri 2000; Albrow 1996; Coulmas 1990; Connolly 1995; Hitzler 1996; Fichte 1918; Randeria 2001; Cohen 1999; Stichweh 2000; Youngs 1999; Beck et al. 2001; Bornschier 1988, 2002; Cutler et al. 1999; Cohen and Kennedy 2000; Czada and Lütz 2000; Drucker 1997; Embong 2000; Greven 1999; Lash 2002b; Latour 2001, 2003; Luard 1990; Luhmann 1975; Luhmann and Scharpf 1989; Machiavelli 1985; Macropoulos 1989; Meier 1990; Meyer et al. 1997; Palonen 1995, 1998; Plessner 1981a, 1981b; Polanyi 1944; Robertson 1992; Scharpf 1991; Scott 1998; Wallerstein 1991; Wapner and Ruiz 2000a; K.-D. Wolf 2000.

2 It was Helmuth Plessner, with his critical sideswipe at the typical, melancholic German approach to politics – 'Germans do politics with a heavy heart because they are too scared to play' (1981a: 104; 22) – who made the concept of the game into the key concept for analysing the political sphere. By drawing on the concept of the game, Plessner affirms society and the public sphere and uses them against the community idyll – precisely in order to create space for the growing 'possibility of play' (ibid.: 38). For Plessner, this space of play stands for a public space filled with strategic options. These options are more real than reality – which, as Robert Musil noted, is ultimately nothing but a hypothesis we have not yet managed to get beyond. Plessner stresses the historical openness of politics:

In this relation of indeterminacy towards oneself, man conceives of himself as power and discovers himself for his life . . . as an open question. All that he denies himself through this renunciation returns to him as the strength of prowess. All that he gains through this in terms of a fullness of possibilities simultaneously sets him clear limits in relation to endless other possibilities of self-understanding and self-comprehending, which he then no longer has. (ibid.: 188)

The game in question is the reciprocal game with contingencies, its aim being to tame the latter. Ultimately, however, for Plessner it is the system of *conventions* that gains the upper hand over against the extraordinary, boundary-breaking opportunities of the game of politics. Accordingly, this is how Plessner analyses diplomacy, which relies on treaties to rein in the wild contingency of the un-bridled game of politics: 'Diplomacy, on the other hand, is the game of threats and intimidation, cunning and persuasion, acting and negotiating, the methods and arts of power enhancement that are intrinsically and necessarily linked to the arts of defending and justifying power, the game of argumentation, of giving meaning to the meaningless' (1981a: 99). In contrast to this almost unpolitical 'possibility of a political *a priori*', which revolves 'around politics in its human necessity' (ibid.: 142), I use the metaphor of the game in the sense of a *meta-game*, in other words, a game of politics that is about the foundations and basic rules of power and domination in the transition from the first to the second modernity.

3   That which is referred to in the sphere of world politics as the 'meta-game' is known in more general terms as 'reflexive modernization' (Beck et al. 1994; Beck 1996; Beck et al. 2001). The theoretical idea common to both is the *interference of side-effects*, which render the basic institutions and boundary lines of the first modernity invalid and force actors into a meta-politics in which the basic rules and plural boundary constructions of social life are renegotiated. The power game played over the rules that govern power is also dominated by side-effects to the extent that, for example, while global business actors act economically (and not politically), they render the fundamental premises of nation-state politics invalid as a side-effect of their transnational investment decisions (see ch. 3.13, ch. 4 and ch. 5 below).

4   'What we have here is not a rigid straitjacket, but a new and more complex playing field. In many ways the game of *political* globalization is still wide open. Indeed, that game is not a one-off, it is an "iterated" game which continues to be played indefinitely, with strategies and tactics of the players and their episte-mological "shadows of the future" feeding back into an ever-evolving set of opportunities and constraints. Furthermore, this game is characterized by a range of alternative outcomes or "multiple equilibria", from world government to chaos, with a range of diversely structured possibilities in between. Some form of uneven pluralism, or the sectoral hegemony of financial markets and/or multi-national corporations, or even the "durable disorder" that is sometimes called neomedievalism are far more likely scenarios. And the differences among these are immense too' (Cerny 2000: 35).

5   The issue of a cosmopolitan Machiavellianism, which this book raises, should not be confused with some secret recipe for inhuman absolutism. Instead, I am

drawing on the tradition of *republican* Machiavellianism, which, as Pocock shows in his book *The Machiavellian Moment* (1975), gained influence over the fathers of the US constitution and their concept of political freedom and sovereignty. For Machiavelli (1985) power [*Macht*] means power that is embedded in and constituted through society. It can only be adequately understood and practised when its social genesis and dynamic are recognized. In his view, power means power constituted domestically on the basis of republicanism, so that these two concepts (power and republicanism) are virtually synonymous. Power presupposes counter-power – it can only be achieved in interaction with counter-power and always has to be counteracted by counter-power, in a strategic process of interaction based on an institutional order. Machiavelli had to develop this view of things independently, against the pre-modern forms of the unpolitical. Nowadays this issue is distorted by some of the most contradictory thought coalitions of the unpolitical, ranging from the politics of systems theory (Luhmann), through the anti-politics of postmodernism and the neo-liberal self-destruction of the state, to the anti-state theorists (not actors!) of civil society.

6   This policy adjustment breaks with the practice introduced by US President Clinton, who determined that terrorist activities are attributable to individuals and not to states.

7   I coined the term 'military humanism' in an article for the *Süddeutsche Zeitung* about the Kosovo war. Under the heading of *military humanism*, Noam Chomsky (2000) presented a harsh critique of the ideology behind the Kosovo warmongering engaged in by NATO as well as the US military-industrial complex. In doing so, however, he clings on nostalgically to the military logic of methodological nationalism and thereby fails to recognize the real danger contained in the term 'military humanism', namely, that *beyond* the bounds of the national outlook a new threat is emerging in the form of a global military human rights monitoring system, which erases the dividing line between war and peace.

8   Fichte 1918: 28; quoted in Coulmas 1990: 420.

9   The nation-state outlook is also criticized, of course, within economics (see, among many others, Voigt 1999).

10 For a discussion of methodological nationalism, see, among others, Martins 1974; Smith 1995; Beck 2000c, 2002a; Gilroy 1993; Zürn 2003; Scott 1998; Sassen 2000a; Falk 1995; Taylor and Gutman 1992; Shaw 2000; Luard 1990; McNeill 1986.

11 Methodological nationalism is not limited to the social sciences; it is also manifested in a certain set of philosophical assumptions that Jacques Derrida has termed 'national philosophism': 'the claim laid by one country or nation to the privilege of "representing", "embodying", identifying with the universal essence of man, the thought of which is supposedly produced in some way in the philosophy of that people of that nation' (1992: 17). Michael Walzer goes one step further in asserting that at the heart of this national philosophism lies a dialectic of state sovereignty and individuals' rights to liberty:

The recognition of sovereignty is the only way we have of establishing an arena in which freedom can be fought for . . . It is this arena and the activities that can go on within it that we want to protect, and we protect them as much as we protect individual integrity, by marking out boundaries that cannot be crossed, rights that cannot be violated. As with individuals, so with sovereign states, there are things that we cannot do to them, even for their ostensible good. (Walzer 1977: 89)

This national philosophism also guides John Rawls's theory of justice, as the title of his book itself suggests: *The Law of Peoples* (1999). The unit of this theory is 'peoples', not states or individual citizens, and it is in these that Rawls saw the structure of liberal domestic societies as being grounded. National philosophism has an international aspect. 'Peoples' are conceived of as a unity consisting of state, territoriality, morality and memory. This is the only way justice is possible, according to Rawls. Anyone observing the philosophical debates of our time cannot but be gripped by a profound philosophical amazement at how deeply and unreflexively the apparently universalistic conceptual habitus of philosophy is wedded to the national outlook. One can almost hear the words of Carl Schmitt coming through: 'The central concept of democracy is the nation (*Volk*), not humanity. If democracy is to be a form of politics at all, there can only be national democracy (*Volksdemokratie*) and not human democracy' (Schmitt 1983: 234). For a critique of this view, see, e.g., Habermas 1998, ch. 5; Kuper 2000; Gilroy 1993; McCarthy 1999; Held 2000; Held et al. 2000; Bauman 2000; Levy and Sznaider 2001; Cheah and Robbins 1998; Boyarin and Boyarin 1993.

While the concept of a 'national culture' is understood in a territorial and homogeneous – and in borderline cases even essentialist – sense, this is *not* the case with the realm of ideas associated with 'cosmopolitan cultures' (if one wants to take this concept on board at all). Post-national, transnational or cosmopolitan 'cultures' can*not* be conceived of as totalities. It is wrong to picture either cosmopolitan cultures or national cultures as being isolated, more or less complete and grounded in themselves, autonomous up to a point and in any case 'integrated'. In national philosophism, the whole batch of ingredients – cultural norms, values and regulations – is conceived of as being grounded endogenously. The term 'cosmopolitan cultures' *contradicts* a vision of relatively separate cultural worlds in which people live alongside one another – based on the pattern of politically and administratively divided territories. It is *not* the case that when we leave one culture we enter another. It is *not* the case that we can move backwards and forwards between different cultures. And neither is it the case that we can say, at any one time and with reasonable precision, in which culture we are currently located or towards which one we are moving. In the cosmopolitan outlook, 'culture' appears precisely as the absolute negation of this imagined world of natural, self-enclosed totalities that we cannot choose and to which instead we belong or do not belong, as fate decrees. Cosmopolitan realism also negates the notion that being integrated in an ethnic or national totality is the 'natural' and therefore really the 'healthy' state of being in the world, while all other states of being – straddling two or more cultures, drawing on different heritages and being subject to different national loyalties – are 'abnormal', 'hybrid', necessarily 'shallow' – if not 'dangerous', 'morbid' and potentially 'monstrous'. If methodological cosmopolitanism makes any sense or is at all effective, then it is so as a *negation* of the imagined world of cultural 'homogeneity', 'multiculturalism' and 'multi-communitarianism', because these sets of concepts exclude and deny the very element that constitutes cosmopolitan common sense: the search for co-existence in a polyethnic world of mutually exclusive certainties, a world that struggles, often painfully and violently, for recognition and acceptance of difference.

12 The following serves as an example for the method of 'double interpretation' (Beck et al. 2001), which we are developing at the 'Reflexive Modernization' research centre in Munich. This method shows how the same 'realities' of social inequality, viewed first from the national and then from the cosmopolitan point of view, appear to be completely at odds with one another, and how this shift in perspective is helpful in terms of raising new issues, generating challenging hypotheses and illustrating why methodological cosmopolitanism opens up new lines of research as well as practical options in the sense of a 'positive problem shift' (Lakatos 1970).

13 Institutions and organizations focusing on a form of 'cosmopolitan' social science research have a long history, and they have always been in competition with the 'self-confirming circle' of nation-state data and knowledge production. It is remarkable that the consistency with which corresponding attacks on academia have been fended off is in large part based on the claim that academic data production and management has greater integrity compared with procedures of global data production and management in supranational organizations. First of all, then, the scientific ethos appeals to the better quality of nation-state data. In parallel, fears abound that either metaphysics or unscientific practice – usually both – will return to the centre of academic social science as the dreaded 'cosmopolitan turn' takes place. Furthermore, methodological nationalism acquires its superiority from the prevalent conviction, held by many in philosophical and political theory circles, that Western values – democracy, the rule of law, social justice – are possible only in the forms and contexts provided by the nation-state. This leads to the conclusion that the cosmopolitan opening betrays and endangers the democratic ethos.

  The main error in both these scenarios is based on two omissions. On the one hand, the interpretive capacity of classical sociologists and their nation-state premises is dehistoricized and posited as absolute. Those who laud the classical sociologists are masking their own intellectual laziness and committing themselves to an imitator's existence, something they have already long become. On the other hand, there is a repeat of the great mistake of sacrificing scientific curiosity about reality to institutionalized value convictions (following the old maxim '*es darf nicht sein, was nicht sein soll*' – anything that should not be true must not be allowed to be true). Even the most rigorous data, methodologically speaking, can itself be blind and can blind us to the new cosmopolitan realities breaking in upon us (see main text).

14 The notion of 'fine differences' (Bourdieu), followed in the 1970s and 1980s by the 'microscopic' sociology of inequalities that produced a filigree stylization of lifestyles and minute differentiations, is located unreflexively under the research umbrella of methodological nationalism. It is not hard to predict that, from the standpoint of a sociology of inequality renewed by cosmopolitan values, this sociology is certain to come in for severe criticism in retrospect, both on empirical grounds and on account of its normative nation-state bias.

15 It is important, however, to avoid giving the impression that a social scientific revolution is being incited beneath the banner of New Critical Theory with

cosmopolitan intent that has not already long been in progress. Where it began is hard to say. Certainly, Jürgen Habermas aired some crucial issues and built the foundations with his book *The Postnational Constellation* (2001). Before that, Niklas Luhmann also drew our attention to the fact that communication processes do not stop at national borders, taking pleasure in deriding the opposing view and using both argument and irony to construct his theory of the 'world society' as the basic unit and only possibly consistent concept of society. For some years now, John Meyer and his masterfully organized social scientific United States national team have been projecting Emile Durkheim onto the global level, so to speak. It is not hard to reconstruct the steps by which the national perspective is being translated into the global perspective – even if ultimately (by exploiting every possible sophisticated method, including virtually global data sets) it is the imperatives of a *global America* that are being spelt out. In many social scientific circles it has long become a platitude that Max Weber's *Economy and Society* – to single out the high priest of the social sciences – needs to be remodelled and rewritten for the demands of the *cosmopolitan imagination*. Numerous contributions over the past few years support this insight, including the following: Anthony Giddens's far-sighted forays away from linear social science (1990, 1994); Manuel Castells's path-breaking trilogy on the network society (1996); Zygmunt Bauman's tireless efforts to substitute the imagination of a cast-iron modernity with the imagination of a liquid modernity (2000). There have also been some successful attacks and visions emerging from postcolonialism, as well as from anthropology, ethnology and geography, all of which have been startled into an awareness of and have fled from their seemingly autarchic locality and, in their very different specialist contexts, have been replacing the premises of methodological nationalism with new mixed forms of the global local and the local global. Additionally, Martin Albrow's *The Global Age* (1996) is probably the most underestimated classic of cosmopolitan redefinitions of social science; Arjun Appadurai (1998) has proposed that we talk of 'flows' and 'spaces', that is, of financial, migration, information and cultural symbolic flows; and, finally, there is Scott Lash's *Critique of Information* (2002).

Chapter 2   Critique of the National Outlook

1   In this chapter I have used the following literature: Dewey 1954; Krüger 1996; Smith 1995; Goethe 1909; Jens 1992; Albrow 1996; Grande and Risse 2000; Levy and Sznaider 2001; Habermas 2001a; Luhmann 1999; Zürn 1998a; Ottmann 2001; Barry 1999; Hobsbawm 1990; McNeill 1986.

2   Anthony D. Smith (1995) constructed this image and critique of nationalism in order to set it off against and provide grounds for his own 'saving criticism' of nationalism.

3   John Dewey early on described the 'cosmopolitan' quality of US-American self-perception: 'Such terms as Irish-American or Hebrew-American or German-American are false terms because they seem to assume something which is already in existence called America, to which the other factors may be externally hitched on. The fact is, the genuine American, the typical American, is himself a hyphenated character. It does not mean that he is part American and that some foreign ingredient is then added. It means that . . . he is international and inter-

racial in his make-up. He is not American plus Pole or German. But the American is himself Pole-Jew – and so on' (quoted in Kallen 1924: 132f.). How little this applies to Europe becomes clear from a Nietzsche quotation that after more than one hundred years has lost none of its topicality: 'Thanks to the pathological alienation that the madness of nationality has placed – and continues to place – between the peoples of Europe, and thanks also to the short-sighted and quick-acting politicians who are in the ascendant on its account today and who have no inkling of the extent to which the disintegrating politics they are pursuing can necessarily only be an 'intermission' politics – thanks to all this and other things that are quite unspeakable today, the most unequivocal symptoms are now being overlooked or else randomly and falsely reinterpreted which say that *Europe wants to be united*' (Nietzsche 1966: 2.724).

4   The inclusive distinction between nation and cosmopolitanism, between world citizenship and patriotism, is renewed in Goethe's distinction between world literature and national literatures (Albrow 1996: Jens 1992). The phrase 'world literature' appears in an essay by Goethe in the magazine *Kunst und Altertum* (Art and Antiquity) in May 1827, at the end of translated extracts from a French magazine. The title of the latter is *Le Globe* and its editors were known in Europe at that time as 'globists'. Bearing in mind the situation of the intellectual classes at the time, the magazine can be said to have had a global orientation. The *Morgenblatt für gebildete Stände* (Morning Post for the Educated Classes), published by Cotta, reported the following from Paris on 11 December 1824: 'Instead of the familiar "Review", a "Globe" has been produced, published every two days and referred to regularly for the first time in Paris by the "Morgenblatt", the London "Literary Gazette" and the Italian "Antologia".'

Goethe followed *Le Globe* keenly from 1826 onwards and initially translated extracts of some of the articles published in it for his notebooks, including the following:

but nowadays, where through a freely agreed movement and in spite of governments' efforts to the contrary, the peoples are removing all obstacles and are seeking to move closer to one another; nowadays, where nations are inclined to allow themselves to be determined one by the other and are forming a kind of community of like minds, like habits, indeed like literatures; this is where, rather than exchanging interminable expressions of scorn with one another, they have to regard one another from a higher perspective.

'Peoples who are coming closer to one another', 'like habits' – it seems that we are dealing here with an early form of social globalization.

In May 1827 Goethe inserted extracts from a review of a French *Tasso-Stück* in *Le Globe* into his magazine *Kunst und Altertum*. He writes that his contributions from French magazines are not intended to promote his own fame:

One hears and reads everywhere of the progress of the human race, of the further prospects of the world and its peoples. Whatever the general situation is in this regard, the investigation and precise description of which is not of my office, I want nonetheless for my part to make my friends aware that I am convinced that a general world literature is coming into being, in which an honourable role is reserved for us Germans.

This definition of world literature is not yet different from that of a canon, that is, from books in one language being translated into another language. One year later Goethe explains his concept of world literature more precisely, in a welcome address to a gathering of nature researchers in Berlin:

If we have dared to proclaim a European, indeed a general world literature, this does not mean that the different nations take note of one another and of one another's products: in this sense it has existed for a long time, it continues to exist and renews itself more or less. No! what we mean here is that active and hard-working literary figures get to know one another and, through affection and a common mind, realize that they have cause to exert social influence.

What becomes clear from this, first of all, is that world literature does not exclusively mean aesthetics, that is, the classical triad of lyric, epic and drama. Rather, scientists of every kind also seem to contribute to world literature. Yet this remains an inadequate definition of Goethe's concept of world literature. World literature in the sense he means it emerges when literary figures get to know one another and, 'through affection and a common mind, realize that they have cause to exert social influence.' But even this definition does not provide a full answer to the question of what constituted Goethe's concept of world literature. One year before his death, on 25 April 1831, in what we would nowadays call a draft speech for Chancellor Müller, he distinguished between different epochs of social learning: the third epoch, the 'more general' one, is followed, according to him, by a fourth and final one:

For it [the more general one] to become universal, that requires good fortune and favour . . . For while we have loyally fostered the same through all those eras, for many years, so it requires a higher influence to bring about that which we are experiencing today: the unification of all educated circles, which other-wise only touched upon one another, the acknowledgement of one purpose, the conviction of how necessary it is to inform oneself about the current state of the world, with regard to both actual events and ideas.

World literature, which for centuries had been over-inflated, contested or scorned, reveals itself in the eyes of its originator, the so-called classic writer Johann Wolfgang von Goethe, to be nothing other than the necessity for an indi-vidual 'to inform [him or herself] about the the current state of the world, with regard to both actual events and ideas.' Or, to put it another way: world litera-ture exists as soon as the individual informs him- or herself about the state of the world. It was Heinrich Heine who regarded the debate about cosmopoli-tanism as *the* German contribution to the political debates of the time. And it was also he who said if the harmony and opposition of cosmopolitanism and nationality in Germany is forgotten, then the lights in Germany will all go out. This is exactly what happened. The National Socialists labelled all the people they intended to exterminate in gas chambers – Jews, Communists, gypsies – 'cosmopolitans'.

5   Dewey 1954: 147; see also Krüger 1996.
6   Jürgen Habermas argues as follows:

For the sought-after establishment of a cosmopolitan order would not mean that violations of human rights would be judged and combated *immediately* in accordance with moral standards; instead they would be prosecuted like criminal acts within national legal systems. A thoroughgoing juridification of international relations is not possible without established procedures for resolving conflicts. The institutionalization of these legal procedures will itself preserve the judicial processing of human rights violations against a moral de-differentiation of law and prevent a sweeping, *unmediated* moral stigmatization of 'enemies'.

Achieving such a cosmopolitan condition does not require a world state that enjoys a monopoly on the means of violence or a global government. The minimum requirements, however, are a functioning Security Council, the binding jurisdiction of an international criminal court and the complementing of the General Assembly of government representatives by a 'second chamber' made up of representatives of world citizens. Since these reforms of the United Nations are still a long way off, insisting on the distinction between juridification and moralization remains a correct, but double-edged response. For as long as human rights are comparatively weakly institutionalized at the global level, the boundary between law and morality can easily become blurred, as we see in the present case [NATO's military action against Serbia in the Kosovo conflict]. With a deadlocked security Council, NATO can only appeal to the moral validity of international law – to norms for which no effective, internationally recognized institutions of application and enforcement of law exist.

The under-institutionalization of cosmopolitan law finds expression, for example, in the yawning gap between the legitimacy of peacekeeping and peacemaking interventions and their effectiveness. (Habermas, forthcoming)

7 Niklas Luhmann argues as follows:

Lawyers typically think that violations of norms can only be established if the norms themselves already exist. However, sociologists of law, and anthropologists of law in particular, also recognize the converse case: that norms emerge when expectations are disappointed and spectacular occurrences make it clear that this is not acceptable. This applies, for example, to torture in prisons, political murder, perhaps also soon to serious violations of nuclear security or of minimum standards of ecological prudence. It applies today to so-called 'ethnic cleansing', to the expulsion of large populations from their homelands, something that was practised on a large scale in 1945, without legal scruples being voiced. It applies to the legal condemnation of war crimes – independently of whether or not appropriate laws existed at the time of the crime in the legal system of the country concerned (entailing, in other words, a spectacular contravention of the equally valid rule that criminal law should not be brought into effect retrospectively). It certainly is possible, then, to observe processes whereby worldwide norms emerge. Perhaps ethics is just the wrong word for it, because it is not simply an issue of matters of conscience or of moral regard – it is much more about a kind of law for which the possibility of sanctions is sought. (Luhmann 1999: 252)

One might say it is about a cosmopolitan regime whose normativity and binding character come to be clearly established through the process of global public reflexion about violations of it.

8   For example, in 1909 there were about thirty-seven supranational governmental organizations and about 176 non-governmental organizations, whereas in 1989 about 300 supranational governmental organizations and 4,624 non-governmental organizations were jostling for space in the transnational arena. In the middle of the nineteenth century it is possible to identify two or three conferences or congresses organized and financed by supranational organizations; since 1998, around 4,000 such conferences have been taking place every year. When one calls to mind the colourful hurly-burly of the Rio de Janeiro Earth Climate Conference in 1992 and the conference for women's rights in Beijing in 1995, and sees them in the context of this historic leap into the transnational era of political action, then the mere fact that these conferences took place at all – and not simply their potential failure – bears witness to the binding force of a global awareness of risk (see Held et al. 1999).

9   Cf. Keck and Sikkink 1998; Risse et al. 1999; Beetham 1995.

10 Gill 1995; Strange 1996; Narr and Schubert 1994; Hirsch 1995; Altvater and Mahnkopf 1996; Schirm 1999.

11 Andre Gunter Frank (1998), in his exciting book *ReOrient: Global Economy in the Asian Age* (which, by way of an aside, is the most incisive and historically most closely argued anti-Max Weber text I have yet laid eyes on), demonstrates that the equation of historical studies with national historical studies is subject to similar errors and mistakes that can only be systematically revealed and corrected in the context of a cosmopolitan opening of historical studies, that is, through its metamorphosis into *global* historical studies. However, to rule out any misunderstanding, what Frank calls the 'global perspective' does *not* have the same meaning as what I call the 'cosmopolitan perspective'. The latter does not have to be 'global', it can be transnational, 'glocal', etc. In making the case for his 'global perspective' Frank refers to the fact that methodological nationalism (to use my language) gets entangled in two sources of error in particular. First, it commits the circular error of *internal* causality, and, second, it restricts historical developments to the either/or of evolution or decline.

The principal intent is to show why we *need* a global perspective and approach, which we require not only on the history of the world economy itself, but also so that we can locate its subordinate and participant sectors, regions, countries, or whatever segments and processes within the global whole of which they are only parts. Concretely, we need a global perspective to appreciate, understand, account for, explain – in a word, perceive – 'the Rise of the West', 'the development of capitalism', 'the hegemony of Europe', 'the rise and fall of great powers', including formerly 'Great' Britain, the United States, and the former Soviet Union, 'the Third-worldization of Los Angeles', 'the East Asian miracle' ... None of these were caused only or even primarily through the structure or interaction of forces 'internal' to any of the above. All of them were part and parcel of the structure and development of a single world economic system. (p. 4)

Frank turns the Eurocentric self-image held by Europe and European social science the right way up again: '. . . it was the world that made Europe' (p. 3). 'Europe climbed up on the back of Asia, then stood on Asian shoulders – temporarily' (p. 5). Frank's world historical analysis also demonstrates that (to put it in my terms again) the distinction between methodological nationalism and cosmopolitanism is a distinction between wrong and right historical studies and not primarily a normative or political issue.

12   These questions will be taken up again in the final chapter.

Chapter 3   Global Domestic Politics Changes the Rules

1   In this chapter I have made use of the following literature: Arendt 1970, 1993; Beck 1998a; Brace and Hoffman 1997; Bredow 2001; Cerny 2000; Connolly 1995; Cutler et al. 1999; Dworkin 1986; Eppler 1998; Goverde et al. 2000; Günther and Randeria 2002; Hall 1999; Harvey 2000; Höffe 1994; Holzer 1999, 2000; Kaldor 1999; Kant 1964, 1996; Krasner 1999; Kriesi 2001; Leutner 2000; Linklater 1998a, 1998b; Luttwak 1999; Mann 1997, 2001; Mittelman 2000; Palan 2000; Palan and Abbott 1999; Pettman 1996; Picciotto 1991; Pieterse 2000; Randeria 1999b, 2001; Schumpeter 1919; Strange 1996; Teivainen 2000; Walker 2000; Weber 1972; Wolf 2000; Young 1994.

2   The powerful influence of transnational corporations (TNCs) and associated foreign direct investments (FDI) continues to increase (Köhler 2002). Thus, for example, while there were once 7,000 TNCs in fourteen large economies in the developed world, this had increased by 1990 to 24,000, while in 1993 there was a total of 37,000 TNCs with more than 170,000 subsidiaries worldwide. However, these figures are still too low, as transnational activities often take place in the form of subcontracting, franchising, licensing or strategic partnerships and as a result do not necessarily appear in the FDI statistics. There is a strong concentration of FDIs (a) within the triad Europe–USA–Japan and (b) within the largest TNCs – the 100 largest TNCs are responsible for 14 per cent of FDIs. Foreign direct investments are made easier by multilateral treaties (e.g. World Bank 'guidelines') on the one hand, and by bilateral treaties at national level (often leaning towards liberalism) on the other. As far as the regional distribution of FDIs is concerned, direct investments in developed countries do drop off from time to time (due to slower growth and, in some cases, recession) but are on the increase in developing countries (boosted by access to new resources and movements towards liberalism and privatization).

Whereas FDIs in the secondary sector show a marked decline in comparison with robust and growing FDIs in the service sector, FDIs increased in the primary sector in developed countries as well in the 1980s.

At the same time changes are also taking place in organizational structures (spatially separated regional company headquarters, product centres and functional company headquarters, as well as divided responsibilities). There is also an ever increasing degree of temporary collaborations between companies. In general, these emerging links between companies are described quite well by the term 'network'. A distinction exists between integrated international production at company level and at national level (thus about one-third of private assets worldwide is controlled by transnational corporations). At the national level there is both 'horizontal integration' (exchange of goods and services) and 'vertical integration' (international production of goods and services), although the trend – to a large extent driven by the activities of TNCs – is towards vertical methods of integration.

All this means that conventional concepts and approaches to the subject – for example, the concept of which country a company is from – are no longer as telling as they once were, owing especially to the complicated division of labour that exists between companies in different countries, and the loss of autonomy of individual units within transnational company systems.

International integration of companies also leads to difficulties in terms of levying taxes; a potential problem that may crop up here is that of establishing the extent to which a parent company and its subsidiary should be considered as independent companies.

3　It is surely no coincidence, but rather a sign of the predictive power of Arendt's diagnosis, that in elucidating her theory she deals especially with the communist, East European system of violence and formulates sentences that can be read as an anticipation of the 'peaceful revolution':

> In a contest of violence against violence the superiority of the government has always been absolute; but this superiority lasts only as long as the power structure of the government is intact – that is, as long as commands are obeyed and the army or police forces are prepared to use their weapons. When this is no longer the case, the situation changes abruptly. Not only is the rebellion not put down, but the arms themselves change hands – sometimes, as in the Hungarian revolution, within a few hours. . . . Only after this has happened, when the disintegration of the government in power has permitted the rebels to arm themselves, can one speak of an 'armed uprising' . . . Where commands are no longer obeyed, the means of violence are of no use; and the question of this obedience is not decided by the command–obedience relation but by opinion, and, of course, by the number of those who share it. Everything depends on the power behind the violence. The sudden dramatic breakdown of power that ushers in revolutions reveals in a flash how civil obedience – to laws, to rulers, to institutions – is but the outward manifestation of support and consent. . . . Only the development of robot soldiers . . . could change this fundamental ascendancy of power over violence. (Arendt 1970: 48ff.)

4　The OECD offers a good example of the way in which declarations that sound sophisticated can be turned into discriminating practices. While the language of the OECD unreservedly signals neutrality, its mode of interpretation and implementation in concrete situations is often restrictive or even openly Eurocentric. For example, the legitimacy of OECD intervention in the domestic affairs of Eastern European states was announced and enacted in the Geneva Agreement of July 1991. It states that 'issues of national minorities . . . are generally part of the legitimate concern of the international community and in this respect never exclusively constitute the domestic affairs of the state concerned.' In order to contain the far-reaching repercussions of these statements and also to quell resistance against this agreement in the Western camp, a highly flexible interpretation of 'national minorities' was introduced. This part of the report establishes that 'not all ethnic, cultural, linguistic or religious differences necessarily lead to the creation of national minorities.' In this way it was possible to bracket off the issue of minorities in those Western states where they had been classified as 'non-national', so that, for example, the rights of Native Americans in the USA, Turks in Germany, Arabs in France and Asian and African-Caribbean groups in Britain could be removed from the international political agenda.

5 Max Weber identified three types of 'belief in legitimacy' and, correspondingly, 'legitimate domination': 'traditional', 'charismatic' and 'legal' domination. Legality means 'constitutional' domination; here, 'obedience is owed to the legally established impersonal order. It extends to the persons exercising the authority of office under it by virtue of the formal legality of their commands' (Weber 1978: 215–16). Thus legitimacy may be based on legality, but is not necessarily so.

6 As Daniel J. Elazar (1998, 2001) argues, Bodin laid the foundations for a theory of statehood, whereas Althusius, at about the same time, developed a no less systematic theory of federalism that deserves to be rediscovered and brought up to date for the post-national global age.

7 Any talk of a future cosmopolitan state (cosmopolitan regime) requires some historical underpinning and ought therefore to be defined by and grounded in its specific historical features. One way of fulfilling this purpose would be to devise, by analogy to comparative research and nationalism theory, a historically comparative field of *'research on empire'* and to establish corresponding research enterprises, perhaps European ones, perhaps transnational ones. These would explore such questions as: what distinguishes the forerunners of the cosmopolitan regime from the same, and what links them? After all, the dream of 'one world' is a remarkably old-fashioned one. Indeed, it is considerably older than national romanticism, dating back to those universal empires – of Hammurabi and Alexander, Justinian and Harun al-Rashid, Genghis Khan and Charles V, Napoleon and the British Empire – that declared themselves to be the bearers of civilization, under which banner they mounted crusades against those from 'different cultures', 'backward peoples' and 'barbarians'. What is common to them all is something to which the flag bearers of the cosmopolitan regime today also lay claim, namely, that they speak a language that binds all people together – the language of human rights, for example – and thereby embody a 'higher culture' that has no limits, whereas the majority of their subject and subjugated populations live within more restricted cultural horizons and are only partially influenced by such noble goals and traditions. Can, or – to be more precise – *how* can, the cosmopolitan regime avoid the snares of this sort of cultural imperialism? Can a cosmopolitan state really bring together people who speak different languages and have different histories, religions, origins and futures, without the imperial factor? Is it not inevitable that any transnational – and therefore, in particular, global – culture will ultimately be based on the patronage of a hegemonic power? Does all talk of a 'cosmopolitan regime' not amount to an act of courtship towards US Americanization and hegemony?

Incidentally, this kind of comparative research on empire might demonstrate that it is *polyethnicity* that constitutes the norm in world history, rather than ethnic-national homogeneity. People of differing origins have always been thrown together into an ethnically plural and hierarchically organized political order by civilizations.

In the last lecture I analyzed the strange case of national ethnic unity, a barbarous ideal, never perfectly realized in western Europe, yet enthusiastically embraced at exactly the time when western European nations were building world-girdling empires, where diverse peoples met and mingled on a scale never equaled before. The consequent polyethnic hierarchy in all the lands of European expansion contrasted sharply with the ideal of national unity that prevailed in the part of Europe most active in imperial venturing. Such an antithesis was intrinsically unstable, because the special conditions supporting the ideal and partial reality of national ethnic unity ... were transitory, whereas the factors promoting ethnic mixing were enduring. (McNeill 1986)

8   I have taken the following approach, of locating economic globalization's losers in the national context, from Kriesi (2001); see also Grande and Kriesi (2002).
9   This has been formulated by example in the social theory of Max Weber and Talcott Parsons.
10   His point is that decisions do *not* constitute the source of politics, that they are not its central element. Rather, it is controversy over their *consequences*, which irritate and alarm the nervous system of cultural and institutional norms, that creates politics and the public sphere.
11   See chs. 1 to 7.
12   See parts of ch. 1, ch. 2 section 1, ch. 3 section 8 and, in particular, ch. 8.
13   Put in more general terms – that is, not applied solely to the sphere of politics – this is the basic idea of 'reflexive modernization' (Beck et al. 2001).

Chapter 4   Power and Counter-Power in the Global Age

1   In this chapter I have used the following literature: Amin 1998; Altvater and Mahnkopf 1996; Boyer and Drache 1996; Dunning 1993, 1997; Bornschier 2002; Dunkley 1999; Drucker 1997; Easterly 2001; Eichengreen 2000; Featherstone 2000; Frieden 2000; Frieden and Lake 2000; Gill 1995; Goldstein et al. 2000; Gilpin 1987, 2001; Goodman and Pauly 2000; Greider 1997; Cerny 1995; Cooter and Ulen 1999; Günther and Randeria 2002; Hutchinson 1966; IMF 2000; Jessop 1999a, 1999b; Jones 2000; Koch 1995; Korten 1995; Krasner 2000; Krueger 1998; Krugman and Venables 1995; Krugman and Obstfeld 2000; Kindleberger 2000; Lane and Ersson 2002; Lake 2000; Ohmae 1990; Randeria 1999c, 2001; Sassen 1991; Sen 1999; Stalker 2000; Stein 1995; Stiglitz 2002; Smart 1995; Streeck 1998a, 1998b; Stubbs and Underhill 2000; Teivainen 2000; Waddington 1999.
2   Of course, there is always something arbitrary about this restriction to groups of actors. One could imagine, for example, extending the circle to include the Catholic Church on the one side and organized crime (the Mafia) on the other. After all, the Catholic Church is a 'global player' in terms of its origins; and even in the present day it treads in the footsteps of the Communist Internationale in

certain respects, as far as criticism of the neo-liberal global market regime is concerned. At any rate, the pope and his 'transnational corporation' is the only remaining independent internationale when it comes to criticizing 'the idolatory of the pure market' as a global social order (Beck and Willms 20003).

3   I speak here of an initial contribution because, in this and the following chapters, the *strategic military* component of cosmopolitan realism is relegated to the sidelines. Centre stage is taken instead by the new global political economy, which overcomes the shortcomings of a realism restricted within the national outlook and unable to do analytic justice to political economy issues.

4   If, however, self-exclusion is no longer an option for states, then all that remains for the majority of them is the role of 'courtesan state', one which offers itself and the services of its women and men for sale to the rich states of the world, or else the role of a state 'tax haven', using the power of the state to prevent other states from gaining access to capital flows.

5   It should not be assumed here that a kind of universalization or Americanization is being established in national arenas via the transnational route, through the back door of the new non-state, global business legislature. It is certainly correct to say that the basic premises of liberal political theory and jurisprudence are being corroded, that the 'congruence of territory, state and law is collapsing' (Randeria 2001). However, this by no means leads (certainly not necessarily so) to the emergence of a universal global 'legal culture' (of the sort frequently implied in the neo-institutionalist thinking of Meyer et al.). Instead, a *plurality* of legal orders co-exists within individual political units – not only in places where one has long suspected it, namely in the colonial and postcolonial context, but precisely in the so-called strong states of Europe and the USA (Günther and Randeria 2002). The growing prominence of supranational legal orders and regimes, international organizations for conflict regulation and law-making companies, as well as the direct interventions of the World Trade Organization, along with other supranational 'consulting organizations', have all created a complex, ambiguous and polyvalent structure of legal spaces and law-making, adjudicating authorities in which responsibilities and boundaries frequently overlap within and between national territories (Randeria 2001).

6   For detail on this, see Dezalay and Garth (1996).

Chapter 5   State Strategies between Renationalization and Transnationalization

1   In this chapter I have used the following literature: Palan and Abbott 1999; Palan 2000; Bernauer 1998, 2000b; Busch and Plümper 1999; Busch et al. 1994; Barro 1996; Bornschier 2002; Duara 1999; Ellwein 1992; Elkins 1995; Evans 1997; Esser 1999; Fuat 1996; Genschel 2000; Grande 1999, 2001a, 2001b; Grande and Risse 2000; Held 2000; Héritier et al. 1994; Herold et al. 1998; Holton 1998; Jönnson et al. 2000; Kaiser and Schwarz 2000; Katzenstein 1985; Keohane 1989; Kohler-Koch 1998; Laïdi 1998; Luard 1990; Martin and Schumann 1996; Messner 1998; Nölke 2000; Portes 1997; Reinicke 1997; Reinicke et al. 2000; Risse et al. 1999; Risse-Kappen 1995; Young 1986; Schulze and Ursprung 1999; Suter 1999; Weiss 1998; Wolf 2000; Youngs 1999; Yoshikazu 2000; Zürn 1998a, 1998b; Zürn and Wolf 2000; Robinson 1996; Rosenau 1980; Rosenau and Czempiel 1992; Ruggie

1998; Ruigrok and van Tulder 1995; Scott 2000; Schirm 1999; Schlichte and Wilke 2000.

2   On this, see section 5.5, on 'Strategies aimed at repoliticizing politics'.

3   On this point, see various writings by Manuel Castells; Wilhelm Reich similarly distinguishes between 'symbolic analytics' – that is, jobs in which information technology is used reflexively – and the new 'information technology mass labour force', which does the low-skilled, easily replaceable work.

4   I have taken this typology of state strategies and the line of argument that follows from it from Palan and Abbott (1999).

5   See the relevant article by Jacqueline Hénard in *Die Zeit*, no. 26, 21 June 2000, p. 10.

6   On this and the following account, see Viner 1950; Palan and Abbott 1999: 61; Frieden and Lake 2000.

7   See also the closing chapter on this.

Chapter 6   Strategies of Civil Society Movements

1   In this chapter I have made use of the following literature: Allan et al. 2000; Altvater et al. 1999; Anheier et al. 2001; Anderson 2000; Bello et al. 2000; Bernauer 2000a; Boli and Thomas 1999; Bhabha 1999; Broad and Cavanagh 2000; Curbach 2001; Grundmann 2001; Guidry et al. 2000; Janett 1999; Keck and Sikkink 1998; Kriesberg 1997; Scholte and Schnabel 2002; Szerszynski and Toogood 2000; Smith 1997, 2001; Starr 2000.

Chapter 7   Who Wins?

1   In this chapter I have used the following literature: Appadurai 1999; Arendt 1958, 1993; Beck 2000b; Berger and Dore 1996; Berkovitch 2000; Broad and Cavanagh 2000; Castles 2000; Doyle 2000; Eriksen 1993; Giddens 1994; Held 2000; Hobbes 1996; Holmes 2000; Janett 1999; Miller and Slater 2000; Münkler 2001; Patomäki 2001; Patterson 1998; Pettman 1996; Scharpf 1999; Schmitt 1983, 1932; Stichweh 2000; Weber 1988.

2   This hypothesis, however, could and should be subjected to empirical exploration in appropriate case studies.

3   'What is crucial is that only those changes in the basic institutions of the first modernity which do not violate the basic principles themselves ought to be judged to be "modernization". In relation to the sphere of statehood, this could mean that the starting point is taken to be not the nation-state (in the sense of the "Westphalian state") or its constitutive principles (territoriality, sovereignty), but rather modernity's intention that *collective* solutions should be found to *collective* problems beyond traditional forms of shared living (family, guilds, clans). This could be taken as the basic principle of modern statehood. The first modernity in the sense of the theory of reflexive modernization was characterized by the fact that a very particular *institutional* solution was found for this function of collective problem-solving, namely, that of the *nation-state*. The emergence and development of the modern nation-state was characterized by a dual assumption: first, the assumption that collective problems can and must be solved by the *state* (in particular, the dispute was about which problems were in

fact collective problems that could be dealt with better by individuals); and, second, the assumption, indivisibly linked to the first, that the *national* level is the best possible standard for the organization of modern statehood. The crucial point is that both assumptions seem to be losing their validity. This means, on the one hand, that, under certain conditions, individual persons and private organizations are willing and able to solve collective problems; in other words, that the state loses its monopoly on the capacity to solve collective problems; and it means, on the other, that the nation-state no longer necessarily constitutes the best possible framework for action for solving collective problems, and that "governance" in the sense of effective social "problem-solving" increasingly takes place beyond and beneath the nation-state. The result is an emerging system of complex governance in which different levels and different forms of governance are differentiated *and* integrated institutionally. In other words: governance occurs in ever more complex configurations of public and private actors and institutions whose responsibilities and resources are distributed across several levels and across different boundaries' (Grande 2000: 1ff.).

4   Jürgen Habermas (2001b) has shrewdly criticized this in his dispute with Carl Schmitt (1983), on whose work this position ought to be based.

5   On the issues and contradictions associated with the 'modern counter-modernity', see Beck (1996, ch. 14).

6   The main point is this: intra- and inter-state polarizations overlap with and interpenetrate one another so that, behind the old institutional façades, new kinds of conflicts and volatilities of global domestic politics take shape within and between specific national contexts. In order to distinguish between different forms of 'both/and', it is necessary to develop a logic of *inclusive* distinguishing. To put it another way, the 'both/and' itself requires clear conceptual distinctions for it even to be recognizable and verifiable – or falsifiable – as such.

   In this sense, what in this book is called 'cosmopolitan regime' can be defined by means of a *doubled politicization of the 'non'*: *non*-inclusion in a central political authority, *non*-exclusion in the national. The dynamics associated with this – dynamics that undermine, cross and mix boundaries – can then be defined more precisely as domain-specific pluralism, plural compromise, hierarchically ordered pluralism, unstructured plurality, an overlapping of the alternatives, boundary dissolution, or synthesis, sequentialization and reflexive decisionism. These conceptual forms of the 'both/and' have been worked out within the framework of the special research area 'reflexive modernization' by Christoph Lau in particular, among others, using the example of issues and research projects in the sociology of science and technology; but they can certainly be applied to other sets of issues as well, especially to the relationship between the national and the cosmopolitan outlook (cf. Grande and Kriesi 2002).

7   See ch. 1, sections 9, 10, 11; ch. 2; ch. 7, sections 1 and 2, as well as the following.

8   See chs. 1, 3, 4, 5, 6 and 8.

9   See ch. 5; ch. 6, sections 1 and 2.

10   See ch. 7, section 4.

11   See ch. 1, sections 4 and 8; chs. 5; ch. 7, section 5.

12   See ch. 3, section 13; ch. 7; and ch. 8 in particular.

13 Engaging in debate with the authors of Critical Theory is an undertaking in its own right that goes beyond the scope of the present argument.

Chapter 8 A Brief Funeral Oration

1 In this chapter I have used the following literature: Archibugi et al. 1998; Arndt 1845; Assheuer and Perger 2000; Beck 2001; Beetham 1995, 1999; Boyarin and Boyarin 1993; Brunkhorst et al. 1999; Benhabib 1992; Cheah and Robbins 1998; Connolly 1995; Coulmas 1990; Cwerner 2000; Dworkin 1986; Falk 1995; Forsythe 2000; Habermas 1998, 2001a, 2001b; Harvey 2000; Held 2002, unpublished manuscript; Horstmann 1976; Linklater 1998a, 1998b; Nussbaum 1996; Ottmann 2001; McCarthy 1999; Kuper 2000; Waldron 2000.

2 The passage from de Maistre was quoted by Brunctière; these quotations by critics of cosmopolitanism are taken from the book by Peter Coulmas (1990: 421f.).

3 The distinction between universalist universalism and *contextual* universalism is useful here (Beck 2000c: 77–86).

4 See Harvey (2000: 73).

5 'Cosmopolitanism and internationalism have the same intellectual origin; they are in the same global historical tradition; they are varieties of the same human yearning and pursue the same goals: peace through the unity of humanity. This universalist and pacifist motif is determined by the history of theories and activities of all internationales, the "red" (socialist), the polemically named "black" (church) and the "grey" (liberal). The only thing to change was the language used. In place of the somewhat romantic cosmopolitan creed "all people will become brothers" was the class-struggle slogan of the communist manifesto, "Proletarians of the world, unite!" (Coulmas 1990: 485f.).

6 The 'democratic' legitimation of human rights 'from below', through the eye of the needle of nation-state consent, is not only the same as saying that nation-states should disempower themselves; it is also equivalent to demanding that human rights should be used in a non-genuine, instrumental way in the interests of the nation-state.

7 In this sense, one can see the cosmopolitan regime, as Jürgen Habermas does, as a 'tradition-making project', whose democratic sources of legitimation

prove themselves during crucial times of productive change. Times such as these give people the rare experience of emancipation and leave in their wake the memory of an instructive historical example. Contemporaries become aware that groups previously discriminated against have acquired a voice of their own and that previously underprivileged classes have been enabled to take their destiny into their own hands. Once the struggles over interpretation have quietened down, all parties will acknowledge that the reforms – although strongly contested initially – are a genuine achievement. (Habermas 2001b: 144)

References and Bibliography

Adam, B. (1995): *Timewatch: The Social Analysis of Time*. Cambridge: Polity.

Adam, B. (2003): Reflexive Modernization Temporized, *Theory, Culture and Society* 20/2, pp. 59–78.

Adam, B., Beck, U., and van Loon, J. (eds) (2000): *The Risk Society and Beyond*. London: Sage.

Agnew, J. (1998): *Geopolitics: Re-visioning World Politics*. London and New York: Routledge.

Ahmed, A. S., and Donnan, H. (1994): *Islam, Globalization, and Postmodernity*. London and New York: Routledge.

Ake, C. (1996): *Democracy and Development in Africa*. Washington, DC: Brookings Institution.

Albrow, M. (1996): *The Global Age*. Cambridge: Polity.

Allan, S., Adam, B., and Carter, C. (eds) (2000): *Environmental Risks and the Media*. London and New York: Routledge.

Almond, G. A. (1999): Review Article: The International-National Connection, *British Journal of Political Science* 19/2, pp. 237–59.

Alt, J. E., and Gillican, M. (2000): The Political Economy of Trading States, in Frieden, J. A., and Lake, D. A. (eds): *International Political Economy*. London and New York: Routledge, pp. 327–42.

Altvater, E., and Mahnkopf, B. (1996): *Grenzen der Globalisierung: Ökologie, Ökonomie und Politik in der Weltgesellschaft*. Münster: Westfälisches Dampfboot.

Altvater, E., Brunnengräber, A., Haake, M., and Walk, H. (eds) (1999): *Vernetzt und verstrickt: Nicht-Regierungs-Organisationen als gesellschaftliche Produktivkraft*. Münster: Westfälisches Dampfboot.

Alund, A., and Schierup, C.-U. (1991): *Paradoxes of Multiculturalism: Essays on Swedish Society*. Aldershot: Avebury.

Amason, J. P. (1990): Nationalism, Globalization and Modernity, *Theory, Culture and Society* 7, pp. 207–36.

Amin, Z. (1998): *Capitalism in the Age of Globalization*. London and New York: Zed.

Anderson, A. (2000): Environmental Pressure Politics and the 'Risk Society', in Allan, S., Adam, B., and Carter, C. (eds): *Environmental Risks and the Media*. London and New York: Routledge, pp. 93–105.

Anderson, B. (1996): *Die Erfindung der Nation*. Frankfurt am Main: Deutsche Verlagsanstalt.

Anheier, H., Glasius, M., and Kaldor, M. (2001): Introduction, in *Global Civil Society*. Oxford: Oxford University Press, pp. 3–22.

Appadurai, A. (1998): Globale ethnische Räume, in Beck, U. (ed.): *Perspektiven der Weltgesellschaft*. Frankfurt am Main: Suhrkamp, pp. 11–40.

Appadurai, A. (1999): Dead Certainty: Ethnic Violence in the Era of Globalization, in Meyer, B., and Geschiere, P. (eds): *Globalization and Identity*. Oxford: Blackwell, pp. 305–25.

Appadurai, A. (2002): Grassroots, Globalization and the Research Imagination, in Vincent, J. (ed.): *The Anthropology of Politics*. Oxford: Blackwell, pp. 271–84.

Archibugi, D. (2000): Cosmopolitical Democracy, *New Left Review* 4, pp. 137–50.

Archibugi, D., and Held, D. (eds) (1995): *Cosmopolitan Democracy*. Cambridge: Polity.

Archibugi, D., Held, D., and Köhler, M. (eds) (1998): *Re-imagining Political Community*. Cambridge: Polity.

Arendt, H. (1958): Freiheit und Politik, in *Zwischen Vergangenheit und Zukunft*. Munich: Piper, pp. 201–26.

Arendt, H. (1970): *On Violence*. New York: Harcourt, Brace & World.

Arendt, H. (1993): *Was ist Politik? Aus dem Nachlaß*. ed. U. Ludz. Munich: Piper.

Arendt, H., and Jaspers, K. (1993): *Briefwechsel 1926–1969*, ed. L. Köhler and H. Saner. Munich: Piper.

Arndt, E. M. (1845): Über Volkshass und über den Gebrauch einer fremden Sprache, in *E. M. Arndts Schriften für und an seine lieben Deutschen*. 1. Teil. Leipzig: Fleischer.

Ashley, R. K. (1984): The Poverty of Neorealism, *International Organization* 38, pp. 225–86.

Assheuer, T., and Perger, W. A. (eds) (2000): *Was wird aus der Demokratie?* Opladen: Westdeutscher Verlag.

Atkinson, A. (1999): *Is Rising Inequality Inevitable? A Critique of the Transatlantic Consensus*. Helsinki: UN University and WIDER.

Barber, B. R. (1995): *Jihad versus McWorld: How Globalism and Tribalism are Reshaping the World*. New York: Random House.

Barro, R. (1996): Democracy and Growth, *Journal of Economic Growth* 1/1, pp. 1–27.

Barry, B. (1999): Statism and Nationalism: A Cosmopolitan Critique, in Shapiro, I., and Brilmayer, L. (eds): *Global Justice*. New York: New York University Press, pp. 12–66.

Bauman, Z. (1998): *Globalization: The Human Consequences*. Cambridge: Polity.

Bauman, Z. (1999): *In Search of Politics*. Cambridge: Polity.

Bauman, Z. (2000): *Liquid Modernity*. Cambridge: Polity.

Beck, U. (1988): *Gegengifte: Die organisierte Unverantwortlichkeit*. Frankfurt am Main: Suhrkamp.

Beck, U. (1992): *Risk Society: Towards a New Modernity*. London: Sage.

Beck, U. (1996): *The Reinvention of Politics: Rethinking Modernity in the Global Social Order*. Cambridge: Polity.

Beck, U. (ed.) (1998a): *Politik der Globalisierung*. Frankfurt am Main: Suhrkamp.

Beck, U. (1998b): Weltbürger aller Länder, vereinigt Euch!, *Die Zeit*, No. 30, 16 July, p. 43.

Beck, U. (2000a): The Cosmopolitan Perspective: Sociology for the Second Age of Modernity, *British Journal of Sociology* 51, pp. 79–106.

Beck, U. (2000b): *World Risk Society.* Cambridge: Polity.

Beck, U. (2000c): *What is Globalization?.* Cambridge: Polity.

Beck, U. (2001): Redefining Power in the Global Age: Eight Theses, *Dissent,* fall, pp. 83–90.

Beck, U. (2002a): Cosmopolitan Society and its Enemies, *Theory, Culture and Society* 19/1–2, pp. 17–44.

Beck, U. (2002b): The Terrorist Threat: World Risk Society Revisited, *Theory, Culture and Society* 19/4, pp. 39–55.

Beck, U. (2004): *Der kosmopolitische Blick, oder: Krieg ist Frieden.* Frankfurt am Main: Suhrkamp.

Beck, U., and Beck-Gernsheim, E. (2001): *Individualization – Institutionalized Individualism and its Social and Political Consequences.* London: Sage.

Beck, U., and Willms, J. (2003): *Conversations with Ulrich Beck.* Cambridge: Polity [adapted from the German: *Freiheit oder Kapitalismus,* Frankfurt am Main, Suhrkamp, 2000].

Beck, U., Bonss, W., and Lau C. (2001): Theorie reflexiver Modernisierung, in: Beck, U., and Bonss, W. (eds): *Die Modernisierung der Moderne.* Frankfurt am Main: Suhrkamp.

Beck, U., Giddens, A., and Lash, S. (1994): *Reflexive Modernization – Politics, Tradition and Aesthetics in the Modern Social Order.* Cambridge: Polity.

Beck-Gernsheim, E. (2000): *Juden, Deutsche und andere Erinnerungslandschaften – Im Dschungel ethnischer Kategorien.* Frankfurt am Main: Suhrkamp.

Beetham, D. (1995): Human Rights and Political Theory: What Future for Economic and Social Rights?, *Political Studies* 43 [special issue], pp. 41–60.

Beetham, D. (ed.) (1999): *Democracy and Human Rights.* Cambridge: Polity.

Beisheim, M., et al. (1999): *Im Zeitalter der Globalisierung? Thesen und Daten zur gesellschaftlichen und politischen Denationalisierung.* Baden-Baden: Nomos.

Bello, W., Buller, N., and Malhotra, K. (eds) (2000) *Global Finance: New Thinking on Regulating Speculative Capital Markets.* London: Zed.

Benhabib, S. (1992): *Situating the Self.* Cambridge: Polity.

Benjamin, W. (1980): Über den Begriff der Geschichte, in *Illuminationen,* Frankfurt am Main: Suhrkamp, pp. 251–62.

Berger, S., and Dore, R. (eds) (1996): *National Diversity and Global Capitalism.* Ithaca, NY: Cornell University Press.

Berkovitch, N. (2000): The Emergence and Transformation of the International Women's Movement, in Lechner, F., and Boli, J. (eds): *The Globalization Reader.* Oxford: Blackwell.

Bernauer, T. (1998): Globalisierung und staatliche Handlungsspielräume, in Ruloff, D. (ed.): *Globalisierung – eine Standortbestimmung.* Chur and Zurich: Rüegger.

Bernauer, T. (2000a): Protecting Consumers in an Open World Economy, *Swiss Political Science Review* 6/2, pp. 79–99.

Bernauer, T. (2000b): *Staaten im Weltmarkt.* Opladen: Leske & Budrich.

Berry, A., Bourguignon, F., and Morris, C. (1991): Global Economic Inequality and its Trends Since 1950, in Osberg, L. (ed.): *Economic Inequality and Poverty: International Perspectives.* Armonk, NY, and London: M. E. Sharpe, pp. 60–91.

Beynon, J., and Dunkerley, D. (eds) (2000): *Globalization: The Reader.* London: Athlone.

Bhabba, J. (1999): Enforcing the Human Rights of Citizens and Non-Citizens in the Era of Maastricht: Some Reflections on the Importance of States, in Meyer, B., and Geschiere, P. (eds): *Globalization and Identity*. Oxford: Blackwell, pp. 97–124.

Boli, J., and Thomas, G. M. (eds) (1999): *Constructing World Culture: International Non-Governmental Organizations since 1875*. Stanford, CA: Stanford University Press.

Bornschier, V. (1988): *Westliche Gesellschaft im Wandel*. Frankfurt am Main: Campus.

Bornschier, V. (2002): *Weltgesellschaft – grundlegende soziale Wandlung*. Zurich: Loreto.

Boswell, T. (1999): Hegemony and Bifurcation Points in World History, in Bornschier, V., and Chase-Dunn, C. (eds): *The Future of Global Conflict*. London: Sage, pp. 263–84.

Bourguignon, F., and Morrisson, C. (1992): *Adjustment and Equity in Developing Countries: A New Approach*. Paris: OECD.

Boyarin, D., and Boyarin, J. (1993): Diaspora: Generation and the Ground of Jewish Identity, *Critical Inquiry* 19/4, pp. 693–725.

Boyer, R., and Drache, D. (1996): *States Against Markets: The Limits of Globalization*. London and New York: Routledge.

Brace, L., and Hoffman, J. (eds) (1997): *Reclaiming Sovereignty*. London and Washington, DC: Pinter.

Bradshaw, Y. W., and Wallace, M. (1996): *Global Inequalities*. Thousand Oaks, CA: Pine Forge Press.

Braithwaite, J., and Drahos, P. (1999): *Global Business Regulation*. Cambridge: Cambridge University Press.

Bredow, W. von (2001): Die Zukunft des Krieges: Gewalt, Politik, Staat, *Frankfurter Allgemeine Zeitung*, 27 September.

Brenner, N. (1998): Global Cities, Glocal States: Global City Formation and State Territorial Restructuring in Contemporary Europe, *Review of International Political Economy* 5/1, pp. 1–37.

Broad, R., and Cavanagh, J. (2000): Global Backlash: Citizen Initiatives to Counter Corporate-Led Globalization, in Wapner, P. K., and Ruiz, L. E. J. (eds): *Principled World Politics*. Oxford: Rowman & Littlefield, pp. 191–208.

Brock, L., and Albert, M. (1995): Entgrenzung der Staatenwelt: Zur Analyse weltgesellschaftlicher Entwicklungstendenzen, *Zeitschrift für Internationale Beziehung* 2/2, pp. 259–85.

Brown, W. (1995): *States of Injury: Power and Freedom in Late Modernity*. Princeton, NJ: Princeton University Press.

Brubaker, R. (1994): *Staats-Bürger: Frankreich und Deutschland im historischen Vergleich*. Hamburg: Junius.

Brunetière, F. (1895): Le Cosmopolitisme et la littérature nationale, *Revue des Deux Mondes*.

Brunkhorst, H., Köhler, W. R., and Lutz-Bachmann, M. (eds) (1999): *Recht auf Menschenrechte: Menschenrechte, Demokratie und internationale Politik*. Frankfurt am Main: Suhrkamp.

Burtless, G., Lawrence, R. Z., and Litan, R. E. (2000): Globaphobia: Confronting Fears about Open Trade, in Lechner, F., and Boli, J. (eds): *The Globalization Reader*. Oxford: Blackwell.

Busch, A., and Plümper, T. (eds) (1999): *Nationaler Staat und internationale Wirtschaft: Anmerkungen zum Thema Globalisierung.* Baden-Baden: Nomos.

Busch, L., Schiller, N., and Szanton Blanc, C. (1994): *Nations Unbound: Transnational Projects, Postcolonial Predicaments, and Deterritorialized Nation States.* Amsterdam: Gordon & Breach.

Butler, J., Laclau, E., and Žižek, S. (2000): *Contingency, Hegemony, Universality.* London: Verso.

Campbell, D., and Shapiro, M. J. (eds) (1999): *Moral Spaces: Rethinking Ethics and World Politics.* Minneapolis and London: University of Minnesota Press.

Carens, J. H. (1987): Aliens and Citizens: the Case for Open Borders, *Review of Politics* 49/2, pp. 251–73.

Castells, M. (1996, 1997, 1998): *The Information Age: Economy, Society and Culture,* Vol. 1: *The Rise of the Network Society:* Vol. 2: *The Power of Identity;* Vol. 3: *End of Millennium.* Oxford, and Malden, MA: Blackwell.

Castles, F. G. (2000): *Ethnicity and Globalization.* London: Sage.

Castles, S., and Miller, M. (1998): *The Age of Migration.* Basingstoke: Macmillan.

Caterbow, A., and Holzer, B. (2001): Babylonische Sprachverwirrung, *Politische Ökologie* 72, pp. 37–49.

Cerny, P. G. (1998): Neomedievalism, Civil War and the New Security Dilemma: Globalisation as Durable Disorder, *Civil Wars* 1/1, pp. 36–64.

Cerny, P. G. (1995): Globalization and the Changing Logic of Collective Action, *International Organization* 49/4, pp. 595–625.

Cerny, P. G. (2000): Structuring the Political Arena, in Palan, R. (ed.): *Global Political Economy.* London and New York: Routledge, pp. 21–35.

Cerny, P. G., Goverde, H., Haugaard, M., and Leutner, H. (eds) (2000): *Power in Contemporary Politics: Theories, Practices, Globalizations.* London: Sage.

Cheah, P., and Robbins, B. (eds) (1998): *Cosmopolitics: Thinking and Feeling Beyond the Nation.* Minneapolis: University of Minnesota Press.

Chero, F. (2000): The Local Dimensions of Global Reform, in Pieterse, J. N. (ed.): *Global Futures.* London: Zed.

Chomsky, N. (2000): *Der neue militärische Humanismus: Lektionen aus dem Kosovo.* Zurich: Ed. 8.

Chossudovsky, M. (1997): *The Globalization of Poverty.* London: Zed.

Clark, M. (1996): Creativity Unbound: Engaging with the Molecular Revolution of Nanotechnology. Mimeo.

Clarke, S., and Gaile, G. L. (1998): *The Work of Cities.* Minneapolis: University of Minnesota Press.

Clifford, J. (1994): Diasporas, *Cultural Anthropology* 9/9, pp. 302–37.

Cohen, J. L. (1999): Changing Paradigms of Citizenship and the Exclusiveness of Demos, *International Sociology* 14/3, pp. 245–86.

Cohen, R. (1997): *Global Diasporas: An Introduction.* London: UCL Press.

Cohen, R., and Kennedy, P. (2000): *Global Sociology.* Basingstoke and New York: Palgrave.

Coleman, J. (1982): *Die asymmetrische Gesellschaft.* Weinheim: Beltz.

Commission of Global Governance (1995): *Our Global Neighbourhood.* Oxford: Oxford University Press.

Connolly, W. E. (1995): *The Ethos of Pluralization.* Minneapolis: University of Minnesota Press.

Cooter, R., and Ulen, T. (1999): *Law and Economics*. Reading, MA: Addison-Wesley.

Coughlin, C. C., Chrystal, K. A., and Wood, G. E. (2000): Protectionist Trade Politics, in Frieden, J. A., and Lake, D. A. (eds): *International Political Economy.* London and New York: Routledge, pp. 303–17.

Coulmas, P. (1990): *Weltbürger: Geschichte einer Menschheitssehnsucht*. Reinbek: Rowohlt.

Cox, K. (ed.) (1997): *Spaces of Globalization: Re-Asserting the Power of the Local.* New York: Guilford.

Crozier, M., and Friedberg, E. (1979): *Macht und Organisation: Die Zwänge kollektiven Handelns.* Königstein: Athenaeum-Verlag.

Curbach, J. (2001): Global Governance und Transnationale Zivilgesellschaft. Diss., University of Munich.

Cutler, A. C., Haufler, V., and Porter, T. (eds) (1999) *Private Authority and International Affairs.* New York: State University of New York Press.

Cwerner, S. B. (2000): Chronopolitan Ideal: Time, Belonging and Globalization, *Time & Society* 9/2–3, pp. 331–45.

Czada, R., and Lütz, S. (eds) (2000): *Die politische Konstitution von Märkten.* Wiesbaden: Westdeutscher Verlag.

Czempiel, E.-O., and Rosenau, J. (eds) (1992): *Governance Without Government: Order and Change in World Politics.* Cambridge: Cambridge University Press.

Dahrendorf, R. (1970): Zu einer Theorie des sozialen Konflikts, in Zapf, W. (ed.): *Theorien des sozialen Wandels.* Cologne and Berlin: Kiepenheuer & Witsch.

Dahrendorf, R. (2000): Die globale Klasse und die neue Ungleichheit, *Merkur* 54/11.

De Boeck, F. (1999): Domesticating Diamonds and Dollars: Identity, Expenditure and Sharing in Southwestern Zaire (1984–1997), in Meyer, B., and Geschiere, P. (eds): *Globalization and Identity.* Oxford: Blackwell, pp. 177–211.

Deacon, B. (1997): *Global Social Policy: International Organizations and the Future of Welfare.* London: Sage.

Delanty, G. (2000): *Citizenship in a Global Age: Society, Culture, Politics.* Buckingham: Open University Press.

Denemark, R. A., Friedman, J., Gills, B. K., and Modelski, G. (eds) (2000): *World System History: The Social Science of Long-Term Change.* London and New York: Routledge.

Derrida, J. (1992): Onto-Theology of National-Humanism, *Oxford Literary Review* 14, pp. 1–26.

Dewey, J. (1954): *The Public and its Problems.* Chicago: Swallow Press.

Dewey, J. (1996): *Die Öffentlichkeit und ihre Probleme.* Bodenheim: Philo.

Dezalay, Y., and Garth, B. G. (1996): *Dealing in Virtue: International Commercial Arbitration and the Construction of a Transnational Legal Order.* Chicago: University of Chicago Press.

Dharwadker, V. (2001): *Cosmopolitan Geographies.* London: Routledge.

Diamond, L. (2000): The Globalization of Democracy, in Lechner, F., and Boli, J. (eds): *The Globalization Reader.* Oxford: Blackwell, pp. 246–54.

Dickens, P. (1999): *Global Shift: The Internationalization of Economic Activity.* London: Chapman.

Dickens, P. (2000): *Social Darwinism.* Buckingham: Open University Press.

Dixon, W. J., and Boswell, T. (1996): Dependency, Disarticulation, and Denominator Effects: Another Look at Foreign Capital Penetration, *American Journal of Sociology* 102/2, pp. 543–62.

Doyle, M. (2000): Global Economic Inequalities, in Wapner, P. K., and Ruiz, L. E. J. (eds): *Principled World Politics*. Oxford: Rowman & Littlefield, pp. 79–97.

Drucker, P. F. (1997): The Global Economy and the Nation-State, *Foreign Affairs* 76/5, pp. 159–71.

Duara, P. (1999): Transnationalism in the Era of Nation-States: China, 1900–1945, in Meyer, B., and Geschiere, P. (eds): *Globalization and Identity*. Oxford: Blackwell, pp. 47–71.

Dunkley, G. (1999): *The Free Trade Adventure: The WTO, GATT and Globalism: A Critique*. London: Zed.

Dunning, J. H. (1993): *The Globalization of Business*. London and New York: Routledge.

Dunning, J. H. (1997): *Alliance Capitalism and Global Business*. London and New York: Routledge.

Dürrschmidt, J. (2000): *Everyday Lives in the Global City: The Delinking of Locale and Milieu*. London and New York: Routledge.

Dworkin, R. (1986): *Law's Empire*. Cambridge, MA: Harvard University Press.

Eade, J. (ed.) (1997): *Living in the Global City*. London and New York: Routledge.

Easterly, W. R. (2001): *The Effect of International Monetary Fund and World Bank Programs on Poverty*. Washington, DC: World Bank.

Eichengreen, B. (2000): Hegemonic Stability Theories of the International Money System, in Frieden, J. A., and Lake, D. A. (eds): *International Political Economy*. London and New York: Routledge, pp. 220–44.

Elazar, D. J. (1998): *Constitutionalizing Globalization*. Lanham, MD: Rowman & Littlefield.

Elazar, D. J. (2001): The United States and the European Union, in Nicolaidis, K., and Howse, R. (eds): *The Federal Vision*. Oxford: Oxford University Press.

Eleftheriadis, P. (2000): The European Constitution and Cosmopolitan Ideals, *Columbia Journal of European Law* 7, pp. 21–39.

Elkins, D. J. (1995): *Beyond Sovereignty: Territory and Political Economy in the Twenty-First Century*. Toronto: University of Toronto Press.

Ellwein, T. (1992): Staatlichkeit im Wandel: Das Staatsmodell des 19. Jahrhunderts als Verständnisbarriere, in Kohler-Koch, B. (ed.): *Staat und Demokratie in Europa*. Opladen: Leske & Budrich, pp. 47–69.

Embong, A. R. (2000): Globalization and Transnational Class Relations: Some Problems of Conceptualization, *Third World Quarterly* 21/6, pp. 989–1001.

Eppler, E. (1998): *Die Wiederkehr der Politik*. Frankfurt am Main: Insel.

Eriksen, T. (1993): *Ethnicity and Nationalism: Anthropological Perspectives*. London: Pluto Press.

Erne, R., Gross, A., Kaufmann, B., and Kleger, H. (eds) (1995): *Transnationale Demokratie*. Zurich: Realutopia Verlags-Genossenschaft.

Esping-Andersen, G. (1991): *The Three Worlds of Welfare Capitalism*. Cambridge: Polity.

Esser, J. (1999): Der kooperative Nationalstaat im Zeitalter der Globalisierung, in Döring, D. (ed.): *Sozialstaat in der Globalisierung*. Frankfurt am Main: Suhrkamp, pp. 117–44.

Evans, P. B. (1997): The Eclipse of the State? Reflections on Stateness in an Era of Globalization, *World Politics* 50/1, pp. 62–87.

Falk, R. (1995): *Humane Governance*. Cambridge: Polity.

Falk, R. (1999): *Predatory Globalization*. Cambridge: Polity.

Featherstone, M. (2000): Technologies of Post-Human Development and the Potential for Global Citizenship, in Pieterse, J. N. (ed.): *Global Futures*. London: Zed, pp. 203–23.

Fengler, W. (2001): *Politische Reformhemmnisse und ökonomische Blockierung in Afrika*. Baden-Baden: Nomos.

Fichte, J. G. (1918 [1806]): *Der Patriotismus und sein Gegenteil: Patriotische Dialogen*. ed. Hans Schulz. Leipzig: Meiner.

Fishman, T. C. (2000): The Joys of Global Investment, in Lechner, F., and Boli, J. (eds): *The Globalization Reader*. Oxford: Blackwell.

Flyvbjerg, B. (2001): *Making Social Science Matter*. Cambridge: Cambridge University Press.

Forschungsgruppe Weltgesellschaft (1996): Weltgesellschaft: Identifizierung eines Phantoms, *Politische Vierteljahresschrift* 37/1, pp. 5–23.

Forsythe, D. (2000): *Human Rights in International Relations*. Cambridge: Cambridge University Press.

Frank, A. G. (1998): *ReOrient: Global Economy in the Asian Age*. Berkeley: University of California Press.

Franklin, J. (ed.) (1998): *The Politics of Risk Society*. Cambridge: Polity.

Franklin, S., Stacey, J., and Lury, C. (2000): *Global Nature, Global Culture*. London: Sage.

Frei, N. (1999): *Vergangenheitspolitik*. Munich: Deutscher Taschenbuch Verlag.

Frieden, J. A. (2000): Exchange Rate Politics, in Frieden, J. A., and Lake, D. A.(eds): *International Political Economy*. London and New York: Routledge, pp. 257–69.

Frieden, J. A., and Lake, D. A. (eds) (2000): *International Political Economy: Perspectives on Global Power and Wealth*. London and New York: Routledge.

Friedmann, J. (2002): Transnationalization, Socio-political Disorder, and Ethnification as Expression of Declining Global Hegemony, in Vincent, J. (ed.): *The Anthropology of Politics*. Oxford: Blackwell, pp. 285–300.

Friedmann, M. (1999): *Consumer Boycotts*. London and New York: Routledge.

Fröbel, F. et al. (2000 [1980]): The New International Division of Labor in the World Economy, in Roberts, T., and Hite, L. (eds): *From Modernization to Globalization*. Oxford: Blackwell.

Fuat, K. (1996): *Globalization, State, Identity and Difference: Toward a Critical Social Theory of International Relations*. Atlantic Highlands, NJ: Humanities Press.

Garrett, G. (2000): Partisan Politics in the Global Economy, in Lechner, F., and Boli, J. (eds): *The Globalization Reader*. Oxford: Blackwell, pp. 227–35.

Geddes, A., and Favell, A. (1999): *The Politics of Belonging: Migrants and Minorities in Contemporary Europe*. Aldershot: Ashgate.

Geertz, C. (1996): *Welt in Stücken: Kultur und Politik am Ende des 20. Jahrhunderts*. Vienna: Passagen Verlag.

Gell, A. (1998): *Art and Agency: An Anthropological Theory*. Oxford: Clarendon Press.

Genschel, P. (2000): Der Wohlfahrtsstaat im Steuerwettbewerb, *Zeitschrift für Internationale Beziehungen* 2, pp. 267–97.

Gereffi, G. (1989): Rethinking Development Theory: Insights from East Asia and Latin America, *Sociological Forum* 4/4, pp. 505–33.

Giddens, A. (1990): *Consequences of Modernity*. Cambridge: Polity.

Giddens, A. (1994): *Beyond Left and Right: The Future of Radical Politics*. Cambridge: Polity.

Giddens, A. (1998): *The Third Way: The Renewal of Social Democracy*. Cambridge: Polity.

Giddens, A. (1999): *Runaway World: How Globalization is Reshaping our Lives*. London: Profile.

Giddens, A. (ed.) (2001): *The Global Third Way Debate*. Cambridge: Polity.

Gilbert, A., and Gugler, J. (1992): *Cities, Poverty and Development: Urbanization in the Third World*. Oxford: Oxford University Press.

Gill, S. (1995): Globalization, Market Civilization and Disciplinary Neoliberalism, *Millennium – Journal of International Studies* 24/3, pp. 399–423.

Gills, B. K. (ed.) (2000): *Globalization and the Politics of Resistance*. New York: Macmillan Press.

Gilpin, R. (1987): *The Political Economy of International Relations*. Princeton, NJ: Princeton University Press.

Gilpin, R. (2001): *Global Political Economy*. Princeton, NJ: Princeton University Press.

Gilroy, P. (1993): *Black Atlantic*. London: Verso.

Gilroy, P. (2000): *Against Race*. Cambridge, MA: Harvard University Press.

Goethe, J. W. von (1909): *Briefwechsel mit Wilhelm und Alexander von Humboldt*. ed. L. Geiger. Berlin.

Goldstein, J., Kahler, M., Keohane, R. O., and Slaughter, A.-M. (2000): The Concept of Legalization, *International Organization* 54/3.

Goodman, J. B., and Pauly, L. W. (2000): The Obsolescence of Capital Controls, in Frieden, J. A., and Lake, D. A. (eds): *International Political Economy*. London and New York: Routledge, pp. 280–98.

Görg, C., and Hirsch, J. (1998): Is International Democracy Possible?, *Review of International Political Economy* 5/4, pp. 585–615.

Goverde, H., et al. (eds) (2000): *Power in Contemporary Politics: Theories, Practices, Globalizations*. London: Sage.

Grande, E. (1995): Regieren in verflochtenen Verhandlungssystemen, in Mayntz, R., and Scharpf, F. W. (eds): *Gesellschaftliche Selbstregelung und politische Steuerung*. Frankfurt am Main: Suhrkamp, pp. 327–68.

Grande, E. (1999): Die Aufhebung des Nationalstaates: Perspektiven des Regierens in Europa, in Fricke, W. (ed.): *Jahrbuch Arbeit und Technik 1999 + 2000* [Bonn], pp. 378–91.

Grande, E. (2000): Anmerkungen zur reflexiven Modernisierung der Staatlichkeit. Unpublished manuscript, Munich.

Grande, E. (2001a): Die neue Unregierbarkeit: Globalisierung und die Grenzen des Regierens jenseits des Nationalstaats, *Working Paper no. 2*, Munich: Munich Technical University.

Grande, E. (2001b): Globalisierung und die Zukunft des Nationalstaates, in Beck, U., and Bonss, W. (eds): *Die Modernisierung der Moderne*. Frankfurt am Main: Suhrkamp.

Grande, E., and Jachtenfuchs, M. (eds) (2000): *Wie problemlösungsfähig ist die EU? Regieren im europäischen Mehrebenensystem*. Baden-Baden: Nomos.

Grande, E., and Kriesi, H. (2002): Nationaler politischer Wandel in entgrenzten Räumen, *Research Centre 536 Reflexive Modernization: Application for Funding for the Years 2002 – 2005*, sub-project C6, Munich University, pp. 767–816.

Grande, E., and Risse, T. (2000): Bridging the Gap: Conceptual challenges for the Analysis of Globalization Processes in Political Science, *ZIB* [German Journal of International Relations] 7/2, pp. 235–67.

Gray, J. (1998): *False Dawn: The Delusion of Global Capitalism*. London: Granta Books.

Greider, W. (1997): *One World, Ready or Not: The Manic Logic of Globalization*. New York: Simon & Schuster.

Greven, M. (1999): *Die politische Gesellschaft*. Opladen: Leske & Budrich.

Grundmann, R. (2001): *Transnational Environmental Policy: Reconstructing Ozone*. London and New York: Routledge.

Guidry, J. A., Kennedy, M. D., and Zald M. N. (eds) (2000): *Globalizations and Social Movements: Culture, Power, and the Transnational Public Sphere*. Ann Arbor: University of Michigan Press.

Günther, K., and Randeria, S. (2002): *Das Recht im Globalisierungsprozeß*. Frankfurt am Main: Suhrkamp.

Gustafsson, B., and Johansson, M. (1999): In Search of Smoking Guns: What Makes Income Inequality Vary Over Time in Different Countries?, *American Sociological Review* 64, pp. 585–605.

Habermas, J. (1998): *The Inclusion of the Other: Studies in Political Theory*. Cambridge, MA: MIT Press.

Habermas, J. (2001a): *The Postnational Constellation*. Cambridge, MA: MIT Press.

Habermas, J. (2001b): *Zeit der Übergänge*. Frankfurt am Main: Suhrkamp; forthcoming as *Time of Transitions*, trans. Ciaran Cronin and Max Pensky. Cambridge: Polity.

Hajer, M. (1995): *The Politics of Environmental Discourse: Ecological Modernization and the Policy Process*. Oxford: Oxford University Press.

Hajer, M., and Gomart, E. (2002): Is that Politics? An inquiry into forms in contemporary politics, in *Looking Back, Ahead – The 2002 Yearbook of Sociology of the Sciences*. ed. B. Joerges and H. Nowotny. Dordrecht: Kluwer.

Hall, P. (1996): The Global City, *International Social Science Journal* 147, pp. 15–23.

Hall, S. (1999): Ethnicity: Identity and Difference, in Eley, G., and Suny, R. G. (eds): *Becoming National*. Oxford: Oxford University Press, pp. 339–51.

Hardin, G. (1974): Living on a Lifeboat, *BioScience* 24/10, pp. 561–8.

Hardt, M., and Negri, A. (eds) (2000): *Empire*. Cambridge, MA: Harvard University Press.

Hart, J. A., and Prakash, A. (2000): Strategic Trade and Investment Politics, in Frieden, J. A., and Lake, D. A. (eds): *International Political Economy*. London and New York: Routledge, pp. 180–92.

Harvey, D. (1989): *The Condition of Postmodernity: An Enquiry into the Origins of Cultural Change*. Oxford: Blackwell.

Harvey, D. (2000): *Spaces of Hope*. Edinburgh: Edinburgh University Press.

Hauchler, I., Messner, D., and Nuscheler, F. (eds) (2000): *Globale Trends 2000: Fakten, Analysen, Prognosen*. Frankfurt am Main: Fischer Taschenbuch Verlag.

Heintz, P. (1982): *Die Weltgesellschaft im Spiegel von Ereignissen*. Diessenhofen: Rüegger.

Held, D. (1992): Democracy: From City-States to a Cosmopolitan Order?, *Political Studies* 40 [special issue], pp. 10–39.

Held, D. (1995): *Democracy and the Global Order*. Cambridge: Polity.

Held, D. (ed.) (2000): *A Globalizing World? Culture, Economics, Politics*. London and New York: Routledge in association with the Open University.

Held, D. (2002): Law of States, Law of Peoples, *Legal Theory* 8/2, pp. 1–44.

Held, D., McGrew, A., Goldblatt, D., and Perraton, J. (1999): *Global Transformations: Politics, Economics and Culture*. Cambridge: Polity.

Held, D. et al. (2000): Die Rückkehr der Politik, in Assheuer, T., and Perger, W. A. (eds): *Was wird aus der Demokratie?*. Opladen: Leske & Budrich.

Héritier, W., Knill, C., and Mingers, S. (1994): *Die Veränderung von Staatlichkeit in Europa*. Opladen: Leske & Budrich.

Herold, A., Ó Tuathail, G., and Roberts, S. (1998): *An Unruly World? Globalization, Governance and Geography*. London and New York: Routledge.

Hirsch, J. (1995): *Der nationale Wettbewerbstaat: Staat, Demokratie und Politik im globalen Kapitalismus*. Berlin: Ed. ID-Archiv.

Hirst, P. Q., and Thompson, G. (1999): *Globalization in Question: The International Economy and the Possibilities of Governance*. Cambridge: Polity.

Hitzler, Ronald (1996): Der gemeine Machiavellismus. Unpublished thesis, University of Munich.

Hobbes, T. (1996 [1651]): *Leviathan*, ed. J. C. A. Gaskin. Oxford: Oxford University Press.

Hobsbawm, E. (1990): *Nations and Nationalism since 1780: Programme, Myth, Reality*. Cambridge: Cambridge University Press.

Höffe, O. (1994): *Demokratie im Zeitalter der Globalisierung*. Munich: Beck.

Hofmann, G. (2002): *Abschiede, Anfänge*. Munich: Kunstmann.

Hofmannsthal, H. von (2000): *Der Brief des Lord Chandos*. Stuttgart: Reclam.

Holden, B. (ed.) (2000): *Global Democracy: Key Debates*. London: Routledge.

Holmes, D. (2000): *Integral Europe: Fast-Capitalism, Multiculturalism, Neofascism*. Princeton, NJ: Princeton University Press.

Holton, R. (1998): *Globalization and the Nation State*. Basingstoke: Macmillan.

Holzer, B. (1999): *Die Fabrikation von Wundern: Modernisierung, wirtschaftliche Entwicklung und kultureller Wandel in Ostasien*. Opladen: Leske & Budrich.

Holzer, B. (2000): Miracles with a System: The Economic Rise of East Asia and the Role of Sociocultural Patterns, *International Sociology* 15/3, pp. 455–76.

Holzer, B. (2001): Transnational Subpolitics and Corporate Discourse. PhD diss., London School of Economics.

Holzer, B., and Sørensen, M. (2001): *Subpolitics and Subpoliticians* (Working Paper No. 4). Munich: Research Centre 536.

Horsman, M., and Marshall, A. (1994): *After the Nation-State: Citizens, Tribalism, and the New World Disorder*. London: Harper & Collins.

Horstmann, A. (1976): Kosmopolit, Kosmopolitismus, in: *Historisches Wörterbuch der Philosophie*, Vol. 4. Basel: Schwabe, pp. 1156–68.

Hove, C. (2002): Ein toter Traum: Warum die Afrikanische Union Irrsinn ist, *Frank-furter Allgemeine Zeitung*, 12 August, p. 31.

Hutchinson, C. (1966): Corporate Strategy and the Environment, in Welford, R., and Starkey, R. (eds): *Business and the Environment*. London: Earthscan, pp. 85–103.

IMF (2000): *World Economic Outlook*. Washington, DC: IMF.

International Office of Migration (2000): *World Migration Report 2000*. Geneva: IOM.

Jameson, F. (2000): Globalization and Strategy, *New Left Review* 4, pp. 49–68.

Jameson, F., and Miyoshi, M. (eds) (1999): *The Culture of Globalization*. Durham, NC: Duke University Press.

Janett, D. (1999): Vielfalt als Strategievorteil: Zur Handlungskompetenz von Nicht-Regierungs-Organisationen in komplexen sozialen Umwelten, in Altvater, E., et al. (eds): *Vernetzt und verstrickt: Nicht-Regierungs-Organisationen als gesellschaftliche Produktivkraft*. Münster: Westfälisches Dampfboot, pp. 146–75.

Jens, W. (1992): *Nationalliteratur und Weltliteratur – von Goethe aus gesehen*. Munich: Kindler.

Jessop, B. (1999a): Reflections on the (Il)logics of Globalization, in Olds, K. (ed.): *Globalization and the Asia Pacific*. London: Routledge, pp. 19–38.

Jessop. B. (1999b): Globalisierung und Nationalstaat: Imperialismus und Staat bei Nicos Poulantzas – 20 Jahre später, *Prokla* 29/3, pp. 469–95.

Jessop, B. (2000): Regulationist and Autopoeticist, *New Political Economy* 6/2, pp. 213–32.

Jones, C. (1999): *Global Justice: Defending Cosmopolitanism*. Oxford: Oxford University Press.

Jones, R. J. B. (2000): *The World Turned Upside Down: Globalization and the Future of the Nation State*. Manchester: Manchester University Press.

Jones, R. J. B. (2001): The Political Sociology of World Society, *European Journal of International Affairs* 7/4, pp. 443–74.

Jönnson, C., Tägil, S., and Tönqvist, G. (2000): *Organizing European Space*. London: Sage.

Joy, B. (2000): Manche Experimente sollten wir nur auf dem Mond wagen, *Frankfurter Allgemeine Zeitung*, 13 June.

Kaiser, K., and Schwarz, H.-P. (eds) (2000): *Weltpolitik im neuen Jahrhundert*. Bonn: Bundeszentrale für politische Bildung.

Kaldor, M. (1999): *New and Old Wars: Organized Violence in a Global Era*. Cambridge: Polity.

Kallen, H. (1924): *Culture and Democracy in the United States*. New York: Boni & Liveright.

Kant, I. (1964): *Werke*, Vol. 11: *Geheimer Artikel zum ewigen Frieden*. Frankfurt am Main: Suhrkamp.

Kant, I. (1983): *Perpetual Peace, and Other Essays on Politics, History and Morals*. Indianapolis: Hackett.

Kant, I. (1996): *The Metaphysics of Morals*, trans. and ed. Mary Gregor. Cambridge: Cambridge University Press.

Katzenstein, P. J. (1978): *Between Power and Plenty: Foreign Economic Policies of Advanced Industrial States*. Madison: University of Wisconsin Press.

Katzenstein, P. J. (1985): *Small States in World Markets*. Ithaca, NY: Cornell University Press.

Kaul, I., Grunber I., and Stern, M. A. (eds) (1999): *Global Public Goods: International Cooperation in the 21st Century.* Oxford: Oxford University Press.

Kautsky, K. (1907): *Patriotismus und Sozialdemokratie.* Leipzig: Verlag der Leipziger Buchdruckerei.

Keck, M. E., and Sikkink, K. (1998): *Activists Beyond Borders: Transnational Advocacy Networks in International Politics.* Ithaca, NY: Cornell University Press.

Keil, R. (1993): *Weltstadt – Stadt der Welt: Internationalisierung und lokale Politik in Los Angeles.* Münster: Westfälisches Dampfboot.

Kennedy, P. (1987): *The Rise and Fall of the Great Powers.* New York: Random House.

Keohane, R. O. (1988): International Institutions: Two Approaches, *International Studies Quarterly* 32, pp. 379–96.

Keohane, R. O. (1989): *International Institutions and State Power.* Boulder, CO: Westview Press.

Keohane, R. O., and Nye, J. S. (eds) (1971): *Transnational Relations and World Politics.* Cambridge, MA: Harvard University Press.

Kieser, A. (ed.) (1999): *Organisationstheorien.* Stuttgart, Berlin and Cologne: Kohlhammer.

Kindleberger, C. P. (2000): The Rise of Free Trade in Western Europe, in Frieden, J. A., and Lake, D. A. (eds). *International Political Economy.* London and New York: Routledge, pp. 73–89.

Knight, F. H. (1967 [1921]): *Risk, Uncertainty, and Profit.* New York: Kelley.

Koch, C. (1995): Die Gier des Marktes: Die Ohnmacht des Staates im Kampf der Weltwirtschaft. Munich: Hanser.

Koch, K. (2000): Leviathan, ade! (Bye bye, Leviathan!), *Süddeutsche Zeitung,* 22–23 July.

Köhler, B. (2002): Soziologie transnationaler Konzerne: Eine empirische Untersuchung der inneren Globalisierung. Diss., Munich University.

Kohler-Koch, B. (ed.) (1998): *Regieren in entgrenzten Räumen.* Opladen: Westdeutscher Verlag [special issue 29 of *Politische Vierteljahresschrift*].

Korten, D. C. (1995): *When Corporations Rule the World.* West Hartford, CT: Berrett-Koehler.

Korzeniewicz, M. (2000): Commodity Chains and Marketing Strategies: Nike and the Global Athletic Footwear Industry, in Lechner, F., and Boli, J. (eds): *The Globalization Reader.* Oxford: Blackwell, pp. 155–66.

Korzeniewicz, R. P., and Moran, T. P. (1997): The Global Distribution of Income, 1965–1992, *American Journal of Sociology* 102/4, pp. 1000–39.

Koselleck, R. (1979): *Vergangene Zukunft.* Frankfurt am Main: Suhrkamp.

Krasner, S. D. (1999): *Sovereignty: Organized Hypocrisy.* Princeton, NJ: Princeton University Press.

Krasner, S. D. (2000): State Power and the Structure of International Trade, in Frieden, J. A., and Lake, D. A. (eds): *International Political Economy.* London and New York: Routledge, pp. 19–36.

Kratochwil, F. (1989): *Rules, Norms, and Decisions.* Cambridge: Cambridge University Press.

Kriesberg, L. (1997): Social Movements and Global Transformation, in Smith, J., Chatfield, C., and Pagnucco, R. (eds): *Transnational Social Movements and Global Politics.* Syracuse, NY: Syracuse University Press, pp. 3–18.

Kriesi, H. (2001): Nationaler politischer Wandel in einer sich denationalisierenden Welt, *Blätter für deutsche und internationale Politik* 26/2.

Kriesi, H., Koopmans, J. W., and Giugni, M. G. (1992): New Social Movements and Political Opportunities in Western Europe, *European Journal of Political Research* 22, pp. 219–44.

Krueger, A. (1998): *The WTO as an Institutional Organization*. Chicago: Chicago University Press.

Krüger, H.-P. (1996): Nachwort, in Dewey, J.: *Die Öffentlichkeit und ihre Probleme*. Bodenheim: Philo, pp. 193–211.

Krugman, P. R., and Obstfeld, M. (2000): *International Economics: Theory and Policy*. Reading, MA: Addison-Wesley

Krugman, P. R., and Venables, A. (1995): Globalization and the Inequality of Nations, *Quarterly Journal of Economics* 110/4, pp. 857–80.

Kuper, A. (2000): Rawlsian Global Justice: Beyond the Law of Peoples to a Cosmopolitan Law of Persons, *Political Theory* 28, pp. 640–74.

Laïdi, Z. (1998): *A World Without Meaning: The Crisis of Meaning in International Politics*. London and New York: Routledge.

Lakatos, I. (1970): Falsification and the Methodology of Scientific Research Programmes, in: Lakatos, I., and Musgrave, A. (eds): *Criticism and the Growth of Knowledge*. Cambridge: Cambridge University Press.

Lake, D. A. (2000): British and American Hegemony Compared, in Frieden, J. A., and Lake, D. A. (eds): *International Political Economy*. London and New York: Routledge, pp. 127–44.

Lane, J. E., and Ersson, S. (2002): *Government and the Economy: A Global Perspective*. London: Continuum.

Lash, S. (1999): *Another Modernity*. Oxford: Blackwell.

Lash, S. (2002a): *Critique of Information*. London: Sage.

Lash, S. (2002b): Foreword: Individualization in a Non-linear Mode, in Beck, U., and Beck-Gernsheim, E.: *Individualization*. London: Sage.

Lash, S., and Urry, J. (1994): *Economies of Signs and Space*. London: Sage.

Latour, B. (1993): *We Have Never Been Modern*. Cambridge, MA: Harvard University Press.

Latour, B. (2001): *Das Parlament der Dinge*. Frankfurt am Main: Suhrkamp.

Latour, B. (2003): Is Remodernization Occurring – And if So, How to Prove it?, *Theory, Culture and Society* 20/2, pp. 35–48.

Lechner, F., and Boli, J. (eds) (2000): *The Globalization Reader*. Oxford: Blackwell.

Lerner, D. (2000 [1958]): The Passing of Traditional Society, in Roberts, T., and Hite, A. (eds): *From Modernization to Globalization*. Oxford: Blackwell.

Leutner, H. (2000): Politics, Power and States in Globalization, in Goverde, H. (ed.): *Power in Contemporary Politics*. London: Sage.

Levett, R. (1966): Business, the Environment and Local Government, in Welford, R., and Starkey, R. (eds): *Business and the Environment*. London: Earthscan, pp. 251–69.

Levy, D., and Sznaider, N. (2001): *Erinnerung im globalen Zeitalter: Der Holocaust*. Frankfurt am Main: Suhrkamp.

Linklater, A. (1998a): Cosmopolitan Citizenship, *Citizenship Studies* 2/1, pp. 23–41.

Linklater, A. (1998b): *The Transformation of Political Community*. Cambridge: Polity.

Lipschutz, R. D. (1992): Reconstructing World Polity: The Emergence of Global Civil Society, *Millennium* 21/3, pp. 389–420.

Long, N., and Villarreal, M. (1999): Small Products, Big Issues: Value Contestations and Cultural Identities in Cross-Border Commodity Networks, in Meyer, B., and Geschiere, P. (eds): *Globalization and Identity*. Oxford: Blackwell, pp. 125–51.

Luard, E. (1990): *The Globalization of Politics*. London: Macmillan.

Luhmann, N. (1975): Die Weltgesellschaft, in *Soziologische Aufklärung*. Opladen: Westdeutscher Verlag.

Luhmann, N. (1999): Ethik in internationalen Beziehungen, *Soziale Welt* 50/3, pp. 247–54.

Luhmann, N., and Scharpf, F. W. (1989): Politische Steuerung: Ein Streitgespräch, *Politische Vierteljahresschrift* 30, pp. 4–21.

Luttwak, E. (1999): *Turbo-Capitalism*. London: Orion Books.

McBride, S., and Wiseman, J. (eds) (2000): *Globalization and its Discontents*. Basingstoke: Macmillan.

McBride, S., and Roach, C. (2000): The New International Information Order, in Lechner, F., and Boli, J. (eds): *The Globalization Reader*. Oxford: Blackwell.

McCarthy, T. (1999): On Reconciling Cosmopolitan Unity and National Diversity, *Public Culture* 11, pp. 175–208.

McGrew, A. (ed.) (1997): *The Transformation of Democracy*. Cambridge: Polity.

Machiavelli, N. (1985): *The Prince*. Chicago: University of Chicago Press.

McNeill, W. H. (1986): *Polyethnicity and National Unity in World History*. Toronto: University of Toronto Press.

McRobbie, A. (1999): *In the Culture Society*. London: Routledge.

Macropoulos, M. (1989): *Modernität als ontologischer Ausnahmezustand? Walter Benjamins Theorie der Moderne*. Munich: Fink.

Mann, M. (1986, 1993): *The Sources of Social Power*, 2 vols. Cambridge: Cambridge University Press.

Mann, M. (1997): Hat die Globalisierung den Siegeszug des Nationalstaates beendet?, *Prokla* 27/1, pp. 113–41.

Mann, M. (2001): Globalization and September 11, *New Left Review* 12, pp. 51–72.

March, J. G., and Olsen, J. P. (1989): *Rediscovering Institutions: The Organizational Basis of Politics*. New York: Free Press.

Marchand, M., and Runyan, A. S. (eds) (1999): *Gender and Global Restructuring: Sightings, Sites and Resistance*. London: Routledge.

Margalit, A. (2000): *Ethik der Erinnerung*. Frankfurt am Main: Fischer [English edition: *The Ethics of Memory*. Cambridge, MA: Harvard University Press, 2002].

Markl, H. (1988): *Wissenschaft gegen Zukunftsangst*. Munich: Hanser.

Martin, H.-P., and Schumann, H. (1996): *Die Globalisierungsfalle: Der Angriff auf Demokratie und Wohlstand*. Reinbek: Rowohlt.

Martins, H. (1974): Time and Theory in Sociology, in Rex, J. (ed.): *Approaches in Sociology*. London: Routledge.

Marx, K., and Engels, F. (1982): *The Communist Manifesto*. Harmondsworth: Penguin.

Mayntz, R. (1996): Politische Steuerung: Aufstieg, Niedergang und Transformation einer Theorie, in Beyme K. von, and Offe, C. (eds): *Politische Theorien in der Ära der Transformation*. Opladen, Westdeutscher Verlag [special issue 26 of *Politische Vierteljahresschrift*], pp. 148–68.

Meier, C. (1990): *The Greek Discovery of Politics*, trans. David McLintock. Cambridge, MA: Harvard University Press.

Meinecke, F. (1922): *Weltbürgertum und Nationalstaat*. Munich: Oldenbourg.

Merkel, R. (ed.) (2000): *Der Kosovokrieg und das Völkerrecht*. Frankfurt am Main: Suhrkamp.

Messner, D. (ed.) (1998): *Die Zukunft des Staates und der Politik*. Bonn: Dietz.

Meyer, B., and Geschiere, P. (eds) (1999): *Globalization and Identity: Dialectics of Flow and Closure*. Oxford: Blackwell.

Meyer, J. W. (2000): Globalization: Sources and Effects on National Societies and States, *International Sociology* 15, pp. 233–48.

Meyer, J. W., Boli, J., Thomas, G., and Ramirez, F. (1997): World Society and the Nation-State, *American Journal of Sociology* 103/1, pp. 144–81.

Mies, M. (2001): *Globalisierung von unten: Der Kampf gegen die Herrschaft der Konzerne*. Hamburg: Rotbuch.

Miller, D. (1988): The Ethical Significance of Nationality, *Ethics* 98, pp. 647–62.

Miller, D., and Slater, D. (2000): *The Internet – An Ethnographical Approach*. Oxford: Berg.

Missbach, A. (1998): NGO-Netzwerke – transnationale Zivilgesellschaft im Entstehen? Research as part of the project 'Das Klima zwischen Nord und Süd', under the directorship of Volker Bornschier, Soziologisches Institut der Universität Zürich, lecture given on 21 January.

Missbach, A. (1999): *Das Klima zwischen Nord und Süd: Eine regulationstheoretische Untersuchung des Nord-Süd-Konflikts in der Klimapolitik der Vereinten Nationen*. Münster: Westfälisches Dampfboot.

Mittelman, J. (2000): *The Globalization Syndrome*. Princeton, NJ: Princeton University Press.

Mlinar, Z. (1997): Globalization as a Research Agenda. Paper presented at European Sociological Association Third Conference, University of Essex, Colchester.

Modelski, G. (1972): *Principles of World Politics*. New York: Free Press.

Modelski, G. (1999): From Leadership to Organization: The Evolution of Global Politics, in Bornschier, V., and Chase-Dunn (eds): *The Future of Global Conflict*. London: Sage.

Modelski, G., and Thompson, W. R. (1995): *Leading Sectors and World Powers: The Co-evolution of Global Politics and Economics*. Columbia: University of South Carolina Press.

Mol, A. P. J., and Sonnenfeld, D. A. (eds) (2000): *Ecological Modernisation Around the World: Perspectives and Critical Debates*. London: Frank Cass.

Munck, R., and Waterman, P. (eds) (1999): *Labour Worldwide in the Era of Globalization: Alternative Union Models in the New World Order*. Basingstoke: Macmillan.

Münkler, H. (2001): *Thomas Hobbes*. Frankfurt am Main: Campus.

Narr, W.-D., and Schubert, A. (1994): *Weltökonomie: Die Misere der Politik*. Frankfurt am Main: Suhrkamp.

Nicolaidis, K., and Howse, R. (eds) (2001): *The Federal Vision*. Oxford: Oxford University Press.

Nietzsche, F. (1966): *Werke*, 3 vols. Munich: Hanser.

Nölke, A. (2000): Regieren in transnationalen Politiknetzwerken? Kritik postnationaler Governance-Konzepte aus der Perspektive einer transnationalen (Inter-)

Organisationssoziologie, *Zeitschrift für Internationale Beziehungen* 7/2, pp. 331–59.

Nowotny, H., Scott, P., and Gibbons, M. (2001): *Re-Thinking Science*. Cambridge: Polity.

Nussbaum, M. C. (1996): Patriotism and Cosmopolitism, in *For Love of Country: Debating the Limits of Patriotism*. Boston: Beacon Press.

O'Briek, R., Goetz, A. M., Scholte, J. A., and Williams, M. (2000): *Consulting Global Governance*. Cambridge: Cambridge University Press.

O'Neill, O. (2000a): Bounded and Cosmopolitan Justice, *Review of International Studies* 26, pp. 45–61.

O'Neill, O. (2000b): *Bounds of Justice*. Cambridge: Cambridge University Press.

O'Rourke, K., and Williamson, J. (1999): *Globalization and History*. Cambridge, MA: MIT Press.

OECD (2000): *OECD Economic Outlook June 2000*. Paris: OECD.

Offe, C. (1975): *Strukturprobleme des kapitalistischen Staates: Aufsätze zur politischen Soziologie*. Frankfurt am Main: Suhrkamp.

Ohmae, K. (1990): *The Borderless World: Power and Strategy in the Interlinked Economy*. New York: Harper Business.

Ohmae, K. (1995): *The End of the Nation-State: The Rise of Regional Economies*. New York: Harper Collins.

Ong, A. (1999): *Flexible Citizenship – The Cultural Logics of Transnationality*. Durham, NC: Duke University Press.

Ortmann, G. (1994): Dark Stars – Institutionelles Vergessen in der Industriesoziologie, in Beckenbach, N., and van Treek, W. (eds): *Umbrüche gesellschaftlicher Arbeit* [*Soziale Welt*, Sonderband 9], Göttingen: Schwartz, pp. 85–115.

Ottmann, H. (1987): *Philosophie und Politik bei Nietzsche*. Berlin: de Gruyter.

Ottmann, H. (2001): *Die Geschichte des politischen Denkens*, Vol. 1/1. Stuttgart: Metzler.

Palan, R. (ed.) (2000): *Global Political Economy: Contemporary Theories*. London and New York: Routledge.

Palan, R., and Abbott, J. (1999): *State Strategies in the Global Political Economy*. London and New York: Routledge.

Palonen, K. (1995): Die jüngste Erfindung des Politischen: Ulrich Becks 'Neues Wörterbuch des Politischen' aus der Sicht der Begriffsgeschichte, *Leviathan* 23, pp. 417–36.

Palonen, K. (1998): *Das Webersche Moment: zur Kontingenz des Politischen*. Opladen and Wiesbaden: Westdeutscher Verlag.

Parsons, T. (1970): Das Problem des Strukturwandels, in Zapf, W. (ed.): *Theorien des sozialen Wandels*. Cologne and Berlin: Kiepenheuer & Witsch.

Patomäki, H. (2001): *Democratizing Globalization*. London: Zed.

Patterson, O. (1998): *Rituals of Blood*. Washington, DC: Civitas and Counterpoint.

Peirano, M. G. S. (1998): When Anthropology is at Home: The different contexts of a single discipline, *Annual Review of Anthropology* 27, pp. 105–28.

Penttinen, E. (2000): Capitalism as a System of Global Power, in Goverde, H., et al. (eds): *Power in Contemporary Politics*. London: Sage.

Pettman, J. (1996): *Worlding Women: A Feminist International Politics*. London: Routledge.

Pfleiderer, E. (1874): Kosmopolitismus und Patriotismus, *Zeit- und Streitfragen: Deutsche Hefte*, no. 6 [Berlin].

Picciotto, S. (1991): The Internationalisation of the State, *Capital and Class* 43, pp. 43–64.

Pierre, J., and Peters, B. G. (2000): *Governance, Politics and the State*. London: Palgrave.

Pieterse, J. N. (ed.) (2000): *Global Futures: Shaping Globalization*. London: Zed.

Plessner, H. (1981a [1931]): Macht und menschliche Natur, *Gesammelte Schriften*, V, Frankfurt am Main: Suhrkamp, pp. 135–234.

Plessner, H. (1981b [1962]): Die Emanzipation der Macht, *Gesammelte Schriften*, V, Frankfurt am Main: Suhrkamp, pp. 259–82.

Pocock, J. G. (1975): *The Machiavellian Moment*. Princeton, NJ: Princeton University Press.

Pogge, T. W. (1992): Cosmopolitanism and Sovereignty, *Ethics* 103, pp. 48–75.

Pogge, T. W. (2001): *Global Justice*. Oxford: Blackwell.

Polanyi, K. (1944): *The Great Transformation: The Political and Economic Origins of our Time*. Boston: Beacon Press.

Porter, M. E. (1990): *Wettbewerbsvorteile: Spitzenleistungen erreichen und behaupten*. Frankfurt am Main: Campus.

Portes, A. (1997): Neoliberalism and the Sociology of Development: Emerging Trends and Unanticipated Facts, *Population and Development Review* 23/2, pp. 229–59.

Poster, M. (1995): *The Second Media Age*. Oxford: Blackwell.

Pries, L. (1997): Globalisierung und Demokratie: Chancen und Risiken aus ökonomischer Sicht. Unpublished MS, Ruhr-Universität Bochum.

Pries, L. (1998): Transnationale soziale Räume, in Beck, U. (ed.): *Perspektiven der Weltgesellschaft*. Frankfurt am Main: Suhrkamp, pp. 55–86.

Pries, L. (2000a): 'Transmigranten' als ein Typ von Arbeitswanderern in pluri-lokalen sozialen Räumen, in Goglin, I., and Nauck, B. (eds): *Migration, gesellschaftliche Differenzierung und Bildung*. Opladen: Leske & Budrich, pp. 415–37.

Pries, L. (2000b): Globalisierung und Wandel internationaler Unternehmen: Konzeptionelle Überlegungen am Beispiel der deutschen Automobilindustrie, *Kölner Zeitschrift für Soziologie und Sozialpsychologie* 4/52, pp. 670–96.

Ramirez, F. O., Soysal, Y., and Shanahan, S. (1997): The Changing Logic of Political Citizenship: Cross-National Acquisitions of Women's Suffrage Rights, 1890 to 1990, *American Sociological Review* 62, pp. 735–45.

Randeria, S. (1999a): Jenseits von Soziologie und soziokultureller Anthropologie: Zur Ortsbestimmung der nichtwestlichen Welt in einer zukünftigen Sozialtheorie, *Soziale Welt* 4, pp. 373–82.

Randeria, S. (1999b): Geteilte Geschichte und verwobene Moderne, in Rüsen, J., Leitgeb, H., and Jegelka, N. (eds): *Zukunftsentwürf: Ideen für eine Kultur der Veränderung*. Frankfurt am Main: Campus, pp. 87–96.

Randeria, S. (1999c): Globalization, Modernity and the Nation-State, in Füllberg-Stollberg, K., Heidrich, P., and Schöne, E. (eds): *Dissociation and Appropriation: Responses to Globalization in Asia and Africa*. Berlin: Das arabische Buch.

Randeria, S. (2001): Local Refractions of Global Governance: Legal Plurality, International Institutions, the Post-colonial State and NGOs in India. Unpublished thesis, University of Berlin.

Randeria, S. (2003): Cunning States and Unaccountable International Institutions: Social Movements and the Rights of Local Communities to Common Property Resources, *European Journal of Sociology*, 16/1, pp. 27–60.

Rawls, J. (1999): *The Law of Peoples*. Cambridge, MA: Harvard University Press.

Redding, S. G. (1990): *The Spirit of Chinese Capitalism*. Berlin and New York: de Gruyter.

Reich, R. (1991): *The Work of Nations*. New York: Knopf.

Reinicke, W. H. (1997): *Global Public Policy: Governing Without Government?* Washington, DC: Brookings Institution.

Reinicke, W. H., and Deng, F. (eds) (2000): *Critical Choices: The United Nations, Networks, and the Future of Global Governance*. Ottawa: International Development Research Centre.

Reinicke, W. H., Brenner, T., and Witte, J. M. (2000): Beyond Multinationalism: Global Policy Networks, *International Politics and Society* 2.

Rex, J. (1998) Transnational Migrant Communities and the Modern Nation-State, in Axtmann, R. (ed.): *Globalization and Europe: Theoretical and Empirical Investigations*. London: Pinter, pp. 59–76.

Richter, F.-J. (ed.) (2000): *The East Asian Development Model: Economic Growth, Institutional Failure and the Aftermath of the Crisis*. London: Macmillan.

Risse, T., Ropp, S., and Sikkink, K. (eds) (1999): *The Power of Human Rights: International Norms and Domestic Change*. Cambridge: Cambridge University Press.

Risse-Kappen, T. (ed.) (1995): *Bringing Transnational Relations Back In: Non-state Actors, Domestic Structures and International Institutions*. Cambridge: Cambridge University Press.

Ritzer, G. (1999): *The MacDonaldisation Thesis*. London: Sage.

Roberts, T., and Hite, A. (eds) (2000): *From Modernization to Globalization: Perspectives on Development and Social Change*. Oxford: Blackwell.

Robertson, R. (1992): *Globalization, Social Theory and Global Culture*. London: Sage.

Robertson, R. (1998): Glokalisierung, Homogenität und Heterogenität in Raum und Zeit, in Beck, U. (ed.): *Perspektiven der Weltgesellschaft*. Frankfurt am Main: Suhrkamp, pp. 191–220.

Robinson, W. I. (1996): *Promoting Polyarchy: Globalization, US Intervention, and Hegemony*. Cambridge: Cambridge University Press.

Robinson, W. I. (1998): Beyond Nation-State Paradigms: Globalization, Sociology, and the Challenge of Transnational Studies, *Sociological Forum* 13/4, pp. 561–94.

Rodrik, D. (1997): *Has Globalization Gone Too Far?* Washington, DC: Institute for International Economics.

Rorty, R. (1989): *Contingency, Irony and Solidarity*. Cambridge: Cambridge University Press.

Rosenau, J. (1980): *The Study of Global Interdependence*. London: Pinter.

Rosenau, J. (1990): *Turbulence in World Politics: A Theory of Change and Continuity*. Princeton, NJ: Princeton University Press.

Rosenau, J., and Czempiel, E.-O. (eds) (1992): *Governance Without Government*. Cambridge: Cambridge University Press.

Ruggie, J. (1998): *Constructing the World Polity*. London: Routledge.

Ruigrok, W., and van Tulder, R. (1995): *The Logic of International Restructuring*. London and New York: Routledge.

Rupert, M. (2000): *The Ideologies of Globalization.* London and New York: Routledge.

Said, E. W. (1993): *Culture and Imperialism.* New York: Knopf.

Sassen, S. (1991): *The Global City.* Princeton, NJ: Princeton University Press.

Sassen, S. (1998): *Globalization and its Discontents.* New York: New Press.

Sassen, S. (2000a): New Frontiers Facing Urban Sociology in the Millennium, *British Journal of Sociology* 51/1, pp. 143–61.

Sassen, S. (2000b): *Machtbeben.* Munich: Deutsche Verlagsanstalt.

Scaff, L. (1989): *Fleeing the Iron Cage: Culture, Politics and Modernity in the Thought of Max Weber.* Berkeley: University of California Press.

Scharpf, F. W. (1991): Die Handlungsfähigkeit des Staates am Ende des zwanzigsten Jahrhunderts, *Politische Vierteljahresschrift* 32/4, pp. 621–34.

Scharpf, F. W. (1999): *Regieren in Europa – effektiv und demokratisch?* Frankfurt am Main: Campus.

Scharpf, F. W. (2000): The Viability of Advanced Welfare States in the International Economy: Vulnerabilities and Options, *Journal of European Public Policy* 7/2, pp. 190–228.

Schirm, S. (1999): *Globale Märkte, nationale Politik und regionale Kooperation – in Europa und den Amerikas.* Baden-Baden: Nomos.

Schlichte, K., and Wilke, B. (2000): Der Staat und einige seiner Zeitgenossen: Die Zukunft des Regierens in der 'Dritten Welt', *Zeitschrift für Internationale Beziehungen* 7/2, pp. 359–84.

Schlosser, J. G. (2000 [1784]): *Kleine Schriften*, Vol. 2. Marburg: Metropolis-Verlag.

Schmidt, K.-D. (1999): Auf dem Weg zum Minimalstaat? Nationale Wirtschaftsord-nungen im Wettbewerb, *Bürger im Staat* 49/4, pp. 212–16.

Schmitt, C. (1932): *Der Begriff des Politischen.* Berlin: Duncker & Humblot.

Schmitt, C. (1983): *Verfassungslehre.* Berlin: Duncker & Humblot.

Scholte, J. A., and Schnabel, A. (2002): *Civil Society and Global Finance.* London and New York: Routledge.

Schulze, G. (2001): *Europa und der Globus.* Stuttgart: Deutsche Verlagsanstalt.

Schulze, G., and Ursprung, H. W. (1999): Globalisierung contra Nationalstaat? Ein Überblick über die empirische Evidenz, in Busch, A., and Plümper, T. (eds): *Nationaler Staat und internationale Wirtschaft: Anmerkungen zum Thema Globalisierung.* Baden-Baden: Nomos.

Schumpeter, J. (1919): Zur Soziologie des Imperialismus, *Archiv für Sozialwissenschaft und Sozialpolitik* 46.

Schumpeter, J. (1950 [1942]): *Capitalism, Socialism and Democracy.* New York: Harper & Row.

Scott, A. J. (2000): *Regions and the World Economy: The Coming Shape of Global Production, Competition and Political Order.* Oxford: Oxford University Press.

Scott, J. C. (1998): *Seeing Like a State.* New Haven, CT: Yale University Press.

Sen, A. (1992): *Inequality Re-examined.* Cambridge, MA: Harvard University Press.

Sen, A. (1999): *Development as Freedom.* Oxford: Oxford University Press.

Senghaas, D. (1994): *Wohin driftet die Welt?* Frankfurt am Main: Suhrkamp.

Sennett, R. (1998): *Der flexible Mensch.* Berlin: Berlin-Verlag.

Shaw, M. (1992): Global Society and Global Responsibility: The Historical and Political Limits of 'International Society', *Millennium* 21/3.

Shaw, M. (2000): *Theory of the Global State: Globality as Unfinished Revolution*. Cambridge: Cambridge University Press.

Short, J. R., and Kim, Y.-H. (1999): *Globalization and the City*. Harlow: Longman.

Silverstone, R. (1999): *Why Study the Media?* London: Sage.

Simmel, G. (1900): *Philosophie des Geldes*. Leipzig: Duncker & Humblot.

Simmel, G. (1968 [1908]): Exkurs über den Fremden, in *Soziologie: Untersuchungen über die Formen der Vergesellschaftung*, Berlin: Duncker & Humblot.

Skinner, Q. (1981): *Machiavelli*. Oxford: Oxford University Press.

Sklair, L. (2000): *The Transnational Capitalist Class*. Oxford: Blackwell.

Smart, B. (1995): *Globalization and Interdependence in the International Political Economy: Rhetoric and Reality*. London and New York: Pinter.

Smith, A. D. (1975): *The Wealth of Nations*. new edn, 2 vols. London: Dent.

Smith, A. D. (1995): *Nations and Nationalism in the Global Era*. Cambridge: Polity.

Smith, A. D., Solinger, D. J., and Topik, S. C. (eds) (1999): *States and Sovereignty in the Global Economy*. London and New York: Routledge.

Smith, J. (1997): Characteristics of the Modern Transnational Social Movement Sector, in Smith, J., Chatfield, C., and Pagnucco, R. (eds): *Transnational Social Movements and Global Politics*. Syracuse, NY: Syracuse University Press, pp. 42–58.

Smith, J. (ed.) (2001): Globalization and Resistance, *Mobilization* 6/19 [special issue], pp. 1–110.

Soeffner, H.-G. (2000): *Gesellschaft ohne Baldachin*. Göttingen: Velbrück.

Soysal, Y. (1994): *Limits of Citizenship*. Cambridge, MA: Harvard University Press.

Spaargaren, G., Mo., A. P. J., and Buttel, F. H. (eds) (2000): *Environment and Global Modernity*. London: Sage.

Spengler, O. (1979): *Der Untergang des Abendlandes*. Munich: Beck.

Stalker, P. (2000): *Workers without Frontiers*. Boulder, CO: Lynne Rienner.

Starr, A. (2000): *Naming the Enemy: Anti-Corporate Movements Confront Globalization*. London and New York: Zed.

Stein, U. (1995): *Lex Mercatoria – Realität und Theorie*. Frankfurt am Main: Klostermann.

Stewart, A. (2001): *Theories of Power and Domination*. London: Sage.

Stichweh, R. (2000): *Die Weltgesellschaft: Soziologische Analysen*. Frankfurt am Main: Suhrkamp.

Stiglitz, J. E. (2002): *Globalization and its Discontents*. New York: W. W. Norton.

Stiglitz, J. E., and Squire, L. (2000): International Development: Is it Possible?, in Frieden, J. A., and Lake, D. A. (eds): *International Political Economy*. London and New York: Routledge, pp. 383–91.

Storper, M. (1997): *Regional Worlds*. New York: Guilford.

Strange, S. (1996): *The Retreat of the State: The Diffusion of Power in the World Economy*. Cambridge: Cambridge University Press.

Strange, S. (1998): *Mad Money*. Manchester: Manchester University Press.

Strange, S. (2000): States, Firms, and Diplomacy, in Frieden, J. A., and Lake, D. A. (eds): *International Political Economy*. London and New York: Routledge.

Streeck, W. (1998a): Industrial Relations in an International Economy, in Dettke, D. (ed.): *The Challenge of Globalization for Germany's Social Democracy*. New York and Oxford: Berghahn Books, pp. 85–112.

Streeck, W. (1998b): *Internationale Wirtschaft, nationale Demokratie.* Frankfurt am Main: Campus.

Stubbs, R., and Underhill, G. (eds) (2000): *Political Economy of the Changing Global Order.* 2nd edn, Oxford: Oxford University Press.

Suter, C. (1999): *Gute und schlechte Regimes: Staat und Politik Lateinamerikas zwischen globaler Ökonomie und nationaler Gesellschaft.* Frankfurt am Main: Vervuert.

Szerszyniski, B., and Toogood, M. (2000): Global Citizenship, the Environment and the Media, in Allan, S., Adam, B., and Carter, C. (eds): *Environmental Risks and the Media.* London and New York: Routledge.

Sznaider, N. (2000): *The Compassionate Temperament: Care and Cruelty in Modern Society.* Lanham, MD: Rowman & Littlefield.

Tamás, G. M. (1996): Ethnarchy and Ethno-Anarchism, *Social Research* 63/1, pp. 147–90.

Tamás, G. M. (2000): On Post-fascism – How Citizenship is Becoming an Exclusive Privilege, *Boston Review*, summer, pp. 42–8.

Tarzi, S. M. (2000): Third World Governments and Multinational Corporations: Dynamics of Host's Bargaining Power, in Frieden, J. A., and Lake, D. A. (eds): *International Political Economy.* London and New York: Routledge, pp. 156–66.

Taylor, C., and Gutman, A. (1992): *Multiculturalism and the Politics of Recognition: An Essay.* Princeton, NJ: Princeton University Press.

Teivainen, T. (1999): Globalization of Economic Surveillance, *Passages – Journal of Transnational and Transcultural Studies* 1/1, pp. 84–116.

Teivainen, T. (2000): *Enter Economy, Exit Politics.* Helsinki: Helsinki University Press.

Teubner, G. (ed.) (1997): *Global Law Without a State.* Dartmouth: Aldershot.

Teubner, G. (2000): Des Königs viele Leiber: Selbstdekonstruktion der Hierarchie des Rechts, in Brunkhorst, H., and Kettner, M. (eds): *Globalisierung und Demokratie.* Frankfurt am Main: Suhrkamp, pp. 240–73.

Thaa, W. (2001): 'Lean Citizenship': The Fading of the Political in Transnational Democracy, *European Journal of International Relations* 7/4, pp. 503–24.

Therborn, G. (1995): *European Modernity and Beyond: The Trajectory of European Societies 1945–2000.* London: Sage.

Therborn, G. (1999): The Atlantic Diagonal in the Labyrinths of Modernities and Globalizations, in *Globalization and Modernities.* Stockholm: FRN.

Therborn, G. (2000): At the Birth of Second Century Sociology: Times of Reflexivity, Spaces of Identity and Modes of Knowledge, *British Journal of Sociology* 51, pp. 37–58.

Tilly, C. (1993): *Die europäische Revolution.* Munich: Beck.

Tilly, C. (1998): *Durable Inequality.* Berkeley: University of California Press.

Toffler, A. (1990): *Powershift.* New York: Bantam.

Tomlinson, J. (1999): *Globalization and Culture.* Cambridge: Polity.

Toynbee, A. (1946, 1957): *A Study of History*, abridgement by D. C. Somervell, 2 vols. Oxford: Oxford University Press.

Toynbee, A. (1958): *Gang der Weltgeschichte*, Vol. 2: *Kulturen im Übergang.* Zurich: Europa-Verlag.

Trotha, T. von, (2000): Die Zukunft liegt in Afrika: Vom Zerfall des Staates, von der Vorherrschaft der konzentrischen Ordnung und vom Aufstieg der Parastaatlichkeit, *Leviathan* 28/2.

Tshiyembe, M. (2000): Vom Postkolonialen Staat zum Multinationenstaat (From postcolonial state to multi-nation state), *Le Monde diplomatique*, September.

United Nations Development Programme (2002): *Human Development Report 2002.* New York: Oxford University Press.

Urry, J. (2000): *Sociology Beyond Societies.* London and New York: Routledge.

van der Pijl, K. (1998): *Transnational Classes and International Relations.* London and New York: Routledge.

Vincent, J. (ed.) (2002): *The Anthropology of Politics.* Oxford: Blackwell.

Viner, J. (1950): *The Customs Union Issue.* New York: Carnegie Endowment for International Peace.

Voigt, S. (1999): *Exploiting Constitutional Change.* Cheltenham: Edward Elgar.

Waddington, J. (ed.) (1999): *Globalization and Patterns of Labour Resistance.* London: Mansell.

Wade, R. (1996): Globalization and its Limits: Reports of the Death of the National Economy are Greatly Exaggerated, in Berger, S., and Dore, R. (eds): *National Diversity and Global Capitalism.* Ithaca, NY: Cornell University Press, pp. 60–88.

Waldron, J. (2000): What is Cosmopolitan?, *Journal of Political Philosophy* 8, pp. 227–43.

Walker, R. (1994): Social Movements/World Politics, *Millennium* 23/3, pp. 669–700.

Walker, R. (2000): Both Globalization and Sovereignty, in Wapner, P. K., and Ruiz, L. E. J. (eds), *Principled World Politics.* Oxford: Rowman & Littlefield, pp. 23–34.

Wallerstein, I. (1991): *Unthinking Social Science: The Limits of Nineteenth-Century Paradigms.* Cambridge: Polity.

Walzer, M. (1977): *Just and Unjust Wars.* New York: Basic Books.

Walzer, M. (1983): *Spheres of Justice.* New York: Basic Books.

Wapner, P. K., and Ruiz, L. E. J. (eds) (2000a): *Principled World Politics.* Oxford: Rowman & Littlefield.

Wapner, P., and Ruiz, L. E. J. (2000b): Greenpeace and Political Globalism, in Lechner, F., and Boli, J. (eds): *The Globalization Reader.* Oxford: Blackwell.

Weber, M. (1923): *Wirtschaftsgeschichte: Abriß der universalen Sozial- und Wirtschaftsgeschichte, in den nachgelassenen Vorlesungen*, ed. S. Hellmann and M. Papyi. Munich and Leipzig: Duncker & Humblot.

Weber, M. (1946): *From Max Weber: Essays in Sociology*, ed. and trans. H. Gerth and C. Wright Mills. Oxford: Oxford University Press.

Weber, M. (1972): *Wirtschaft und Gesellschaft.* Tübingen: Mohr.

Weber, M. (1978): *Economy and Society: An Outline of Interpretive Sociology*, ed. Guenther Roth and Claus Wittich. Berkeley and Los Angeles: University of California Press.

Weber, M. (1988): *Gesammelte Aufsätze zur Sozial- und Wirtschaftsgeschichte.* Tübingen: Mohr.

Weiss, L. (1998): *The Myth of the Powerless State: Governing the Economy in a Global Era.* New York: Cornell University Press.

Weiss, T. G. (2000): Governance, Good Governance and Global Governance: Conceptual and Actual Challenges, *Third World Quarterly* 21/5, pp. 795–814.

Welford, R., and Starkey, R. (eds) (1966): *Business and the Environment.* London: Earthscan.

Welskopp, T. (1998): Die Sozialgeschichte der Väter, *Geschichte und Gesellschaft* 24, pp. 173–98.

Whitaker, R. (1999): *The End of Privacy: How Total Surveillance is Becoming a Reality.* New York: New Press.

Wichterich, C. (2000): *The Globalized Woman: Reports from a Future of Inequality.* London: Zed.

Wiener, J. (1999): *Globalization and the Harmonization of Law.* London: Pinter.

Wiesenthal, H. (1999): Die Globalisierung als Epochenbruch – Maximaldimensionen eines Nicht-Nullsummen-Spiels, in Schmidt, G., and Trinczek, R. (eds): *Globalisierung – Ökonomische und soziale Herausforderung am Ende des 20. Jahrhunderts,* [*Sozialen Welt,* Sonderband 13].

Willke, H. (1992): *Die Ironie des Staates.* Frankfurt am Main: Suhrkamp.

Willms, J. (2001): *Die deutsche Krankheit.* Munich: Hanser.

Willms, J. (2002): Glasperlenspieler: Frankreichs große Lebenslüge, *Süddeutsche Zeitung,* 7 May, p. 13.

Wobbe, T. (2000): *Weltgesellschaft.* Bielefeld: Transcript Verlag.

Wolf, E. R. (2002): Facing Power – Old Insights, New Questions, in Vincent, J. (ed.): *The Anthropology of Politics.* Oxford: Blackwell, pp. 222–33.

Wolf, K.-D. (2000): *Die Neue Staatsräson – zwischenstaatliche Kooperation als Demokratieproblem in der Weltgesellschaft.* Baden-Baden: Nomos.

Wolf, M. (2000): Why this Hatred of the Market?, in Lechner, F., and Boli, J. (eds): *The Globalization Reader.* Oxford: Blackwell, pp. 9–12.

Wood, A. (1994): *North–South Trade, Employment and Inequality.* Oxford: Clarendon Press.

Woods, L. T. (1993): Nongovernmental Organizations and the United Nations System: Reflecting Upon the Earth Summit Experience, *International Studies Notes* 18/1, p. 10.

World Bank (1999): *Global Economic Prospects.* Washington, DC: World Bank.

World Bank (2000a): *World Development Indicators.* Washington, DC: World Bank.

World Bank (2000b): *World Development Report 2000/2001.* New York: Oxford University Press.

World Trade Organization (2000): *Annual Report.* Geneva: WTO.

Yearley, S. (1996): *Sociology – Environmentalism – Globalization.* London: Sage.

Yoshikazu, S. (2000): An Alternative to Global Marketization, in Pieterse, J. N. (ed.): *Global Futures.* London: Zed, pp. 98–116.

Young, O. (1986): International Regimes: Toward a New Theory of Institutions, *World Politics* 39/1, pp. 105–22.

Young, O. (1994): *International Governance: Protecting the Environment in a Stateless Society.* Ithaca, NY: Cornell University Press.

Youngs, G. (1999): *International Relations in a Global Age.* Cambridge: Polity.

Ziltener, P. (1999): *Strukturwandel der europäischen Integration: Die Europäische Union und die Veränderung von Staatlichkeit.* Münster: Westfälisches Dampfboot.

Zolo, D. (1997): *Cosmopolis: Prospects for World Government.* Cambridge: Polity.

Zürn, M. (1998a): *Regieren jenseits des Nationalstaates: Globalisierung und Denationalisierung als Chance.* Frankfurt am Main: Suhrkamp.

Zürn, M. (1998b): Schwarz-Rot-Grün-Braun: Reaktionsweisen auf Denationalisierung, in Beck, U. (ed.): *Politik der Globalisierung.* Frankfurt am Main: Suhrkamp, pp. 297–331.

Zürn, M. (2003): Globalization and Global Governance: From Societal to Political Denationalization, *European Review* 11/3, pp. 341–64.

Zürn, M., and Wolf, D. (2000): Europarecht und internationale Regime, in Grande, E., and Jachtenfuchs, M. (eds): *Wie problemlösungsfähig ist die EU?* Baden-Baden: Nomos, pp. 113–40.

Zürn, M., and Zysman, J. (1996): The Myth of a 'Global' Economy: Enduring National Foundations and Emerging Regional Realities, *New Political Economy* 1/3, pp. 157–84.

Zürn, M., Walter. G., Dreher, S., and Beisheim, M. (2000): Postnationale Politik? Über den Umgang mit den Denationalisierungs-Herausforderungen Internet, Klimawandel und Migration, *Zeitschrift für Internationale Beziehung* 2, pp. 297–331.

Index